Flowers, Guns, and Money

AMERICAN BEGINNINGS, 1500–1900

A series edited by Hannah Farber, Stephen Mihm, and Mark Peterson

Also in the series:

Banking on Slavery: Financing Southern Expansion in the Antebellum United States
by Sharon Ann Murphy

A Great and Rising Nation: Naval Exploration and Global Empire in the Early US Republic
by Michael A. Verney

Trading Freedom: How Trade with China Defined Early America
by Dael A. Norwood

Wives Not Slaves: Patriarchy and Modernity in the Age of Revolutions
by Kirsten Sword

Accidental Pluralism: America and the Religious Politics of English Expansion, 1497–1662
by Evan Haefeli

The Province of Affliction: Illness and the Making of Early New England
by Ben Mutschler

Puritan Spirits in the Abolitionist Imagination
by Kenyon Gradert

Trading Spaces: The Colonial Marketplace and the Foundations of American Capitalism
by Emma Hart

Urban Dreams, Rural Commonwealth: The Rise of Plantation Society in the Chesapeake
by Paul Musselwhite

Building a Revolutionary State: The Legal Transformation of New York, 1776–1783
by Howard Pashman

Sovereign of the Market: The Money Question in Early America
by Jeffrey Sklansky

National Duties: Custom Houses and the Making of the American State
by Gautham Rao

Liberty Power: Antislavery Third Parties and the Transformation of American Politics
by Corey M. Brooks

The Making of Tocqueville's America: Law and Association in the Early United States
by Kevin Butterfield

A complete list of series titles is available on the University of Chicago Press website.

Flowers, Guns, and Money

*Joel Roberts Poinsett and the Paradoxes of
American Patriotism*

Lindsay Schakenbach Regele

*The University of Chicago Press
Chicago and London*

SPECIAL EDITION FOR MIAMI UNIVERSITY

The University of Chicago Press, Chicago 60637
The University of Chicago Press, Ltd., London
© 2023 by The University of Chicago
Published 2023
Printed in the United States of America

ISBN-13: 978-0-226-82960-9 (cloth)
ISBN-13: 978-0-226-82962-3 (paper)
ISBN-13: 978-0-226-82961-6 (e-book)
DOI: https://doi.org/10.7208/chicago/9780226829616.001.0001

Library of Congress Cataloging-in-Publication Data

Names: Schakenbach Regele, Lindsay, 1984– author.
Title: Flowers, guns, and money : Joel Roberts Poinsett and the paradoxes of American patriotism / Lindsay Schakenbach Regele.
Other titles: Joel Roberts Poinsett and the paradoxes of American patriotism | American beginnings, 1500–1900.
Description: Chicago : The University of Chicago Press, 2023. | Series: American beginnings, 1500–1900 | Includes bibliographical references and index.
Identifiers: LCCN 2023013587 | ISBN 9780226829609 (cloth) | ISBN 9780226829623 (paperback) | ISBN 9780226829616 (ebook)
Subjects: LCSH: Poinsett, Joel Roberts, 1779–1851. | Cabinet officers—United States—Biography. | Statesmen—United States—Biography.
Classification: LCC E340.P77 S33 2023 | DDC 973.5092 [B]—dc23/eng/20230403
LC record available at https://lccn.loc.gov/2023013587

♾ This paper meets the requirements of ANSI/NISO Z39.48-1992 (Permanence of Paper).

For my family

Contents

....

Contents

Introduction

Joel Roberts Poinsett is and was everywhere if we look for him. The Smithsonian, Trail of Tears National Historic Trail, the American Philosophical Society, the oldest stone bridge in the South. The War and State Departments, US Congress, the South Carolina General Assembly, Europe, Russia, South America, Mexico, the Caribbean. Andrew Jackson confided in him about military matters, and Emperor Alexander of Russia discussed US claims to the Pacific Northwest with him.[1] He fought in Chile's War for Independence and orchestrated the United States' longest and costliest war against Native Americans in history. Today Poinsett's primary visible traces are on the tags of the world's most economically important potted plant: the Christmas flower called the "Poinsettia," which he took from the Mexican state of Guerrero in 1828 on a business trip during his controversial tenure as America's first minister plenipotentiary to the country. The story of how the United States appropriated the Aztec plant the *Cuitlaxochitl,* named it after Poinsett, and commercialized it speaks to the process by which American foreign relations and political economy developed in the nineteenth century, as well as to the role that Poinsett played in this development.[2]

He worked as a secret agent in South America, ambassador to Mexico, South Carolina state legislator, US congressman, and secretary of war. His three-decade career included military planning for Chilean independence leaders, asserting US commercial interests in Mexico, and advocating the use of federal force against tariff opponents in his home state. All of these activities reflected an emerging form of political economy rooted in opportunism, chauvinism, and international competition. Poinsett personified a type of patriotism that emerged in the decades following the American Revolution, in which statesmen claimed to act in the service of the new American republic by securing economic prosperity and military security.

In many ways, we could call Poinsett a nationalist for his commitment to whiteness, Anglo-American culture, and militarism, but this word is steeped in twentieth-century meaning, and it was not a word that Poinsett or his correspondents used; instead, they used patriotism and patriot often.[3] Early in his career, he used these words most frequently to refer to revolutionaries in South America, equating their independence movements with that of the "patriots" of the American Revolution. Patriotism was a value judgment used to compare individuals' actions to those of the "patriot Washington"[4] and to praise the "military spirit" that marked the "patriotism of the soldiers."[5] It could also be used to refer to any activity that advanced commercial or national interests, such as when South Carolina botanist Stephen Elliott referred to Amos Eaton's work on geological surveys as a "patriotic pursuit."[6] Poinsett's own friends and allies referred to his patriotism. Fellow Mason, South Carolina slave owner, and unionist Chapman Levy, for example, wrote to Poinsett in reference to his actions during the nullification crisis: "These feelings of high respect and kindness and regard for you, which sunk deep into my bosom in those trying times which evinced your exalted patriotism and devotion to our country, as well as your firmness and talents in its support, has remained unchanged."[7] And Commissioner of Indian Affairs Thomas Hartley Crawford wrote to Poinsett at the end of Poinsett's term as secretary of war, "Your administration of the department was in the true spirit of patriotism."[8] When South Carolinians began seriously debating secession, Poinsett wrote that at least the "fanatics of the north" had "patriotism" and an "attachment to the union."[9] Finally, nine years before South Carolina's threats became reality, Poinsett's tombstone proclaimed his life and death as those of "a pure patriot, an honest man, and a good Christian."

Poinsett matters, but not because he was "a pure patriot, an honest man," or "a good Christian."[10] He was never fully any of those things. He matters because he embodied the contradictions and inconsistencies at the heart of the American experiment. He was born in South Carolina while it fought for independence from Great Britain, and he died as it debated secession from the Union on the eve of the Civil War. He was a southerner who lived much of his life elsewhere—in Europe, Mexico, South America, and Washington, DC. In his time, he was the subject of newspaper articles, presidential correspondence, diplomatic memos, and congressional proceedings. A eulogist credited him with "sav[ing] the country" from disunion over a tax crisis; members of the Mexican public lambasted his self-interested interference in local politics.[11]

An elite enslaver, statesman, and world traveler who was on familiar terms with such individuals as James Madison; John Quincy Adams; King Louis XVI's finance minister, Jacques Necker; and Chilean independence leader José Miguel Carrera, Poinsett was certainly not an everyman. He descended from French Huguenots who, on his father's side, immigrated to Charleston in the late 1600s and, on his mother's side, lived in England. During the American Revolution, his family switched loyalties, siding with Britain and temporarily moving there after the rebels won. As a teenager, Poinsett returned to England for some of his education, before traveling back to the United States with the hope of fighting against his mother's home country in the War of 1812. Then, as ambassador in Mexico, he colluded with British bankers on land schemes to the detriment of other Americans, even as he was considered a great patriot by some.[12] He was cosmopolitan, nationalistic, and, above all, self-serving, and his life experiences intersected with the major tragedies and relative triumphs of the era, including Native expulsion and the growth of slavery, diplomatic and military expansion, and imperial acquisition and exploration. The unique span of his career, which traversed multiple branches and localities of the government over the course of the early national era, reveals how power operated in different geographies and jurisdictions of the law during the United States' foundational years. Poinsett's experience navigating the postcolonial transition to imperial nationhood at the state, national, and international levels exemplified the emergence of self-interested patriotism among US officials.[13]

Commitment to the Union did not preclude other interests, and Poinsett's range of activities helps illustrate the various guises of "patriotism" among government agents in the early republic. Even as Poinsett believed he was doing what was best for the nation, he simultaneously worked to achieve his own ambitions and fulfill his various obligations in ways that benefited his own agenda and finances. Poinsett was representative of many of the men who governed domestic and international affairs at a time when individual advancement superseded old ideals about a virtuous citizenry and when the actions associated with white masculinity focused less on community and more on self-improvement and physical dominance.[14] In general, the men who shaped American political economy and statecraft valued economic opportunism and martial competition. They contributed to what might be called martial capitalism.

Poinsett came of age in a world at war, and, like many men born during the Revolution, he courted military conflict.[15] He was too young to re-member the Revolution but spent much of his life jealous of British influ-ence and covetous of military recognition. Poinsett left medical school in his late teens to pursue military arts, and although he never served in the armed forces, at age fifty-eight, he oversaw the nation's military affairs as secretary of war. Militarism informed his various roles as a public servant, and it is precisely because he was never a bona fide military man that his career so powerfully illustrates the extent to which militarism pervaded early American politics and the economy. While very few Americans par-ticipated directly in the military and many white Americans made preten-sions to their nation being a reluctant wielder of military power, there was a martial quality to economic life and domestic and international politics, from aggressive land speculation, bank wars, coercive trade agreements, and dueling in Congress to forced labor camps and "frontier" violence. Poinsett embodied this martial dominance, as he intervened aggressively in Mexican politics on behalf of personal and American interests, esca-lated violence against Natives in Georgia and Florida, and managed slave labor.

Although some men practiced extreme forms of this martial domi-nance, like Andrew Jackson, who massacred Native peoples, invaded Florida, and executed two British subjects, Poinsett was less wanton in his aggression. His patriotism was rooted in his ability to capitalize on governmental powers to profit beyond national borders, which meant subscribing to a "transnational business masculinity" that depended on a reputation for not just dominance but decorum. To fit into an inter-national class of capitalists who invested in banking, agriculture, inter-national commerce, mining, whaling, manufacturing, railroads, and land, Poinsett tempered some of the bellicose aspects of his manhood with gentility.[16] He purchased expensive Madeira and dining room carpets, for example, at the same time as he approved the use of bloodhounds against Seminoles in Florida.[17] Wine, along with plants and mineral specimens, connected Poinsett to an international elite. For example, British banker Francis Baring sent mail to Poinsett through Robert Gilmore & Son, mer-chants and collectors of art and minerals. Gilmore would later invest in Poinsett's mining venture in Mexico.[18] This gentility also made it easier for Poinsett to engage in what historian Laurel Clark Shire calls "sentimen-tal racism," assuaging the violent actions that accompanied the belief in his racial and cultural superiority.[19] Because Poinsett belonged to learned societies, contributed to botanists' collections, and purchased art from Europe, he could more readily justify the expulsion of Natives from their homes.

Poinsett learned this refined aspect of his masculinity from his genteel upbringing. He descended from wealthy French Huguenots, who, on his father's side, settled in Charleston in the 1670s and became elite property owners and prominent members of the urban social scene. Poinsett's grandfather and great-grandfather were vintners (Poinsett himself was well known for his appreciation of fine wine, and in 1899 a Charleston resident still possessed a bottle of "Poinsett wine" that Poinsett had brought home from Madeira in 1816) and traveled often.[20] His grandfather had briefly moved to Newport, Rhode Island, in the 1730s and married a local woman, who gave birth to Poinsett's father, Elisha, before the family returned to Charleston. Elisha became one of the wealthiest men in Charleston, owning slaves and multiple properties. He was also a physician, and he completed his medical education at Edinburgh and in London, where he met Poinsett's mother, Ann Roberts, also of French Protestant descent. Poinsett's parents connected him to elites throughout the United States and in England and provided him with travels and education in New England and Europe.

Poinsett's early life was shaped both by cosmopolitan experiences and by the traditional honor culture associated with southern plantation life, which revolved around reputation, sociability, and strict codes for masculine and feminine behavior. Young southern gentlemen were supposed to dress elegantly and display proper education and manners.[21] Honor culture praised virility, but taken too far, this masculine aggression could sabotage business ventures and diplomatic negotiations, which is why Poinsett often harnessed his genteel cosmopolitanism rather than southern masculinity in his political and financial undertakings. Additionally, Poinsett's father derided military life and strongly discouraged Poinsett from pursuing military education. Poinsett, however, found ways to fulfill his military ambitions. Although he did not receive formal military training or serve in the War of 1812, he participated in some of the United States' major military developments, such as expanding the United States' military forces, and escalating wars against Native peoples, as well as in activities outside the United States, like Chile's War for Independence. Poinsett's lifelong interest in the military reflected his reverence for order. From his early travels in Europe, Poinsett believed in the virtues of the military for quelling dissension, enforcing stability, imposing regulation on society, and growing the economy (in ways that benefited his national and international associates and interests).

Poinsett channeled his love of order and regulation into another of his lifelong interests: agriculture. As historian Courtney Fullilove has defined it, "the history of agriculture is the process by which people have

attempted to impose order on the generation of plants, attempting to manipulate the rules and habits of other organisms by selecting and modifying them for human exploitation."[22] Throughout his life, Poinsett was interested in plants for their intrinsic, functional, and economic values. He
carefully studied the writings of Alexander von Humboldt, the German
naturalist who traveled to Spanish America at the turn of the nineteenth
century on an environmental reconnaissance mission for the Spanish
Crown. Humboldt recorded his observations of plants, animals, and minerals; assessed economic potential; and collected plants and seeds for
Spain's Royal Botanical Garden.[23] Poinsett would do the same thing for
the US government during his South American and Mexican diplomatic
posts over the following two decades. In addition to sending the "Christmas flower" to the United States, Poinsett collected seeds to grow in his
own greenhouse and often exchanged plants and seeds with elites in the
United States and Britain. He cared about collecting materials for the sake
of knowledge and diplomacy; he also cared about marketable crops.[24]

Over the course of his life, agriculture became increasingly associated
with improvement for the sake of profit.[25] Poinsett was a member of the
Agricultural Society of Charleston, and one of his goals was to find "useful" crops to help diversify the United States' main agricultural staples:
cotton, tobacco, sugar, and grains.[26] Although Poinsett sent some seeds
to his southern planter friends, he shipped the majority of plant specimens to northern reformers and scientifically minded individuals. The
wife of one of his South Carolina friends was "vexed" that Poinsett had
sent so many plant clippings and seeds to northern gardeners rather than
to her and his other local friends.[27] Philadelphia in particular was a center
of commercial horticulture, and its Bartram's Garden would be the first
recipient of the poinsettia. Philadelphia philanthropist James Ronaldson
wrote to Poinsett in Mexico, "You will benefit the union by sending us all
the useful plants and seeds; if there are any grapes that would thrive in
the poor sandy or worn out lands, they would be a valuable compliment
to this country." He also suggested exporting Mexico's "cochineal insect
and its favorite plant" to see if they would "thrive in Florida."[28] Ronaldson
expressed his concern that the United States relied so heavily on only a
few agricultural staples (tobacco, cotton, and sugar). Poinsett agreed. Agricultural diversification was one of Poinsett's goals for state and national
economic development. Although he eventually owned a rice plantation,
he hoped to wean the South off such cash crops and was always looking for potentially profitable alternatives, such as grapes for wine, exotic
seedlings, and dye plants. He used his privileged position to procure and

disseminate these things, such as when he took a clipping of the *Cuitlaxo-chitl* from southwestern Mexico and sent it along with other plants to Bartram's Garden in Philadelphia. The poinsettia was not mass-marketed in his lifetime, but its eventual commercialization reflected his ambitions.

Poinsett's other ambitions centered on internal improvements, favorable trade deals, and the extermination of Native peoples for territorial exploration and acquisition. Poinsett's stance on these issues defied what one would expect from a typical "southerner," "expansionist," or "Democrat," categories that he identified with throughout much of his life. We must then understand the nuances of his behaviors and decisions and recognize that there were others like him, who did not completely fit the era's categories. His defiance of categorization—as a slave owner, for example, who opposed states' rights doctrine and the annexation of Texas—suggests greater fluidity in political actions and ideologies than histories of US expansion, empire, and politics usually ascribe to individuals of the era. Poinsett's experiences in the overlapping jurisdictions and competing arenas of the early American state and economy are especially instructive because they do not map neatly onto the familiar types and tropes of the era, such as "southerner," "slave owner," "expansionist," and "Jacksonian Democrat." His seemingly contradictory positions and the way he cultivated relationships with individuals of different political leanings at home and abroad reveal how the promotion of military and economic power, both real and perceived, dominated early national development. It superseded other divisive agendas because "patriotic" members of any party could advocate prosperity and military strength.

Poinsett thus helps explain political inconsistencies of the era. He was from a state that was known for its virulent distrust of government power yet whose residents also committed "more funds per capita to the project of state development than did any of their peers across the nation," as historian Ryan Quintana shows, and "were among the first Americans to transition to the modern practices of governance."[29] Throughout his career, Poinsett tended to favor federal over state power, but for political reasons, he always had to at least acknowledge the virtues of limited government. Although Poinsett promoted military power, he was not equivalently in favor of war, opposing, for example, both war against Mexico and southern secession and rebellion. Politically and geographically, Poinsett crossed boundaries. At different times, Poinsett and the United States contended with Britain for influence in hemispheric affairs and worked with various British officials to secure mutually beneficial trade deals and political stability. Poinsett kept in touch with a large number of northerners, and, like many southerners, he had close ties to Philadelphia, at once the birthplace of American abolitionism and an appealing market-place for wealthy southerners.[30] He received much of his education from Federalist Charlestonians and New Englanders and would later become a Democratic-Republican and then a Jacksonian Democrat. Although he was from a state not known for industrial development, he worked to advance it by endorsing railroads in South Carolina and supporting some protectionist tariffs.[31] His position on any given issue, like those of others of his cohort, reflected political and economic pragmatism. In general, there was little ideological consistency among public figures of the era.[32] Historians question why Calhoun switched from being a nationalist to a states' rights proponent and why John Quincy Adams championed anti-slavery and also sometimes defended slaveholders' interests.[33] Poinsett's and others' partisanship was rooted in a political pragmatism that some-times defied one's status as a slaveholder or abolitionist, northerner or southerner.

Take the tariff, for example. During South Carolina's nullification cri-sis in 1832–1833, Poinsett challenged provincial Carolinians by coordinat-ing military preparations that would compel tariff collection in his home state. In this conflict between states' rights and federal intervention, he aligned with President Andrew Jackson rather than South Carolina's sym-bolic leader John C. Calhoun because of his ambitions and personal eco-nomic interests. His decision contradicted the position he took less than ten years earlier, when he had given a speech on the floor of Congress (a rare occurrence for him) against a bill to increase the tariff. In this April 1824 speech, he had said that, "the Government having kept steadily in view the spirit of the Constitution . . . the law now contemplated in the reverse of all this" would create "hostile feelings . . . between the differ-ent interests in various parts of this union."[34] Poinsett was correct about the hostile feelings; in the early 1830s, he contributed to the exacerbation of this sentiment when he favored a coercive national government over the consumerist preferences of slaveholders. Although he had inherited slaveholder wealth and spent liberally on art, wine, and home furnish-ings—a mahogany bed, marble-top desk and washstand, a host of maple furniture, leather chairs, expensive carpets, dining and bedroom china, large mirrors, clocks, and a gold tea set—he did not make his livelihood on slave-grown commodities; a regular shortage of cash led him to find new ways to settle debts and accumulate capital outside of South Caro-lina.[35] Like other elites with diversified and far-flung economic portfolios, he tended to support federal, over state, strength because it was better for his business interests.[36]

Poinsett's published speeches and addresses to Congress, his home state, and the learned societies to which he belonged, as well as his reports on South America and Mexico, allow us to understand how he presented his ideas on political economy, race, and military size to a wide audience; however, they do not disclose his financial motives. Historical accident and Poinsett himself have limited what we can know about his business dealings. For one, many of Poinsett's financial records were destroyed during the Civil War. We know he traveled outside the state frequently, collected rent on the roughly fifteen properties that he owned in Charleston, hired individuals to manage them, and acquired a large plantation when he married at age fifty-four.[37] We don't know much about his finances. He was close to Francis Baring, a member of the famous British banking family, who likely invested money for him. After Poinsett returned from Mexico the first time, Baring informed him, "It is not impossible that to my speculating spirit you may indirectly owe the improvement of your rank on the Savannah and the Pee Dee."[38]

Poinsett did not spend much time writing about his finances or himself, in general. Unlike statesmen who were known for prolific and judicious writing, such as John Quincy Adams, Poinsett read more than he wrote. He considered himself too busy to sit down and write more than perfunctory letters, except when he was bored at sea and wrote detailed accounts of his travels. Additionally, Poinsett was cagey. While serving as secretary of war, he instructed one of his friends that his business in Texas had to be "managed quietly. It is important to my position not to be assailable in such matters."[39] His writings also obscure much of his private life, which he worked to conceal, praising "discretion and prudence" in conducting affairs with women.[40]

Yet we get glimpses of what he tried to hide. For example, he had a son, whose existence appears only in three letters to a man in Charleston named Isaac A. Johnson. These letters are located not in the main collections of Poinsett's papers at the Historical Society of Pennsylvania but in a smaller collection at the South Carolina Historical Society. Johnson, a founder of the Charleston Antiquarian Society, was most likely the brother of Poinsett's closest friend, Joseph.[41] In 1821, when Poinsett was forty-two, he wrote to Johnson to let him know that the infant's mother had died and to request that Johnson serve as caretaker. Poinsett had set aside funds for this purpose and asked that Johnson keep the whole matter a secret, particularly the identity of the mother.[42] Poinsett's earlier biographers did not mention this arrangement, perhaps because they never came across the letters to Johnson or perhaps because they preferred to ignore personal details that might detract from Poinsett's political record.

The secrecy of this relationship among Poinsett, his son, and Johnson reveals the clandestine aspects of Poinsett's life. Poinsett had surreptitious visits with his son in the summers, while Johnson provided regular care. One of the reasons Poinsett could rely on Johnson was that they both belonged to the Freemasons and were bound by "obligations as a brother."[43] It is unclear exactly when Poinsett joined the secret fraternal society, but by 1818, he had reached the rank of Master Mason. That year, he received a certificate from Lodge No. 1 in Charleston affirming that he had achieved the degree of Royal Arch Mason, part of the York Rite system of the Masonic degrees.[44]

Poinsett's involvement with Freemasonry waxed and waned over his life, but it shaped his relationships, such as with Johnson, and guided many of his political and personal decisions.[45] It also caused controversy at several points in his career. Masons privileged loyalty to their brothers over all else, which made outsiders uneasy.[46] By the 1820s and 1830s, there emerged a strong opposition movement against Freemasonry's intervention in US culture and politics. Poinsett himself attracted criticism for his alleged establishment of York Rite lodges in Mexico as a means to counter the influence of his political rivals during his tenure as minister to Mexico in the 1820s.[47] Yet just like other aspects of his identity, his status as a Freemason did not define him. For example, although he worried about the influence of the Anti-Mason Party in the United States, he was able to collaborate with prominent anti-Masons, such as Edward Everett. Maybe because the society's internal favoritism gave Poinsett common ground with Masons of different political parties and nationalities, he was able to find this mutuality with men outside the fraternity as well, collaborating politically and economically with men whose background varied significantly from his.

Despite his readiness to interact with men of different political leanings, he expressed his insecurities, prejudices, and household concerns to very few people outside the Masons. One of these confidants was his closest friend, Joseph Johnson; another was James Butler Campbell, a Charleston attorney and politician from Massachusetts almost thirty years Poinsett's junior, whom Poinsett mentored.[48] Both men later wrote biographical manuscripts of Poinsett. Poinsett relied on Johnson and Campbell to manage his properties in Charleston when he was away, which was often.

He also shared personal information with them. Johnson, once a student of Poinsett's father, was one of the only men to whom Poinsett wrote throughout the course of his life. The few letters that Poinsett wrote during his tour of Europe as a young man were to Johnson. Early on, he established the norm of discussing financial issues and career objectives with Johnson, requesting money from his inheritance and expressing his desire to join the military. Throughout his life, he offered honest opinions about his various professional decisions, such as not wanting to go to Mexico because there were no government funds for him to employ a private secretary. When he did go to Mexico, he confided in Johnson that he had aroused the suspicions of Mexican and British officials.[49] In turn, Johnson kept him apprised of Charleston gossip and provided political advice that would allow Poinsett to reenter local politics when he returned: "Let it be seen and known and felt that you are among us and are cooperating with us."[50] Johnson also collected correspondence and wine for Poinsett.

Conversely, Poinsett did not meet Campbell until the 1830s. Campbell was a former Massachusetts teacher who had moved to Charleston and was courting the daughter of one of Poinsett's friends. Campbell managed Poinsett's correspondence in the city, checked on rental properties, and arranged repairs at Poinsett's request. Poinsett counseled Campbell as an older man speaking to a junior, offering relationship and life advice. The two became so close that Poinsett explained to Campbell that "some of our Carolina friends knowing the intimacy which subsisted between us asked me if I knew who you were, of what family, where brought up and educated and seemed surprised that I could give no satisfactory answers." To allay their concerns, Poinsett solicited a letter of recommendation from Massachusetts Whig senator Daniel Webster (with whom Poinsett maintained collegial relations).[51] His friends were not necessarily mollified, but, undeterred by their disquiet, Poinsett trusted Campbell with many of his household matters. He wrote to Campbell frequently with explicit instructions for paint colors, furniture stains, and flower cuttings. Relaying instructions for his cabinetmaker, Poinsett wrote, "Let him abstain from cleaning them up and making them look new—a thing I abhor—I like old looking furniture."[52] After moving to his wife's plantation north of Charleston, Poinsett asked Campbell to ship a variety of flower cuttings from his various properties in the city because the lack of flowers at his new home appalled him.

In his letters to Campbell, Poinsett always mentioned the plantation's vineyards and gardens before or instead of rice, which was the cash crop his plantation produced. This could partly be explained by the fact that, to some extent, he harbored an old-fashioned, elitist view of wealth and moneymaking, preferring to talk about aesthetic aspects of his plantation rather than its economic status. Yet he readily discussed the profitability of steamboat competition and the value of real estate in US cities and Mexico, and he was not above asking for current prices for cash crops.[53] It seems more likely that he was embarrassed, at least among some individuals, to be associated with slaveholding. Although his father had owned slaves and he had inherited some of them, he conducted business for much of his adult life without owning slaves and traveled in countries with little or no slavery, and many of his friends in the United States and abroad opposed the institution of slavery (Campbell did not own slaves, but he defended slave owners in court). Unlike some other slave owners, Poinsett spent minimal time engaging in a paternalistic defense of his ownership of human beings and calculating their economic worth. He instead worked to downplay their presence in his life. An antislavery visitor to his estate described the slave quarters, noting the peach-tree-lined streets and whitewashed houses, which Poinsett no doubt intended to disguise the brutality of human bondage.[54]

He did not acquire a large plantation until his marriage to Mary Izard Pringle at age fifty-four. Pringle, the fifty-two-year-old widow of John Julius Pringle Jr., owned a 160-acre rice plantation about sixty miles north of Charleston, as well as almost one hundred slaves.[55] Poinsett and Pringle married soon after Poinsett befriended Campbell, to whom he lamented that by marrying, he had "abandoned the very respectable fraternity of Bachelors."[56] In general, though, Poinsett viewed marriage positively, advising Campbell "to do the same earlier than I did, indeed as soon as you can find some good natured person to have you." That good-natured person, Poinsett and Campbell agreed, was the daughter of Poinsett's friend Thomas Bennett. Poinsett cautioned that "womankind are strange inexplicable creatures, and the more lovely, loveable and loved they are the more strange and capricious," and advised him to ally with her brothers.[57] He also advised Campbell not to "wait until you can support your wife in comfort and independence." Instead, Campbell should use marriage as the means to his financial stability and independence. Poinsett told him, "If you were once a member of the family everyone would be interested in promoting your views; and Mr. Bennett who is as generous as he is able would place you in a situation at once to render you independent of him."[58]

Poinsett's advice suggests that he viewed his marriage to Mary, who was "possessed in her own rights of considerable real and personal estate," through an economic lens.[59] Poinsett came of age in an era when companionate marriages predominated, and he was too distracted for companionship.[60] He devoted less articulation to girls and women than many of his peers did—having sexual relations with women, rather than courting them or writing about them—and his masculinity was shaped more by comparison to other males than it was in opposition to females. By the time he reached his fifties, he traveled less and was more inclined toward domestic life; his preferences coincided with the Victorian era's widened divide between the sexes and increased emphasis on the home as a sanctuary.[61] Pringle made possible Poinsett's increasing reliance on the comforts of domestic life, yet it was her material wealth more than her domesticity that sheltered Poinsett from the vulgarity of public life. He was a chronic overspender and was often in debt. Access to her plantation, slaves, and rice crops gave him a steadier source of income.

The couple had a complicated financial arrangement. Before their marriage, Poinsett gave her a piece of land in Charleston as collateral. Once they married, the law of coverture, which existed in South Carolina until the end of the nineteenth century, prohibited Pringle from legally owning property in her own name.[62] Aware of the discrepancies in their respective assets, the couple protected her wealth by entering a marriage settlement that established a trust to manage their possessions.[63] The settlement permitted Pringle to acquire the profits and interest from her property "as if she were femme sole and unmarried." Additionally, she was not "in any manner liable for or subject to the debts contracts or control of Mr. Poinsett."[64] Although this arrangement protected Pringle's interests, it also benefited Poinsett, who profited from his wife's assets. Pringle owned bank stock, which the couple sold soon after their marriage, using the cash to pay off debt and purchase additional land for their plantation.[65] Her inheritance and her status as a slaveholder made possible Poinsett's ascent to plantation gentleman at the age of fifty-four.[66]

Although the couple did not have children together, they remained close to Mary's son from her first marriage.[67] This relationship offered Poinsett the opportunity to serve as a paternal figure in a way that he could not for his own son. Poinsett said little about his wife, other than to remark on her health or whereabouts, but he clearly cared for his step-grandchildren, looking forward to their visits and worrying when they were sick. He also extended to them his obsession with self-presentation. In the only existing letter from Poinsett to a grandchild, he told his granddaughter that he "liked best young ladies with their hair cut short and turned up in front with a comb to keep it out of their eyes, especially when the eyes are bright and cheeks tinged with health like those of my own dear grandchild."[68]

Self-presentation was essential to Poinsett's balancing act between political reputation and personal profit. Just as he wanted his granddaughter to look the part of a neatly groomed young lady, he worked to project an image of himself as a cosmopolitan, curious, honorable statesman who cared about his state and nation. In this aspiration, he was no different from all the statesmen who had come before him. Yet his career marked a shift in governance, away from republicanism. Although he worked to maintain the facade of a virtuous, republican public servant, he embodied the transition to self-interested autonomy common among many state agents. Other individuals took similar initiative in the service of economic development; their actions were often either hidden or in direct opposition to US policy.

Take, for example, Philadelphia merchant Joseph Ray, who served twice as US consul to Recife, from 1817 to 1825 and from 1836 to 1842.[69] He furthered US economic interests by helping American merchants yet also undermined US foreign policy by aiding revolutionaries in their struggles against the Brazilian monarchy. The process by which Ray created commercial and political links between Brazil and the United States was controversial. He was popular among elite merchants and revolutionaries, but in 1825, Emperor Pedro exiled him, and in 1842, the US State Department removed him from his post. There are parallels between Ray's meddling (including his involvement with Freemasons in Brazil) and Poinsett's divisive intervention in both Chilean and Mexican affairs.

Likewise, the political activities of Decius Wadsworth, who served as chief of ordnance from 1815 to 1821, offer an example of individual autonomy within the War Department. Wadsworth used his power to establish military depots and coordinate the supply and inspection of arms to simulate military buildup. He aggressively promoted arms production, arguing that "measures ought to be taken so we can wage a vigorous war."[70] Congress dictated the amount of money spent on arms production, but Wadsworth privately ordered the superintendent of the federal armory in Springfield, Massachusetts, to produce at least twelve thousand stands of arms, even if it meant exceeding the $199,834 Congress had provided for the annual production of arms for the militia. He instructed the superintendent, in preparing the quarterly return for congressional review, to make it look as if less money had been spent.[71] Wadsworth's actions enhanced the state's capacity for violence against perceived impediments to economic opportunity for white Americans.

Ferdinand Hassler, appointed by Thomas Jefferson as the first superintendent of the US Coast Survey and later reappointed by Andrew

Jackson, also exemplified the sort of government agent who effected change outside the purview of legislators.[72] Although many congressmen considered a general survey of all the coasts of the United States "of urgent necessity" because of "the interest of our merchants, and the benefits to the revenue," Hassler still took it upon himself to plan and execute aspects of the surveys clandestinely. On a trip to Europe, Hassler purchased an extensive array of tools and books that he believed would enable him to carry out the most accurate coast survey. Congressional leaders were none too pleased when they discovered he had spent about $55,000 without authorization.[73] Congress attempted to curtail Hassler's and the survey's powers by limiting employment in the coast survey to army and navy personnel, but the survey was fully revived in the 1830s, and Jackson reappointed Hassler to lead it.[74] Ultimately, although Hassler acted without congressional permission, the army and navy adopted his surveying plans for the systematic mapping of the United States' newly expanded territory. His successor, Alexander Dallas Bache, enlarged the work and the budget of the survey, ensuring that Hassler's bureaucratic legacy lived on.[75]

Just as Hassler exploited his limited federal power to leave his mark on the US Coast Survey, William Thornton did so with the US patent system. Thornton was an inventor, physician, and architect who served as the official administrator of patents from 1802 until his death in 1828, and, with little input from Congress, he used his authority to establish a patent bureau that advanced American invention.[76] Thornton saw himself as the mediator of the contract between inventor and the public and believed that in generously dispensing patents he was protecting the public from the loss of important inventions. He unilaterally eased the application process by publishing guidelines for inventors and developing the practice of reissue. Legislators resented Thornton's liberal administration of patents, and soon after he died, the Senate's Committee on Patents and the Patent Office reported that the Department of State issued too many patents and that "the evils which necessarily result from the law as it now exists, must continue to increase and multiply daily until Congress shall put a stop to them." Although a new law in 1836 made patents more difficult to obtain by implementing stricter standards for the examination of patents, Thornton had already shaped the nature of early national invention.[77]

Thornton, Ray, Wadsworth, and Hassler, like Poinsett, exemplified the far-reaching effects of public servants' individual autonomy on military and economic development. Poinsett did not spend as long in any position as these men; instead, he moved throughout levels and branches of government and worked in different locations in and outside the United States. For this reason, he is the ideal tour guide for different arenas of nation building.

This book will follow Poinsett's travels throughout the Americas and Europe in between his birth and death in South Carolina. The first chapter examines his childhood and adolescence in Charleston, England, and Connecticut and his education and travels in Europe during the Napoleonic Wars. European conflict shaped Poinsett's understanding of military power and foreign relations, and his exposure to international trade and diplomacy laid the groundwork for his future involvement in military and political economic development. Subsequent chapters explain how Poinsett intervened in political and military affairs in South America and Mexico, sponsored internal improvements in South Carolina while serving as a state legislator and US congressman, aided President Andrew Jackson during the nullification crisis, oversaw Native expulsion and continental exploration as secretary of war, and promoted Cuban annexation and the establishment of a national scientific institution. He spent the last eighteen years of his life as a husband and slave labor camp owner.

When he died on December 12, 1851, he was buried near his summer home, at the Vestry of Christ Church in Greenville. On Christmas Day, the church sent his widow a letter. "Society at large," the letter read, had lost "a generous sympathizer with the wants and ills of humanity."[78] The letter may have hyperbolized Poinsett's virtues, but it was right about his familiarity with the "wants and ills of humanity." Poinsett's life explains the "ills" that resulted when individuals and their government pursued their "wants." From the post-revolutionary to the pre–Civil War era, Poinsett helped make both a reality.

A Note about Poinsett's Biographers

Poinsett's early biographers were men who knew him personally and employed firsthand knowledge in the absence of autobiographical reflections. The first was Henry D. Gilpin, a Pennsylvania lawyer and attorney general under Martin Van Buren. In 1838, Gilpin wrote a brief sketch of Poinsett's career that appeared in *Political Portraits*, a collection of short biographies of notable individuals in the *United States Magazine and Democratic Review*.[79] In the 1850s, he corresponded with Poinsett's widow and collected material for a longer biography that was never completed.[80] In 1851, John Belton O'Neal, a judge, plantation owner, and author of *Negro Law of the Carolinas*, wrote a short biography of Poinsett for an obituary.[81] Poinsett's oldest and closest friend, Joseph Johnson, a medical doctor who had been a student of Poinsett's father and later served a term as Charleston mayor, wrote an unpublished biography of Poinsett sometime after his death. Gabriel E. Manigault, a descendant of Poinsett's wife's family, also wrote a biographical sketch of Poinsett that appeared in the Charleston yearbook in the late 1880s.

The first person outside of his family, friends, and professional pool to write a biography of Poinsett was Charles Janeway Stillé, a biographer, historian, and provost of the University of Pennsylvania from 1868 to 1880. Stillé based his biography on the collection of Poinsett's papers at the Historical Society of Pennsylvania, which the society acquired from Poinsett's stepdaughter-in-law, Mrs. John Julius Pringle, in 1885. Stillé's "The Life and Services of Joel R. Poinsett, the Confidential Agent in South Carolina of President Jackson during the Nullification Troubles of 1832" appeared as a series of articles in the *Pennsylvania Magazine of History and Biography* in 1888. Over thirty years later, the *Pennsylvania Magazine of History and Biography* published another series on Poinsett, written by Charles Lyon Chandler, a historian of US–Latin American relations and former US consul to Buenos Aires and Callou. Chandler paid a woman in South Carolina named Emma Bull to conduct significant research on Poinsett's life, although he did not credit her in the journal series. He intended for an academic press to publish his biography, but it was rejected; two other biographies appeared around the same time, by James Fred Rippy and Herbert Putnam, as did a study of Poinsett's diplomatic career by Dorothy Parton.[82] Since then, there have been no book-length studies of Poinsett.

Most of Poinsett's biographers praised him, examining his actions through the lenses of his "mania for republicanism," "ardent nationalism," and "democratic principles."[83] They neglected the less savory aspects of Poinsett's career, as well as details about his personal life. This book aims to change that.

1

Founding a Man,
1779–1810

When Joel Roberts Poinsett was a teenager, he traveled throughout the Russian Empire and central Asia with a twenty-two-year-old British viscount titled Lord Royston.[1] As Poinsett and Royston sailed down the Volga to the Caspian Sea on a luxuriously furnished merchandise ship, outfitted with guns, they encountered a fishing boat whose crew "denied that they had caught anything." Poinsett and Royston demanded their fish at gunpoint or, in Royston's words, "immediately presented [their] double barreled guns and compelled a delivery." They softened their belligerence by offering to pay for the fish at a price set by the fisherman, which, according to Poinsett and Royston, seemed to "astonish and please" the sellers.[2]

With this incident, we can see the formation of Poinsett's attitude toward power and economic relations, as well as a microcosm of the United States' emerging role in commercial relations: Poinsett and Royston effectively combined coercion and liberalism to secure resources. They used guns to force a sale but assumed that the transaction worked out for all parties because they paid what the fisherman asked. This type of transaction would be carried out again and again as the US government acquired land from Native Americans through unequal treaties, as wealthy capitalists purchased farmland and water rights from less well-off citizens, and as US travelers extracted plants, minerals, and other raw goods both within and beyond their national borders. And it would sometimes take place in cooperation with the British, as in the case of Poinsett with Royston, and at other times, in competition.

Seventeen years before this armed encounter with foreign fishermen, on March 2, 1779, Joel Roberts Poinsett was born in Charleston, South

Carolina, a prime target of the British during the Revolution. Shortly after Poinsett's first birthday, the British occupied the city, and his family, one of the most affluent in the city, switched loyalties. Although his father, Dr. Elisha Poinsett, had traveled with the American army to Savannah as an attending physician several months after Poinsett's birth, the Americans' failure to retake the city from the British prompted Elisha's shift in allegiance. The British capitalized on their victory by marching to Charleston and laying siege the following spring, in one of the worst American defeats of the war. When the British army promised property and status protection in exchange for allegiance, Elisha prioritized his family's safety and economic well-being over American patriotism.[3]

Fearing what American victory meant for Loyalists, in 1782 Elisha took his family to England, where the family lived for six years and where, from age three to nine, Joel Roberts received his basic elementary education. Elisha had done his medical training in London. There, he met Joel Roberts's mother, Ann Roberts. Like Elisha, she descended from French Huguenots, Protestants who had fled persecution in the late seventeenth century, but while Elisha's family had lived in America for over a century, becoming one of the wealthiest families in Charleston, she came from an elite English family, whose members included the royal optician John Dollond, the inventor of a type of telescope lens that challenged the findings of Isaac Newton.[4] Ann's family provided community and resources while the Poinsetts resided overseas.

The family returned to Charleston in 1788. Despite Elisha's changing allegiances during the war, he was able to reintegrate into Charlestonian life, partly because, as a philanthropist who owned slaves and multiple properties, he had already established himself as a patron of some of the city's most elite societies. When he returned, he helped found the Medical Society of South Carolina on Christmas Eve, 1789, and in 1792, he became president of the South Carolina Society.[5] Like most privileged children, Joel Roberts would benefit from his father's reputation and cultural circles.

The Charleston to which the Poinsetts returned was booming again. Although it ceased to be the state capital when the seat moved to Columbia in 1790, it was a major cultural center, a hub of the slave trade, and the most populous southern city, with a population of over sixteen thousand (half of that population was enslaved). It was the United States' preeminent winter port and did a thriving business with the Caribbean. Charleston was a center of natural history that almost rivaled New York and Philadelphia. One of the nation's first historians, David Ramsay, was a medical colleague of Elisha Poinsett.[6] The state in general was wealthy from rice, and soon cotton would become king. Much of the land around Charleston was occupied by large plantations worked by enslaved laborers.

Although Poinsett's father was a wealthy property holder who owned slaves, he was not a rice or cotton planter; regardless, the honor culture associated with southern plantation life influenced the Poinsett family.[7] Within this racialized culture, property ownership bestowed on all white men the duty to control their families and reputations, with violence if necessary, and to be courteous and hospitable.[8] For elites like the Poinsetts, the culture included expectations about piety and erudition.[9] Their family attended an Episcopal church but were not especially dogmatic and could abide by most Christian sects, so long as they were not Catholic. Poinsett absorbed this viewpoint and remained deeply prejudiced against Catholics his whole life. He also inherited his family's intellectualism. Poinsett's father, as a physician, had more scientific training than many elites. The medical profession was Charleston's most intellectually rigorous profession, and its physicians also pursued training in natural history and maintained ties to an intellectual community that spanned Philadelphia, New York, Boston, and some European cities.[10] Poinsett grew up exposed to his father's scholarly activities and developed a lifelong interest in language and science. Although economic value would later be attached to Poinsett's intellectual pursuits, he seems to have possessed a genuine curiosity for learning.

When he was fourteen, Poinsett's parents sent him to Greenfield Academy in Connecticut for what they considered a first-rate education. It was not uncommon for elite southerners to enroll their sons at academies and universities in the North. As a Federalist stronghold, Charleston in particular had close ties to elites in New England. Early on, Poinsett established connections with influential northerners. While riding on a stagecoach in Connecticut, he met prominent Boston Federalist Harrison Gray Otis, with whom he maintained a friendly relationship until Otis's death in 1848. At Greenfield, Poinsett was taught by Timothy Dwight Jr., a Congregationalist theologian and leader of the Second Great Awakening. Dwight taught rationalism and natural science alongside religious doctrine, a multidisciplinary curriculum that pleased Poinsett's father.[11]

Dwight was a leading member of the New England Federalist establishment. Although Poinsett was too young for political affiliation, he would eventually be associated with the Jacksonian Democrats, whose predecessors despised the Federalists. This early experience in Connecticut solidified for Poinsett the value of cross-sectional relationships. Dwight took a liking to Poinsett, whom he found to be a good listener. Dwight believed Poinsett was destined for an impressive career (and incorrectly predicted that Poinsett might one day be president). He encouraged Poinsett's early intellectual interests and initiated him into the northern intellectual milieu.[12] Poinsett was curious about different subjects but easily bored. As an adult, Poinsett would change occupations every few years.

Poinsett was somewhat of a loner. Throughout his life, he was generally well liked by elite white men and women, often of different regions and political persuasions, yet beginning in his youth, he rarely fit in with any one group. At Greenfield, he often preferred wandering alone and reading poetry to socializing with the other boys. For the rest of his life, Poinsett would avoid cliques. He wrote occasionally about girls, and at one point, he was smitten with the "prettiest little flirt" in Greenfield, but after she and other girls snubbed him at a ball in favor of "several smart young men from New York," Poinsett prioritized his studies.[13] Perhaps this incident influenced his later efforts to display expensive taste and martial masculinity.

He also spent much of his time at school dreaming of travel, so when doctors recommended a trip to England, Poinsett was delighted. Earlier in the century, physicians had begun prescribing a change of climate to improve one's health. England's milder climate seemed the ideal antidote to New England, especially since Poinsett had relatives there. The fact that his parents encouraged and financed his travel reveals his privilege; they helped set him up for a diplomatic career. Poinsett attended school outside London, where he continued to study languages and mastered them quickly, a skill that later gave him an advantage for State Department employment. Poinsett spent a lot of time with his mother's cousins, who took him to balls and exposed him to English nobility. Poinsett began to pay attention to social class and appearances, writing to his sister that the differences between the English aristocracy and working classes were "as great as that between blood horses on the Charleston race course and the heavy brutes that draw our carriage."[14]

Poinsett's military interests also began to develop. His instructor, a man he referred to as Mr. Roberts, had been in the army, and Poinsett spent a lot of time with Roberts's family, learning how to fence. His grandfather took him to Enfield, the site of a major English armory, for several days.[15]

In the fall of 1797, Poinsett went to Edinburgh to study medicine like his father, but he burned himself out studying a subject he did not enjoy. When his health worsened that winter, one of his professors recommended a trip to Portugal. His stay in Portugal was brief, and once back in England, he committed to studying military arts.[16] War seemed to be everywhere that year, as the French army invaded Italy, Egypt, and Switzerland and the Quasi War between the United States and France intensified. Although Poinsett failed to gain admittance to the Royal Military Academy at Woolwich, he contented himself with studying military arts under one of the academy's former professors.

Poinsett was hoping to join the army when he returned to the United States. His father, however, had different plans for him, and in 1800, Poinsett returned home to study law under Henry William DeSaussure, a prominent Federalist in Charleston. Of the classic texts that DeSaussure recommended that Poinsett study, Vattel's *Law of Nations* and John Joseph Powell's *Essay upon the Law of Contracts and Agreements* would be especially useful to Poinsett's future endeavors as a diplomat and investor. DeSaussure knew that Poinsett was determined to pursue an alternative career. When sending him a catalog of books, DeSaussure wrote, "But as circumstances make it doubtful whether you will venture to engage deeply in so laborious a profession [as law] I have solicited most of these books with a view to your general improvement as a gentleman and a citizen, who has rights to vindicate and duties to perform."[17]

Knowing that Poinsett planned to travel to Europe before finishing his legal studies, DeSaussure enclosed with that letter a note for Robert Livingston, a wealthy New York statesman whom President Jefferson had just appointed as US minister to France, one of the nation's most important diplomatic positions.[18] Poinsett received extra assistance from Thomas Sumter Jr., the son of a prominent South Carolinian Revolutionary War officer and US congressman, who introduced him to Secretary of State James Madison and forwarded a letter to President Jefferson to secure for Poinsett passage on the ship that would take Livingston to France.[19] Poinsett's father approved of this travel because it would prevent his son from joining the military.

Poinsett spent the winter of 1801–1802 in Paris, where he developed some of his conflicted sentiment between republicanism and militarism. Napoleon had recently established authoritarian rule and was in the process of reforming the legal code. Poinsett thus witnessed the restoration of stability and the impact of strong government measures. He left no written record of his thoughts, but for the rest of his life, despite affiliating with the party associated with minimal government, Poinsett generally favored state-imposed order.

He made exceptions, however, for opportunities for military engagement. His appreciation for the restoration of order in France, for example, was overshadowed by military enthusiasm when he encountered Swiss troops marching to retake their government from the French. Poinsett paused his travels through Switzerland to join Swiss military officer Alois Reding's camp, where he spoke enthusiastically with some of the men about republicanism. The fact that the troops were unsuccessful early on had little consequence for Poinsett, who quickly left for a small town near Geneva, where he socialized with Livingston and several French exiles. Poinsett and Livingston attended a dinner hosted by the French writer Madame de Staël, who had taken refuge near Geneva at the outset of the French Revolution with her father, the former French finance minister Jacques Necker. Although Europe was mostly at peace for much of 1802, there were a series of Swiss uprisings against their French-controlled government. Necker and Staël organized political and intellectual salons for supporters of the Swiss resistance. They welcomed Poinsett, who was fluent in French and told stories of his extensive travels. When Livingston visited during his tour through Switzerland, Staël and Poinsett worked together as translators for him and Necker, who was toothless by then and quite difficult to understand.[20]

Poinsett's stay in Switzerland influenced his later political behavior. His collaboration with Reding was his first exposure to foreign warfare and only added to his desire for a life of military glory. Additionally, he spent much time conversing with Necker, from whom he learned to appreciate the importance of reputation, appearances, and pragmatism. During the French Revolution, Necker had worked to appease both King Louis XVI and the revolutionaries and had, all things considered, fared okay (when the French army invaded Switzerland in 1798, for example, they treated Necker with respect). Poinsett would adopt this approach to political posturing in his own career.

After several months in Switzerland, Poinsett traveled to Italy, France, and Vienna. Sometime before Christmas 1803, he learned that his father had died in Boston. He reunited with his sister Susan in Charleston that winter, only to lose her several months later. Poinsett had taken her to New York City by boat, hoping that sea travel would improve her health, but she died soon after they arrived in the city. Poinsett spent the rest of the year traveling in the northern United States and Canada, stopping in Boston to settle some of his father's business. He left no records for the year 1805, but his father's will indicates that Poinsett inherited a yearly income that secured his status as a wealthy man. His father left to him and Susannah—Poinsett acquired her inheritance when she died—over a dozen rent-yielding properties and a small fortune in bank shares and interest-bearing English funds.[21]

Poinsett used some of his bequeathed funds to travel back to Europe, which, after the Peace of Amiens had broken down, was back at war. He was especially keen to visit Russia, where Joseph Allen Smith, an elite Charlestonian ten years Poinsett's senior, had been the first American traveler in the 1790s; Smith connected Poinsett with some of his contacts.[22] As a reflection of Russia's importance for US trade, particularly as a source of hemp and sailcloth for America's navy and merchant ships, the United States had appointed its first consul to Saint Petersburg in 1803.[23] Poinsett, however, was more interested in military affairs than in securing a post like Smith's because he still had little interest in personal profit (during the nation's first decades, consuls did not receive a salary but were expected to profit from their service).[24] For now, at least, Poinsett could live easily off his inheritance. He asked his closest friend from home, Joseph Johnson, to send him military credentials so that Russian officials would be more willing to bestow on him certain access and privileges.

Poinsett wrote that it would "save me an immense expense in clothes, etc., but I wish it chiefly as a mean of procuring military information." Specifically, he wanted a certificate stating that he was an aide-de-camp to South Carolina governor Charles Pinckney. Poinsett knew this might prove difficult, as he had no military service. If Pinckney did not comply, Poinsett instructed Johnson to turn to "some of the brigadier generals," writing, "It is in fact essentially necessary to my future plans, spare no pains to procure it, and you will add another obligation to the many I am already under to you."[25] Johnson and Pinckney complied, and Poinsett received his official paperwork, dated December 10, 1806, as aide-de-camp to Governor Pinckney.[26] If this were not enough to win over Russian officials, "Colonel" Poinsett also asked Johnson to send some plants and seeds from Carolina for the empress. For the rest of his life, Poinsett would incorporate botany into his diplomacy. As elites throughout the world became increasingly interested in exotic natural products, plants and seeds served as a sort of international diplomatic currency.

With his credentials in place, and having "at length conquered the Russian language," Poinsett made plans to travel throughout the Russian Empire and central Asia with twenty-two-year-old Philip Yorke, a British viscount with the title Lord Royston.[27] Royston, the oldest son of a member of Parliament and Earl of Hardwick, referred to Poinsett as "one of the few liberal and literary gentlemanlike men I have seen emerge from the forests of the New World." They planned a trip to reflect their "gentlemanlike" status. Royston was in regular contact with his father about outfitting their tour and planned to "float down the Volga, luxuriously sitting upon a sofa." They purchased a large merchandise bark and furnished it with comfortable pillows and fine upholstery. They also hired guides, a Tatar interpreter, military escorts, and several servants, whom they armed with pistols and broadswords. Although Russia and Napoleonic France signed a peace treaty in July 1807, Russia remained at war against the Persian and Ottoman Empires, which made travel dangerous. Poinsett and Royston each carried a double-barreled gun, a brace of pistols, a dagger, and a saber.[28]

They sailed down the Volga to the Caspian Sea, along the way taking landed excursions to hunt, purchase food and supplies, and visit former Greek colonies and Zoroaster worship sites. They sent letters ahead to local leaders to inform them that two "distinguished" foreigners were visiting, hoping for special greetings and comfortable lodgings. According to one of Poinsett's rare accounts of his trip, people traveled specifically to "see two European travelers, a sight most rare."[29] Regardless of whether the people Poinsett encountered actually thought he was a European traveler, Poinsett felt like one. He had spent a large portion of his life overseas.

Although Poinsett was notorious among his friends as having an "unconquerable indolence for writing," he sent one very long letter to Johnson, narrating the details of his trip (partly because, as he wrote, "I feel so far removed from you all that I fear to be forgotten").[30] These writings reflect his curiosity about geography and cultural diversity, as well as his chauvinism. He wrote to Johnson from the Russian-occupied city of Baku on the Caspian Sea, which he described as having "extraordinary appearance," before detailing its architecture and the worship sites associated with Zoroaster.[31] He also enjoyed trying a variety of Georgian wines, which seemed comparable to brandy; Royston preferred them to "most French wines imported into Russia."[32]

Although he appreciated aspects of other cultures, Poinsett's chauvinism often won out. When visiting a Persian khan, Poinsett felt "obliged to give [the khan] a long geographical lecture." Poinsett was amused that the people he encountered knew almost nothing about the United States and that they referred to Thomas Jefferson as "shah of America." Poinsett's condescension reflects his and Royston's entitled attitudes. Before launching into his geography lesson, Poinsett "immediately harangued" the khan because he and Royston felt slighted by their interactions with locals prior to their visit to the court. A local chief had permitted the theft of their horses, before forcing them to wait to see the shah. As Poinsett and Royston traveled, they expected to have their needs met, as evidenced by the armed fishing incident that opened this chapter.

Throughout his travels, Poinsett focused on resources, not just for his own provisions but for economic reconnaissance. When he wrote to Johnson from Baku, he devoted a considerable amount of space in his letter to detailing the structure of the port, as well as the "sources of naptha, which are within 15 miles of Baku and constitute its chief branch of commerce."[33] He explained that naphtha was used to light lamps all over Persia. Poinsett predicted that Baku would eventually become a major oil exporter. In noting that Russia's ongoing conquest of the Caucasus region would give the empire access to this lucrative resource, Poinsett acknowledged the role of military force for resource acquisition.[34] This phenomenon was simultaneously a holdover from mercantilism and a harbinger of state-sponsored capitalism.

Poinsett's letter more generally reflects a preoccupation with war. Russia was formally at war with Persia, and more recently with the Ottoman Empire; it also dealt with Napoleon to the west. Poinsett saw thousands of men marching to join armies, and he chose to forgo a trip into Persia in favor of following the path of the Russian military on a treacherous trip in freezing weather over the Caucasus Mountains. Accompanied by fifty soldiers and equipped with a cannon, the group "fell in with an army of Circassians" (indigenous highlanders) who requested their assistance "to repulse a tribe, which had invaded them." Although they avoided serious fighting, Poinsett, Royston, and their servants caught debilitating fevers several times. Three of their servants ended up dying; "only a stout negro of Poinsett's" survived.[35] Even after this ordeal, Poinsett wanted to join the military. He and Royston spent part of January 1808 in Moscow recovering, and at the end of the month, Poinsett left Royston for Petersburg. Poinsett stayed alert to US-Russo opportunities.[36] Years later, Poinsett remembered speaking to the emperor about signing a treaty of mutual protection for both countries' claims to the Pacific Northwest; he brought it up to President James Madison and Secretary of State James Monroe, but without results.[37]

Poinsett traveled back to Paris, where he attended Napoleon's birthday celebration in August 1808 and witnessed a famous argument between Napoleon and Austrian chancellor Prince Klemens von Metternich.[38] Soon after, he learned that the British had fired on the USS *Chesapeake* off the coast of Virginia over a year earlier. He had built up a collection of military books and wanted to join the US military.[39] At that point in his life, Poinsett made decisions based on desires, not pecuniary needs. He was still dependent on his father's money and had not yet begun to worry about generating his own income, even as he got himself into debt.[40] He wrote to Johnson to send him money from his trust (which Johnson sent through a French banker who had been involved in the XYZ Affair—an illustrative example of the complexity of dubious international financial connections among US statesmen) while also writing that he would enlist as a volunteer if the United States declared war against Britain. Poinsett wanted to be an aide-de-camp rather than an engineer because the latter would preclude him from promotion. Status still mattered more to Poinsett than financial gain.

Poinsett sailed for the United States, assuming incorrectly that he would be entering military service. He had no real home and spent the next year in limbo. He now owned his father's thirteen city properties, plus 310 acres on the Ashley River, but he had no family with whom to share any of the responsibility.[41] He inherited an enslaved individual named Samuel, likely the "stout negro of Poinsett's" whom he took on his travels in Europe and Asia.[42] Partway through his time in Paris, however, Poinsett had sent Samuel back to Charleston for the sake of appearances. He claimed that Samuel had "been fool enough to many," but Poinsett also may have been embarrassed to have an enslaved African in Europe.[43] In general, at that point in his life, Poinsett viewed slaves more as status objects than as capital. His father's slaves were all household servants, and since Poinsett was never at home, it seemed proper to him to free them. Poinsett did note derisively later on that they all struggled with freedom, so perhaps he figured they were not valuable enough to sell.[44] Poinsett always harbored reservations about the institution, but when he became a plantation owner later in life, he began to view enslaved laborers as valuable assets.

At age thirty, however, Poinsett was little more than the privileged, urbane son of a "gentleman" and had no clue about managing a household. He made a brief attempt to settle down when he returned from Europe. According to Nathalie de Lage de Volude, the wife of Thomas Sumter Jr. (who had introduced Poinsett to Madison and socialized with him in France), Poinsett hoped to marry a woman named Nancy Elliott. There is little historical record of her, other than that Nathalie Sumter told another South Carolina woman that Poinsett, a close friend of the Sumters, spoke often of his love for her. He did this confidentially and allegedly was heartbroken that she preferred Ralph Izard.[45] The Izards were a powerful South Carolina family; there were at least two Ralph Izards among Poinsett's peers. One inherited a large rice plantation on the Pee

Dee River; the other, just returned from naval service, was a hero for his role in the Battle of Tripoli. The former was the brother of Poinsett's future wife, Mary; the latter was her cousin.[46] Neither Izard ended up marrying Nancy, but the threat dashed Poinsett's hopes. Although Poinsett "felt diffident as to his own merits" and assumed he was not "acceptable" to Nancy's father, Nathalie Sumter held out hope for Nancy and Poinsett. In fact, Sumter had at one point wanted her sister to marry Poinsett, writing that "there are few gentlemen in our country in which so many advantages are combined . . . he has the best of education, has been at all courts of Europe, his merits were distinguished by the Emperor Paul."[47]

As Poinsett dawdled between Washington and Charleston, waiting to see if his dreams of military service or marriage to Nancy Elliott would become reality, his prospects grew dimmer. The qualities Sumter listed may not have made Poinsett marriage material, but they qualified him for diplomatic service. Poinsett hoped that because he had "picked up some military knowledge" while overseas, he could get a position in the army, but as much as Poinsett thought he was fit for military service, the administration did not agree.[48] They saw a diplomat. When Madison proposed his name for quartermaster general, Secretary of War William Eustis allegedly protested. When Secretary of Treasury Albert Gallatin proposed his name for a diplomatic mission to South America, it stuck. It was well known that Poinsett had made a good impression abroad. When serving as minister to Saint Petersburg in 1809, for example, John Quincy Adams noted that Russian royalty spoke highly of Poinsett.[49] Also, as Gallatin pointed out to Madison, Poinsett was fluent in French and was "so far versed in Spanish that a few weeks practice will enable him to speak it fluently." In addition to Poinsett's language skills and cosmopolitanism, another benefit of his was "his object being reputation and not money."[50] Consular agents were supposed to be financially independent so that they had motivations beyond earning a salary. At that point, Poinsett was still financed by his father's wealth (it was not until he served as ambassador to Mexico that he used the privileges of his position to make personal investments). This, combined with the fact that he was unattached to family in the United States, made him the perfect choice for an intelligence-gathering mission in South America, where Spain's colonies were in the beginning stages of independence movements.

When Napoleon invaded Spain and installed his brother on the Spanish throne in 1808, opposition movements sprang up throughout South America. Some aimed to restore a reformed version of the Spanish monarchy; others, to establish complete independence. People in the United

States had very little understanding of what was going on because Spain prohibited diplomatic agents in all colonial cities except Havana and La Guaira, and the little US citizens knew about the continent came. from mercantile news and travel accounts.[51] The United States had to decide whether the commercial and ideological appeal of Latin American independence outweighed the strategic advantages of continued colonial rule.

Many Americans were interested in their southern neighbors, especially for business. Spanish American mines were the major source of the world's silver, an essential commodity for trade with China and 80 percent of legal tender in the United States.[52] US merchants hoped that Spain's colonists would abolish monopolies and allow them to acquire silver directly from their mines. In the face of escalating military and economic tensions with Great Britain, Americans also hoped to take advantage of new markets for their exports—particularly grains and some manufactured goods.[53]

US leaders, however, had to balance revolutionary enthusiasm with practical diplomatic considerations. They could not openly support revolution if there was a chance that Spain might not lose. Conversely, they feared that in the absence of Spanish rule, new sovereign republics might threaten the integrity of the Union, especially if British naval and commercial influence dominated the region.[54]

The overthrow of the Spanish viceroy and establishment of an independent junta by Buenos Aires revolutionaries in May 1810 prompted the Madison administration to make sure the United States had influence. At the very least, it had to take action to protect the small US business community there. Madison struggled to find qualified men who were willing to go. He prematurely had instructions printed with one candidate's name on them, only to learn that the man had turned down the post in Buenos Aires. Gallatin then suggested Poinsett to Madison. Poinsett had said he was open to diplomatic employment but tried to stress that "his studies & views had been more particularly directed to the army, specially in relation to its organisation and general staff." Gallatin knew that despite Poinsett's enthusiasm for war, a diplomatic post, especially this one, would be a more useful fit.[55]

Poinsett said yes. Nathalie Sumter thought he might have stayed in the United States if he had believed Nancy would marry him. With no military post and no prospect of marriage, however, Poinsett decided to cut his losses and accept the South American post as a gateway to career advancement later on. His freedom from family and occupational obligations permitted him to act in his own self-interest, which at this point in his life meant adventure, status advancement, and, if possible, military engagement. Poinsett hoped this position would prove his ability to serve the United States and help him secure a military post if war broke out with Britain. He was fortunate to receive this diplomatic position at a time when the US government was eager to expand its power at home and overseas yet unable to tightly manage its employees. The State Department, for example, in addition to its foreign service, oversaw the superintendent of patents and allowed William Thornton almost free rein in administering the rights for inventions.[56] This bureaucratic precedent continued with Poinsett, who would have the latitude to serve US interests as he saw fit.

At the end of August 1810, Secretary of State Robert Smith sent him the official instructions "to proceed without delay to Buenos Aires and there if convenient to Lima in Peru, or St. Iago in Chile, or both." Poinsett would be furnished with letters, but it was understood that "the authorities thereof may possibly refuse to give a public recognition and character to a consul of the United States."[57] The United States had been appointing consular representatives, diplomatic agents who were charged with giving their "attention to whatever can promote the commerce and navigation of our country," to port cities throughout the world since it declared independence from Britain. Although the United States had consuls in places as far away as Canton and Cape Town (Poinsett's fellow Charlestonian Joseph Allen Smith was consul in Saint Petersburg), it struggled to establish a consular service in the Americas. The Spanish Crown denied foreign nations consular presence in its empire, except for Havana and La Guaira.[58] To appease Spanish officials, the US government gave Poinsett the title "agent for seamen and commerce," a rank lower than consul. In practice, however, the State Department expected Poinsett to exercise more power than a mere agent, as he was supposed to "attend to the commercial and other concerns of our citizens in all the cases where they would fall under the patronage of a consul and . . . appoint deputies wheresoever it may be found necessary."[59]

Smith informed Poinsett that he would receive a cipher that would allow him to communicate secretly with the US government, as well as with the handful of confidential agents scattered throughout the Americas.[60] With this cipher, Poinsett joined the shadowy world of early US foreign relations, much of which were conducted secretly.[61] The US government, like those of other nations, had been using secret code since the Revolution as a way to shield information from foreign powers and sometimes from the American public.[62] By the late 1700s, critics in the United States and Europe condemned government secrecy, but this did little to stop the practice.[63] In fact, as Poinsett was preparing for his South American mission, President Madison had initiated a series of secret plans to invade contested territory in Florida. (Although Seminoles controlled the Florida peninsula, Spain claimed to "own" it, and white Americans steadily moved into the territory throughout the 1790s and 1800s.)[64] Madison issued a public proclamation in October declaring his intention to claim the Florida territory, which he maintained belonged to the United Sates as per the Louisiana Purchase. In January, Congress passed a secret act for acquisition of the area, and, later that year, Madison gave secret approval for an insurrection against Spain in East Florida, of which he later claimed ignorance.[65] And earlier, Thomas Jefferson, while serving as secretary of state, had seriously considered cooperating with France to take Florida from Spain.[66] He had also tacitly condoned French ambassador Edmond-Charles Genet's 1793 plans to employ American soldiers in the liberation of Spanish New Orleans.[67] During Jefferson's presidency, Venezuelan patriot Francisco de Miranda had secretly recruited financiers and soldiers in the United States for a colonial rebellion in northern South America, which Spanish officials assumed the Jefferson administration had knowingly permitted. It is unclear how much Jefferson knew about Miranda's clandestine expedition, but he claimed ignorance so as not to anger Spain, hoping Spain might willingly cede some of its land to the United States if the United States respected its sovereignty in the hemisphere.[68]

As Smith warned Poinsett, "under the varying aspect of the affairs of Spain, it has been the anxious endeavor of the president to regulate his conduct by the rules of the most exact neutrality."[69] Although the United States was rarely ever "neutral," its agents were supposed to minimize the nation's imperial designs.[70] Smith instructed Poinsett to emphasize the US government's "prompt suppression of unlawful enterprises carried on by certain privateers bearing the French flag clandestinely fitted out in the ports of the Unites States and calculated to annoy the pride of the subjects of Spain."[71] Poinsett would be affirming US neutrality at the same time as Madison justified the US annexation of West Florida.

The State Department's main goal for its new agents in South America was to maintain the fiction of US citizens as detached republicans because their economic success in the region depended on it. The United States, as of yet, had no territorial aims in South America, but neither was it unambitious, a fact that the State Department worked to minimize for the sake of revolutionaries, who sought sympathetic allies, and Europeans, who did not want potential rivals.[72]

When the new opposition parliament in Cádiz, which formed on September 24, 1810, during French occupation, denied equal representation
to members from South America, Spain's colonies began to talk more seriously of war. The impending wars called into question commercial relationships, simultaneously threatening to disrupt business and to usher
in "free" trade without Spanish restrictions. Both Britain and the United
States sought to establish lucrative trade relationships with whoever
emerged victorious, which meant maintaining the appearance of neutrality while events played out.

If Smith and others had known the extent of Poinsett's military desires,
they might have found him less suitable for the task. Fresh from imperial warfare in Europe and the Caucasus, and eager for revenge against
the British, Poinsett was primed for violence. Yet he was also becoming
a master of pretension. He looked and acted the part of a cosmopolitan
diplomat and had the proper breeding and education to interact amicably
with influential foreigners. This meant he could keep his bellicosity under
wraps, at least until military opportunity presented itself. He would put
to work his experiences in Europe, traveling, observing, socializing with
dignitaries, and extracting information from locals.

On October 15, 1810, Poinsett sailed from New York to South America.
He headed in what many ways felt to him like the wrong direction—away
from Nancy and away from the possibility of war against Britain. Poinsett
was hopeful that if war broke out, President Madison would let him return home to fight. War did break out less than two years later, and Poinsett had to content himself with fighting against British interests in a different theater of the Napoleonic Wars.

2

....

International and Domestic
Politics, 1811–1819

Poinsett arrived in Rio de Janeiro on Christmas Day, 1810, after seventy days at sea. The *Niagara* had struggled to navigate from the Caribbean down to the coast of Brazil. "By entreaties and threats," Poinsett and his fellow passengers convinced a group of locals who were fishing off the coast of the West Indies to come aboard and help them. They "induced" one man to pilot them around the cape and later "dismissed [him] off Pernambuco" before steering for Rio. As they approached Rio de Janeiro, Poinsett sighted the "high rock in the shape of a sugar loaf." He was impressed by the lush vegetation, the bustling business on the street, and the "silversmiths and jewelers who make a great display of the precious stones of the Brazils such as topaz, amethysts and Brazil diamonds."[1]

However, the sight of Afro-Brazilians jarred the southerner, who had spent years away from South Carolina's Black majority: "The streets swarm with blacks who from neglect are a prey to all the diseases of tropical climate. . . . The treatment of these unfortunate people throughout Brazil is inconceivably barbarous and constantly intrude itself upon the stranger whose compassion and indignation are alternately excited at every step."[2] Poinsett derived his pretentious compassion from years of privileged education and travel and seemed to assume that no visitors to the United States were ever appalled by the brutality of the American plantation or slave market. Poinsett would later turn his observations into a journal to submit to the State Department, blending these observations with commentary on geography, topography, demography, politics, and economics.

He also paid special attention to commercial opportunities and obstacles (like competition from the British). In his first letter to the State

Department, Poinsett warned of British efforts to "procure a temporary commercial advantage" in different cities and wrote that they "are more to be feared" than any other foreign powers.[3] Napoleon's occupation of Spain had inadvertently created a power vacuum in the Americas that Spanish America's juntas sought to fill. Both the United States and Britain hoped to have influence; the United States, however, operated from a mostly defensive position. The State Department regularly received letters from mercantile agents like Mathew Arnold Hoevel, begging for diplomatic representatives to protect their interests against British privilege. Hovel pleaded the necessity of "an agent to treat with the new government of Chile."[4] Poinsett was the first diplomatic agent to do so in Chile, as the federal government began employing consuls and other agents below the level of minister plenipotentiary to compete for influence in this new arena of economic opportunity.

State Department goals for Poinsett's mission were commercial and informational. He was expected to "inquire into the state, the characteristics and the proportions as to numbers, intelligence and wealth of the several parties, the amount of population, the extent and organization of the military force, and the pecuniary resources of the country," as well as "explain the mutual advantages of a commerce with the United States, promote liberal and stable regulations, and transmit seasonable information on the subject."[5] As Poinsett traveled throughout the future nations of Brazil, Argentina, Chile, Peru, and Uruguay, he wrote down his observations for the State Department. At that point, the writings of German naturalist Alexander von Humboldt, who had traveled around Latin America from 1799 to 1804, were US officials' main source of information on the region. Like Humboldt, Poinsett was interested in the "natural" world, and he blended scientific curiosity with utilitarianism, writing about geography, climate, natural resources, political events, valuable resources, and influential people.[6] His writings, like Humboldt's, would be used in the service of imperialism, as US policy centered on gathering intelligence to benefit private American interests.

Poinsett also sent regular updates to Washington, summarizing his activities and observations and reporting on the activities of British diplomatic agents. Poinsett relayed information essential for a government that knew so little about the region and yet desired to compete with other world powers for new economic opportunities for its citizens.[7] The manuscript drafts of Poinsett's reports to the State Department, as well as the letters he wrote to and received from businessmen and political figures, highlight nascent US interests and US officials' attempts to take advantage of the opportunities posed by new nations. Many of the letters were hastily written, a result of Poinsett writing in snatched moments of time and in potentially insecure locations. He often wrote in cipher to protect his letters from British and Spanish interception and to hide the embarrassing state of foreign relations from the American public.

Poinsett served as the government version of a business manager, what business historian Alfred Chandler referred to as the "visible hand" of the economy.[8] As Poinsett acted as the "hand" of the US state, he guided the abstract forces of economic integration, sometimes steered by the US government, other times self-directed.[9] Even when he occasionally bucked protocol, he received approbation from officials in Washington. He both acted autonomously and cooperated with other State Department agents. This was not unusual. American consuls to the Barbary States, for example, had been working on behalf of their own, their friends', and their nation's interests since the 1790s.[10] In Spanish America, where the United States did not yet place authorized consuls, quasi-official US citizens dealt with issues of property and security. James Wilkinson, for example, whom Poinsett would later encounter in Mexico, negotiated independently with Spanish officials in Natchez to counter Choctaw and Chickasaw presence in the region.[11] These sorts of negotiations on behalf of US economic advantages would continue as more consuls were appointed to the region.[12]

While Poinsett was not, as of yet, especially motivated by money, he did know that South America was the perfect site for patriotism and profit to overlap.[13] Philadelphia and Baltimore had become hot spots for exactly this type of intersecting interest. Men like Stephen Girard invested fortunes in Spanish American independence, shipping arms and supplies in the hope of patriot profits and lucrative future trading relationships. They curried favor with revolutionaries, who themselves had something to offer. Chilean leader José Miguel Carrera, for example, whom Poinsett would befriend, was from a wealthy mining family. In some ways, Poinsett was similar to men like Girard, favoring economic opportunity and military intervention.[14] Poinsett's support, however, reflected a stronger military desire. While some Americans violated US neutrality by sending arms and munitions, Poinsett violated US neutrality by fighting in Chile for the cause of US free trade. His patriotism intersected with, and was perhaps overshadowed by, not only American business interests but his own unrequited military dreams. Fighting against Britain preoccupied Poinsett the whole time he was in South America.

Travels

Poinsett spent weeks in Rio de Janeiro, waiting for his real work to begin. His first major problem had to do with passports. He received clearance at Rio but did not know whether he would get a passport to travel to Buenos Aires. The United States had a different relationship with Brazil, where US merchants traded flour and grains for animal hides, sugar, and other raw goods, than it did with Spanish America.[15] Portugal had allowed the United States to maintain a consul in colonial Brazil at Rio de Janeiro, while the Spanish Crown denied foreign nations consular presence at any of its colonies, except for in Cuba and for one post at La Guaira in the Viceroyalty of New Granada.[16] With the Portuguese royal crown firmly ensconced in Rio after fleeing from Napoleon, there was little serious hope of a successful independence movement and therefore less diplomatic ambiguity for the United States.

Soon after arriving in Rio, Poinsett connected with fellow South Carolinian Thomas Sumter Jr., who was serving as US consul to Rio and could help Poinsett procure passports for his travels to the Rio de la Plata region. Sumter, like Poinsett, was the privileged son of an elite Revolutionary War veteran. He had declined an "extraordinary offer" for a lavish city home and "retired to the country until he could procure a habitation in a less despotic manner." To avoid displacing a local family, Sumter moved into a monastery, where he attempted to reform the "profligacy" of the monks there. This "excited their hatred," and Sumter left. In his journal, Poinsett declined to say where Sumter went, although in January 1811, Poinsett stayed with Sumter and his wife in Rio.[17]

After writing about Sumter's experience in the monastery, Poinsett launched into a critique of Rio as mostly "broken and incapable of cultivation." He affirmed Sumter's views on the monks and wrote that "the prince although said to be a good man and desirous to promote the welfare of his subjects is incapable of governing he is entirely occupied with the ceremonies of the Catholic religions and in the gratification of his appetite." Poinsett crossed out the section about the prince, perhaps considering that opinion to be unnecessary, even though he would continue to pepper his journal with negative comments about Catholicism.[18] Poinsett seemed to be balancing his own opinions with the information he thought the State Department wanted. Although it was relatively common for Americans to criticize the social and political effects of Catholicism, Catholicism was not a major concern of the US government.[19] Instead, Poinsett's religious critiques reflected his own prejudices.

After setting the scene with condescending commentary, Poinsett got to the point. England had helped the Portuguese court take refuge from Napoleon in Rio de Janeiro. The Portuguese government in Brazil subsequently signed a treaty with England that gave England favorable trade preferences in exchange for support of its independence. This was a problem for US traders, who paid 10 percent higher duties than British merchants. Unequal trade policies would be a constant issue throughout South America, as the United States struggled to compete with British influence. Poinsett knew, however, that Brazil did not necessarily need any foreign help. Unlike Portugal, which recognized "the necessity of depending on a foreign power," Brazil's "population and resources will shew what it is capable of under an active intelligent government."[20] Here, Poinsett recognized the power of government and also the obstacle of competing factions. The royal court in Brazil was divided, with Princess Carlota (born in Spain, married to the Portuguese prince regent, João VI) initially offering revolutionaries throughout Spanish America her alliance, then reneging and aiding the royalists.[21] Poinsett feared the combined power of Brazil and England; he wanted all of Spanish America to form a federation to check their influence.[22] If Poinsett could not challenge the British at home, he wanted to do it in South America.

The first place on his State Department itinerary was Buenos Aires, where US business struggled without a representative. The city had been the capital of the Viceroyalty of Rio de la Plata until nonseparatist patriots had set up a junta the previous year. Carlota was in talks with royalists in Montevideo—the new capital of Rio de la Plata—to challenge the junta in Buenos Aires. Poinsett wrote his first secret-code letter to the State Department in January, expressing his concern with traveling from Rio de Janeiro to the Rio de la Plata region, based on the limited information he received from a few foreign merchants he met in Rio. Poinsett managed to keep his destination a secret from foreign powers and "found no difficulty in obtaining a passport to embark for the South."[23]

Twenty-five days after leaving Brazil, Poinsett entered the Rio de la Plata. He wrote detailed instructions relating to its difficult navigation for the State Department, intending future merchant ventures to consult them. His ship approached Rio at the "height of summer," and he observed that "many people were bathing, some of whom sat with the water up to their chins and held an umbrella over their heads." Poinsett described everything he saw, from the height of houses on the shoreline to the ponchos Indigenous people wore. As always, he fixated on appearances, objectifying those he considered beneath him. Of Buenos Aires' Indigenous population, Poinsett "observed in passing that their complex-

ions were darker than that of our Indians and their forms not so slight."
Of women, he wrote, "They are well formed and although I saw few faces
regularly beautiful they had generally fine dark eyes and an animated
expression."[24]

At first, the junta in Buenos Aires would not accept Poinsett's commission. It looked unofficial and was not directly addressed to the junta—
partly a reflection of the US State Department's ignorance of who was in
power. After Poinsett convinced city officials that the document was the
same type of commission that the US consul had in Havana, which was
recognized by Spain, Poinsett was accepted as an agent of commerce.[25]
The commission did not solve the problem of finance, however. The
State Department allowed Poinsett "reasonable expenses" so long as he
kept "a regular account," including vouchers "and where vouchers cannot be obtained . . . a statement of the details."[26] Yet he could not at first
access federal monies to fund his stay because the US State Department
had no bankers in Buenos Aires with whom to open credit.[27] Everything
the United States did in South America was ad hoc, and Poinsett had to
construct a financial arrangement that involved Sumter in Rio and mercantile agents in Charleston, Boston, and London.[28] Poinsett and the US
government ultimately depended on Barings Bank, a prominent British
bank that funded many American enterprises—an arrangement that symbolized the complexities of the United States' cooperative/competitive
relationship with Britain.[29] As the United States was on the brink of war
with Britain, it relied on British bankers for its solvency.

Word quickly spread that a new American was in the city, and Poinsett
was invited to parties held by the Creole upper class. Although he had
applauded Sumter for choosing republican simplicity over lavish lodgings, Poinsett took advantage of luxurious accommodations. He used
elite gatherings to ingratiate himself with men and women alike, danc-
ing and making conversation. His ultimate goal was to gain political contacts and convince Creoles to give up their allegiance to King Ferdinand
VII and separate from Spain.

As pretentious as Poinsett could be, he found the women intelligent,
and, because he needed people to like him, he tried local customs, such as
drinking the caffeine-infused maté and participating in carnival celebrations. Of his trip to a bull fight, Poinsett wrote, "The streets [were] lined
with ladies, armed with basins of water, squirts, or wax eggs filled with
scented water. Finding that there was no hope of escape I furnished myself with some of the latter and defending myself as well as I could passed
through this file. I was assailed with showers of scented water and arrived

totally soaked." At the fight, he "conformed to the custom by throwing money into the arena," but his gentlemanly pretenses caused him to disdain that "the frequent exhibition of this sanguinary spectacle familiarizes the people to scenes of blood and tends to augment the ferocious character of the lower orders."[30] Poinsett mentally separated this type of bloodshed with the bloodshed that he had willingly chosen to observe while following the Russian military.

For all his efforts socializing, Poinsett noted that people were still guarded around him. He had trouble getting detailed answers to his questions, until he had spent several months living in the country house of military leader Manuel Luzuriaga, who was "more communicative than most of his countrymen and of more import not attached to any party." Luzuriaga gave Poinsett information about the revolution and about social and economic conditions of the city, which Poinsett began writing down to send to the State Department.

It was not enough to learn about politics; Poinsett wanted to influence them. He claimed that he convinced the junta to place "the vessels of the United States nearly upon footing with the British."[31] However, he was not allowed to publicize the change of policy, lest it anger the British. To combat Britain's influence, Poinsett wanted the United States to supply the patriots with arms, which would shift the power dynamics in favor of the United States.[32] Because the US government could not openly support colonies in rebellion by providing weapons (it would be a violation of the country's official policy of neutrality), Poinsett encouraged arms deals between private merchants from the United States and the junta at Buenos Aires.[33]

His strategy blended cooperation and subtle coercion. In addition to offering support, Poinsett made indirect threats, such as "the United States never would suppose it necessary to have an armed force to protect her commerce in the rivers and harbors of a friendly power." These actions were precursors to techniques future US consuls would employ when negotiating for favorable trade deals with newly independent nations.[34] As yet, however, the threats carried little weight, so Poinsett attempted cooperation with the British. At first, he had lobbied the Buenos Aires patriot government, in opposition to several dozen British merchants, to adopt liberal trade policies. The British merchants had already paid heavy tariffs on the goods they had recently imported and did not want to see the tariffs removed. Poinsett, though, was able to convince them that if the high tariffs continued, all future trade would suffer. Some agreed to cooperate, but Poinsett still urged the State Department to station a per-

manent commercial agent at Buenos Aires, insisting that "otherwise the
English will obtain exclusive commercial privilege."[35] Poinsett was there
only temporarily, and by the time he made that request, he had already
decided to move on. In April, Poinsett wrote to the department that if he
did not hear from them, he would plan to cross the *Cordillera* into Chile
in October.[36]

He left Buenos Aires in November. In the months before his departure, Poinsett finished collecting information. He wrote about flora and
fauna, houses and customs, marketable commodities and revolutionary
developments. He focused particularly on military intelligence, providing specifics on troop numbers and weapon supplies. When possible, he
included copies of intercepted communications, such as a letter from a
British captain at Montevideo addressed to British merchants at Buenos
Aires about Montevideo's plan to blockade the port. War had broken out
between the patriot junta in Buenos Aires and royalist forces in Montevideo.[37] Poinsett's hopes for a patriot victory were dashed when royalist forces defeated patriot efforts in Uruguay, Paraguay, and Upper Peru;
however, "the differences so long existing between this place and monte
video are finally adjusted. The only condition with which we are yet ac-
quainted is to us the most important: the free commerce in the River of
Plate."[38]

"Free trade," or at least trade without prohibitive restrictions on merchandise from the United States, was the State Department agents' main
goal everywhere.[39] Chile had liberalized its trade the previous February,
but royalist ships from Peru harassed American ships entering Chilean
ports.[40] Poinsett determined to do something about this.

He arrived in Chile in December, after taking the arduous overland
route so that he could observe the region's infrastructure and natural
resources. Before setting out, Poinsett had informed the State Department that his travel expenses would be considerable because of "insecure
roads."[41] His writings throughout Argentina, Uruguay, and Chile reflect
a preoccupation with what would become two of his career interests:
internal improvements and Indigenous conflict.[42] He wrote frequently
about bad roads and Native violence, revealing the development of his
thoughts on political economy. He saw the presence of Native peoples
and the absence of transportation infrastructure as detriments to white
people's ability to travel and trade. Both could be overcome with government intervention, and, as South Carolina legislator and US secretary of
war, Poinsett would put into practice his belief in funding economic development projects and violence against Natives.

In February, Poinsett was received as consul general by José Miguel Carrera, who had fought in the Spanish Army against Napoleon in Europe and had recently risen to power through a coup. Eager for good commercial relations with the United States, Carrera organized a lavish ceremony for Poinsett.[43] Poinsett was hopeful. He wrote to the State Department about Chile's economic potential, once Carrera's government liberalized trade: "The people now use their own coarse expensive manufactures whose custom must cease with the introduction of free commerce."[44] Poinsett had no qualms about stifling domestic industry, and he resolved to have more influence than he had in Rio or Bueno Aires. He attempted to force this influence by choosing military interference over cooperative diplomacy.

First, he befriended Carrera, a controversial leader whose tactics bordered on dictatorial.[45] A keen student of appearances, Poinsett encouraged Carrera to more fully embrace symbols of republicanism. One of these was a "free" press. Carrera had purchased a printing press from Mathew Hoevel, who was in Chile representing the illegal interests of a US whaler and whom President James Monroe had recently given Poinsett permission to employ as a consular agent.[46] Carrera used the press to set up the *Aurora*, a pro-revolution newspaper that printed pieces on popular sovereignty, separation of powers, and the US founders. Poinsett encouraged its use as a mouthpiece for the regime, especially for the promotion of another major symbol of republicanism: Chile's new constitution.

After Carrera's coup nullified the National Congress of Chile's Decree for the Provisional Executive Authority, Chile lacked a liberal constitution to balance his authoritarian-style rule.[47] Poinsett, unbeknownst to the US State Department, hosted meetings to draft a new constitution.[48] He was mostly responsible for the first draft, which, like the US Constitution, provided for representative democracy, separation of powers, and religious liberty. Of particular import to Poinsett was the last. He feared "the evil . . . which grows out of the Catholic institutions" and devoted a lot of space in his travel journals to disparaging Catholic rituals, priests' influence on politics, and the church's ownership of large amounts of valuable property.[49] In Poinsett's view, the church stifled political development. On this point, he was disappointed with the final draft, which made Catholicism the official religion.

As a whole, however, Poinsett was pleased with the new constitution. It succeeded at liberalizing Carrera's government—at least on paper—and bolstered the United States' capitalist agenda by codifying a free press and individual freedoms. The constitution also gave the *Gran Jefe* authority over warfare and foreign relations. With Carrera in power, this authority boded well for US-Chilean relations. As much as Poinsett touted republicanism, he recognized the importance of sovereign executive power, especially when it was exercised by Carrera, whom he believed was the Chilean leader most likely to support US interests.

Poinsett was pleased that Carrera agreed to take a census because a more accurate account of the country's population and resources would doubly aid the independence movement and the US State Department—that is, if the department was even interested anymore.[50] Poinsett complained about the lack of attention he received. It was common for State Department agents to receive minimal correspondence, and things were especially slow because of conflict with Great Britain. Additionally, the State Department did not know enough about the region to give Poinsett instructions; they expected him to figure things out himself. He was happy to take his own initiative, but he wanted to know that his service was valued. Despite the occasional amusement of parties, such as the July 4 celebration in which an American was accidentally shot in a drunken fight, Poinsett was "tired of being shut up here without any communication."[51]

Poinsett became even more despondent when he learned that war had broken out between the United States and Great Britain in June 1812, months before he heard about it. Commodore David Porter, who had been sent down to the South Pacific to harass British ships, brought the news.[52] Poinsett wanted nothing more than to go home and fight; the US government wanted him to stay. His language skills were more valuable than his military ones.

When royalist troops from the Viceroyalty of Peru invaded Chile in early 1813, Poinsett got his wish for military service.[53] In April, Poinsett rode south with Carrera to Talca to attempt to repel the invaders.[54] Poinsett's stated motive was the detainment of American ships under the orders of the viceroy of Peru, who had nullified the free trade provisions of Chile's new constitution, and as he would later claim, he "could not wait tamely and see our flag insulted, our ships seized and our citizens loaded with irons."[55] At the time, however, Poinsett simply chose to stop corresponding with the State Department. US law prohibited him from joining Chile's military, but Poinsett's desire to fight trumped official policy.

Poinsett was not alone. Americans were increasingly getting involved in South America's independence struggles. Filibustering attempts in Spanish-controlled Western lands were not uncommon. In 1806, Aaron Burr had allegedly tried to set up an independent republic in the North

American southwest, and Francisco de Miranda, a Venezuelan patriot, had recruited financiers and workforces in the United States for his attempt to depose the colonial government in Venezuela.[56] When Mathew Hoevel arrived in Chile in 1811 with a printing press, his ship also contained a concealed supply of pistols and rifles.[57] Arms shipments increased throughout the independence wars, and several American merchant ships aided the Chilean Navy.[58] Enterprising men from the United States took advantage of the wars as an opportunity for adventure and financial profit.[59]

Poinsett was no different, except that he was a commissioned agent of the state, not a private profiteer. He used his status and friendship with Carrera to intervene aggressively in Chile's political and military affairs. Poinsett believed that his brief military training in Europe had instilled in him the requisite knowledge to determine strategy and command troop movements. When Colonel Juan Mackenna suggested an attack on the Spanish forces who had retreated to Chillán, Poinsett urged them to take Talcahuano instead.[60] Poinsett's reasons were selfish: Americans from whaling ships had been taken prisoner in Talcahuano. In the short term, the attack brought a victory: the royalists surrendered at Talcahuano and Concepción, and the prisoners were released. Poinsett's strategy came with a long-term cost, however. Because the patriots failed to defeat the royalists while they were at Chillán, the Spanish ultimately reclaimed the region that fall. The patriot junta replaced Carrera with Bernardo O'Higgins, who was Carrera's off-and-on rival. O'Higgins actually thanked Poinsett for his service, but many Chileans called for Poinsett's removal.[61] Royalist colonel Juan Frances Sanchez wrote to Poinsett, "Your conduct is notorious in separating yourself from the duties incumbent on the character of an American consul, you have fomented in the capital of Chile the discords which have produced the present war."[62]

As a royalist, Sanchez was obviously opposed to Poinsett's activities, but he was not wrong about their defying proper decorum. Poinsett knew this. After boasting to a friend, "I returned last night from the army of Chile whose movements I had directed in a short and brilliant campaign during which the province of Concepción has been reconquered," he wrote, "the motives which induced me to take up arms would lead me into a long detail which I have only time to give to the government. I may be blamed by government and by my fellow citizens but I have acted right and I have been so long a solitary wanderer that I am accustomed to conduct myself with my own approbation."[63] Poinsett's self-righteousness stemmed from months of operating as an individual agent without official instructions. Even as he knew his interventionism bucked State Department expectations, he could assume that he was doing what was necessary, since the secretary of state had no real way of checking up on him.

Part of his justification for participating in war also rested on the fact that he had been shut out of military service at home. He wrote that he joined Chile's forces "at the moment when my country was engaged in a glorious struggle against her natural enemy a moment which I had always looked forward to with hope and anxiety."[64] Poinsett exploited Chile's independence movement for his own military ambitions and simultaneously equated his actions with patriotism. He later wrote to the State Department, "Although my conduct does not appear to have been that of a neutral agent it is justified by my country from insult and the property of her citizens from lawless and piratical depredation," and, "measures which however violent they may seem were fully justified by the repeated insult . . . I could not wait tamely and see our flag insulted, our ships seized and our citizens loaded with irons."[65] Poinsett knew his actions were illegal according to the Neutrality Act of 1794; that was why he appealed to patriotic virtue and why he waited so long to inform the State Department about his military involvement.

Poinsett's appeals to patriotism were not entirely disingenuous because he conflated his individual welfare with the common good. In addition to acting in his own self-interest, he was also serving the interests of his constituents. Boston merchant Samuel Curson asked Poinsett to pursue the release of two Americans, which "would enable [him] to form with them a party against the commandant to which in turn he would inevitably fall a victim and a more liberal system might then be taken up which would very possibly lay the foundation for having an almost exclusive trade to this quarter."[66] Curson wrote to him from Lima about the prospects for American business, insisting that "the only hope of a change in system is in the removal of [the viceroy's] counsellors from whom once separated we may hope for better days. As Rivero is the most important among these his separation would be the gaining of half the battle. Should overtures be therefore made to Chile I should recommend the attempt to remove this man." If that did not work, Curson wrote, "another measure might likewise be taken, which is the gaining over to our interests." He was trying to convince Peruvians that "all the holders of barks, cocoa, copper, etc., whose capitals in these articles is completely dead and gradually disappearing," would see the benefits of open trade with the United States.[67]

Poinsett, however, gave up. After the royalist victory, he retired to the countryside, staying at the Carrera estate.[68] He cited poor health, which was a recurring issue throughout his life, but he was also likely embarrassed. He wrote that there was little hope: "As the present state of Spain will allow her efforts to be directed towards the recovery of these provinces and as the character of these people will not bear them a revolution but under the most favorable circumstances I have taken no steps to prevent a peace with Lima, although certain that submission to Spain must be the consequence. Buenos Aires appears to me to be negotiating with Spain and England and will ultimately submit to one or the other."[69] Having failed at diplomatic initiatives, Poinsett finally got his chance for a military engagement against the British, when Commodore Porter and the *Essex* arrived in Valparaiso in January 1814. Porter, bringing news of the war between the United States and Britain, planned to meet Poinsett in the city. The *Essex* bore the slogan "Free Trade and Sailors' Rights!"— the rallying cry for American patriots who wanted naval respect and safe commerce.[70] After a British commander set up a blockade to prohibit the *Essex* from leaving, Poinsett tried and failed to get a Chilean commander to agree to open fire on the British.[71] When Porter attempted to exit the port, the British attacked and forced him to surrender after a brief naval skirmish.[72] The British commander permitted the Americans to be accompanied by patrol back to the United States.[73]

Poinsett was not included in this allowance. In fact, the British commander referred to Poinsett as the "archenemy of England" because he had conspired against British initiatives.[74] Porter tried to convince Poinsett to travel overland to Buenos Aires and then to Rio. Porter thought it would be safer for Poinsett; he also wanted him to make notes about an important British commercial route. Porter said he hoped that, on their way home from Rio, they could drink the excellent wine Poinsett had given him.[75] Poinsett stayed behind. He gave Porter a collection of his papers to bring back to Washington and, knowing his military engagement would come to light, composed a lengthy defense of his actions to mail to the State Department.[76]

Soon after, the Chilean government, under pressure from the British, informed Poinsett that he was no longer welcome there. He traveled to Buenos Aires to wait for passage home. There, he received updates from Carrera, who had been released from prison and asked Poinsett to convince the Buenos Aires junta to supply him with arms.[77] While Poinsett unsuccessfully pleaded Carrera's case to the Buenos Aires government and waited to leave for home, he wrote up more of his observations of and thoughts on South America. Many had to do with political upheaval and the immense trade opportunities—and potential losses: "In the present unsettled state of that country our trade has been immense . . . yet the whole is lost to us the moment Spanish power is again affianced there." He was beginning to understand how new markets were created. He wrote, for example, about the Argentine city of Mendoza, which had become the "entrepot of the trade between Buenos Aires and Chile." The independence movement had increased trade in the area and exposed them to "luxuries which were before unknown to them." Poinsett wrote, "All they could hope for under the colonial government was to maintain their families and the bare necessaries of life and no exertions were made to go beyond this limit, but now that luxuries are within their reach this powerful incentive to industry is visible in the improvement of agriculture and manufactures."[78] Poinsett hoped that the combination of new consumer desires and "free trade" would increase imports from the United States and reduce local manufacturing initiatives.

This scenario was starting to become a reality, particularly between South America and Philadelphia. Philadelphia, the unofficial center of Hispanic studies, was fast becoming an important exporter of goods to the patriot cause as South American patriots traveled to the city and US merchants sent ships south.[79] Poinsett had specifically recommended a Philadelphian, William Gilchrist Miller, as consul to Buenos Aires. According to Poinsett, he was a well-connected businessman from Philadelphia who was familiar with South American trade.[80] Additionally, his firm shipped arms.[81]

Poinsett knew that the selection of consuls could help determine the future of US trade. He made recommendations based on business experience and connections. He also had nativist prejudices, writing, "Mr Hoevel is a Swede formerly a citizen of that state and now a citizen of Chile. In our relations with these countries it will be highly politic to appoint native American citizens consul and agents of the United States."[82] Ultimately, however, business acumen won out, and Hoevel proved himself an able advocate of US whaling interests and Spanish American independence for the sake of US trade.

As the United States began appointing more consular agents to the region, this cohort helped cement new trade links. Rhode Island merchant Thomas Lloyd Halsey arrived as the new consul to Buenos Aires soon after Poinsett's departure. Halsey informed the State Department that Poinsett had provided valuable information on political factions, trade potential, and natural resources and had left US-Argentine trade relations in a promising state. The junta was favorably disposed to easing up trade restrictions, and the "duties on many articles . . . and manufactures of the United States should be reduced."[83]

By the time Halsey wrote this, Poinsett was heading home by way of Madeira.[84] Out of curiosity, he requested an update on the "present state of our affairs with the Barbary States" from the US consul there, James Leander Cathcart.[85] Cathcart had been a privateer and merchant, was enslaved in Algiers for over a decade, and served as a diplomat in the Mediterranean since the late 1790s. He had a mercantile business in Cádiz and illegally exported bills out of Madeira, and he greeted Poinsett with a lengthy letter that reflected views on political economy and state power that matched Poinsett's.[86] The Mediterranean was an important region for US commerce, but North African tribute requirements resulted in ongoing conflict and a war a decade earlier. Cathcart wrote that the United States, after the Treaty of Ghent, had the perfect opportunity to display naval force in the region. He advised escalating US strategy from one of defense to one of offense to subdue these states into submission to US commerce. Cathcart suggested using Robert Fulton's torpedo "to have the whole of their Navy destroyed by an invisible agent."[87] If the United States succeeded, they would beat England and other European powers to favorable negotiations with the Barbary States. Cathcart viewed war and trade as perpetual cycles. War with Tripoli had helped the United States win against Great Britain, and now the War of 1812 would help the United States against Algeria. Victory would usher in profitable trade, made more feasible by peace with Britain and the resumption of Mediterranean business through London.

Cathcart wanted Poinsett to convey his enthusiasm for war and his willingness to facilitate his plan for US-Barbary relations to the government. Cathcart argued that he would be able to "convert their embarrassments to our own interest and advantage" and that the United States "must act independent of every nation on earth and trust to God and the strength of our own arms for a happy result."[88] Cathcart got his wish when Congress voted to send naval power to Algiers in March and won a battle against Algiers several months later. The subsequent peace treaty ended tribute payments.[89] It is unclear how much of a role Poinsett played, but later, when Poinsett was serving in Congress, he presented Cathcart's pecuniary claim on the Spanish government to the Committee on Foreign Relations. The claim was awarded.[90]

Cathcart and Poinsett were part of the United States' small army of capitalist consuls—they were on the front lines advocating for American commerce and dubious military action. They operated both within and beyond the legitimacy of the state, often acting first and explaining later.

When Poinsett finally returned home in the spring of 1815, he had to relinquish his military ambitions, at least for a time. The Treaty of Ghent had already been ratified, and Poinsett resigned himself to state politics. He transitioned from writing about his observations on the South American political economy and infrastructure to administering internal improvements in South Carolina, overseeing the construction of hundreds of miles of roads and canals. By then, he had cooled on his enthusiasm for Spanish American independence, but he continued to work behind the scenes to promote revolution.

Home

Poinsett arrived in Charleston on May 30, 1815, and wrote to Monroe that he would be in Washington within a couple of weeks. Poinsett enclosed the commercial regulations that had been agreed upon in Buenos Aires, proudly noting that "articles of our produce of the greatest consumption are free of duty."[91] After reviewing Poinsett's reports, Monroe was pleased with his service.[92] Because the Spanish government did not notice or care, as it had with Francisco de Miranda's expedition, Monroe seemed to brush aside the fact that Poinsett had taken up arms in another nation's imperial struggle. It would become increasingly common for the US government to look the other way when its employees took unsanctioned actions.

In fact, as Monroe wrote to him, Poinsett was in Philadelphia, once again abetting revolution without the consent of his government. Before Poinsett left South America, he had written to Carrera, "The people of Chile will always live in my memory and I shall have the greatest pleasure whenever it may be in my power to contribute in any manner to their prosperity and felicity."[93] This he did by helping organize money and supplies from the United States. Poinsett met with Carrera in New York on July 4 and connected him with financiers, such as John Jacob Astor and the firm D'Arcy and Didier.[94] On this trip Carrera joined the Freemasons, the secret fraternal organization to which such statesmen as Benjamin Franklin and George Washington had belonged, at St. John's Lodge No. 1.[95] He may have done so at the recommendation of Poinsett, who around that time became a Freemason and likely would have visited a lodge in New York.[96] Although Poinsett was a member at the Grand Lodge of Ancient Free Masons of South Carolina, it was common for Masons to attend other lodges. Masonic ties transcended other affiliations, such as citizenship, and allowed members to form business—or revolutionary—connections.

Poinsett continued his organizing activities in Philadelphia, which was quickly becoming one of his favorite cities.[97] While there, he met several other men from Charleston (Philadelphia was a popular city for both revolutionaries and South Carolinians) and convinced them to take a tour of the West, a part of the country he had not yet traveled. Poinsett's motives may have been political; it would be a chance to visit the homesteads of two influential leaders. It was also an opportunity to observe trade routes and infrastructure, which could be put to political use later.

The four white men and an enslaved man headed west out of Philadelphia on horseback. The roads in Pennsylvania were atrocious, not any better than the difficult roads in Chile. His travels in some ways paralleled those he had undertaken in South America. Just as in the pampas, he was confronted with the effects of Native warfare. His party came across the aging General Arthur St. Clair, who had retired to the mountains in poverty after his disastrous defeat in 1791 by the Northwestern Confederacy. This was especially upsetting to Poinsett and his white companions.

The roads were so rough on the horses' hooves that Poinsett bought two rough flat-bottomed boats to float down the Ohio River. Always keenly interested in wine, he observed industry and visited a vineyard in Indiana, and he chatted about South American affairs with Henry Clay, who invited them to a dinner party in Lexington. Before heading home, he had breakfast with Andrew Jackson in Louisville.[98] There is little record of this encounter, but the two men would later become quite close.

When Poinsett returned to South Carolina, he got his first experience in local politics and investing. He arrived in Greenville in November and learned that he had been elected to the South Carolina House of Representatives (he had been named as a candidate back in September).[99] This was the era of "good feelings," when the majority of Americans identified as Republicans, and Poinsett indeed had requested to be listed on the ticket as one.[100] He wanted to be clear that he was not a member of the dying Federalist Party, despite the party's traditional popularity in South Carolina and despite Poinsett's support of some vigorous government programs, especially regarding internal improvements.[101] This election was his first real opportunity to identify with a political party (he had been in Europe during turn-of-the-century battles between Federalists and Jeffersonians).

For the rest of his career, Poinsett would associate with the party that traced its lineage to Jefferson, but like many Americans (and Jefferson himself), his actual stance on political issues belied party purity. Despite associating with the party that championed the common man and small government, Poinsett often favored a strong military and a government that intervened in the economy. He would also increasingly ally with men of different political leanings for various political and business pursuits.

As a newly elected state official—and as a private investor—Poinsett put his experience with poor travel infrastructure in South America and the western US states into action. Like much of what he did, his involvement in state transportation was controversial. In December, the General Assembly acceded to the requests of nine petitioners, of whom Poinsett was one, to incorporate the Winyaw and Wando Canal Company. The following year, the assembly formed a committee for internal improvements, of which Poinsett was a member, and purchased seven of the Winyaw and Wando Canal Company's twenty shares. Canals were subject to inspection by the state's civil and military engineer, until the engineer's office was abolished and replaced in 1819 by the Board of Public Works, of which Poinsett became president.[102] The board was charged with constructing a series of canals and highways to link trade throughout and between states.

Internal improvements were costly: they involved tax breaks and taxpayer money and subsequently attracted much skepticism and criticism. As president of the Board of Public Works, Poinsett received some of the blame. He traveled around inspecting public works and was allowed to draw out of the state treasury as needs arose and to make contracts nationally.[103] For example, this provision allowed him to seek out preferred suppliers in New York and Philadelphia.[104] Lackluster progress prompted the state legislature to abolish the Board of Public Works in 1822 and replace it with a superintendent who was required to pay a $50,000 bond to guarantee his performance.[105]

Poinsett's private venture, which intersected somewhat with his public duties, had more significant legal and financial ramifications. Poinsett was one of the principal shareholders of the Winyaw and Wando Canal Company, whose charter permitted it to build canals and locks that connected the Santee and Wando Rivers with Winyaw Bay.[106] The company was allowed to purchase land for construction and control all the lands through which the canals passed, and it was granted a monopoly on steamboat travel for ten years. Members of the company could take 25 percent profit above what they expended on maintaining the infrastructure. Despite all these incentives, five of the shareholders neglected to make their payments, leaving a burden on the company's contractors and remaining shareholders. Their negligence threatened the company's ability to carry out one of the charter's stipulations: commencing construction within two years and completing it within seven years.[107]

Thomas Pinckney Jr., company backer and son of the well-known Federalist statesman, wrote to Poinsett that, with more money and a little more time, they could finish the canal system and entice more investors. He asked Poinsett to convince the negligent shareholders to pay.[108] Whether Poinsett did this or not, the public accused the company of prioritizing individual interests over public ones.[109] In May 1826, Poinsett and several other shareholders (General Wade Hampton, Colonel Abram Blanding, and William Matthews) were sued for failing to pay contractors and for generally neglecting to carry out the actual object of the corporation. In a decision that was upheld two years later in the court of appeals, the shareholders were required to pay.[110] This may have been one of the issues that led to Poinsett's financial troubles in the 1820s.

Administrating the public and private sides of state infrastructure and dealing with public criticism gave Poinsett experience that he would later use to organize and reorganize the militia during South Carolina's nullification crisis and as secretary of war. He also got his first major experience dealing with enslaved labor. Poinsett owned slaves and had inherited some from his father, yet he had scarcely lived as an adult in South Carolina. He usually traveled with enslaved servants but did not buy or sell plantation slaves. One of the provisions of the incorporation was that the company could buy and sell "negroes or other goods and chattels."[111] As antislavery sentiment grew internationally, southerners sought to "modernize" the institution by using slave labor for internal improvement projects. They purchased enslaved individuals or rented them from plantation owners.[112] Poinsett, like many southerners, was simultaneously market oriented and feudal.

Throughout his involvement in state politics and infrastructure, his identity as an "expert" on South America dominated. News of Poinsett's time there appeared in newspapers, and Monroe asked him for updates on developments in the region.[113] David Porter wrote to Poinsett for help convincing Carrera, and any other interested leaders, to offer positions in the patriot armies to American officers, who, "in consequences of the intended reduction of our army . . . will be thrown out of employ—their half pay will not be sufficient to support them."[114] Porter's proposal would simultaneously offer profitable employment for unemployed officers (Charles Whiting Wooster, Connecticut native and captain of the port of New York, for example, served as a privateer during the War of 1812, and in 1818 he became a captain in the Chilean Navy[115]) and facilitate favorable trade relations with South America. Even as the US economy depended on foreign nations for military employment and commercial outlets, chauvinism predominated. Just as Poinsett disparaged many of the people he encountered while traveling, Porter believed American officers should be given higher posts in Chile and other countries than they had in the United States (an expectation he would take to Mexico ten years later when he served in the Mexican Navy).

In 1817, revolutionaries had some success in Argentina and Chile, and the US government decided to send another commission to assess the status of the independence movements. In April, President Monroe asked Poinsett to serve as the sole agent, as he had before. Poinsett declined, writing only that he had taken a seat in the state legislature.[116] In a private letter to an unnamed friend, Poinsett explained that he would be of more use in the United States, where he could drum up support for the patriot cause. Also, he wrote that he "never will again leave America in a subaltern capacity, or as an unauthorized agent of the Government," reflecting his concern with status.[117] Other than that, he said little about his decision to stay home. Perhaps he did not want to miss any more action in the United States.

In his place, the State Department sent John Graham, Theodorick Bland, and Caesar Augustus Rodney as commissioners, with Henry M. Brackenridge as secretary.[118] The mission sailed on December 4, 1817, and arrived in Rio de Janeiro on January 29, 1818.[119] Like Poinsett, they traveled to the Rio de la Plata region and overland to Chile and wrote much about natural resources. They collected samples of plants, which were later displayed at the Academy of Natural Sciences in Philadelphia, and tested samples of Georgia cotton in Argentina.[120] Their activities were a precursor to later agricultural imperialism.[121] When William Miller wrote to Poinsett about having met up with one of the commissioners, he asked Poinsett to send Sea Island cotton to experiment with on the cotton plantation on which he was living.[122] This collection of and experimentation with natural flora was part of Poinsett's overarching agenda and would continue throughout his career.[123]

Upon the commission's return, the State Department wanted a report on the viability of South American independence. In September 1818, State Department clerk Daniel Brent sent Poinsett his letters and journal from South America, which Poinsett used to compile an official report two months later. Poinsett wrote it while serving in the legislature in Columbia; he claimed the majority of his papers were at home. Additionally, many of Poinsett's original letters were "missing" and never made it to Washington. (Perhaps they were intercepted by foreign officers, but there are no duplicates, either. He might never have sent the alleged letters.)

Poinsett wanted much about his tenure to remain unreported. Nonetheless, his package for the department, which was published, included some original letters and undated reports on politics, geography, demography, and economics.[124] He reiterated his warnings about British influence in Argentina and also expressed some skepticism about the region's capacity for self-government. Despite his previous enthusiasm for revolution, he cautioned, "They will require subsidies of Money and Arms and by their incompetence will embarrass our operations."[125] Poinsett might have resented not being the hero he wished to be, or he might have wanted government funds spent on other things, such as internal improvements. Either way, he denied the type of support the United States had gotten from France and others during its own war for independence.

The State Department compiled Poinsett's writings and a collection of other documents from South American leaders and US diplomatic agents to show Congress. The opinions were mixed. Brackenridge had written a pamphlet about the "common American interest" while he waited for the commission to depart for Rio. He recommended that the United States "establish official relations with the republics of La Plata and Chili" and argued that "the United States will be the natural head of the New World."[126] Secretary of State John Quincy Adams would echo Brackenridge's opinion several years later in the Monroe Doctrine, but in the meantime, he was swayed by Poinsett's and Bland's reservations.[127] Adams was in the process of negotiating a treaty with Spain that had major ramifications for American claims against the Spanish government and business interests generally, and so the United States would wait to recognize Spanish American independence.[128]

News of the South American report reached various cities in South America, and William Miller wrote to Poinsett from Buenos Aires that patriots now viewed the United States as "determined to assist Spain in the reconquest of the country."[129] In short, the opinion was that Americans were self-interested, scheming hypocrites. Miller did not specifically blame Poinsett for this, but he was slightly rebuffed that Poinsett had not mailed the report to Miller himself.

Carrera was still grateful for Poinsett's aid. He continued to write to him secretly, updating Poinsett on factions among the nationalists in Chile. Carrera would be imprisoned within the year and executed shortly after, in September 1821.[130] Poinsett continued to work behind the scenes. In the fall of 1819, Poinsett offered Bank of the United States president Langdon Cheves specie in some kind of deal relating to the service of naval captain Charles Morris.[131] This most likely had to do with aiding independence; Morris was involved with negotiations in Venezuela. Two years later, Poinsett exchanged cryptic letters with Secretary of War John C. Calhoun about this.[132]

Poinsett's correspondence often obfuscated exactly what was going on. It is clear, however, that during and after his mission to South America, he became known as someone who could make things happen within and outside the channels of official government. Poinsett was finished traveling in South America, but he was not done with Spain's crumbling empire. Nor was he done with secrecy. First, he would go to Congress.

3

....

Domestic and International
Politics, 1820–1825

Five years after Poinsett left South America, Harvard professor Edward
Everett requested his expertise on the region. Everett had received a copy
of Henry Brackenridge's reports on South America and hoped Poinsett
would review it for the *North American Review*.[1] Everett also wanted
Poinsett's thoughts on canals; he had read Poinsett's reports on internal
improvements in South Carolina, and he was eager to get more detail for
an article in the *Review*.[2]

Poinsett was becoming a reputable figure nationwide—across partisan
and regional divides—particularly within elite knowledge networks. Not
only were local intellectuals like Stephen Elliott, president of South Carolina's Literary and Philosophical Society, writing to him about plants,
books, and art but well-known northerners, like Everett, were as well.
For example, Peter Du Ponceau, a member of Philadelphia's American
Philosophical Society, became a regular correspondent.[3] Ponceau sought
out Poinsett for his status as a cosmopolitan man of science and culture.
He wrote to Poinsett to introduce him to a young mineralogist named
L. C. Varnum, who planned to travel from Pennsylvania to South Carolina.[4] Ponceau knew that Poinsett was an important contact for this scientist, owing to Poinsett's societal connections, membership in the South
Carolina Philosophical Society, and credentials as a collector of naturalist
objects. Five years later, Poinsett would employ Varnum in mining ventures in Mexico.

By 1820, Poinsett had traveled extensively throughout three continents
and was considered an expert on South America, internal improvements,
and naturalist pursuits. This reputation set Poinsett up for national politics and another foreign tour. He was elected as a US representative from

the Charleston district in 1820 and again in 1822 and 1824.[5] His first term was interrupted by a secret mission to Mexico, and he resigned from his last term to serve as the nation's first minister plenipotentiary to Mexico. While he was in Congress, men from around the country wrote to Poinsett asking him to push his fellow lawmakers to increase the nation's military and naval presence. At home and in Mexico, Poinsett would have the opportunity to explore the stakes of US dominion and prove himself as an advocate of economic and military strength. US pretensions to power, as embodied by Poinsett, increasingly depended on secrecy, coercion, and commercial connections.

Seventeenth Congress

In the fall of 1820, President James Monroe was reelected for his second term. It was still ostensibly the "era of good feelings," when the vast majority of legislators identified as "Democratic-Republican." However, feelings were not all good. There were issues over the size of the military, taxation, South American and Greek independence, and the spread of slavery.

Poinsett was a candidate for the first time in a national election, and he faced public scrutiny in a way he had not before. Poinsett was criticized for working on internal improvements solely to improve his own reputation. His critics argued that any achievements of the Board of Public Works were the result of engineers and skilled workers, rather than Poinsett's management.[6] Worse, laborers in his district accused him of hiring northern workers for public works projects, thereby taxing people in South Carolina for work they could do themselves. One newspaper article charged, "Was there any necessity for Mr. Poinsett to look abroad for Mechanics? Would not many of you who have been for a long time idle, been glad to get the jobs Mr. Poinsett had the power to give you on the part of the State? And would you not have worked as cheap, if not cheaper, than the men imported?"[7] The article was correct. Poinsett commissioned workers from his friend Colonel James Burn, a former South Carolina naval officer who now lived outside Philadelphia in Frankfort, Pennsylvania.[8]

Poinsett's supporters, meanwhile, touted his foreign travels, military involvement in South America for the cause of "rational freedom," and "warm approbation of the war and his distinguished services abroad for the promotion of its objects."[9] He won, beating Governor John Geddes in a narrow victory: 1,326 votes to 1,287.[10] As soon as US district attorney for Pennsylvania Charles Ingersoll heard the election news, he wrote Poinsett a congratulatory letter. Ingersoll was a member of the Philadelphia elite with strong ties to the South.[11] Ingersoll told Poinsett he hoped he would serve for ten or fifteen years, long enough to have an impact beyond yearly reelection concerns. Ingersoll and Burn had electioneered together in South Carolina on Poinsett's behalf.[12] This was their way of thanking him for providing business support and safeguarding their future interests.

After Poinsett won his congressional seat, he was reelected as president of the Board of Public Works on December 20.[13] Although some Carolinians had criticized Poinsett's motivations for his involvement in internal improvements during the election, many credited him with improved infrastructure. One traveler's letter, reprinted in newspapers, extolled the "beauties and excellencies" of "Mr. Poinsett's celebrated road."[14] Over a decade later, a reputable engineer and architect would write to Poinsett that South Carolina's infrastructure kept the state "at the pinnacle of the union for enterprise."[15]

Poinsett's ambitions, however, were bigger than public works. One of his friends remarked that his aspirations had "grown too fast for the ambition of some men."[16] He resigned as president at the end of spring, citing health reasons, and Robert Mills, the famous architect who designed the Washington Monument, took over as acting commissioner. Even as Mills complained about some of the decisions made under Poinsett—contracts went to the lowest bidder and work was shoddy—he asked Poinsett for his opinions, saying that he wanted "to be guided in decisions of this nature by those whose judgment is best calculated to direct."[17] Poinsett's career in public works gave him national credibility as a statesman who was knowledgeable about applied science, just as he was about foreign languages and natural philosophy.

After resigning from South Carolina's Board of Public Works, Poinsett left the country. His doctor suggested a sea voyage for his health. Although his knee had improved from earlier that spring, when it caused him to miss board meetings, his doctor now worried about tuberculosis. Poinsett always had liked going to England, so that was where he chose.[18]

Before he left, he sent a letter to Isaac Johnson, a fellow Mason in Charleston, about a secret matter. Poinsett had an infant son who needed a caretaker. He wrote to Johnson, "In the event of any accident befalling me I have provided for my son who is under your charge." Poinsett also requested, "by your obligations as a brother and companion never to reveal the name of the mother." The woman Poinsett had recently gotten pregnant had passed away; as Poinsett wrote, "the reputation of a woman even after her death ought to be sacred."[19] This is one of the few glimpses we get of Poinsett's private life. He did not marry until he was fifty-four. He and his correspondents wrote little about women, other than to comment briefly on their appearance, intellect, or mere presence in a location. However, he most likely took advantage of women when he could. Upon his appointment in Mexico as minister in 1825, one friend instructed him not only to "make a good commercial treaty for us" but to "take care of the ladies."[20] He corresponded with more than one female friend later in life, and he was respectful of his wife. In general, however, Poinsett viewed women at best as complementary objects—useful but not necessary for a meaningful life—and at worst as a corrupting influence. For example, he later wrote derisively about a Mexican politician, saying, "He is sometimes influenced by a woman."[21]

The mother of Poinsett's child has remained unknown, and the existence of his son only appears in three letters to Isaac Johnson (it was never mentioned by Poinsett's earlier biographers). Poinsett's concern for her reputation suggests that the woman was white because he most likely would not have considered that a Black woman could have a reputation to protect. Also, it is likely that he met the woman in Philadelphia and conceived the child there, since he visited frequently and was known to "form or renew acquaintances" with "ladies" there.[22] It is difficult to ascertain her social class. On the basis of his correspondence, it seems that he socialized with elite women, whom he would consider to have a reputation to protect. It is entirely possible, however, that he impregnated a woman of lower status. Unfortunately, Poinsett never mentioned her name in writing. He said slightly more about his son, with whom he spent some time in the summer of 1824 (when he remained in Charleston to defend his congressional seat), writing, "The little fellow has become very dear to me."[23] But although we know he instructed Johnson to christen the child James Burn, the name of the South Carolina naval officer who had electioneered with Charles Ingersoll for Poinsett, it is difficult to pick Poinsett's son out of all the James Burns listed in the census over the course of the nineteenth century. There exists an 1898 death certificate for a James Burn who might have been Poinsett's son because he was born "abt 1819" in Philadelphia.[24] All we know about him is that he was white and married at the time of his death and was buried in the Mount Moriah Cemetery. Poinsett's experience having at least one child out of wedlock reveals the convergence of sex and power and the importance of male networks in his career. Had the boy's mother lived, she would have been responsible for raising him. Poinsett felt obligated enough not to completely abandon James, but he relied on his fraternal connections, and their Masonic oaths of secrecy, to absolve himself of the responsibility of identifying as James's father, other than providing occasional sums of money "for this precious charge."[25]

After Poinsett sent one hundred dollars to Johnson and arranged for him to take charge of James's baptism, he escaped to Europe. He said little about what he did while he was away. He expressed interest in going to Spain to observe the effects of its revolution but figured he did not have enough time to justify such a long trip. He may have been charged with some State Department business, as indicated by his note telling a friend he could be reached through Richard Rush, US minister to England.[26] Decades later, he wrote that he visited the English seaside town of Hastings.[27] Poinsett also went to France, where he collected plants that might be profitable in the South. He was particularly optimistic about poppy seeds and the seeds from the "Colzat" cabbage, which he said were used for painting and culinary purposes and were preferable to sperm oil in lamps. Poinsett met with the famous botanist François Michaux, who offered to send New Zealand flax to South Carolina, which he claimed would do well in the rice-growing regions of the state, and olive plants for the Sea Islands. Before Poinsett came home, he asked Johnson to send some of his wine to Washington or Alexandria so it would be ready for him during the congressional session.[28]

Poinsett's return in time for the legislative season must have been a relief to Secretary of War John C. Calhoun, who asked him to hurry back from Europe so he could defend the military. That summer, Calhoun had written to Poinsett that he feared that congressional opposition to the military would result in more cuts.[29] There was a persistent tension between Congress and the military establishment, and in the years following the War of 1812, Congress frequently debated military size and cost. On March 2, 1821, Congress had reduced its size, and Calhoun wanted Poinsett's help to "resist and put down" any further opposition.[30]

Although Poinsett had never served in the US military, he was viewed as an ally of military interests. His expertise was in foreign relations, and he served on the Committee on Foreign Relations, but he made himself known as an advocate of armed force. When he began serving in Congress, government employees and citizens wrote to him about national security matters. Supreme Court Justice William Johnson, for example, who was familiar with court cases relating to piracy off the coast of Florida, wanted Poinsett to promote the idea of stationing a vessel of war at

Key West: "You would do an excellent thing if you would keep the subject in the memory of the administration until they did something of the kind. Nothing else will put a stop to the piracies in that quarter."[31] Likewise, Louis McLane, serving on the Naval Affairs Committee in Congress, recruited Poinsett's support for naval strength in the West Indies. He shared with Poinsett a letter he received from W. B. Finch, a master commandant of the naval court-martial in Philadelphia. Finch had written to McLane about the necessity of increasing US naval presence in the West Indies and the Gulf of Mexico to protect American commerce.[32] McLane forwarded this letter to Poinsett, hoping Poinsett would promote Finch's request. In April, Poinsett gave a speech arguing that, "instead of creating a new army with all its inexperience and want of discipline, and adding it to the old army, as was done at the commencement of the last war," the United States should bolster the current army.[33] Although his campaign against reducing the army did not succeed, his naval resolution would be adopted the following year.[34] Also, several months after Poinsett advocated for more naval power in Key West, Commodore Matthew Perry sailed to the island and claimed it for the United States; the following year, the United States established a naval base there.

National security issues also hit closer to home. In June 1822, white South Carolinians allegedly discovered plans for a slave uprising, led by the free Black carpenter Denmark Vesey.[35] Charleston mayor James Hamilton Jr. called for the arrest of suspects, who were tried by a court made up of two magistrates and five freeholders.[36] All told, thirty-five men were hanged and thirty-seven were expelled from the state. The sentences resulted from two separate courts. The first court met secretly for over a month and made the majority of decisions.[37] After the initial proceedings, another trial was held for William Garner, the remaining "ringleader" who had managed to escape. Poinsett was chosen as one of this court's five freeholders, who, according to Hamilton, "were known to possess, deservedly, a large share of the publick confidence."[38]

The court met on August 2 and sentenced Garner to execution. Then, "after a short adjournment of three or four days, recommenced their session, disposed of twelve cases more, involving a minor degree of guilt, and adjourned finally on the 8th of August." Hamilton noted that, "as enough had been done for publick example, they determined to visit capital punishment on none but ringleaders."[39] Here, Hamilton acknowledged the main objective of the trials: to set a horrifying example for enslaved individuals in order to bolster white social control. Some historians in fact have argued that the Denmark Vesey conspiracy may have been fabricated by whites as a means of legitimizing the expulsion and execution of Blacks who were deemed a threat.[40] Whether it was real or not, many whites were terrified of slaves' ability to organize and transmit knowledge secretly. Poinsett most likely did not associate slaves' covert organizational strategies with his own, yet his own career continuously involved secrecy and armed organization. The court ruled in favor of social control.

It was not a foregone conclusion that Poinsett should have voted the way he did. His track record on slavery was mixed. In some ways, he agreed with his Pennsylvanian friend Charles Ingersoll, who supported the institution as a "vast, stupendous and vital American reality."[41] Several years prior, Poinsett had voted to repeal a bill to prohibit importation of slaves, a bill he had previously been in favor of.[42] Many of his acquaintances were opposed to slavery, and his friend William Johnson advocated leniency for the rebellion's alleged conspirators.[43]

Poinsett, however, believed first and foremost in social control and, increasingly, the sanctity of white Americans' property, which he had done his best to protect in South America. Before the trial, Poinsett's former law tutor, Henry William DeSaussure, had written to Poinsett, "This kind of property is fast losing its value on the sea cost for its proximity to the West Indies . . . and scenes of blood." DeSaussure approved the first court's decision, writing, "Hamilton and the council have acted with discretion and firmness," and "the court was wisely selected from among the best informed, most reasonable and firm of the community; men neither to be misled by violent popular rumors nor deterred from the performance of painful duties, by a false humanity."[44] DeSaussure was right about the court's not being deterred by a sense of humanity, but he missed the influence of fear. As DeSaussure himself had acknowledged, coastal slaves were losing value because of white fears about Blacks' ability to travel and collaborate in violence. Fear of economic loss and the forfeiture of racial control certainly affected Poinsett's and others' decision to sentence the suspected conspiracy leaders to death.

Despite the economic and social importance of slavery in South Carolina, some white Carolinians opposed the outcome of the Denmark Vesey trials, objecting especially to the freeholders' secret proceedings. In state politics, however, the court's sentiment ultimately won out. After the executions and exile of many of the "conspirators," the South Carolina legislature outlawed the presence of free Black men in Charleston.[45] Soon after Poinsett limited the liberties of African Americans in South Carolina, President James Monroe sent him to Mexico to assess the status of liberty there.

Mexico

Monroe interrupted Poinsett's tenure in Congress because he needed Poinsett's help with another foreign mission. A decade of independence warfare in Mexico had ended the previous August, in 1821. The political elites serving in the new Mexican Congress sought to avoid the social radicalism of earlier revolutionaries like Hidalgo and Morelos and hoped they could install a member of one of Europe's royal families as head of state. Under the Plan of Iguala, they created a constitutional monarchy as the legitimate descendant of the historical Mexican Empire. When no European ruler materialized, they elected Augustín de Iturbide as emperor.[46]

This change added to the US government's urgency to announce its stance on independence, as more policymakers, like Clay, began to endorse official recognition. Shortly before Iturbide became emperor, Poinsett publicly articulated his views on Spanish American independence, which had changed since his travels in South America, when he claimed it was too soon. Now, he thought the revolutionaries finally had a legitimate chance at success, and he gave a speech in Congress supporting Monroe's request for appropriations from the House of Representatives for official diplomatic missions to Spain's former colonies. The economic benefits outweighed all else. He argued:

> It is our interest that they should be free. With an extensive line
> of coast, with numerous navigable rivers, facilitating their inter-
> nal trade, with a population of more than fifteen millions, almost
> without manufactures, with a demand for one hundred millions of
> dollars, and without the means of carrying on their foreign com-
> merce, these countries present a market for the skill and industry of
> our merchants, which promises the greatest advantages. . . . With the
> increase of knowledge, will arise free and well-organized institu-
> tions, the refinements and various wants of civilization. This cannot
> fail to produce a demand for all the manufactures of this country,
> and for all the objects of trade.[47]

Mexico's proximity to the United States made recognition more problematic. Many Americans were settling in the Mexican province of Texas because while the United States had begun requiring full cash payment up front for new lands in 1820, Texan authorities did not.[48] This was a major boon to aspiring American landowners but also a source of jealousy and tension between the United States and Mexico. Monroe hoped that Poinsett would be able to suggest a policy plan after assessing these different challenges for the two countries' relations.[49] Stephen Elliott wanted Poinsett to procure minerals to correct the "imperfect state of our knowledge of the mineral treasures of Mexico."[50]

Poinsett left for Mexico on August 28, 1822, on the *John Adams*.[51] The small warship first went to Puerto Rico, a detour that irritated Poinsett. He made the best of it by writing about everything he saw. With Denmark Vesey still fresh in his mind, his notes reflected his paranoia about slavery and race, and he wrote, "Although the slaves are not numerous, the vicinity of the republic of Hayti renders [an insurrection] a probable event." Just a few weeks after the Vesey executions, Poinsett arrived in San Juan in time to see sixty Black men being marched to trial for an intended insurrection. He was even more attentive to race, status, and appearances than usual. He wrote that the men in the several garrisons he saw were "of all colors, from the fairest European to the blackest son of Africa."[52] He saw young officers, returned from a ball, "delighted with the charming faces, delicate figures and graceful movements of the Creole ladies. Those I saw in the street had good persons, and delicate and well-formed features, but very sallow complexions."[53]

Poinsett was also preoccupied with the effects of privateering on American business in Puerto Rico, and his comments reflected his growing belief in the value and legitimacy of state power. When the governor told him that pirates would be duly punished, Poinsett was skeptical, writing, "I . . . am of opinion that these acts of piracy ought to be restrained by the strong arms of power . . . the dominion exercised by the mother country over these colonies is too remote and inconsiderable to enable her to control the lawless banditti that inhabit the coast of Puerto Rico and Cuba."[54] He was also disgusted with private revolutionary expeditions that set out from the United States, writing, "We ought to exercise a more vigilant police, and if possible prevent adventurers from disgracing us." These US adventurers were later termed *filibusteros* by the Spanish, which became filibusters in the United States. They illegally participated in revolutionary upheaval, usually with the hope of personal profit. Despite, or perhaps because of, Poinsett's own extralegal military involvement, he doubted that these expeditions had liberty as the true goal. The real object, according to Poinsett, was usually plunder.[55] All revolutions had economic motives, but Poinsett now preferred to pursue them through ostensibly legitimate channels. This was a change from his days as an aspiring Chilean revolutionary. As he gained more political legitimacy, he came to believe support for revolutionaries should originate with the state.

On September 30, Poinsett began his journal entry with "Farewell to

Puerto Rico!"[56] He was eager to get to Mexico, which took a little over two weeks. They passed Santo Domingo, where they picked up newspapers from Boston and Liverpool ships and read updates about warfare in Spain and various independence struggles from Greece to Brazil.[57] They landed at Vera Cruz, where two American businessmen joined them from the capital. Poinsett sympathized with them: "What difficulties perils and privations, they have suffered encountered and overcome! Nothing to eat but *tasajo*—dried beef—nothing to drink but *pulque*, the fermented juice of the *agave*. Inns destitute of all accommodation and execrably dirty." He "listened seriously to a long catalogue of miseries and dangers which I am doomed to encounter, for I have advanced too far to be frightened from my purpose by these terrible relations."[58]

He met with the US vice consul at Vera Cruz, who filled him in on the problems for American commerce. Mexico was the third-largest source of exports from Latin America, but US ships paid an 8 percent duty to the castle and another tariff that seemed to be arbitrarily assessed. At the capital, goods were hit with an additional 12.5 percent duty.[59] Mexico, like other nations, used tariffs as political weapons and as protection for domestic industries.[60] These prohibitive duties made it more difficult for US merchants to sell goods in exchange for Mexican silver, which was important for the US money supply.[61] That was why Poinsett became interested in silver mining in Mexico and why, as minister, he would cooperate with the British when it might facilitate specie transfer to the United States, while also competing with them for commercial advantage.

Poinsett met with the governor of Vera Cruz Antonio López de Santa Anna, whom he would encounter many times over the next decade. Poinsett remarked that Santa Anna was "slightly yet well made and possessing a very expressive countenance, but evidently suffering from fatigue and the effects of climate." After the governor asked Poinsett to dine with him, Poinsett wrote, "A ceremonious Spanish dinner is of all things most odious to me, and I endeavored to excuse myself, on the ground of my extreme haste to set out."[62] Poinsett's tone was often supercilious. He wrote that he would "rather fall into the hand of the banditti than into those of a Mexican physician."[63] He was dismissive of most artwork he saw. After seeing a portrait of Iturbide, Poinsett wrote, "From this daub I can form no idea of his physiognomy."[64]

Poinsett then traveled to the village of Plan de Rio, where "the people are every shade of color between white and black." As always, he was observant of racial appearance, noting that he had "seen very few of the former since I left Vera Cruz, and none of the latter."[65] He visited the largest house in the village and observed a "clean, tidy Mestizo woman" in the kitchen as she cooked the "fowl [they] had brought with [them], and served it up with a sauce *piquante*, made of tomatoes and Chili pepper." When a traveler stopped by, the man told Poinsett and his companions of the "tyrannical conduct of the emperor." They met with the general of Puebla, Vera Cruz, and Oaxaca, and Poinsett lamented that the general was assisted by two Americans, whom he wished would "fill the stations they aspire to in other countries before they leave their own."[66] He derided the men he saw gambling at a game called *monte*, writing, "As you know I never touch a card, I cannot describe the manner in which a great deal of money was won and lost. There is no exhibition of the human passions that disgusts me so thoroughly and I very soon retired to scribble in my journal."[67] Poinsett missed the parallels to his own investments. He believed business could be manipulated and controlled, and he prided himself on a Protestant aversion to gambling as he mocked these men's amusement.

Poinsett was not always so disdainful; more often than not, he was snobbishly mystified or chauvinistically curious. At an inn, Poinsett was bemused by the servants and described how one of them gathered up the tablecloth, writing in parentheses, "(which from its appearance is changed semi-annually)."[68] When they traveled to a "cottage in the suburbs," he sat with a family huddled around a fire and watched "four damsels industriously making tortillas of Indian corn."[69] These two brief anecdotes reveal an elite world traveler, who was accustomed to fine dining, observing the culinary practices of a culture he found inferior. After dinner at the cottage, Poinsett's observations turned to voyeurism. The girls' parents went to bed, and Poinsett "was curious to see how the young ladies would go to bed in [their] presence, for a candle was burning before an image of the Virgin. They . . . contrived to undress under the clothes with great decency."[70] This is one of the more disturbing example of Poinsett's chauvinism. He felt entitled to watch them and had a conception of how they should behave—as well as a condescending approval of this behavior—according to his own prejudices about Catholicism. Poinsett and his companions slept on mattresses on a boarded floor and left before sunrise.

After almost a month of traveling inland from the coast, Poinsett arrived in Mexico City in late October. He was struck by inequality, crime, and the abundance of game at markets.[71] He also visited the city's mint and included notes on production and profits. He explained how things had functioned under the royal government: "The government formerly sold quicksilver to the miners at a certain price. This was objectionable as a monopoly, but it always insured a supply of that necessary article."[72] Here, Poinsett demonstrated his preference for economic stability and order over republican government. Poinsett observed festivities during the Day of All Saints and remarked on pretty ladies smoking cigars: "It appears to me a detestable habit for young ladies, but I suppose my fastidiousness is the effect of early prejudice."[73]

Poinsett was formally presented to Iturbide on November 3.[74] He was anxious to meet the emperor, but "from his sudden elevation to the throne, I fear he is extraordinarily bad."[75] Despite being impressed by Iturbide's generosity in releasing thirty-nine Americans from prison, Poinsett was pessimistic. His perception was shaped by the fact that he had arrived at a particularly tumultuous time. The previous year, after members of the Mexican populace declared Iturbide emperor, elections for the first independent Congress resulted in a heterogeneous Congress divided among a range of liberals and conservatives, not all of whom were Iturbistas.[76] Iturbide, however, dissolved Congress at the end of October because of legislative obstacles to his reforms and, according to Poinsett, ruled by "corruption and violence."[77] In reality, Iturbide had both passionate supporters and fierce opponents, and although much of his support came from conservative members of the military, nobility, and clergy, he also received endorsement from strategic liberals, like Lorenzo Zavala, who would become Poinsett's political and business ally.

According to Poinsett, Iturbide depended on "ample means to pay the soldiery," means that seemed likely to continue because Iturbide was courting English financiers, who were favorable to the Mexican cause.[78] Poinsett was jealous of this British influence. He wrote, "There exists with all the governments of Spanish America, a great desire to conciliate Great Britain; and although the people everywhere are more attached to us, the governments seek uniformly and anxiously to form diplomatic relations, and to connect themselves with that of Great Britain. They are afraid of the power of that nation, and are aware that their commercial interests require the support of a great manufacturing and commercial people. We shall glean something of the commerce of those countries, but the harvest will be for the British."[79] Even his pet project of collecting plants and minerals was not safe from British competition. He heard "with great dismay" from "the professors of Botany and Mineralogy . . . that they had received orders from his majesty to prepare collections to be sent to England."[80]

After meeting Iturbide, Poinsett visited these two professors at the Minería School of Mines. Poinsett knew from Humboldt's account, as did English capitalists, that Mexico was rich in gold, silver, copper, mercury, and iron. The mines, however, either had been destroyed or had fallen into disrepair during the independence wars.[81] He was frustrated minerals could not be bought in the market, only taken directly from the source.[82] Poinsett was looking for new opportunities to revive minerals as commodities. So too were English capitalists. Mexican mining laws prohibited foreigners from owning mines or shares in the mines, but investors began offering deals to serve as financial backers for mining proprietors, resuscitating the mines in exchange for profits.[83] For the time being, Poinsett worked to procure minerals, with the help of the professors. He would become involved in mining on his next trip to Mexico.

Before leaving the city, Poinsett met Iturbide's father and sister, whom he referred to as a "plain good sort of woman, dressed in a dark striped calico gown." Yet Poinsett could "scarcely restrain a smile, when I gave her the '*tratamiento*' (highness) due to her rank. These people can have no idea, how ridiculous this miserable representation of royalty appears to a republican."[84] He always prided himself on being a good "republican," even as his political preferences often fell short.

Poinsett and his companions headed for the coast. They "stopped to breakfast at a collection of wretched hovels," where he took the opportunity to observe and describe the process of making corn tortillas. Poinsett blended cultural curiosity with jealous economic scouting. He remarked that Humboldt had predicted that the Mexicans "will one day undersell [the United States] in bread corn, in the West Indies and other markets."[85] Poinsett was skeptical but could not deny that there was an abundance of corn. In Querétaro, he noted that people were unlikely to purchase foreign manufactures because they seemed to prefer such simple things.[86] He remarked on the burdens of price-fixing for US merchants, who struggled to profit from selling large cargoes wholesale. He met several merchants who had opened their own shops so they could sell directly to consumers.[87] Poinsett was sympathetic to the international merchants and financiers who opposed Iturbide's rule, observing that from the economic standpoint of many Creoles, Iturbide's rule was worse than Spain's.[88]

In another village, Poinsett went "strolling about the village, and into every hut in it." He did so to escape the smoke from servants' dinner preparations in the barn, where he was lodging, but used the opportunity to disparage their homes and inflate the benevolence of southern slaveholders, writing, "I certainly never saw a negro-house in Carolina so comfortless. Any master, who, in our country, should lodge his slaves in this manner would be considered barbarous and inhuman."[89] He occasionally remarked on seeing men and women "well dressed" or "neatly dressed" but said that "not even the crowd of well dressed peasantry, that fill the streets, could enliven its appearance."[90]

On the journey to the coast, he was pleasantly surprised by the "great natural politeness" of the Native people and castes and observed that they were "humble to their superiors, submissive, and docile" except when drunk.[91] In general, the people Poinsett encountered were kind and hospitable to him, but they were also suspicious of him. At one cottage, a woman accused Poinsett of making her baby cry. He had "patted its cheek and complimented the mother on its beauty," and when "the little urchin shortly after began to squall," the woman "attributed its uneasiness to [his] having touched it with an evil hand." Poinsett agreed to dip his hand in a cup of water; the mother gave the baby some of the water, and the baby stopped crying.[92]

In the days after the baby incident, Poinsett grew increasingly irritable. He was disgusted by the sickness near the coast and by his surroundings in general. He complained about his lodgings, the bugs, the food, and the sounds of dying men. He wrote that only organizing his notes and translating "Iturbide's absurd proclamations and speeches has enabled [him] to bear with this detestable place."[93] Poinsett rode every day to the lookout to see if he could spot the ship that would take him home. He was so desperate that he almost decided to leave on a Baltimore schooner, a type of vessel he had once had an accident in and "dislike[d] very much"; it departed, though, before he had a chance.[94] Although some of the prisoners whom Poinsett had helped free resented having to return to the United States (criticizing the United States as a nation of "robbers and Jews" and speaking ill of American officers and of Poinsett), Poinsett was anxious to go.[95]

When he finally boarded a ship bound for the United States, the crew had to wait several days for the winds to be right. Poinsett used the delay to finish sorting through his notes on Mexico and to reflect on the political and economic takeaways of his trip. His notes revealed his preoccupation with race, his mixed feelings on government, and his economic agenda. Describing one of the towns he liked most, he said, "There were more whites than in any other town we have passed through since we left Mexico." For this reason, he found "the women are generally pretty and very well made."[96] He liked the artist he met, partly because he looked on "his countrymen" with the "utmost contempt."[97] One of the few compliments he gave was that he liked what he perceived to be the equality with which all people attended Mass.[98] This may have been more a reflection of his own elitist experience with church in the United States than of the reality in Mexico.

Poinsett remarked on commerce and mining, as well as potential opportunities for the United States. As in South America, he noted transportation issues, comparing the advantages of the United States over
Mexico: "The superior fertility of [Mexico's] soil and cheapness of labour,
will not compensate for the difference between land and water carriage,
and that flour might be brought from the Genessee country, in the state of
New York, by the canal, shipped at the port of New York for either Tampico or Vera Cruz, and sold there at a lower rate than the flour of the table
island." He also remarked on the inferiority of Mexican flour mills and
said he had "no doubt that if the importation of flour were permitted, we
would for many years be able to undersell the Mexicans in their own markets."[99] Poinsett sketched out information on mining districts, noting that
there were three thousand mines and that "under a good government"
mining would increase.[100] For example, at Valencia, which was now in
ruins, Poinsett had seen the plans of the mines; he wrote out detailed information on the shapes and directions of mining shafts, as if to serve as
a reference for future investors. He noted that "the state of these mines is
deplorable . . . it will require a large capital to establish forcing pumps to
extract the water."[101] Poinsett would use those observations several years
later as minister to Mexico and mining investor.

On Christmas Eve, Poinsett and his companions finally set sail for
Cuba, where he caught up on US news and gathered Cuban intelligence
he thought would be pertinent to US interests.[102] They were only supposed to be on the island for one day, so to make the most of his time, he
went straight to the house of an elite Creole, to whom he had a letter of
introduction, to ask questions about trade and politics. When the winds
delayed their departure, Poinsett went to Regla, "this city of pirates."[103]
He collected economic and demographic information, as usual, but
wrote, "To do this well in a Spanish colony is always difficult, and requires
time. If, therefore, you find what I have been able to collect but a meagre
account, you must make all due allowances for the situation in which I
am placed."[104] Regardless, he knew that "Cuba is not only the key of the
Gulph of Mexico, but of all the maritime frontier south of Savannah, and
some of our highest interests, political and commercial, are involved in its
fate."[105] He therefore preferred continued Spanish rule to occupation by
a great maritime power because he predicted that Spain would keep the
Black population down. This would not be the last time Poinsett offered
his thoughts on Cuban sovereignty.

Poinsett left Cuba on January 11. As he viewed Cuba in the distance,
more favorably than he had when he had been on shore, he took a few
moments to write several pages about the "scandalous system of piracy."

He argued, "All the great commercial nations of the world, ought to unite to induce or to compel Spain to adopt some such [antipiracy] measure. If that nation does not possess the power of carrying it into effect, the United States ought to lend the necessary aid to insure its execution."[106]

Poinsett submitted his notes to the president, conveying the message that Iturbide's administration was unstable and that the United States should wait to recognize independence. It was too late. By that point, the majority of policymakers had decided that recognition was necessary, and Monroe had received José Manuel Zozaya as Mexican minister to the United States in December. He did so unaware that as Poinsett was leaving Mexico, an uprising in Vera Cruz occurred. Antonio López de Santa Anna and Guadalupe Victoria had signed the Plan of Casa Mata to delegitimize Iturbide's rule and establish a new congress, marking the slow unraveling of Iturbide's rule. Poinsett warned Andrew Jackson, whom Monroe planned to appoint as minister to Mexico, that now was not the right time to accept such a post. He said negotiations would be impossible and the US minister would ultimately be embarrassed. Jackson declined Monroe's offer.[107]

Poinsett's writings about Mexico reached a broader audience than Monroe and Jackson, highlighting the fact that both politicians and the public received skewed information about their southern neighbors. Over the next two years, his notes were published nationally, as well as in Britain. In American editions, the author was listed as "citizen of the United States"; in Britain, his full name appeared in print.[108] The publication included an extract of his friend's journey from Tampico to the capital, a historical sketch of Mexico, several executive reports and decrees, and trade memoranda from both a Spanish and an American merchant. Poinsett also included material from Alexander von Humboldt's writings, which he had referenced during his travels, as he had in South America.[109] Poinsett's writings provided readers in the United States the most complete, albeit flawed, collection of information on Mexico they had yet received, and these were reviewed extensively in New England.[110] They also inaugurated the decades of racist, capitalist writings on Mexico that would follow Poinsett's *Notes*.[111] Poinsett's opinions formed the basis for Alexis de Tocqueville's statements in *Democracy in America* about Mexico's inability to sustain democracy (Tocqueville never visited Mexico himself).[112]

Poinsett sent advance copies to some of his business acquaintances, including a T. Ford, who wrote Poinsett a letter "on Cuba and Piracy." Ford appreciated reading about Poinsett's opinions on Cuban piracy and was adamant about the need to stop the "depredations" to "our increasing commerce." He said the current "plan of guarding our commerce and arm of attacking the indirect aggressor when caught in the fact is too lean and feeble."[113] The "increasing commerce" to which Ford referred was the illegal slave trade, which was a frequent target of pirates.[114] Both Ford's request and Poinsett's response illustrate the intersection of different aspects of Poinsett's career. When Poinsett returned to Congress, he advocated for more naval power, his months in Mexico and the Caribbean having intersected with security issues and business interests at home.

Return to Congress

Poinsett resumed his seat in Congress on Wednesday, January 29. Over the next two years, he would bring concerns like Ford's before Congress. In general, he took a more active role than he had before Mexico. Despite his reputation as a lackluster orator, he gave longer speeches on economic matters and foreign relations.[115] By the next election, his opponents managed to brand him an "anti–slave holding candidate," even as he pursued enslavers' "security" concerns by endorsing their tariff preferences and advocating strategic military and naval expansion.[116] He also remained a Democratic-Republican, along with the majority of politicians, while he simultaneously moved closer to Andrew Jackson *and* advocated policies in line with future National Republicans and Whigs.

Although the "second party system" did not exist until 1828, Poinsett began displaying political behavior that would persist throughout this system, behavior that defied the limits of party and sectionalism.[117] The second party system allegedly curbed sectionalism and was characterized by "improbable alliances."[118] If the two-party system that emerged managed to evade sectional divide, it also failed to fully unite people. Poinsett would become a Jacksonian Democrat, but his position on any given issue, like others', reflected political and economic pragmatism. In general, there was little ideological consistency among politicians of the era, and political expediency often trumped moral and ideological stability (for example, John Quincy Adams championed antislavery and sometimes defended slaveholders' interests).[119] Before Poinsett was reelected in 1824, he pledged to support John Quincy Adams over southern enslaver William H. Crawford, should the election become a contest between the two men. He correctly gambled that Adams was more likely to win and might reward his show of support, which Adams did by appointing Poinsett minister to Mexico.

Even though Poinsett would profess preference for the antislavery northerner over the southern enslaver, one of the first things he did after being reelected was present a memorial from the South Carolina legislature to establish a municipal guard to protect Charleston. This guard would "carry into effect the laws of the State and the city ordinances for the government of negroes and free persons of color; but the members of said corps shall have no military power over the white inhabitants of the State."[120] Two days after Poinsett's presentation, a group of American ship captains petitioned Congress to "interpose in their behalf" and rescind the Negro Seamen Act.[121] Instead, Congress signed Charleston's municipal guard into law less than a month later.[122]

Poinsett also advocated on behalf of enslavers' requests for increased naval strength. President of the Literary and Philosophical Society of South Carolina Stephen Elliott, for example, asked Poinsett to advocate for a navy yard in Charleston. Elliott was a plantation owner and botanist who corresponded with Poinsett about plants and minerals, especially once Poinsett was made an honorary member of the Franklin Library Society—Charleston's version of the American Philosophical Society—in the spring of 1823.[123] Their correspondence exemplified how the cultural, intellectual, and financial interests of Poinsett and his associates intersected in Poinsett's political efforts.[124] In one letter, Elliott updated Poinsett on the recent plans of the society and informed Poinsett that he had received two boxes of minerals from New York but had not received the painting Poinsett had selected from the Comte de Survilliers's collection (which he hoped to use in the next exhibition). Elliott followed this with an argument for the practicality of a navy yard. It would, he wrote, both provide work for Charleston's mechanics, who could build vessels "as cheap or cheaper than at the north," and "necessarily add some military and some physical force to our white population."[125] Charleston did not end up getting a navy yard, but that spring the navy undertook an examination of the harbor, and the resolution Poinsett put forward to increase the navy, in response to his business contacts in Cuba, was adopted.[126]

Perhaps more significant, his stance on naval strength and his writings on Cuban piracy influenced the executive's articulation of US policy in the Americas in what became known as the Monroe Doctrine. In his annual address to Congress at the end of 1823, President Monroe declared the hemisphere closed to "future colonization by any European powers."[127] British foreign minister George Canning had suggested that the two nations issue a joint statement against European intervention in the Americas, which former presidents Jefferson and Madison supported.[128]

Poinsett's *Notes on Mexico*, however, warned of the influence of Great Britain in Spanish America, noting that "the harvest will be for the British."[129] Adams likewise urged against a joint declaration with Great Britain. Despite denouncing slavery, Adams, like Poinsett, feared British interference in the illegal slave trade, which many of their constituents and colleagues profited from. Monroe's address to Congress ultimately reflected these concerns. At the time of his address, almost 50 percent of all commissioned US naval forces were deployed in the Caribbean, and Poinsett would continue to advocate for additional naval resources on behalf of the interests of enslavers, noting that "the commerce of the United States with the island of Cuba . . . claims in a peculiar manner the protection of the Government."[130]

While he advocated for additional government intervention in the Americas, Poinsett made a speech *against* similar intervention in Greece. There was a popular movement in the United States to support Greek independence from the Ottoman Empire on the basis of shared cultural and revolutionary experiences, and many private citizens sent aid to the revolutionaries. While some influential politicians, like Edward Everett and Henry Clay, were major proponents, Poinsett was not.[131] In his speech, he argued against recognition of Greek independence. He recognized racial and cultural similarities between the United States and Greece but said the duty of a statesman was a "stern" one. The United States, he said, would need to conserve its resources to defend liberty in the Americas.[132] Poinsett believed martial resources should be used to further economic interests, and by getting involved in Greece, the United States would potentially harm the interests of some of his associates, like Baring, who did business with the Ottoman Empire.[133]

In fact, opium exports from the Ottoman Empire were a major reason not to upset Turkish leaders. Poinsett had initially faced off against Massachusetts senator Daniel Webster, who gave a moving speech in favor of Greek independence because at first he equated Greek sovereignty with business opportunities for some of his constituents. Webster reversed his position once it became apparent that some of his financial allies relied on Turkish support of the opium trade (like Thomas Handasyd Perkins, to whom Webster owed money) and were opposed to independence.[134] Webster, like Poinsett, ultimately chose political expediency over revolutionary sympathy. Other influential congressmen, like John Quincy Adams, did the same, and the United States declined to recognize Greek independence until 1837.

Throughout his career, Poinsett's agenda focused on social control in

South Carolina, the interests of his business contacts, and the acquisition of exclusive goods. He had increasingly expensive taste, and he argued for legislation that seemed to have little relevance for enslavers but that ultimately benefited the purchases of elite enslavers. For example, in March 1823, Poinsett opposed a tariff on wine. He was recorded in the House journal as arguing that "he did not desire to see this country a wine growing country, as, in comparison with corn growing countries, they were always poor and miserable."[135] Not recorded in the minutes was the fact that he loved imported fine wines. In fact, when English banker Francis Baring wrote to him that summer for news on South America, Baring noted that the only thing that would induce him "to cross the Atlantic again will be the prospect of drinking a bottle of red south with you on the summit of that volcano with a hard name who is within 3 days march on Veracruz."[136]

Poinsett's success on the Greek issue would not be matched by commercial policy. His next major speech addressed a controversial tariff bill introduced early in 1824. The bill aimed to protect American industry with duties on cotton and wool textiles, iron, and agricultural goods. This would be the first protectionist tariff since 1820, when the 1816 tariff expired. In general, the tariff was popular among northern and western states and opposed by southerners, especially South Carolinians. Poinsett's speech called attention to the potential ruin to the South: "We now supply Great Britain because we are her best customer: she may not refuse to take our cotton, but her manufacturers, who are many of them shipping merchants, will bring their cotton from those places where they sell their fabrics—from Brazil and from Mexico."[137] With this argument, Poinsett used his knowledge of trade in the Americas to favor the cotton interest.

The anti-tariff stance went beyond the cotton interest, however. Throughout the nation, men with international business connections opposed the tariff, and just as a nonpartisan campaign succeeded in raising the tariff, there was a nonpartisan resistance to it.[138] In February, Poinsett received a letter from a group of northern merchants requesting his support in opposing the tariff. They "resolved that the labor and capital of the country will naturally be applied to the most profitable objects and that all legislative interference has a tendency to divert them to unprofitable objects and of course to diminish the national wealth."[139] Here was a laissez-faire argument that Poinsett supported because it was expedient. However, he used his diplomatic experience to justify his position: "The consumption of our manufactures is already great in Buenos Ayres and Peru, in the Brazils and in Mexico, and whenever our interests shall be properly attended to in those countries that consumption will be increased, unless, indeed, the policy we are about to pursue deprive us of those markets."[140]

Poinsett actually found himself on the same side of the debate as Daniel Webster. Both men catered to merchants. (Although Webster's wealthiest constituents were manufacturers, these manufacturers still made the bulk of their wealth from trade.) Poinsett's position on the tariff was based on more than his constituents' interests. He was clearly in conversation with businessmen outside of South Carolina, sending privileged information on tariff negotiations to New York merchants.[141]

The tariff passed on May 19, after a debate about "negro cloth," the coarse woolen manufacture used to make cheap slave clothing. An amendment to the tariff that would have operated against these textiles was rejected.[142] Aside from that small victory, the amendments Poinsett voted in favor of were rejected, and the protectionist tariff passed.[143] Although Poinsett voted with his state against the tariff, eight years later he would support the tariff over the South Carolina free trade contingent.

Before Congress recessed for the summer, it passed legislation relating to internal improvements, which offset Poinsett's disappointment in the tariff law. Poinsett's colleague from the South Carolina Board of Public Works, Abram Blanding, wrote to him in February asking him to support an initiative to facilitate communication between the east and west.[144] Despite complaints by Poinsett's opponents about unnecessary public works projects, Poinsett and Blanding had had some success together. When Poinsett was president of the Board of Public Works in 1820, they had overseen construction of the Poinsett Bridge, a unique gothic arch bridge (the oldest surviving in the state) that helped connect Charleston and Columbia to upstate South Carolina and North Carolina. It is not clear whether Poinsett presented Blanding's suggestion to Congress, but on April 30, legislators approved a bill that authorized the president to have surveys made of routes throughout the nation and to improve mail carry.[145] When Poinsett became secretary of war, these routes would be essential for military communication and so-called "Indian removal."

Poinsett planned to travel to London again in the summer of 1824 and ended up staying local. He spent at least a little time that summer visiting his orphaned son, but the more likely cause of his decision to remain in South Carolina was the upcoming election. Since the start of Monroe's second term, Americans had wondered who would succeed him and what fate the Democratic-Republican Party would meet. Four major candidates from the party were running, and there was no clear frontrunner among John Quincy Adams, Andrew Jackson, William Crawford, and Henry Clay. Congressmen and aspiring officeholders gambled on whom to support; party patronage was at stake. Poinsett himself had ambitions for the cabinet, and he needed to spend the summer monitoring the political mood.

Although these aspirations for the cabinet were premature, he was a candidate for minister to Mexico. President Monroe presented the offer through Secretary of War John C. Calhoun, who tempered it with a note of caution relating to the upcoming election.[146] There was talk among Calhoun's supporters that perhaps Poinsett could be made secretary of state to thwart Henry Clay's ambitions for the postelection cabinet.[147] Soon after reading Calhoun's letter, Poinsett received a similar letter from Secretary of Navy Samuel Southard requesting him to consider a post to Mexico while also asking, "Would your absence endanger the vote of the state so as perhaps to give it in a way not satisfactory to the majority of the people?"[148] Southard cautioned Poinsett about leaving Congress for Mexico because even months before voters went to the polls, it seemed a definite possibility that the electoral votes would be split in such a way that the House of Representatives would have to decide the results. This made congressmen especially important, which is why Calhoun preferred Poinsett to stay where he "will be at least useful."[149]

Poinsett ran for office again. He was branded as being part of the moneyed aristocracy; at the same time, he was criticized for remaining ambiguous on slaveholding and for being a Jackson man rather than a southern Crawfordite.[150] Voters were obsessed with what the congressional election meant for the presidential election because they rightly predicted that it would get thrown to the House.[151] They feared that Poinsett would choose Adams over Crawford.[152] Others disdained his international experience and called him the "anti–slave holding candidate."[153] Despite the opposition, Poinsett captured 58 percent of the vote on his pledge to vote for Jackson, endorse Calhoun as vice president, support the army and the navy, and "assert the freedom and independence of North and South America."[154] Even though he resigned before taking his seat, Poinsett would follow through on the last two promises when he finally accepted the position as minister to Mexico.

The presidential election did indeed end up in the House, resulting in a compromise that would be called the "corrupt bargain."[155] Just as Poinsett's supporters had hoped, he was part of the private conversations and backroom deals that dominated politics in early winter, despite his criticism of Iturbide's "corrupt" administration. Not only his Carolina constituents but also his colleagues in Philadelphia asked him to vote for Jackson.[156] Individual votes were anonymous, but both South Carolina and Pennsylvania ended up giving their votes to Jackson, for which Poinsett would be rewarded when Jackson became president.[157]

Adams, however, won the election.[158] Clay, for his role in securing Adams's presidency, became secretary of state. With Poinsett's ambitions for secretary dashed, he accepted the position as minister to Mexico. As late as February 28, he thought he might be going to Greece on business for the House Committee on Foreign Relations, but the day after Adams's inauguration, Adams approached Poinsett about Mexico.[159] Adams might have intended the invitation to be a reward; Poinsett had shared his position on Greece and had supported Adams over Crawford. Or perhaps Adams wanted to get another Jacksonian out of Washington.[160]

Soon after Adams's offer, Poinsett got a letter from Edward Everett, the editor of the *North American Review* who had earlier solicited material from Poinsett (and who had ties to New England's most influential intellectuals and capitalists).[161] Everett had corresponded with Daniel Webster and wanted Poinsett to travel to Greece to assess the status of independence, much the way he had in Mexico. Everett seemed convinced that Poinsett would now advocate for Greek independence. Poinsett left no writing to confirm Everett's assumption, but Everett's deduction, and his confidence in Poinsett, suggests the extent to which Poinsett had cemented his reputation as an international man who could be counted on by different political interests. Poinsett's ability to move among interest groups and to take political initiative was perhaps the main reason Adams chose him for the position of minister to Mexico.

Poinsett's domestic and international experience over the previous five years revealed the agenda that would shape the rest of his career. It was based on political pragmatism, economic expansion, white supremacy, and state power. His ability to ally with different groups domestically and internationally gave him an advantage in the manipulation of US power. As minister plenipotentiary to Mexico, Poinsett would have the opportunity to use this advantage more fully than he ever had before. This was just the start.

4
....

Interest in Mexico,
1825–1830

James Madison was glad that Poinsett would be returning to Mexico. The former president, now in his seventies, had read Poinsett's "authentic" account of Mexico at his home in Montpelier during the 1824 election season. He worried when he had trouble tracking down Poinsett to compliment him.[1] Poinsett had left Washington several months earlier, abandoning his "friends" in Congress during the tumultuous election.[2] However, he returned in time for the "corrupt bargain" and for the answer to the question that had been asked since the United States had officially received José Manuel Zozaya y Bermúdez as Mexico's first envoy in 1822: Who would represent the United States in Mexico?

Poinsett was an obvious choice because of his service in South America and Mexico, but he was not the first one. When Adams was serving as secretary of state, he had wanted to send Andrew Jackson to Mexico, partly to get Jackson out of the way before the election and partly because he wanted someone to take an aggressive stance regarding North American relations. Adams was not as militaristically aggressive as Jackson, but he was a shrewd expansionist and nationalist with grand ambitions for US hemispheric relations. Adams knew Poinsett took initiative in diplomatic affairs and could be counted on to help shape, and potentially assume the blame for, US policy. Some had thought Poinsett was holding out for the position of secretary of state in the new administration because he had declined President Monroe's request for him to serve in Mexico, but when Adams called on Poinsett the day after inauguration, he accepted within twenty-four hours.[3] This would be Poinsett's first time in Spain's former empire acting in more than a semiofficial capacity. Poinsett's friends were glad he decided to go to Mexico, with the full powers of the state behind him, because they predicted their "connections with that government may well become highly important."[4]

Mexico was important diplomatically for the United States, as evidenced by the fact that by 1827 the State Department had stationed twelve other officials there besides Poinsett. This was more than in any other country save England, France, and Spain.[5] The State Department's main goals for Poinsett's tenure in Mexico were favorable treaties of commerce and limits. In all of Spain's former colonies, the United States wanted good trade terms; in Mexico, they also wanted land, particularly part of the Mexican province Coahuila y Tejas.

Texas, which "belonged" at various times to the Comanche, Kiowas, Apache, and other Native tribes, Spain, and Mexico, occupied a significant amount of American resources, imagination, and diplomatic energies throughout the first half of the nineteenth century.[6] Much has been written about how both Cuba and Texas fit into a US agenda driven by Manifest Destiny ideology and the expansion of slavery.[7] While it was true that some Americans' aspirations for slaveholder dominance and territorial expansion influenced US aggression in the region, desires for this territory were not unique to Americans. Cuba and Texas were battlegrounds for international capitalists.[8] France, England, and the United States were all interested in the sugar plantations of Cuba, while Mexico was eager to disrupt Spanish rule on the island.[9] Likewise, investing in Texas land was becoming popular not only for land-hungry Americans but also for British speculators, as well as for prominent Mexican military and political leaders who saw Texas assets as a kind of safeguard against the risks of revolutionary instability.[10] Manifest Destiny exceptionalism does not quite explain either US national goals in the region or Poinsett's.

Whether or not Texas was officially part of the United States was less important than fostering business ties and securing investment opportunities. Poinsett's interests did not depend on acquisition, just access. He had long been interested in the science and profits of mining; his writings on South America and Mexico are filled with his observations of mining regions, as well as information from his conversations with mineralogists.[11] For example, he was on friendly terms with famous Spanish Mexican professor of mineralogy Andrés Manuel del Río and introduced him to the scientific community of Philadelphia, where del Río hoped to publish some of his findings.[12] Poinsett was keen to promote anyone and anything that would lead to new knowledge of, and business opportunities regarding, mining. The work did not map neatly onto his official agenda because mines were not unilaterally good or bad for either the

United States or the Mexican state. Because mining ventures transcended national identities, Poinsett made strategic alliances based on investment motives rather than nationality.

It is fitting that he served as minister to Mexico for an administration that from the outset was labeled as "corrupt." In the early nineteenth century, practices and perceptions of "interest" and corruption were in flux.[13] US interests were a morass of economic, cultural, and military concerns at the individual and national levels. Although historians generally agree that the value placed on "disinterest," or impartiality, in politics faded away by the early 1800s—replaced by a tacit acknowledgment that self-interest could and should be compatible with national interest—Poinsett and his peers continued to tout traditional understandings of disinterest.[14] They used it as a standard by which to judge political leadership of newly independent Latin American nations, as well as their own behavior.[15] It served as a cover, whether intentional or not, of actions that might be described as corrupt. Poinsett professed to value old-fashioned disinterestedness but violated the trust associated with his authority to use political institutions and business ventures for private gains.[16] Although Poinsett and his correspondents wrote about corruption in antiquated terms, focusing on the debasement of morals and institutions, their business activities more closely resembled the Civil War–era intersection of politics and financial fraud.[17]

Poinsett used his post as minister plenipotentiary to advance common American interests, such as land acquisition and favorable trade agreements, as well as his and his business connections' individual interests, such as mining. In both cases, his activities crossed national allegiances and revealed the centrality of capital and coercion for foreign relations. Poinsett's early biographers tended to portray him as a nationalist who also had the best interests of the Mexican population at heart.[18] Less sympathetic historians characterize Poinsett's diplomatic tenure as injurious to Mexican welfare.[19] Poinsett did not practice disinterested diplomacy; instead, he tried to present himself as a disinterested statesman. He worked with private individuals and public officials to advance access to commercial and investment opportunities for his constituents. He and other US officials attempted to manipulate local politics and brought military intervention into the diplomatic arena, however slight, to achieve economic aims. In doing so, they built off, and reinforced, what some private American citizens were already doing in other countries. At home and abroad, corruption, concealment, and interest politics functioned as pillars of US political economy.

Poinsett did not have time to go home to Charleston before he left for Mexico at the end of March. His mercantile contact in New York, however, was hard at work purchasing items for Poinsett's South Carolina home, including flower vases, a crumb cloth for the dining room table, and a dark-green carpet with wicking that would allow for the easy cleaning of any tobacco "squirts."[20] His friend Joseph Johnson arranged to have his personal things packed and sent to Norfolk, where Poinsett would embark for Vera Cruz. Johnson collected Poinsett's rents, dealt with bad tenants, and boxed up some of Poinsett's favorite wines.[21] While Poinsett waited to depart from Norfolk, he sent one last business letter to Johnson. He needed Johnson to track down Vice President John C. Calhoun, a fellow South Carolinian, for the $1,000 Calhoun owed him.[22] Johnson, as always, complied, connecting Poinsett, wherever he was, to South Carolina.

Johnson also filled Poinsett in on the major social event in his absence: the Marquis de Lafayette's visit to Charleston. As the last surviving general of the Revolution, Lafayette was on a grand tour of the United States, and he had stopped in Charleston for a party. Although Poinsett missed Lafayette in person, the general wrote to him before Poinsett had a chance to reach Mexico. Lafayette wanted Poinsett to know that he was following one of Poinsett's favored travel routes. He also, like so many others, had a patronage request. He asked Poinsett to find employment in a Mexican mercantile house for the son of a French official.[23] Poinsett would receive many more of these types of requests.

When Poinsett arrived in Mexico at the beginning of May, US capitalism was waiting for rescue. While the Monroe administration had dallied in appointing a minister, American businessmen had been "suffering here for the want of an able representative."[24] Things were bad. Not only had Americans recently been murdered in the middle of the day but, according to one American resident, "British adventurers are overrunning this country" and soon US "commerce will be cut up."[25] American newspapers, likewise, printed reports about the threat of British merchants, who sold at a loss to drive American competition out of the market.[26] Even worse, the British had concluded a treaty with the Mexican government while Poinsett was still in Washington. If Poinsett did not take action, Lafayette, never mind American citizens, would not be able to secure positions in mercantile houses.

Poinsett should have rushed to Mexico's capital, 250 miles away from

Vera Cruz, where he disembarked the US frigate Constellation. His instructions from the State Department were to promote trade with the United States and convince Mexico not to privilege any European powers over the United States, an agenda that required official diplomatic recognition.[27] Before Poinsett left Vera Cruz, he started practicing the unsanctioned part of his strategy for American prosperity in Mexico: covert interference. Treaties would mean little if Spain reconquered Mexico, an outcome that seemed possible on the basis of the ongoing conflict between Spanish and Mexican forces at the Castle of San Juan de Ulúa in Vera Cruz. Poinsett sent clandestine orders to US naval officer Melancthon T. Woolsey to negotiate a peace between Spanish commander José María Coppinger and Mexican general Miguel Barragán. Poinsett instructed Woolsey to tout US neutrality; the aim, however, was Spanish defeat. Poinsett feared that reconquest would benefit Britain more than it would the United States, whereas Spain's surrender of the castle would promote both US and Mexican trade interests. He in fact had been secretly discussing the situation with Barragán, who offered suggestions on how Woolsey should approach Coppinger. All of this was to be done quietly, at night if possible. Coppinger, for his part, refused to negotiate secretly. Poinsett, Woolsey, and Barragán would have to wait until autumn for Coppinger's official surrender.[28]

Poinsett turned his attention to arrangements for Mexico City. After sending word to the Mexican government that he had arrived in the country and would like to be received by the president, Poinsett was instructed to delay his visit to the city. A multiday religious festival occupied the nation's leaders. Poinsett brought his entourage, which included his twenty-two-year-old secretary, Edward Thornton Tayloe, and John Mason Jr., secretary of legation, as well as Dr. Rich, D. A. Smith, and Stephen Elliot, to the nearby hacienda of James Smith Wilcocks, a wealthy Philadelphian who had served as US consul to Mexico since 1822.[29] Wilcocks had offered up his estate as soon as Poinsett got to Mexico, even though he was still in the city on business. Poinsett requested that Wilcocks finish settling American landowner James Wilkinson's business before joining them in the country.

Wilcocks and Wilkinson embodied two types of American venturers for whom Mexico was a land of opportunity. Poinsett saw the world— and his role in Mexico—in a way that reflected and blended both of their outlooks. Wilkinson was a former army officer and rogue schemer who twenty years earlier had been tried for treason for conspiring with Aaron Burr to seize Spanish land in North America. When Poinsett arrived in

Mexico, Wilkinson was living in the capital, waiting for the government to approve his request for a land grant in Texas. In the 1820s, the Mexican government attracted foreign investment to Texas by allowing individuals to control large plots of land in exchange for assuming the cost of their settlement. Wilcocks was a successful Philadelphia merchant who had served as a commercial agent for the United States in Canton before moving to Mexico. He owned several mines in Mexico and had sent bricks of gold and silver ore back to the State Department.[30] Wilkinson saw opportunity chiefly in land; Wilcocks, in capital. Wilkinson was known for engaging in extralegal pursuits; Wilcocks was more likely to advance his agenda through channels that at least appeared legitimate. They occupied flip sides of the US agenda in Mexico.

Wilcocks's and Wilkinson's interests converged in settling American claims, especially those of a Baltimore company that had lent money to Mexican revolutionary Francisco Xavier Mina in 1816. When Spanish forces executed Mina the following year, it seemed to destroy his investors' chances for profits, but after the Mexican independence struggle succeeded in 1821, these men moved to capitalize on their investments by presenting their claims, usually through US agents, to the new Mexican government. Mina's biggest investor was Dennis A. Smith, former loan contractor during the War of 1812, who afterward was involved in an embezzlement scandal and costly lawsuits in his role as a director of the Baltimore branch of the Second Bank of the United States.[31] Smith had paid for the heavy artillery, munitions, construction supplies, and eighteen-gun brig for Mina's expedition and had recently employed both Wilkinson and Wilcocks to represent his claims to the Mexican government.[32] Smith arrived at Wilcocks's place with Poinsett.

It is not clear whether Wilkinson and Wilcocks were meeting about Smith, but it is clear that business dominated Poinsett's agenda. Poinsett was familiar with the importance of claims issues and had worked with Wilcocks on behalf of American cases when he was in Mexico several years before.[33] Claims were a mainstay on the diplomatic circuit. Merchants sent countless letters to the State Department requesting aid in pursuing remuneration from various foreign governments. These sorts of claims requested compensation or exemption from payment in response to a variety of grievances, which included the alleged unlawful seizure of cargo, application of a duty or custom house fees, damage to property, or loan repayments.

In Mexico, claims against the government for revolutionary aid were common. For example, the recently deceased A. L. Duncan of New Orleans had lent the Mexican government about $90,000 in cash and supplies.[34] Poinsett had barely commenced his duties when five men sent him introductory letters on behalf of the "most reputable" Captain Joseph Vidal from New Orleans, who was on his way to Mexico to pursue Duncan's claims.[35] Duncan had lent money to the Mexican government to aid the independence movement, and Vidal, "from motives altogether disinterested," sought to collect the claims for Duncan's family. The disinterestedness, according to Vidal's recommenders, qualified him for the benefits of Poinsett's "public capacity," a sign that perceptions of "disinterest" still mattered even though profiteering self-interest was the norm.[36] Claimants, by the very nature of their requests, were never disinterested. When successful, claimants and their representatives received a reward, and Vidal's case was no different.

Consular agents often represented American citizens, but claims were best pursued by a higher-ranking diplomat. Poinsett's arrival, therefore, was a relief, especially because Smith wanted to start a Mexican mining company in Baltimore and hoped a cash windfall from the Mexican government would provide the capital.[37] Although Smith would have to wait over fifteen years for his settlement, Poinsett would advance his interests in other ways.[38]

After Wilcocks and Wilkinson's meeting, Wilcocks returned to his hacienda to visit with Poinsett. The others went ahead to Mexico City with some of Poinsett's luggage.[39] From there, they planned to visit the mining district of Tepalcatepec to evaluate business prospects.[40] If Poinsett had not had to prepare for his official reception with the president, he would have gone with them. Poinsett was considering investing and wanted to get his companions' assessment of British and German mining companies in the region. Wilcocks, on the other hand, planned to divest. He worried that Mexico's mines were being exhausted. Although he had imported steam engines to improve their drainage, he wanted to sell some of his mines, as a hedge.[41] This was fortuitous for Smith, who was eager to start a US-based mining company, one that need not be aware of the day-to-day functioning of the mines. He and Wilcocks agreed that Poinsett would hold the titles to the mining lands until Smith raised the capital to purchase them. Poinsett meanwhile wrote to a friend in New York, "The great merchants and capitalists of the United States appear to me to be neglecting this very important country," and he recommended they form mining companies, "as others have done in England" because of the potential for significant profits.[42] Five years later, Poinsett and Smith would be under investigation for collusion and deception.[43]

When President Victoria formally received Poinsett as minister pleni-potentiary and envoy extraordinary on June 1, Poinsett emphasized the two nations' revolutionary and republican similarities. He said the United States was flattered Mexico had modeled its new constitution on theirs.[44] These pretensions to shared republicanism served as a justification for political meddling and a cover for business activities that crossed the line between national interest and self-interested profiteering.

While Poinsett acted the part of the United States' highest-ranking diplomat in Mexico City, Smith sent him updates from mining country. It was rainy, the mosquitos were out, and several Americans had died from the black vomit. Smith could not convince the driver of his coach to take him to Vera Cruz because so many people were ill. Smith was glad he would be leaving soon.[45]

Poinsett crafted Smith's miserable experience into a positive adver-tisement for Mexican mines. He wrote to New York investors that after extensive research he had selected a mine that "was formerly one of the most productive in the kingdom" and that "if this business is properly managed, it must prove profitable." He strongly urged the formation of an investment company, making the case that "operations of the mines will be of service to the country; the bullion will go there direct." Poinsett chided Americans for not taking advantage of Mexico as the British had, calling himself "anxious as you know I am to promote to wealth of our country."[46] Yet when Smith asked about purchasing equipment from the British, Poinsett readily agreed. Smith had asked Poinsett's opinion about whether to introduce water into the mines they now controlled. Water was used for mineral processing, and its management required costly machinery. Smith had conversed with the agent of another company and learned that iron pumps could be purchased from England for much less than in the United States. Smith would avoid the mistakes British min-ers had made by overspending on expensive machinery with minimal re-turns, by purchasing machinery from the British.[47]

Diplomatic historians have written about the Anglo-American rivalry in Mexico and about Poinsett's conflicts with British diplomats, yet they have failed to see that these conflicts obscured many of Poinsett's and his associates' economic activities, in which there was not always a clear enemy or protagonist. Wilcocks, for example, bought and sold mines to whomever he could profit from, whether they be American or British.[48] Poinsett claimed he could not "bear to see the English and German deriv-ing all the profits of these mining transactions," yet he and Smith agreed it made the most business sense to spend money on British machinery.[49]

Profit usually trumped nationality, and sometimes business with British merchants was a good thing.

Soon after learning that Smith expected to be in Baltimore in less than three weeks to get finances in order for the mines, Poinsett wrote to wealthy Baltimore merchant Robert Oliver. Oliver was the kind of investor they wanted involved in the new company. He had been one of the few Americans to export specie from Mexican mines before Mexico's independence, a privilege of his brother-in-law's influence in the Spanish court. Oliver also had a reputation for prudence and for prioritizing business over politics.[50] Although Oliver declined at first, he soon became a major subscriber of mine stock.[51] Later, when Poinsett stood accused of deceiving investors about the mines' profitability, his correspondence with Oliver would be cited as proof that Poinsett truly believed the mines were a sound investment.[52] Poinsett certainly talked up the mines. The plan was also to get New York merchants interested and to contract with people there.

However, Poinsett knew that mines, like all investments, were risky. The best he could do was diversify his investments and establish ties with the right people. As things got underway with the mining business in Baltimore, Poinsett worked to cover all his economic and political bases in Mexico. This meant investing in mines to the southeast of Mexico City and lands to the northwest; infiltrating Masonic lodge culture to undermine pro-British political support and simultaneously currying favor with British financiers; and aiding President Victoria's efforts to stifle Spain's commerce in Cuba while also thwarting Mexican attempts to take the island. Despite the Monroe Doctrine's assertion of unilateral dominance over Spain's crumbling empire, Poinsett needed to develop strategic alliances to manage US interests in the region.[53] His interactions with British diplomats were in line with official US-British relations: an uneasy cooperation around shared hemispheric interests, punctuated by periods of competition. His financial connections, which would extend far beyond purchasing mining equipment from British sellers, were his own doing.

Soon after his recognition ceremony in Mexico City, Poinsett began discussing a new treaty with the Mexican minster of foreign relations, Lucas Alamán, hoping to readjust the boundary fixed by the United States' 1819 treaty with Spain to include land as close to the Rio Grande as possible. If Victoria was ambivalent to Poinsett, Alamán was not. Alamán was unreceptive to Poinsett's agenda, partly because Poinsett was also dodging suspicions over Cuba. Poinsett told a half lie to Alamán when he said that the United States had no intentions to take the island.[54]

Many Americans sought to annex Cuba for reasons that blended slavery and commerce, military security, and Manifest Destiny impulses, but the US government's primary goal was the island's independence, with the assumption that annexation might follow naturally. In the meantime, Poinsett collaborated with British minister Henry Ward to secure the British and American objectives of preventing France from taking the island from Spain. For a brief period, their interests overlapped enough that Ward shared his knowledge of French ambitions. Poinsett took advantage of the information, transmitting it back to the State Department in secret code. The information became moot several months later when the French government announced that it would not invest in a military expedition in the Caribbean.[55] By then, Poinsett was working on new British and Mexican alliances.

Many Mexicans grew increasingly suspicious of Poinsett, and rightfully so.[56] He removed himself from Ward's good graces, and confirmed Alamán's suspicions, when he helped establish a Masonic lodge in Mexico City and allegedly used it for political ends. Freemasonry has a complicated and contentious history in early nineteenth-century Mexico. As secret fraternities, Masonic organizations are difficult to parse; sources for early nineteenth-century Mexico are particularly scarce. Lodges may have existed as early as the late eighteenth century, and they became institutionalized shortly before Poinsett's arrival. From 1816 to 1820, the Grand Lodge of Louisiana granted charters for York Rite lodges in Vera Cruz, Campeche, and Mérida.[57] Soon after, these lodges dissolved or became associated with the Scottish Rite.[58] Freemasonry became politicized as different Scottish groups united in opposition to Iturbide and then, after his fall, around plans for the new republican government. Members of the Scottish Rite Lodges were known as Escocés, and tended to favor a strong, centralist government with close ties to British business and politics. Opponents of these political views left the Scottish Rite and established the York Rite in Mexico City.[59] Around the time of Poinsett's arrival, the York Rite lodge became a meeting ground for opponents of the Escocés, including General Vicente Guerrero, Senator Lorenzo Zavala, and Secretary of Treasury Jose Ignacio Esteva.[60] Yorkinos wanted a liberal, federalist system of government. Poinsett himself had been a member of the Freemason Lodge in Charleston for years and had become a Royal Arch Mason, an advanced degree within the York Rite, in 1818.[61] The South Carolina Grand Lodge wanted Poinsett to establish ties in Mexico and sent Masonry literature to the State Department for Secretary of State Henry Clay to dispatch with Poinsett.[62]

Poinsett took advantage of his status as a Royal Arch Mason to join the York Rite lodge in Mexico City. The lodge did not yet have a charter from a grand lodge, which Poinsett secured from Philadelphia.[63] He later claimed that the timing was coincidental, that his involvement with the Masons had nothing to do with politics. In his initial correspondence with Clay on the political shift, he claimed success in helping establish an American Party but omitted his involvement with the Freemasons.[64] Yet he hosted dinners for members, many of whom were politicians, and soon, pro-American sentiment prevailed among Victoria's administration. Several pro-British members resigned, including Alamán. Victoria himself increasingly leaned liberal.[65] Privately, Poinsett claimed credit for this change. He wrote to US minister to England Rufus King that he had helped organize the Yorkinos and boasted to a Charleston friend, "We have established Masonic lodges and priests and soldiers and statesmen all disposed to be Masons . . . this institution has grown up under my patronage." Poinsett was, of course, capable of overstating his significance. Unironically, he followed this boast with the remark "I am desperately afraid of having my picture made by a Mexican painter. They imitate human nature abominably."[66]

Regardless of Poinsett's actual influence, the Mexican public believed Poinsett was using the organization to advance his own agenda.[67] His involvement with the Yorkinos irritated the political opposition, especially that spring, when Poinsett was appointed through the Masonic District of Pennsylvania as the district deputy grand master for Mexico and Central America, which gave him the power to inspect lodges, congregate meetings, and promote ranks.[68] It also ended his collaboration with Ward. Ward, for his part, played a similar role in the Scotch Rite Masons (although he had a personal conflict with Alamán).

While Poinsett's Masonic activities countered politics that tended to favor general British interests, he dealt personally with individual British interests. For example, an agent of the General Pearl and Coral Fishery Association of London attended balls hosted by Poinsett.[69] Privately, Poinsett corresponded with British banker Francis Baring, who that summer purchased an estate near the Texas border. Barings Bank was certainly familiar to Poinsett and other state agents as an institution that was necessary for business. It had long been involved in American economic development, first marketing US government debt on the international market in the 1790s and then facilitating the sale of the Louisiana Purchase in 1803. American merchants regularly used the bank for international commercial transactions, which Poinsett had done while he was in

South America.[70] Baring lent significant sums of money to the Mexican government, earning him a privileged position in the eyes of many Mexican politicians and businessmen.[71] Poinsett hoped to take advantage of this privilege, along with the obvious benefit of dealing with reputable bankers.

Baring also needed Poinsett's help, first to stall passage of a bill that would nullify foreigners' land titles and then to take charge of his estate ownership when his father, who wanted the firm to remain a "house of trade," instructed him to pull out of Mexico.[72] In general, British financiers were starting to sour on Mexican investment, owing to Mexico's debt-payment difficulties and an economic downturn caused by reckless speculation in the region.[73] Poinsett was not deterred; he was all too pleased to help Baring.[74]

Baring chose Poinsett instead of Britain's minister as his agent because although Ward had slightly more political sway at that point, Poinsett was a better business contact.[75] Ward was more cautious, more wedded to official diplomatic channels. Also, the political tide was changing, especially as Poinsett used American naval resources to ingratiate himself with Victoria's administration. While Poinsett was forging business ties with Baring and establishing mining ventures, he was serving as a liaison between the administration and a seasoned US naval captain. Even after Coppinger's surrender, there was still a chance that Spain would reconquer Mexico. Poinsett knew that President Victoria was concerned about this and connected him with David Porter, who had fought in the War of 1812 and had recently been court-martialed for invading Puerto Rico in an act of retaliation. When Victoria offered Porter a commission in the Mexican Navy, Porter resigned from the US Navy and began organizing expeditions to interfere with Spanish commerce in the Caribbean. Although Porter's insults and harsh disciplinary tactics would eventually prompt his resignation, his service helped prevent Spanish reconquest, which ultimately advanced Poinsett's business aims. Naval power simultaneously made Victoria's administration more amenable to US political influence and offered a sort of shield for US economic activities.[76]

According to Ward, Poinsett wanted hundreds of American families to colonize Baring's estate.[77] It was common for land contracts to contain a provision for colonization, and although many Mexicans opposed the ability of foreigners to control so much land, it was legal until 1830. When Poinsett took up his post as minister plenipotentiary, Stephen F. Austin, whose father, Moses, was the first American to receive a grant from the Mexican government to settle a colony in Texas, was in the process of securing from Mexico's congress his inheritance to the grant. Poinsett began helping Kentucky native Benjamin R. Milam obtain a contract for land in Texas on which three hundred families would settle.[78] Both Milam and Austin saw slavery as essential to the function of their colonies.[79] In helping these men, Poinsett contributed to the beginning of the intersection of cotton, slavery, and settler colonialism in Texas.[80] Poinsett himself was more interested in speculative capitalism than he was in settler colonialism, however. He knew that most colonizers were failures by any profit standards.[81]

Additionally, Poinsett had to be careful about personal land acquisition. When he received a portion of a land grant as gratitude for his diplomatic services, his concern with appearing disinterested prevented him from taking it. He decided to transfer the land to Baring, who he thought could add it to his estate. It had good pasture for sheep, which might offer a source of income to offset the sluggish mines Baring owned. Poinsett also "opened a negotiation with the commander . . . for the purpose of getting [Baring his] bargain."[82]

As Poinsett became more involved with Baring, mining, and certain Mexican politicians and American businessmen, it became increasingly difficult to keep up appearances of disinterestedness. By the end of 1825, the mines that Poinsett had purchased on behalf of Smith—and whose riches he had touted to investors in Baltimore—still were not producing. When Poinsett was later accused of deceiving investors by overselling the mines' value as an investment, his defenders would say he had no interest in the mines; he simply was holding them until Smith paid him back. Yet Poinsett also assembled a mining investment portfolio for the New York mercantile firm LeRoy, Bayard & Co., for whom he served as a debt agent. It is hard to make the case that Poinsett had no interest in the mining venture when he stood to benefit if the firm invested in the mines and if additional stockholder interest raised the value of shares. There was a commission involved. Whether he misrepresented value is another issue, but considering he knew from Wilcocks about the struggles to make the mines productive, it seems likely that he engaged in at least a bit of overselling. Wilcocks's agent in fact peddled flooded mines to foreign investors.[83] Poinsett wrote to LeRoy and Bayard that he was working to get silver from the mines before those in the hands of other companies produced any.[84] While it was in Poinsett's interests if the mines produced, of greater importance was that potential investors thought they would produce.

This illusion was achieved with strategic advertising. Poinsett had suc-

ceeded in attaching the name of Robert Oliver, a respectable merchant, to
the venture. Oliver had not yet invested, but he helped with logistics. He
wrote to Poinsett in March that he was sending William Keating, a professor of mineralogy and chemistry at the University of Pennsylvania, to
oversee the mines.[85] Several days later, an article appeared in a Baltimore
newspaper advertising these mines; the article specifically linked them
to the reputation and qualifications of Keating, who had studied mining
for five years in Europe and had a "tact for business."[86] Science mattered
to Poinsett and others as a subject of interest and as source of societal
advancement, but it was almost always subordinate to business aims. In
this case, it served as reputation management for the mines. If Keating
and his team could not make the mines productive, the company at least
had to make the situation sound promising to shareholders and potential
investors.[87]

Over the next two years, they drummed up a lot of interest in the
mines, even though investors had no idea in what they were investing.
Instead, they trusted scientific experts, like Keating. They also initially
trusted Poinsett.

When profits were not forthcoming, investors grew suspicious about
the information they had received and berated Poinsett for deception.
Although he had tried to maintain a low profile, there was no hiding as
minister plenipotentiary. As a "representative of the nation," according
to investors, Poinsett was "bound to insure them against errors of opinion and the chances of hazardous speculation."[88] Poinsett disagreed. He
cited other failures and information gaps. He wasn't wrong. Other foreign
companies failed, and British minister Henry Ward published a pamphlet
explaining how mines worked specifically because potential investors did
not understand the mining sector.[89] Poinsett claimed investors' decision-
making was not his responsibility, and the company in general defended
its right to profit from misinformation. Congressman Charles J. Ingersoll
criticized the charges against Smith as "absurd, for he sold them at the
price they agreed to pay a commodity he had a right to sell. If he made
money in the bargain it was a fair expectation on his part."[90]

Poinsett saved his most detailed commentary on mining for his reports
to the State Department, in which he admitted that the mines had only
yielded a moderate rate of return in comparison with the capital invested
in them. Poinsett recognized the importance of precious metals for the
economy of the United States, more generally, and thus the need for investment. British capital, he wrote, had made the mines productive, even
at a minimal profit to the investors themselves. According to Poinsett,

when British companies finally tired of lackluster profits and pulled out of the region, Mexicans would resume control of the mines and probably work them with fewer overhead costs. Commercial activity in Mexico and the United States would benefit from more specie in circulation.[91] This formulation suggests that Poinsett (a) did not really care who operated and invested in the mines and (b) had indeed engaged in a bit of investor fraud in his role in the mining companies.

Poinsett's attempt to excuse his role in the mining controversy, just like his decision to transfer his land gift to Baring, revealed his obsession with protecting his reputation. Many were beginning to see through the smoke screen, however. Vera Cruz legislators requested his recall in June 1827, issuing a statement that referred to Poinsett as "sagacious and hypocritical" and accused him of organizing the York Rite Masons specifically for the purpose of dividing the country.[92] Poinsett did damage control. He published "Exposition of the Policy of the United States toward the Republics of America," justifying and excusing his behavior to the Mexican people. He wrote to President Adams that President Victoria approved of him but was in a tricky position because of the Vera Cruz petition. Poinsett stated that he was offended by the anonymous reports published in Vera Cruz but was willing to continue serving for the good of US interests.[93] Clay and Secretary of State Adams were oblique in their response to Poinsett and the Mexican government: they were displeased but only asked that he apologize.

Poinsett continued to try to hide his interests, especially the extent to which he was deeply interested in land, not for colonization but for investment. Poinsett had previously supported the annexation of Texas, but as the political tide changed and he became increasingly influential, he grew more reluctant to comply with Clay's and Adams's instructions that he offer to purchase the territory from Mexico. Poinsett claimed that it was insulting to offer Mexico such a sum, that the government would never accept it.[94] That was true, but Poinsett also had little incentive to push Mexico to sell the land. If Texas remained in Mexico, the administration in power would determine land grants, and as the Yorkinos gained control, land grants would go to Poinsett's friends. They could then sell parcels of land to US citizens, regardless of sovereignty, whereas the laws, fees, and taxes that would accompany US annexation would likely disrupt their profits.

There was uncertainty over the border following the United States' 1819 treaty with Spain. Mexico set up a commission to investigate American lands in Texas and to investigate the ambiguous border.[95] Poinsett tried to tell the president and secretaries that the commission was useless without an actual treaty. They went ahead with it anyway.[96] The treaty of limits Poinsett signed with Sebastián Camacho and Jose Ignacio Esteva on January 12, 1828, stated that both countries acknowledged the boundaries established by the treaty of 1819. This disappointed many Americans, who wanted a more aggressive treaty. They viewed Poinsett's diplomacy as ineffectual, especially when treaty ratification was delayed because Mexican documentation reached Washington after the four-month deadline stipulated by the treaty.[97] From an official standpoint, Poinsett was indeed ineffectual. Mexico dictated the terms of the treaty and delayed its ratification. Poinsett prioritized individual investments over the popular national goals of settler colonialism. In terms of his own goals, he was successful. Texas remained Mexican.

That fall, Zavala, Poinsett, and fellow Yorkinos worked to control politics in Mexico by contesting the election of moderate Manuel Gómez Pedraza over their preferred candidate, Vicente Guerrero, in what became known as the Acordada Revolt. Poinsett's behavior and preferences during this uprising are instructive of his paradoxical and at times hypocritical diplomatic actions. He and Zavala had first established shared political interests when Poinsett visited Mexico in 1822.[98] Although Zavala had a history of aligning himself with radical liberal groups, who promoted social equality and equal rights for the Mayan peoples, Poinsett—who could only be considered anything close to egalitarian by an extreme stretch of the imagination—very much approved of Zavala's opposition to clerical and monarchical power and preference for the United States, rather than Europe, as Mexico's model for development.[99] When state legislatures declared Pedraza, who as minister of war was backed by the military, winner in September 1828, Poinsett, Zavala, and fellow Yorkinos took advantage of popular opposition to his weak stance against Spanish residents.[100] At the beginning of December 1828, some of Guerrero's supporters occupied the Acordada barracks, where arms and munitions were stored, and mobs ransacked the markets in the Zócalo. Wealthy residents either fled the city or barricaded themselves at home. Zavala clandestinely led the rebels, while also negotiating with the government.[101] After several days of fighting between the rebels and government forces, Pedraza fled, and Congress declared Guerrero the president.[102] Poinsett had remained locked up at home, and although mob action made him nervous, he ultimately approved of the riots. In his words, "it was necessary to remove this cause of discord at any sacrifice. It might have been done with more mildness but in time of high revolutionary excitement it is difficult to moderate passion."[103]

Many Americans claimed their property had been destroyed in the riots at the Parián market, but Poinsett informed the US State Department that no damage had occurred because he did not want any interference with the political changes that would bring Guerrero to power.[104] Later, he mediated Americans' claims against the Mexican government, especially those of people with whom he conducted banking business, proof that his representation of American business had to accord with his own terms.[105] He ultimately supported a politician whose plans for the presidency did not line up with overarching US goals of commercial expansion. Guerrero favored commercial policies that protected domestic industry (something Poinsett had recently argued against in the US Congress) and ultimately made it more difficult to sell US goods in Mexico.[106]

In general, Poinsett's support of Guerrero's presidency typified Poinsett's political contradictions and inconsistencies. Guerrero had little education and was not white (details about his ethnic background are uncertain, but he was considered to be mestizo, possibly part Black and Indian). He was popular with the lower classes, promoted social equality, and, most radically, abolished slavery less than six months after becoming president.[107] And yet Poinsett overlooked whatever clashed with his elitist, racist worldview. He praised Guerrero's "vigorous intellect and determined character" to President John Quincy Adams because he wanted the US government to support the man who would advance his own interests.[108] Guerrero's presidency meant that Lorenzo Zavala, Poinsett's closest Mexican ally, would have more economic and political influence, a reversal of the previous year when Zavala had had to flee during a persecution of Federalists. Once Guerrero took office, Zavala became minister of treasury and received a large land grant in Texas.[109]

Poinsett's mask was becoming transparent. Newspapers in Mexico and the United States speculated that he had influenced Pedraza's coup and was interested in Zavala's land.[110] They were not wrong. It was obvious even to individuals outside Mexico that Poinsett had connections to land. For example, British social reformer Robert Owen visited Mexico with the hope of setting up a utopian colony in Texas and knew Poinsett was an appropriate target.[111] The fact that Owen approached Poinsett with his plans reveals the conflict between Poinsett's personal and national interests; Owen's choice of Texas as the site to establish a moral society based on a self-designed law code was meant to prevent the United States from acquiring additional land.[112] If Poinsett had been a well-known expansionist, it is doubtful that Owen would have bothered with him, but after Owen discussed his plan with President Victoria, who was leaving office, he contacted Poinsett, who offered to speak to Guerrero on Owen's behalf.[113]

Owen never received his colony, which meant that Poinsett either neglected to talk to Guerrero or spoke disparagingly about Owen's plan. Both were equally likely. Poinsett found Owen overly idealistic and uninformed about Mexico, telling him that Mexico was "difficult to be explained and difficult to be understood by a person who has passed his life in Europe in the midst of the civilization of the nineteenth century and under long established governments."[114] He was also wary of Owen's association with a leader of the Fredonian Rebellion who had attempted to get Mexico's permission to settle Cherokee along the Texas-US border. Poinsett shared some of Owen's correspondence with Zavala, who expressed skepticism of Owen's plan.[115] Although Zavala believed in equal social rights for Natives, he did not believe in actual equality. In his response to Owen, Poinsett gave himself an out by saying, "The new administration is not yet entirely formed and the president too much occupied at the moment to attend to us on our representations."[116] Poinsett for his part had wanted to send Natives out of Mexico to New Harmony, Indiana, where Owen had established a utopian community with geologist William Maclure (whose individualistic ideals Poinsett probably preferred over Owen's communitarian ones).[117] The objective was to have state governments in Mexico pay the school in New Harmony to educate small groups of "young Indians" who would then return to Mexico to become productive miners.[118]

Part of Poinsett's and Zavala's scorn for a reform community in Texas, like the one they approved of in Indiana, stemmed from the fear of interference with investment opportunities there. When Owen left Mexico, he traveled to Cincinnati, Ohio, to give a speech, and while there he met with Poinsett and Zavala's future business partner, Texas empresario David Burnet. Burnet was friends with Benjamin Milam, who had previously tried to sell some of his land to Owen. Now, like Poinsett and Zavala, Milam and Burnet disapproved of Owen's plan.[119] They were organizing a joint-stock company, called the Western Colonization and Mining Company, to fund mining operations on their land, and they did not want another competitor. It was already hard enough to make their own colonies profitable, partly because the economic crisis of 1825—a stock market crash precipitated by Latin American speculation—unnerved investors. The English Mining Company had broken its contract with Milam, and several years later, when Milam entered a provisional sale agreement with Baring, Baring decided to hold off until the colony was more established.[120]

The way these various land grants worked was that the Mexican government expected each empresario (land agent) to settle a number of

Christian families within a set number of years (usually six). He received twenty-three thousand acres for every family he settled, which he could then sell to whomever. The entire contract could be sold, but specific parcels of land within it could not. There was a lot of uncertainty about these land grants: *Who was in control? Where were the boundaries? What exactly could be sold?* Milam and Burnet, for example, had to dissolve their company because of misunderstandings with investors who had assumed they would own actual real estate; this was not the case.

Additionally, if the colony was not settled with the requisite number of families within the contracted time frame, the grant was void. This stipulation affected many empresarios, who struggled to attract settlers. As much as Americans were land hungry, there were impediments to seamless colonization. First, there were border issues that remained unsolved by the nonratification of Poinsett's treaty, as well as conflict with Native peoples. Although Anglo-Americans had some Chickasaw and Cherokee allies, settlers resented the Mexican government for abetting, or at least failing to quell, conflict with the Atapaka, Comanche, and Coahuiltecan peoples. Second, after 1827, the Mexican government prohibited the introduction of new slaves into Coahuila y Tejas. Many settlers worked around this law, but it was still a deterrence to aspiring plantation owners. Finally, Mexican officials began resisting US immigration.

In 1824, the Mexican government had instituted an open immigration policy, allowing all foreigners an easy path to citizenship and exempting them from taxes for a number of years. The hope was that the majority of these settlers would be Catholic Europeans. Instead, Americans from states like Tennessee and Kentucky repeatedly clashed with Mexican governance. General Manuel de Mier y Terán traveled to Coahuila y Tejas on a boundary expedition during US-Mexico treaty negotiations. His report, issued in 1828, asserted that Americans were having a detrimental impact on the region. Conflict and resentment culminated in a law passed in 1830 that banned all immigrants from the United States. By the time this happened, Poinsett was back in the United States and Guerrero was no longer president. Much had changed.

Several months after Guerrero became president—during the summer that Owen visited Cincinnati and Burnet and Milam formed the Western Colonization and Mining Company—Spain invaded Mexico. At the same time, Poinsett's influence on Mexican politics finally backfired on him. Many believed that he had too much influence. One satirical periodical asked who had caused the Acordada Revolt and answered that it was Poinsett.[121] A year later, newspapers continued to discuss his role in the attacks.[122] In the spring of 1830, after Poinsett returned to the United States, one news article reported on his Masonic inauguration in Washington and noted his role in bringing the rite to Mexico and thereby causing the ruin of the republic and onset of anarchy.[123] Because of this sentiment, the legislature of the State of Mexico sent a memorial to the president requesting Poinsett's removal from his post. They cited, among other things, Poinsett's interference with Mexico's "liberty and independence" and destruction of the "friendship and confidence between both countries."[124] In response, President Guerrero asked President Andrew Jackson to order Poinsett back to the United States. Rather than recall Poinsett, Jackson allowed him to resign.[125]

As Poinsett lost control in Mexico, Spain threatened Mexico's independence. This was worrisome to foreign investors. Poinsett had been working with British capitalists and Mexican officials to restore the credit of the Mexican government in the British money market. Despite standard narratives about US-British competition, some British investors actually welcomed US influence in the region.[126] Poinsett had been collaborating with Richard Exter until Exter died in June 1829. Exter's brother, John, wrote to Poinsett, lamenting that their plans had been interrupted, both by Richard's death and by the Spanish invasion. The "most opulent capitalists" in Britain wanted to invest in Mexico but had to wait to make a loan until they knew the result of the Spanish expedition.[127] Burnet's land company, for example, dissolved as soon as investors heard about the Spanish invasion.[128]

The situation changed daily. Guerrero himself had grown unpopular with conservatives because of his liberal land reforms and abolition of slavery. He looked especially bad to his detractors in the face of invasion, and during the conflict, he was accused of being a tyrannical dictator. After Antonio López de Santa Anna and Manuel de Mier y Terán led Mexican forces to a victory over Spain in September, they helped Vice President Anastasio Bustamente remove Guerrero from office. Bustamante became president on January 1, 1830. Two days later, Poinsett left Mexico.[129]

All of these political changes might have been disconcerting for investors, but once Spain was defeated, they were relatively inconsequential. Several months after assuming office, Bustamente followed through with Mier y Terán's suggestion to prohibit American immigration. The new law, which passed on April 6, 1830, made things difficult for Americans who wanted to move to Texas. It did not, however, stop the land-speculation game. Americans with diplomatic connections managed to get passports, and international investors found a way to profit.[130] Poinsett himself remained involved in the business of several different empresario grants. He had long been interested in Zavala's land, and in the spring of 1830, he arranged to form a company with him. They signed a contract with Poinsett's successor, Chargé d'Affaires Anthony Butler, who would represent the company's interests in Texas.[131] Butler, a fellow Mason, was friends with President Jackson and had served in the War of 1812.[132] Unlike Poinsett, Butler did not speak Spanish, and he lacked Poinsett's diplomatic cosmopolitanism. Mexicans would dislike him even more than they disliked Poinsett.[133] The deal between Poinsett, Butler, and Zavala fell through, perhaps because of the jealousy that developed between Poinsett and Butler. Butler quickly started accusing Poinsett of ruining things diplomatically with Mexico and spending too much money. He became involved in the Arkansas and Texas Land Company and the Trinity Land Company and would later attempt to undermine Poinsett's mining ventures by organizing a commission to investigate fraud charges.[134]

Poinsett and Zavala then made a separate arrangement with David Burnet and Joseph Vehlein, a German merchant. Combining the grants of Zavala, Burnet, and Vehlein, they formed the Galveston Bay and Texas Land Company with New York– and Boston-based lawyers Anthony Dey, George Curtis, and William H. Sumner, who would manage the colonization of their land.[135] Poinsett, who was on friendly terms with the customs collector at Galveston, was a major stockholder and controlled a portion of land between the Sabine and San Jacinto Rivers.[136] The company, with Dey as president, served as trustee for the land grants, promoting colonization to potential settlers. They sold certificates for hundreds of thousands of acres at five cents per acre. Because of the 1830 law, the company sought European colonists. Zavala went to Europe on a recruiting mission for this purpose, which the company publicized in newspapers.[137] However, they also sold certificates to Americans who did not know about the 1830 law. They claimed that because the empresarios had received the land before 1830, the law did not apply to them. In general, the company flouted the law. The scrips they sold had no legal significance in Texas. Although holders of the scrips viewed them as deeds, Mexican officials did not recognize them as such and instead permitted individual empresarios to grant land to immigrants as they chose.[138] Mexican vice consul James Treat, who was also a company member, received instructions in the fall of 1830 not to issue passports to Coahuila y Tejas; the doubts he expressed, along with the fact that almost half of the settlers were American, suggests that he issued passports anyway.[139]

While Butler aggressively pushed for annexation to benefit his own investments (Trinity Land Company offered him $10 million to secure the cession of Texas to the United States[140]), the Galveston Company preferred that Texas remain Mexican.[141] They commissioned General José Antonio Mexía, secretary of the Legation of Mexico in Washington, to lobby for the removal of the provision of the 1830 law that prohibited US citizens from settling along the border.[142] Soon after the ban on US immigrants was lifted in 1834, the General Land Office of Texas closed without the company having received its premium land for settling the requisite number of families. However, the company continued to profit from land development, and decades later, they received a claims settlement from the United States and Mexican Claims Commission.[143] They were also instrumental in the development of independent Texas.[144]

Despite early setbacks in Coahuila y Tejas, there was much potential profit for those willing and able to hold out and for those with connections. In addition to Poinsett's involvement in the mining companies and the Galveston Bay Company, he managed Richard Exter's estate after his death in June 1829.[145] Exter had received two *empresario* grants in northwestern Texas with Stephen Julian Wilson, a North Carolina native who became a naturalized Mexican citizen. The two requested a fur-trading monopoly from the Mexican government on the grounds that most fur trappers from the United States and Great Britain deprived the government of significant tax revenue by hunting in Mexico and selling elsewhere; Exter and Wilson conversely would employ Mexican citizens and pay Mexican taxes. The government quickly rescinded their license, but the partners retained their land.[146] When Exter died, his land passed to his widow, María Dolores Soto y Saldaña. Several months after Exter's death, she married John Charles Beales, a British doctor and land speculator, who sought Poinsett's help in administering the land.[147] He wanted Poinsett to take charge of settling the land so that his company could claim their prize land before the contract expired. Beales also needed help asserting his right to the grant over Dennis A. Smith, Poinsett's associate in the mining venture, who had entered into a purchase agreement with Exter in 1827. Shortly before Exter's death, Smith organized a $400,000 company to develop the land.[148] Beales argued that Smith's claim to, and investors' shares in, Exter's land was illegitimate because it violated the 1830 colonization law. Exter's brothers wanted Poinsett to ensure that Exter's widow and child secured profits from the land.

Poinsett attempted to represent all his interested constituents by recommending New York congressman Churchill C. Cambreleng, who owned stock in Smith's Tlacotal Mining Company, to oversee the administration of Exter's estate.[149] Poinsett had met Cambreleng, a wealthy businessman and former employee of John Jacob Astor, when he served in Congress, and he relied on Cambreleng for banking services in New York. The Exters declined to give power of attorney to Cambreleng, requesting instead that Poinsett find a "respectable house in the United States" to manage the estate. Beales moved on with his business concerns, transferring the land grants to the Arkansas and Texas Land Company and offering Butler five hundred thousand acres in scrip to protect the company's interests.[150] Butler was unsuccessful, and Beales's brief success establishing the colony Dolores, named after his wife, was destroyed during the Texas Revolution. Beales spent the rest of his life trying to get the Mexican government to recognize his claims to land.[151]

Claims like Beales's would continue to define much of US foreign policy, as all agents of the State Department were charged with representing the interests of American citizens. These interests, however, did not always align with national identity. Butler and Poinsett each had different American, Mexican, and British allies and enemies. US interests were more complex than simple territorial acquisition. That is not to say that territory did not matter in the national consciousness. It did; both Butler and Poinsett were considered diplomatic failures because they did not secure Texas for the United States. Butler wanted Texas more than Poinsett did and pushed for it aggressively. Poinsett focused his energies on mining and investment activities that did not depend on the annexation of Texas. For their actions, they were both vilified by segments of the Mexican population and forced to resign. Butler was accused of fomenting rebellion in Texas.[152] Poinsett was accused of interference. Both men established tense, distrustful diplomatic relations with Mexico and the United States.

They used power and military intervention, however slight, to achieve economic aims. Butler was accused of belligerent and abusive behavior, including toward Mexican women.[153] Poinsett was accused of "being jealous of Mexican prosperity that would soon eclipse that of his own country."[154] It is more accurate to say that Poinsett was jealous of prosperity that did not align with his own perception of national and individual interests. He worked to promote the interests of British merchant Richard Exter, US consul J. S. Wilcocks, Baltimore investor Dennis A. Smith, Mexican statesman Lorenzo de Zavala, and British banker Francis Baring. He did so by using covert political and military power to interfere with Mexican affairs. Poinsett's naval associate Commodore Porter contributed to these efforts by serving in the Mexican Navy and helping defeat

the Spanish invasion.[155] When Porter and Poinsett left Mexico, US influence was still tenuous, but it would become increasingly aggressive over
the coming decades.

On New Year's Day, 1830, Americans in Mexico City threw Poinsett a
"grand public dinner" to celebrate his service in Mexico.[156] To some, he
was a business savior; to others, a self-serving sycophant who jeopardized
American economic interests.[157] Poinsett left Mexico two days after his
party and reached New Orleans a month later. His friends were relieved
when he was finally back in Washington, safe from threats in Mexico and
travel hazards.[158] Business continued as usual. James Wilcocks represented Poinsett's interests as consul in Mexico City; Zavala wrote to him
about land, and Baring dealt with his finances. Although Poinsett failed to
achieve State Department goals, he had helped some American citizens
during his time in Mexico, and, more important, he had helped himself.

5

Southern "Honor,"
1830–1836

Mexico followed Poinsett home. A British pamphlet that cast Poinsett as the villain in US-Mexican-British relations circulated in newspapers throughout the country. The stockholders of the Temascaltepec Mining Company in Baltimore accused Poinsett of fraud.[1] Poinsett had tried so hard to protect his image in Mexico, but now his character was under attack in the United States. He was safe from criticism, at least, with the Masons, who surprised him upon his return from Mexico by making him deputy general grand high priest for the General Grand Royal Arch Chapter of the United States. Poinsett used the installation ceremony in Washington as an opportunity to defend his actions in Mexico, holding up the Ahiman Rezon (Book of Constitutions) and swearing he had never used Masonry as "an engine of political influence" nor engaged in any "anti-republican" activities.[2]

Over the next half decade, he had to reconcile these different aspects of his career and his identity: he was a Mason who upheld republican morality, a cosmopolitan diplomat and a Carolina slaveholder, a worldly bachelor finally ready to marry a plantation heiress, and an international investor home to straighten out local politics. These facets of his identity required more careful management during the 1830s than they had previously, as Poinsett spent more time "at home" than he ever had before. They also prompted a heightened awareness of the importance of control—both personally and militarily.

As news about Poinsett's recall spread around the nation, he asserted control over his reputation on the personal front by enlisting his friend Robert Walsh—influential Philadelphia publisher, founder of the *National Gazette and Literary Register*, and editor for *American Quarterly*

Review—to manage the fallout.[3] Poinsett sent Walsh a written defense of his service in Mexico, which Walsh cleaned up for two printed formats. He ran it in the *National Gazette* and printed an excerpt of it in pamphlet form, which he distributed nationwide. He also sent another 150 copies to Vera Cruz and "caused several of the distant editors to republish the whole defense, which no one can read without being convinced."[4]

Walsh's son-in-law Robert Gibbes handled Poinsett's parallel business defense.[5] Soon after Poinsett returned to the United States, Gibbes sent him a letter saying that the stockholders of the Temascaltepec Mining Company had "mutin[ied]."[6] The stockholders demanded an investigation into the management of the company and claimed they had been given false information about the value and profitability of the mines. Corporate fraud charges were not unusual. The mining company had been founded during a speculative boom in which investors poured money into new financial opportunities, including lending, insurance, and mining ventures.[7] Many of these new companies failed when the bubble burst in 1826—a result of the rapid increase in unregulated incorporation.

While Poinsett oversaw his public defense, wrapped up State Department business, and managed the arrival of his baggage "containing minerals, antiquities, papers, etc." from Mexico, his home state was in the midst of a crisis over federal tariffs.[8] In what would later be known as the nullification crisis, many in South Carolina claimed that the taxes passed in 1828 were unconstitutional. They had hoped Andrew Jackson's election that year would result in a reduction of the tariffs; when it did not, they turned against him. Jackson's vice president and Poinsett's old friend John C. Calhoun led the opposition.[9] At a dinner at Indian Queen Tavern in Washington on April 13 to celebrate Thomas Jefferson's birthday, Jackson and Calhoun each made their position on the tariff controversy clear in what became an infamous toasting clash. Jackson raised his glass to "the federal union: it must be preserved!" To which Calhoun replied, "The Union: next to our Liberty the most dear: may we all remember that it can only be preserved by respecting the rights of the States."[10]

Poinsett was not one of the 150 attendees, but he would spend the next few years fighting nullification. The nullification crisis generally is depicted as a showdown between Jackson and Calhoun; Poinsett, however, was a central player behind the scenes. Poinsett's friends had had high hopes for his post-Mexico career—a diplomatic post in Russia or Naples, or a return to Congress. Instead, he created a political organization in South Carolina to run anti-nullification candidates for city office and the state legislature.[11] As he narrowed his political focus amid larger concerns over his affairs in Mexico and Texas, he remained committed to his vision of American power, choosing federal strength over state loyalty.

This chapter will examine Poinsett's position in the national political economy from his vantage point as a southerner, particularly as a South Carolinian. In many ways, Poinsett was the archetypal southern gentleman. He owned slaves and multiple properties, inherited money, promoted agricultural development, and cared deeply about status and reputation. And he was especially South Carolinian in his commitment to imported goods, to slavery as an incomparable form of wealth, and to his state's prosperity. In many other ways, however, Poinsett defied his status as a South Carolina planter. He was not dedicated to cotton production, nor did he adhere to the insular politics of many other South Carolina elites, who had adopted a paranoid and defensive outlook in response to their slave majority and worsening economic prospects.[12] Poinsett dedicated himself to local politics in alignment with what he saw as the best interests of his state and country—interests that complemented his own financial concerns, as well as his future career goals. Poinsett's economic pursuits depended on a strong nation, not one in which states could nullify federal economic legislation. He was a South Carolina slaveholder, to be sure, but this identity did not define his politics or his economics, especially because the majority of Poinsett's business contacts were not slaveholders and many of them wished slavery abolished. Over the next half decade, Poinsett's biggest challenge was how to reconcile different aspects of his career and his identity—how to resolve business interests and political ambition with his patriotism and southern honor culture.[13] Examining his challenge allows us to see beyond the lens of regionalism, which obscures larger issues of power and political economy. The predominant tensions were not a matter of state versus nation or north versus south but a shifting power struggle over who controlled access to perceived opportunities.

A lot had changed since Poinsett left for Mexico in 1825. His close friend's son wondered whether Poinsett would recognize him, he had been gone so long.[14] More serious than that, the South Carolina to which Poinsett returned was on the decline. The Panic of 1819 hit South Carolina harder and longer than any other state. The state never fully recovered. Cotton production ramped up in the United States, and, globally, prices decreased, which had more serious ramifications for South Carolina than elsewhere. The state faced a series of other challenges, such as soil erosion, out-migration, and a decline in Charleston's status as a port city.[15] As many white South Carolinians felt their economic opportunities contract, they viewed national political decisions as an attack on their way of life.

This became especially true when Congress passed a tariff in 1828 to protect American manufactures. The legislation taxed imports, which upset the balance of trade between South Carolina and Britain. Many South Carolina households found it too expensive to purchase the British manufactured goods they relied on, while their British counterparts subsequently had less income to purchase cotton. During Poinsett's last year and a half in Mexico, some of his friends began organizing against the tariff. In Congress, Senators Robert Y. Hayne of South Carolina and Daniel Webster of Massachusetts vigorously debated protectionist tariffs and the sale of public lands. Hayne accused the government of unfairly favoring the Northeast over the South and West by taxing imports and limiting the ability of Americans to move west. Webster came down on the side of the federal government and his industrialist friends. South Carolina congressman James Hamilton Jr. sent Poinsett a letter that detailed all the negatives of the tariff. Hamilton warned Poinsett that if he were to run for Congress, he would have to "give satisfactory assurances" about his opposition to the tariff.[16] When Jackson was elected president in 1828 and did not repeal the tariff as opponents had hoped, a more radical opposition developed. Hamilton, George McDuffie, Robert Y. Hayne, and John Calhoun led the charge for nullification.[17]

South Carolinians finally experienced deep political division, which Poinsett expedited. He was opposed to the tariff in theory, arguing as he had in 1824 that tariffs should exist to raise revenue, not protect certain sectors of the economy.[18] However, he believed that nullification was unconstitutional and increasingly viewed opposition as futile. At first many unionists and nullifiers considered themselves Jacksonian Democrats, but the crisis soon became a choice between Jackson and Calhoun. Although Poinsett had cooperated politically, made financial agreements, and served in the executive branch with Calhoun, he met with Jackson to tell him he would organize a movement against nullification.[19] While he chose Jackson and union, his colleague James Hamilton Jr. chose Calhoun and nullification.

Poinsett and Hamilton, who had been on amicable business terms and would later collaborate on Texas investments and Cuban annexation, embodied the divergence that existed within the southern elite in response to this issue. Both Poinsett and Hamilton were slaveholders who owned tens of thousands of shares in the Bank of the United States and purchased agricultural equipment from the West Point Foundry in New York.[20] They had been born into wealthy low-country families, educated in New England, and served in the House of Representatives. They were on friendly terms with northern statesman Daniel Webster and such Charleston elites as Daniel Huger, William Drayton, and James Petigru.[21] Both Hamilton and Poinsett had military inclinations, but although Poinsett wanted to fight during the War of 1812, the Madison administration sent him to South America on a diplomatic mission, while Hamilton volunteered and was promoted to major. After the war, Hamilton served as mayor intendant of Charleston, and the two men worked closely during the 1822 Denmark Vesey trial.[22] They overlapped briefly in the South Carolina state legislature and in Congress before Poinsett went to Mexico. While Poinsett cultivated foreign business interests and sought out new agricultural opportunities, Hamilton profited from the three cotton and rice plantations his wife brought to their marriage.[23] When Poinsett returned from Mexico, Hamilton was elected governor of South Carolina on a free trade and states' rights platform, becoming one of the chief administrators for the nullification movement. Hamilton then served as commanding general of the South Carolina militia after his term as governor ended in 1832, coordinating military supplies to deploy against the federal government.[24] Poinsett, conversely, spearheaded a system of unionist committees of correspondence and stockpiled federal arms to use against the nullifiers. After the crisis, they both engaged in land speculation using their wives' trusts as collateral and collaborated once again in the cause of Texan independence.[25]

While Hamilton played a very public role in the nullification crisis from the outset, Poinsett was still dealing with the fallout from his Mexican mining controversy, which influenced his decision not to run for US Congress, even though his friends from other states wanted him there.[26] Instead, he planned to influence elections from behind the scenes.

First, Poinsett faced a lawsuit brought by the stockholders of the Temascaltepec against him and Dennis A. Smith for "large sums of money unaccounted for by them in their transaction with the company."[27] He spent a good part of the spring and summer dodging inquiries and preparing his defense as he traveled among Washington, Philadelphia, and Baltimore. William Keating, his mining scientist, tracked down a speech Poinsett had given and arranged for its circulation in both German- and English-language papers in Pennsylvania. Keating and Poinsett were hoping that publicity and Poinsett's reputation would overshadow questions about his financial behavior. There was precedent for this. When former

New York state senator and founder of the Exchange Bank of New York Jacob Barker, for example, was tried for conspiring to defraud investors of the Life and Fire Insurance Company, he defended his lending practices by declaring the honor and reputation of his debtors. Barker was found guilty but faced no legal repercussions. He was able to continue working as a lawyer and reputable financial investor.[28]

In addition to managing Poinsett's public image, Keating also prepped rooms for Poinsett at "the mansion house" in Philadelphia.[29] Still a bachelor, Poinsett used this opportunity to "form or renew acquaintance" with a number of "ladies."[30] This gives us another glimpse of Poinsett's romantic and sexual life. One of Poinsett's friends claimed that these women asked "about the period of [Poinsett's] return."[31] It seems probable that Poinsett had amorous relationships with multiple women, given that he had at least one child out of wedlock. These relationships were most likely fleeting and sexual, given that no correspondence exists and Poinsett tried to conceal the identity of his son and son's mother. The nature of their occurrences reflected his obsession with reputation, work, and power.

Poinsett and his supporters were worried about his chances of withstanding stockholder scrutiny. His friend Robert Gibbes, a stockholder in the mining company, hosted a dinner in Baltimore for shareholders and other influential men, such as the Mexican minister José María de Tornel. Gibbes specifically delayed the dinner to make sure the right people from Philadelphia had time to arrange travel. The dinner was a success, all the more so because company shares were selling at $250 and $300, which was over twice as much as domestic manufacturing companies.[32] Yet although Poinsett seemed to enjoy "all the honorable notoriety which a diplomat could desire," he refused to face the stockholders in person again.[33] His detractors continued to spread toxic information about him; their lawyers were "vindictive." When the stockholders arranged a series of meetings to examine reports on the actions of the company, Poinsett's friends made excuses for his absence and arranged for a reputable lawyer to attend the meetings by proxy.[34]

Gibbes, Robert Gilmore, and Robert Oliver were especially anxious that the case go favorably for Poinsett. These stockholders had intertwined financial interests that extended beyond Mexico and Baltimore. They saw Poinsett as well positioned to help them, so long as his career was not ruined by the Temascaltepec case.[35] For example, Oliver had over $300,000 of outstanding mercantile claims, and Gilmore, $5,000, on the Kingdom of Naples. Oliver spoke to President Jackson specifically about getting Poinsett appointed on a diplomatic mission to Naples to adjudicate merchants' claims.[36] Interestingly, Oliver was also concerned with nullification and discussed his views on both issues in the same conversation with Jackson. Gibbes, a former South Carolinian, was similarly invested in the outcome of the nullification crisis. As an enslaver whose human property continued to seek their freedom, he was especially motivated to ensure that his other investments panned out and that the national government appeared strong.[37]

Poinsett was these men's chosen agent because of his success at managing American business interests abroad and his ability to transcend region and party at home.[38] Boston merchant Samuel Curson, for example, applauded Poinsett for nonpartisanship.[39] This was not an entirely substantiated compliment, but the fact that Poinsett appeared this way made him a likely ally for diverse constituencies. Curson was secretary of the National Insurance Company and fraternized with New England industrialists.[40] He conducted a lot of his business in the Gulf of Mexico and helped manage Poinsett's reputation in New Orleans. When Poinsett traveled north late in the summer, Curson offered to give him a tour of Lowell, where some of the factories that would benefit from the tariff were located. Not surprisingly, he wanted Poinsett to serve in Congress. Poinsett's connection with Curson reveals how his activities and contacts in Mexico influenced his response to nullification and, more broadly, how the different theaters of his career intersected.

Poinsett settled back into Charleston just in time for election season. The major issue that fall was whether to call a state convention to nullify the 1828 tariff. Men who had common political and economic interests suddenly divided into two parties: candidates designated themselves as "Convention" and "Anti-Convention." Both sides claimed to be Jacksonian and to advocate for state rights. The creation of the "State Rights and Jackson Party" (soon to be renamed "State Rights and Free Trade") and the "Union and State Rights Party" marked a rupture in political norms, and historians have tried to determine why exactly men who had previously been political allies divided over whether to fight for nullification or tariff compromise. As over a century of scholarship has proved, the nullification crisis was a conflict over tariffs, slavery, and states' rights.

One of the dominant explanations has identified fears about interference with slavery as the main catalyst for the formation of the Nullifier Party.[41] Why, though, did not all slaveholders make political decisions based on the calculation that federal policies might interfere with their ability to own humans? In St. Peter's Parish, for example, five of the largest rice planters and enslavers, including James Hamilton Jr. and Daniel

Huger, took contradictory stances on the crisis.[42] Many southern enslavers, accustomed to the federal government bolstering slavery, opposed
nullification. Some of slavery's staunchest defenders, such as William
Drayton and James Pringle, were ardent unionists. The nullification crisis
was a personal contest between those who believed the powers of the
federal government helped the economy and those who believed they
hurt it—a clash over what public policies would best protect slavery and
provide the greatest economic benefit at the individual, state, and national levels.[43] The planter class was evenly split between the two parties.
Unionists, however, occupied over twice as many directorships of banks,
insurance companies, and railroad companies.[44] They tended to foster
national connections that depended on some measure of federal support.
Poinsett's political and economic success depended on both Jackson and
the national mercantile community. In Mexico, he sometimes privileged
international connections over national interests; in South Carolina, he
privileged national interests over state loyalty. The nullification crisis became a power struggle between elites like Poinsett, who had diversified
political and economic interests, and those whose personal measure of
success depended on cotton and Carolina politics.

In early October, Poinsett's name was on the "Anti-Convention" ticket
for the South Carolina House of Representatives. Poinsett had last served
the state legislature over a decade before; now he was elected along with
ten other Anti-Convention Charlestonians. It looked like a victory. Their
party won a majority of seats in the General Assembly, as well as a key seat
in the US Congress. In Charleston city elections in September, unionist
James R. Pringle had won the mayoral race, and unionists took the majority of city offices in September. The overall margin of victory, however,
was small, and four nullifiers made it to Congress.[45]

Poinsett's Temascaltepec crisis faded into the background. Gibbes
wrote to him now with nullification first on the agenda; the lawsuit was
an afterthought (it looked as if it might not be brought until April).[46] As
election results came in, Poinsett wrote a "confidential letter from a gentleman" to explain the gravity of the situation in South Carolina to outsiders.[47] Nullifiers had used Jackson's name to promote their cause, referring
to themselves as "the only true Jackson men."[48] Even after the Jefferson
Day toast in which Jackson exalted union over all else, many people associated him with aggressive states' rights. (Unionists also included "states'
rights" in their party platform, but they needed federal reinforcement for
their state objectives.) Poinsett wrote that Jackson, if he chose, could "restore order and tranquility to the state by a breath."[49]

Gibbes suggested that Poinsett's opinion be shared with Jackson but that Poinsett's name be "kept entirely out of view." Gibbes decided that Oliver, as an influential and apolitical merchant, would be the right person to pass Poinsett's letter on to Jackson. Oliver introduced the letter as from "a gentleman at present in Carolina in whose statement he had most implicit confidence and of whose judgment and character he entertained the most exalted estimate on."[50] Jackson took Poinsett's anonymous words seriously. He assured Oliver that he and Secretary of State Martin van Buren were opposed to nullification.[51] Oliver forwarded Jackson's letter to Gibbes, who sent it to Poinsett. Gibbes suggested that Poinsett find a way to make use of it politically and then destroy the copy. This was the start of secret correspondence between Poinsett and Washington.

The General Assembly began meeting in November. The first order of business was the convention. When the nullification convention failed to achieve the requisite two-thirds majority, things looked good for unionists on the surface. Nullifiers, however, carried through a series of resolutions that essentially legitimized nullification by declaring the state's intention to defend the Constitution and its right to interpose if the federal government overstepped its powers, as in the case of the tariff.[52] They also elected James Hamilton Jr. to the governorship and Stephen Miller to the Senate, where nullifier Robert Hayne was already serving. Poinsett, sick again, had missed the chance to vote to reelect his friend William Smith to the Senate.[53]

In its short session, from November 22 to December 18, the assembly also had to deal with election fraud. Voters petitioned the legislature to clamp down on interference at the polls. Bribery, false counting, and coercion were common during all elections but had gotten especially bad because of the tariff issue. This season, petitioners wanted the legislature to investigate voting issues in St. Philip's and St. Michael's Parishes, which both voted unionist. The hope was to get people to testify to bad votes, but the committee could not find anyone to prosecute. Instead, they passed a law for the better regulation of magistrates and constables of St. Philip's and St. Michael's Parishes that ultimately did little to mitigate fraud in the next election.[54]

The assembly adjourned shortly before Christmas. After the holidays, state politicians turned their attention to the last session of the Twenty-First Congress. In January, the Committee on Manufactures enraged the nullifiers by reporting that the tariff was a success because it simultaneously raised revenue and protected manufactures. Although nullification action died down for the winter, the report served as proof that Congress was unwilling to remove the tariff, providing fodder for nullification speeches that spring. Congressman George McDuffie, for example, blasted the tariff for its unjust effects, arguing that cotton farmers and planters bore the full brunt of import duties.[55] Poinsett exchanged information on the situation in South Carolina for updates on Congress with William Smith, who was finishing his second term as senator (Smith first served from 1816 to 1823), and William Drayton, who had represented South Carolina in the House since 1825. Both men were concerned about the strength of nullification in South Carolina. They were unionists who, like many nullifiers, were tidewater plantation owners. Smith was actually one of the first southerners to argue publicly that slavery was a positive good, and Drayton published a proslavery pamphlet in the 1830s.[56] They were anxious about what nullification meant for their political and economic concerns.

This was a common theme among unionists. They tended to have more economic power—power that depended on federal patronage and national business connections—and wanted to maintain it.[57] Both unionists and nullifiers subscribed to the early national concept of political honor, which emphasized reputation and appearance; nullifiers, however, adhered to an older southern honor code based on plantation violence and Carolina loyalty.[58] Both sides also depended on familial and financial networks, but unionists had farther-reaching connections, as Poinsett did. Other prominent unionists included Hugh S. Legare, attorney general of South Carolina and editor of the *Southern Review*; James R. Pringle, Charleston mayor and customs collector; and state politicians and proslavery planters Daniel Elliott Huger and Alfred Huger. Poinsett also corresponded with men in the western part of the state.[59] He cultivated these local connections while also maintaining his extensive network outside the state.

This network intersected with Poinsett's business in Mexico. The Mexican mining-company lawsuit never materialized, but Poinsett received frequent briefings on the situation in Mexico. While his friend Zavala traveled around the United States and Europe trying to find investors for their land in Texas, US consul James Wilcocks was Poinsett's main source of information. Poinsett also corresponded with his successor in Mexico, Anthony Butler. Although Poinsett and Butler were jealous of each other, and their business relationship was short lived, their overlapping interests and connections kept them in strained contact. Butler told Poinsett that he had finally settled the treaty with Mexico that Poinsett had worked on and that he was on good terms with the administration. To emphasize his own influence in Mexico, Butler wrote that he had convinced Mexican minister Lucas Alamán not to allow public "calumnies" against Poinsett; Butler personally had prevented a particularly "abusive" piece from being printed in the *Registro Oficial*.[60]

In addition to his unabashed boasting, Butler relayed political information that Poinsett needed. Instability affected business, and a rebellion had been going on since shortly before Poinsett left Mexico. In December 1829, President Guerrero was ousted by his vice president, Anastasio Bustamente, in a conservative uprising. Violence in southern Mexico continued throughout the next year, and in February 1831, Guerrero was captured and executed. Guerrero's presidency had made many Americans nervous because he abolished slavery and was the "first Black Indian president."[61] Poinsett and Butler, however, much preferred Guerrero to the conservative regime that threatened to interrupt American business.

Around the time of Guerrero's execution, Poinsett became one of the executors of South Carolina native James Burn's estate, which included debts in Mexico.[62] Burn was a former military officer who had electioneered for Poinsett in 1820. He had extensive investments in real estate, slavery, and international stocks and bonds. When he died in Frankford, Pennsylvania, in the winter of 1831, one of his relatives, Richard Willing, contacted Poinsett to coordinate the settlement of Burn's property and financial obligations. These obligations extended to Mexico, where Burn owed money. Butler helped Poinsett arrange payments through New York banker and Congressman C. C. Cambreleng and Baring and Co. in London.[63] All of these parties wanted stability in Mexico. They also wanted stability in South Carolina. In the same letter in which Butler criticized Guerrero's "abhorrent" executioners, he denounced the nullifiers in South Carolina.[64] Richard Willing, too, was opposed to nullification.[65] Willing was a wealthy Philadelphia merchant who avoided public office, other than serving on the board of an insurance company.[66] He, like most of Poinsett's merchant contacts, had claims on European governments and depended on a fiscally responsible government.[67] Poinsett would help ensure that South Carolina did not interfere with its reputation.

First, Poinsett left the country. As the nullification crisis abated, Poinsett's health worsened, and he decided to go to London. The trip gave him a break from constant communication and political and economic causes. In June 1831, for example, he was appointed to attend a New York railroad convention, which aligned with another of his interests.[68] Railroads had the potential to revive Charleston's economy by making it the southern depot for western trade. Boosters in the state hoped to obtain federal funds for more construction.[69] Poinsett, however, had told some people he was going to Philadelphia, so that in London he would be free from constant contact and could speak privately with financiers.[70]

While Poinsett was gone, he missed most of barbecue season—where many political allegiances were won or lost.[71] Both parties ramped up efforts to lure voters to their cause. The nullifiers organized a statewide system of associations and began appointing delegates to an anti-tariff convention in Philadelphia at the end of September. At one dinner, George McDuffie referred to the Union as a "monster."[72] To combat this vitriol, Congressman William Drayton gave an Independence Day reading of a letter President Jackson had written denouncing nullification.[73] Although there was some internal division among the nullifiers, they generally were more successful politically, particularly in winning the youth and immigrant votes.[74] In the fall election, they took the majority of legislative positions, as well as the mayor's seat in Charleston.[75]

Poinsett was back in Columbia in time for the fall legislative session. He had barely settled in when correspondence started pouring in. A Virginia man wrote to him when he heard that Poinsett had passed through his area on the way from New York to South Carolina. He was distraught at having lost his savings at sea and had been anxiously checking the papers for word of Poinsett's return. He thanked Poinsett for his encouragement and claimed that "one half hour with [him] would have been worth years with all the rest of the world."[76] Their connection was unclear, but the letter exemplified the sort of flattering notes Poinsett occasionally received, despite being maligned by some.

Soon after arriving in Columbia, Poinsett attended a meeting with members of the legislature to discuss the nomination for president.[77] Despite earlier campaign rancor and a movement by the nullifiers to prevent northern and eastern merchants from voting in Charleston, there was minimal acrimony in Columbia.[78] After a relatively civil meeting, members of the legislature from both parties agreed on Jackson as the preferred candidate. Some nullifiers chose to abstain from the campaign. This was their way of making a statement about the futility of participation in national politics. Hamilton encouraged nullifiers to wait for a more opportune time to push nullification aggressively. Unionists, for their part, published an address to reinforce their support for the Union.[79]

Once the assembly adjourned, Poinsett traveled to Washington. He shared part of the journey with Alexis de Tocqueville, the French aristocrat who was touring America for his report on society and democracy.

Tocqueville asked Poinsett about his thoughts on slavery. Poinsett told him he did not think the United States could abolish slavery. The government certainly could not afford to compensate all the slave owners. Perhaps to convince himself and others that the potential of another, bigger Nat Turner uprising was unlikely (several months earlier, slaves in Virginia had killed over fifty white people), he said slaves lacked the organizational capacity for a large-scale revolt.[80] He might not really have believed that slaves did not pose a threat to white dominance, but he at least was not afraid the federal government would undermine the institution.

In Washington, Poinsett and other members of the South Carolina minority submitted a memorial asking for a reduction in the tariff.[81] The memorial was an official attempt at compromise. Unofficially, Poinsett and his colleagues met with the people most able to influence the tariff: President Jackson, Secretary of Treasury Louis McLane, Senator Henry Clay, and Congressman John Quincy Adams. Although Poinsett's conversation with Clay was a disappointment, he and South Carolina representative Thomas R. Mitchell talked to Adams, Jackson's former presidential nemesis and a potential ally in tariff moderation. Adams was agreeable but, always cautious, said he would not be able to report on the likely outcome of the tariff because he needed to wait for word from the Treasury Department, as well as for the committee report from Philadelphia's recent free trade convention.[82] Mitchell then followed up with another northerner, "Mr. [Henry] Lee of Boston, our man of business." Mitchell convinced Lee, an ardent free trade advocate, to give Albert Gallatin, who was drafting the Philadelphia memorial, the "necessary information" that he hoped would temper the free trade argument.[83]

Soon after, their fellow unionist, Robert Cunningham, had a closed-door meeting with Jackson, in which they strategized about how to cajole and coerce South Carolinians to enforce the tariff. Jackson offered up political offices for key Carolinians in the western part of the state. He was known for these sorts of favors. He also believed this situation required force. Jackson told Cunningham that he would arrange for a collection of arms to be available for Poinsett's use, should the nullifiers become violent. He said they should have no problem getting them past South Carolina's military storekeeper.[84] Several years later, as secretary of war, Poinsett refused to sanction the deployment of federal resources in an armed political dispute in Pennsylvania, but for now, the availability of federal weapons seemed to be making his dreams of participating in war come true.[85]

The war against nullification intersected with another political war.[86]

The fate of the Second Bank of the United States was in question that winter, when Henry Clay and other supporters of bank president Nicholas Biddle introduced legislation for an early renewal of the bank's twenty-year charter (due to expire in 1836). It was a political gamble. Jackson had targeted the bank as an undemocratic institution of corruption; at the same time, bank supporters figured Jackson would not risk losing votes in key commercial states like Pennsylvania by vetoing it. The bank was relatively popular in South Carolina: in the 1820s, South Carolinians owned more bank stock than any other group outside the federal government.[87] Poinsett himself had tens of thousands of dollars tied up in it.[88] Poinsett's dearest friend, Joseph Johnson, was serving an eighteen-year tenure as president of Charleston's branch, and many of Poinsett's business associates around the country depended on the bank for financing and profitable stock options. They were all worried about its future.

Just like nullification, bank support defied regional and partisan alliances. For example, South Carolina congressman George McDuffie, a nullifier, headed a committee that supported the bank, while South Carolina's two senators, Robert Y. Hayne and Stephen D. Miller, both nullifiers, opposed it.[89] Poinsett and some of his associates, however, saw both the bank and the end of the nullification crisis as essential for their business prospects. Robert Gilmore, the Baltimore investor who owned stock in the Temascaltepec Company, believed the bank was critical for the economy. He thought Poinsett should invest money from Burn's estate in bank stock. Gilmore also wanted the nullification crisis to end.[90]

Secretary of Treasury Louis McLane was well positioned to help mediate both issues. McLane supported the bank and opposed nullification from a moderate standpoint and was liked by Jackson. After Clay's proposal proved too protectionist, Poinsett and Cunningham supplied McLane with arguments for the reduction of the tariff. McLane produced a report, delayed by his gout, which struck a balance between uniform duties of 12–15 percent across the board and the 1828 tariffs, which were as high as 50 percent on some manufactured goods. Generally lauded as a successful compromise, it was still unacceptable to the free trade contingent.[91]

Robert Gibbes was disgusted by the nullifiers' response to McLane's bill and the fact that the bank's opponents would probably succeed in stalling its recharter.[92] While he and Oliver were in Washington lobbying, John Quincy Adams, as chair of the Committee on Manufactures, worked on the bill that finally passed in early summer. Gibbes was pleased with Adams for eschewing his northern Whig loyalties.

Drayton, Mitchell, and James Blair all voted for the compromise bill and were branded as "betrayers of the state" by the nullifiers. The publicity war intensified. Calhoun used the enaction of the tariff as the basis for a letter to Governor Hamilton in which he laid out the legitimacy of nullification.[93] After the letter was reprinted throughout the state, Poinsett doubled down on newspaper efforts, paying for pro-Union pieces to be published in papers throughout South Carolina. He also used his network to collect voting data and organize vigilante committees all over the state.[94] Nullifiers were known for their rowdy lower classes, but one of Poinsett's correspondents noted that "vigilance is as much required for the higher class as it is for the lower."[95] Paranoia set in.

In September, the Union and States Rights Convention appointed delegates to travel to other southern states to assess the possibility of a southern convention to propose a plan for tariff revisions.[96] They sent Poinsett and Daniel Elliott Huger to North Carolina and Virginia.[97] Nothing significant resulted from these travels other than increased party animosity. During the elections for state and city offices, violence was worse than usual. Gangs of nullifiers attacked men leaving Union Party suppers. Both sides plied voters with liquor, which was common in all elections, but that fall, party leaders lured opponents with free alcohol and then kept them intoxicated long enough to prevent voting.[98]

Despite the best policing efforts of Poinsett and his associates, including appointing extra men on the eve of Sunday nullifier parties, the nullifiers took the majority of state and local offices. After the elections, Hamilton called a special early session. Poinsett knew this meant nullification and took several measures in response. First, he authored the Washington Society's address to the people of South Carolina, denouncing nullification and endorsing the use of arms to put down the movement.[99] Second, he established a secret intelligence network between Charleston and Washington, convinced that spies controlled the Charleston post office. Third, Poinsett gave a speech that reached a national audience, in which he made clear his two main goals for the United States as a nation: international respect and federal protection of capital.

In the speech, Poinsett waxed patriotic about South Carolina and the Union. He said that he had proudly waved the American flag during a political riot in Mexico City in 1828 and asked rhetorically whether it would have done any good to hang "the Palmetto and the single star." Poinsett argued that "to be respected abroad we must maintain our place in the union." He knew from his contact with foreign investors how important national cohesiveness was. He then went on to address slavery: "Let us suppose South Carolina with a population of 25,000 white inhabitants a separate nation. . . . If we were a separate and independent nation without the protection of the Confederacy . . . we should be exposed to the united efforts of the evangelicals of Great Britain and the northern abolitionists."[100] In that brief hypothetical, Poinsett acknowledged that the federal government was the only real protection for the South's most valuable form of capital.

In this, he understood what some southerners would increasingly come to see: that federal power could be used to protect, and potentially expand, slavery.[101] This was already happening as the government funded Native expulsion from cotton-growing lands (just a year prior, the US Army oversaw the forced removal of Choctaw peoples from Alabama under the Indian Removal Act).[102] The use of government force for the prosperity of southern "agriculture" was an outgrowth of the fact that much of the American financial system intermingled with the institution of slavery—the Second Bank of the United States, for example, secured loans using plantations and enslaved humans as collateral.[103] Although historians have long recognized this cross-sectional investment in slavery, contemporaries' understanding of the nation's relationship to slavery still bears illumination, especially when traditional narratives of the nullification crisis portray it as the fear child of paranoid slaveholders.[104] Poinsett later wrote that slavery "cannot be repelled by any act of congress." In his view, even those who opposed slavery were not a threat, so long as South Carolina stayed in the Union, because they "believe in the compact which binds us together and makes us a great nation."[105] In fact, he knew opponents of slavery in the North who reprinted his speech. Just as there was interregional cooperation on slavery, there was interregional cooperation on ending the nullification crisis. Massachusetts antislavery academic George Ticknor, for example, asked Poinsett for a copy of his full speech to publish in New England newspapers, which were only printing excerpts.[106] Richard Willing, meanwhile, read Poinsett's speech from his sickbed in Philadelphia and arranged for Robert Walsh to print and distribute it in Pennsylvania. He was personally invested in ending the crisis because he still needed to collect the debts due on Burn's estate in South Carolina. He wrote that it was imperative for Poinsett to defeat the nullifiers.[107]

Knowing the British might choose South Carolina if the United States appeared weak, Poinsett's strategy involved violence. He told the man known for violence to use more force, writing to Jackson, "I am decidedly of opinion, that whenever the Government is compelled to act it should be done with such an overwhelming force as to put down at once all hopes of successful opposition."[108] When Governor Hamilton called for a twelve-thousand-man state army, Poinsett wrote to Jackson: now was the time for arms.[109] Jackson dispatched five thousand muskets and other military equipment to Charleston Harbor, concealed in camouflaged boxes.[110] Several days later, Jackson issued a statement against nullification, which unionists paid to have printed in as many papers as possible.[111] In confidential correspondence, Jackson made Poinsett the point person for the government's defense against nullification. He instructed military officials to refer, privately, to Poinsett for arms. Poinsett was Jackson's choice because he was in many ways more ruthless than Jackson. Poinsett believed that Calhoun "deserves punishment and I am disposed to inflict it in its most cruel form." He was willing to fight dirty, telling Jackson that "hand grenades and small rockets are excellent weapons in a street fight and I should like to have some of them."[112]

At the same time, however, Poinsett hid behind the facade of a cosmopolitan civilian, which allowed him to move between groups and assess the situation on the ground. Poinsett understood exactly how and when force should be used. He told Jackson to wait out the calls for preemptive violence. The nullifiers had to strike first. Also, he wrote, Jackson should not make too big a deal of Calhoun and other leaders because "in our country a man may be persecuted into consequence . . . to attack him as the arch Rebel might enlist in his favor a feeling he is totally unworthy of."[113] If the nullifiers appeared to be the dangerous enemy and the federal government put "these bad men down by the strong arm," Poinsett told Jackson, "the union will be cemented by . . . the vigour of the government, and you will earn the imperishable glory of having preserved this great confederacy from destruction."[114]

Poinsett seemed to relish making military preparations. He followed up his letter about the "vigour of the government" with this statement to Jackson, which he sent by way of "a gentleman entirely in [his] confidence" instead of by ordinary express: "I should think that with the forces in Augusta and Savannah and at Smithville added to the troops here a movement might be made upon the city at any time—and I repeat my belief, that Charleston once in our possession the Nullifiers will be paralysed. We shall deprive them of their part of artillery and a large part of their arms and ammunition by such a movement."[115]

Jackson told Poinsett he could have as many guns as he wanted. If nullifiers planned to resist with twelve thousand bayonets, the federal government would greet them with twenty-four thousand.[116] Poinsett specifically requested a United States Rifle, fitted with bayonet, which would give him the benefit of long-range accuracy and intimate combat; he offered to instruct men how to use them.[117] In addition to serving as a sort of adjutant general, Poinsett organized and drilled men in Charleston.[118] A Baltimore merchant wrote to Poinsett from Europe that everyone was confident about the state of the Union, with Poinsett in charge.[119]

Poinsett attempted to use the crisis as a platform for implementing political changes in Charleston. He reported on office-holding nullifiers and suggested replacements for them. Men who sacrificed nullifier patronage by supporting the Union Party needed favors, which Poinsett did his best to oblige. He also wanted to make Charleston a naval depot for the West Indian squadron, arguing that it would improve Charleston's economy and make mechanics more amenable to the government. Poinsett's request was given serious consideration by the president and prominent naval captains but was tabled for the time being.[120] Poinsett ended up being satisfied, however, with his request for tariff alterations. He argued that although the 1832 tariff had lowered the protection on "negro cloth," it ultimately hurt planters because the duties on the higher-quality cloth, which planters purchased for their families, remained high.[121]

The compromise that was signed into law on March 2 mandated a reduction in tariffs by about 10 percent per year until 1842.[122] That same day, Jackson signed the Force Act, which legalized the preparations he and Poinsett had already begun; the act allowed the president to use military power to force South Carolina to comply with tariff collection. Jackson referred to it as the Collection Bill and said it "proved to the world the fixed determination of Congress to execute the laws passed in pursuance of the Constitution . . . fully shows to the world that [the United States] was not to be deterred by a faction which if found in rebellion and treason she was prepared to crush in an instant."[123]

For the next two weeks, the situation remained tense. Poinsett readied his militia leaders throughout the state with men and arms. Small skirmishes continued. Any alleged offenders received unfair trials, as nullifiers controlled the courts.[124] On March 15, the South Carolina legislature rescinded the Nullification Ordinance, but even with this abatement of conflict, Poinsett argued that federal force should increase. He reiterated his desire for a navy yard: "The presence of the *Natchez* has had a good effect, but if the government established a navy yard, it would give them better protection from the slave population."[125] Once again, he called on federal protection for the state's most valuable form of capital, giving lie to the argument that a unionist victory endangered the institution of slavery.

Although the unionists technically won when the South Carolina legislature rescinded the Nullification Ordinance, secessionists kept control of much of local politics; as a symbolic gesture, they nullified the Force Act on March 18.[126] Some historians have argued that the crisis was a sort of popular uprising, linked with evangelical revivalism, and that nullifier leaders manipulated the enthusiasm of the lower orders for their own political gain.[127] Poinsett's aspirations, however, were bigger than local or state politics. He always had national and international connections and ambitions in mind. He was rewarded for his efforts. Not only did local militia guards host dinners for him but Robert Walsh wrote to him that people in Philadelphia much admired him and Jackson promised him an office.[128]

Poinsett's success with nullification and good favor with Jackson ultimately secured him a post as secretary of war, even after his business in Mexico threatened once again to destroy his political reputation. Anthony Butler, Jackson's handpicked replacement for Poinsett in Mexico, threatened to destroy his political reputation. During the winter of nullification, Poinsett received a letter from James Wilcocks in Mexico, who reported that Anthony Butler had become Poinsett's "mortal enemy" and was spreading rumors about Poinsett's role in investor fraud in the ongoing Temascaltepec scandal. The case had never gone to trial in the United States, but allegations kept surfacing and were made worse by Butler's meddling.[129] Wilcocks was doing his best to protect Poinsett. He had already secured Poinsett's commission from the mine, and he planned to send a petition to Washington requesting Butler's recall. The petition charged Butler with dishonorable behavior, such as making lewd gestures to women and profiting unfairly from office.[130] Butler went beyond Poinsett's diplomatic practices—he was too overtly aggressive and too obviously self-interested. He also refused to uphold Poinsett's business deals in Mexico. Jackson, however, ignored Wilcocks's request to recall Butler and recalled Wilcocks instead.

By then, Poinsett was married; in his words, he had "abandoned the very respectable fraternity of Bachelors."[131] On October 24, 1833, Poinsett married Mary Izard Pringle, fifty-two-year-old widow of John Julius Pringle Jr. (cousin of Poinsett's nullification ally James R. Pringle), at the harbor-front home of a naval officer at Fort Monroe.[132] Poinsett had avoided marriage for so long; now he told twenty-five-year-old James Butler Campbell "to do the same earlier that I did, indeed as soon as you can find some good natured person to have you. If it was not so cold I would write you a homily upon the subject; but I can scarcely hold my pen."[133]

We know nothing of Mary and Joel's courtship. Two days after his March call for more protection against the slave population, Poinsett expressed regret that he had not married earlier in life.[134] Then his correspondence dropped off precipitously from June to November. Poinsett was gone for much of the summer, traveling with Jackson. Jackson rewarded his service to the Union by inviting him to serve on the board of visitors to examine the cadets at West Point and then taking him to New England. After being invited by numerous Democratic societies in New England, Jackson had agreed to do a northern tour in June.[135] Throughout their travels, the presidential suite was met with celebrations for Jackson's role in the nullification crisis. In Connecticut, several hundred women paraded with a banner that read, "The Union—it must be preserved." Women played a major part in the welcoming committees, and cities cordoned off space for the "ladies" to congregate.[136]

The crowds in Massachusetts were less enthusiastic, but Jackson's stance on nullification was popular, even if he himself was not. Harvard reluctantly gave Jackson an honorary degree. The presidential party was invited aboard the *Constitution*, where Commodore Isaac Hull presented Poinsett, Jackson, Vice President Martin Van Buren, and Massachusetts governor Levi Lincoln with canes made from the wood of his favorite ship.[137] When Jackson and his entourage traveled to Lowell to see the textile factories, they were greeted by five thousand women who waved parasols and wore sashes that indicated the mills in which they worked. The workers had the day off for Jackson's visit, but Jackson requested that a factory be opened so he could observe its operation.[138] He could not refrain from the opportunity to plug free trade. Surely, he said, such fine undertakings as these would not need protectionist tariffs.

As Poinsett traveled with Jackson, northerners mostly celebrated his efforts in the nullification crisis, but he angered others by "intermeddl[ing] politically." Poinsett visited the Grand Lodge of Massachusetts, where he shared Jackson's favorable opinion of Freemasonry and urged them to persevere in the face of opposition.[139] In response to Poinsett's address, the State Anti-Masonic Committee published a letter chastising his position.[140] Anti-Masonry had escalated in the United States after the 1827 disappearance of former Master Mason William Morgan, who had planned to publish a book revealing the organization's secrets. The Anti-Masonic Party had gained enough strength to run William Wirt for president in 1832. Although the party was vehemently anti-Jackson, it ended up helping Jackson get elected because Wirt secured votes that probably would have gone to Henry Clay (interestingly enough, Wirt was only a lukewarm supporter of the anti-Masonry movement and was an admirer of Poinsett's).[141] The Anti-Masonic Party was relatively strong during the 1830s, serving as a low-level threat to Poinsett's national ambitions. After receiving criticism for "intermeddling," Poinsett appropriately "did not avail [himself] of the opportunity to speak of southern affairs when in Boston."[142]

He also perhaps had already moved on, readying himself first for domestic life and then, he hoped, Washington. After the wedding, Poinsett moved to Mary's "White House" plantation, which she had inherited from her father, Ralph Izard, one of the wealthiest rice planters in South Carolina. It was located on the Pee Dee River in Georgetown County, about sixty miles north of Charleston. The next year, the couple bought a summer home in Greenville. When he and Mary married, they had signed a "marriage settlement," whereby the couple assigned their prior assets to two trustees who would manage their estates on their behalf. One of these was James R. Pringle, who would oversee later deals.[143] Poinsett brought to the arrangement a piece of property in St. Philip's Parish; Mary brought the 160-acre White House plantation, several tracts of land in Charleston, 100 shares in the Banks of the United States, 182 shares in the Planters and Mechanics Bank of South Carolina, 10 shares in the Union Bank of South Carolina, and 49 shares in the Camden and Amboy Railroad in New Jersey. As part of the agreement, the trustees gave Mary's only son an income of $1,000 per year, and Mary assumed the profit from her property's income "as if she were a femme sole and unmarried."[144] Poinsett became a plantation owner by virtue of marriage.

Mary also brought eighty-nine enslaved individuals to their marriage. Poinsett, a city landlord who had owned some slaves, now controlled the labor of almost one hundred enslaved African Americans. His new experience helped inform the speech he had to prepare for the anniversary celebration of the Literary and Philosophical Society of South Carolina.[145] This speech was a racist vindication of Jackson's American Indian removal policy, influenced by his status as an enslaver. On March 28, 1830, Jackson had signed into law "An Act to Provide for an Exchange of Lands with the Indians Residing in Any of the States or Territories, and for Their Removal West of the River Mississippi."[146] Although the act codified the demands of aggressive American expansionists, it was far from popular among the white population. It passed the House of Representatives narrowly (102–97) and faced strong opposition nationwide, most visible among women's organizations and in petitions, pamphlets, and religious newspapers and magazines.[147] The act therefore needed justifying. Poinsett said little about the act after its passage but used his presidential address as a platform to argue that Native Americans were incapable of progressing through stages of civilization. In doing so, he challenged the Jeffersonian belief that they could become assimilated. Poinsett said that the hypothesis that all humans started as hunters and gatherers "has always appeared to me erroneous whether we regard the proofs furnished by sacred or profane history."[148] Instead, he said, humans have historically had different habits of civilization, and peoples long unaccustomed to civilized behaviors were incapable of adopting the virtues of more civilized groups. Poinsett drew on his own experience and opinions for evidence. His speech was a racist reflection on the nature of different groups of humans across time and space. His new experience as a large plantation owner made him feel like a feudal lord; he referred to his slaves as vassals.[149] He therefore found it preposterous that any historians could compare North American Indians to medieval Germanic tribes, some of whom had "free institutions themselves but slaves to cultivate the earth." To him, the coexistence of slavery and freedom were the markers of superiority (never mind the fact that Indians owned farms and slaves).

Poinsett also provided judgmental anecdotes from his travels in Europe, Asia, and North and South America, recounting, for instance, the night he spent decades before in the Eurasian Steppe. According to Poinsett, the pastoral tribes there were in some ways superior to the hunters of North America, yet he still scoffed that the "savage who . . . regaled [him] with a singed sheep head . . . pitied the luxurious Frenchman who eats the most delicate food, and drinks the choicest wines, and lives in a palace, because he has no steppes." This was not a nod to cultural relativism; this was Poinsett's prejudiced ranking of the "barbarous" peoples of the world and an assertion that it was futile to hope they could assimilate into higher levels of civilization. He "regret[ted] to state" that American tribes had "resisted the well directed efforts of humane and pious Christians to civilize and convert [them]." Therefore, in everyone's best interests, they must be removed, or else they would "perish under the shade of the white man's settlement."[150] Three years later, Poinsett would have the opportunity to put his opinions into action as secretary of war.

In the meantime, Poinsett settled into his new role as plantation "master," busy fixing an estate that had suffered "17 years of neglect." For the first time in his life, he attempted to control the labor of eighty-nine enslaved individuals. While at the White House plantation, he relied on James Butler Campbell to keep an eye on things for him in Charleston.[151] Campbell was a former Massachusetts teacher turned Charleston unionist who was courting the daughter of one of Poinsett's friends. The two had met during the nullification crisis. Campbell now managed Poinsett's correspondence in the city, checked on rental properties, and arranged repairs at Poinsett's request. He also bolstered Poinsett's ties to northern politicians, such as their "mutual friend" Daniel Webster.[152]

Perhaps because Campbell was so much his junior, Poinsett felt free to discuss business interests candidly and give unsolicited advice, especially related to Campbell's love interest (Poinsett, for example, encouraged Campbell not to delay marriage until he was "independent"; rather, he said, marry soon and have the girl's father help him achieve "independence").[153] Poinsett wrote more openly and more casually to Campbell than he did with many of his correspondents. Some of his friends expressed concern at their closeness and suggested that Poinsett check on Campbell's references, which he did by writing to Daniel Webster for verification.[154]

Had the references not checked out, it would have been too late, because Poinsett had already familiarized Campbell with his personal finances.[155] Poinsett was in debt, and the properties of which he and Mary remained "beneficial owners" were not profitable. He kept hoping Charleston real estate would improve and wished New Yorkers saw value in it the way they did in the West.[156] When he learned of a new business opportunity in Texas in the summer of 1834, he enlisted Campbell to help. General Santa Anna had recently established a dictatorship in Mexico, which upset the political situation in Mexico and Texas. Poinsett's old investment ally Lorenzo Zavala denounced Santa Anna, resigned from the Mexican legation in Paris, and traveled to New York to establish the New Washington Association, a real estate company that would purchase and develop lands in Texas, forming towns from which it would profit. One of its managers was Mexican consul to New York James Treat, who was responsible for issuing passports to the states of Coahuila y Tejas. He had traveled to Charleston on personal business in 1831 and probably met with Poinsett during that time.[157] When Campbell traveled through New York, Poinsett instructed him, "See Mr. Treat as often as you can and get every information from him possible in relation to the lands in Texas."[158] The following year, he offered Campbell one-third of potential earnings to travel to Texas to make purchases for him. The goal was to "secure the fee simple of them" and then sell them for a profit in a few years.[159]

As Texas fought for independence, the major issue was annexation.[160] Many Jacksonians wanted independence to include annexation to the

United States. Interestingly, Poinsett and Hamilton, opponents during the nullification crisis, did not. Hamilton had become involved in the region after his term as governor, buying land with his brother-in-law, Barnard E. Bee, who served on his staff during the nullification crisis. Bee himself had taken advantage of Poinsett's connections in Texas and Mexico, getting a letter of introduction before moving to the region and joining the army in 1836.[161] All three men wanted independence without annexation. When he began his post as minister to Mexico in 1825, Poinsett had supported the annexation of Texas, but as he became increasingly influential in Mexican politics, he grew more reluctant to comply with instructions to offer to purchase the territory from Mexico.[162] Poinsett had little incentive to encourage Mexico to sell the land because if Texas remained in Mexico, the administration in power would determine land grants, which meant that land grants would go to Poinsett's friends, who could sell parcels of land to US citizens. Once Texas gained independence, he did not want US involvement to interfere with the political situation in Texas, since his old associate David Burnet was president and Zavala was vice president.[163]

Poinsett and Hamilton had confidential discussions with a New York real estate investor and former Mexican resident about trying to convince the Mexican government to recognize Texan independence.[164] Taking a more visible stance, Hamilton also contributed his own funds to Texan independence and worked with former foe Daniel Webster to influence Britain's recognition of the republic.[165] Because of his support, Hamilton was offered command of the Texas Army at the end of 1836, but he declined. At that time, he was serving in the South Carolina senate with Poinsett, who had reluctantly agreed to serve.[166] They worked together to oppose former nullifiers like George McDuffie who called for annexation. Pro-annexationists wanted additional slave power in Congress; they also feared that if Texas did not belong to the United States, Britain might influence the abolition of slavery. Hamilton and Poinsett correctly gambled that Britain would not interfere with slavery and that even if it did, British merchants would still want to purchase Texas cotton, which would keep their lands profitable.[167]

The aftermath of the nullification crisis looked good for both men. Hamilton would suffer from financial downfall in the 1840s, but before then, he secured his standing in South Carolina and Texas by negotiating a railroad and fire loan for Charleston and a loan for the new Republic of Texas. Poinsett, meanwhile, had appeased Jackson and his northern friends and was ultimately rewarded in February 1837, when Van Buren offered him the position of secretary of war (a position that would improve his land investments and allow him to help stave off annexation).[168]

Poinsett had claimed that he wanted to avoid public office and that he was happier at home, but when Van Buren appointed him secretary of war, he gladly resigned from the state senate to go to Washington. As soon as Poinsett was made secretary of war, Johnson wrote to him, "The appointment though it may interrupt your farming and such like prospects will result incidentally in your benefit . . . measures may be informally taken to obtain a good location or selection of your Texas lands with a confirmation of your titles from the new sovereign nation."[169] Poinsett would have to be discreet, of course. He was used to that. He instructed Campbell to "not act too boldly in asserting my claim to Texas Lands. I think it may be managed quietly. It is important to my position not to be assailable in such matters."[170]

Poinsett would not, however, have to be discreet with violence. He would soon have control over the growing military resources of the United States. The nullification crisis had been a practice for the large-scale deployment of force in the service of what he perceived as US national security and economic opportunity.

6

....

War,
1837–1841

Poinsett returned to the capital on March 9, 1837, to serve as Martin Van Buren's secretary of war.[1] After over two decades of political service, he was finally at the center of power. He had worked in the executive branch before, as well as in Washington. He had been an American abroad, a South Carolinian in the nation's capital, and a nationalist in South Carolina. He was now a civilian, with lifelong military aspirations, at the head of the country's armed forces. When Van Buren made the official offer on February 4, Poinsett did not hesitate to accept.

Poinsett was Van Buren's lone cabinet appointee and the only newcomer to the White House.[2] Continuing on from Jackson's administration were John Forsyth from Georgia as secretary of state, Levi Woodbury from New Hampshire as secretary of treasury, Mahlon Dickerson from New Jersey as secretary of navy, Amos Kendall from Kentucky as postmaster general, and Benjamin Butler from New York as attorney general (Butler would be replaced by Poinsett's future biographer Henry D. Gilpin in 1840). Van Buren chose Poinsett to mollify disgruntled members of his party and broaden his geographic base. Poinsett was a loyal Jacksonian, a slaveholder, a unionist, and, most important for voting purposes, a southerner.

After serving as Jackson's informant during the nullification debacle, Poinsett had kept a fairly low profile. He tended to his new plantation on the Pee Dee River. He also served as president of the Literary and Philosophical Society of Charleston, where he held weekly breakfasts for patrons, intellectuals, and promising youth, including future explorer John C. Fremont. Over the past year, however, his political activities had picked up. When Texas declared independence in the spring of 1836,

Poinsett was called on as an expert on Mexican affairs. That fall, he was re-elected to the South Carolina state legislature after declining the George-town District's nomination for Congress. Poinsett then gave up his state position for a chance to go north. The stakes of his new office were higher than at his previous posts. He was no longer representing nascent US in-terests overseas, advocating local interests in the nation's capital, or pro-moting federal authority at the state level. He now wielded the nation's military power in a vast territory over which the United States, and he as an executor, claimed jurisdiction.

On February 5, Poinsett headed north out of Georgetown, South Car-olina. He had wanted to go first to Charleston to finish business there and then make the trip from Norfolk by steamship. Van Buren asked that in-stead he hurry to Washington to begin urgent department business. Poin-sett and Mary took the stagecoach, which stopped for a day in Fayetteville. Poinsett worried about how his wife would handle the journey. He also worried about their health in the Washington climate.[3] The capital could be toxic in all sorts of ways. It could destroy marriages and reputations. The Poinsetts, however, were not the Eatons.[4] They were now almost sixty, and health problems were a bigger threat than marriage scandals.

Poinsett started his term more popular than the other cabinet mem-bers. Newspapers of different political bents commented on his military fitness, cosmopolitanism, and bipartisan appeal. He was "eloquent," "courteous," and "the ablest and most accomplished man in the present cabinet." He also practiced "good business habits" and spoke French.[5] He was congratulated by northerners and southerners, states' rights advo-cates and unionists alike.[6] Although he had been a polarizing figure in Mexico, most Americans had forgotten or did not care. Advertisements trumpeted the availability of the plant "introduced into the United States from Mexico, by our former minister, J. Poinsett, Esq," which recently had been named the *Euphorbia poinsettii* in his honor. Poinsett's Mexi-can Christmas flower was "unsurpassed in general effect by the most gor-geous coloring."[7]

This sort of praise made it easier for Poinsett to carry out his agenda, which combined his lifelong interests in scientific endeavors and milita-rism with economic advancement. In what would be his last major po-litical role, this agenda morphed into warfare against obstacles to white Americans' opportunities. These wars were multiple—against Indians, economic limitations, and unknown territory—and he waged them by centralizing military power and employing military resources in the ser-vice of national and individual economic interests. Poinsett carried out his racialized, masculine, and order-driven vision of national interest without ever making it explicit. Although he was not always successful, he attempted to work as a sort of invisible agent, as he had in South Carolina and South America.[8]

Poinsett's first and last orders as secretary of war were regulations for the Corps of Engineers. The first related to the discipline; the last related to maps, the fruits of their labor. That engineering served as the bookends to his tenure symbolized the emphasis he placed on improvement and discovery.[9] In between, he advocated an increase in both the engineering corps and the army.[10] The subtext of this promotion of engineering and discovery was the bolstering of military strength to achieve economic and governing ends. Although the long-term gains from these expeditions would not be realized during Poinsett's time in Washington, during his tenure, military expansion, efficiency, and exploration intersected in the creation of the Manifest Destiny political economy. Poinsett waged war against the inefficiencies and uncertainties associated with an expanding nation in a multipronged campaign that reflected the culmination of his vision for national prosperity. The executions of his plans blended capitalist rationality with old-fashioned fiscal militarism. His influence, perceived and real, extended beyond straight military matters.

Opportunity: The Wars of 1837

Poinsett got to Washington too late to witness Van Buren's inaugural address. On March 4, 1837, Van Buren announced to the nation, "We may not possess, as we should not desire to possess, the extended and ever ready military organization of other nations."[11] This was a common trope in American political rhetoric, and it often served as a challenge and a cover to the nation's military men. Less than two weeks after inauguration, General Edmund P. Gaines, commander of the Western Military Department, sent Poinsett a letter urging greater military presence in Florida. According to Gaines, Van Buren was wrong: "The opinion that small detachments can be made with any advantage to the service or without imminent and useless risk is erroneous," he wrote.[12]

Poinsett had waited his whole life for war in the United States, and Gaines's request would be the first of several opportunities to participate. None involved war declared as such, but the task of overseeing American Indian removal gave Poinsett the chance to carry out violence against Native peoples in a series of military battles and armed marches. Although the forced removal of approximately fifty thousand individuals is usually associated with Jackson, the majority of it happened under Poinsett's watch.[13] He would oversee the forced migration of four-fifths of Native peoples beyond the Mississippi. As Poinsett militarized the process of so-called removal beyond its beginnings as an ad hoc series of protracted frontier conflicts and "voluntary" emigrations, he simultaneously capital-ized on white Americans' desires to exploit more fully this appropriated land—along with the rest of the continent and beyond—by jump-starting stalled exploratory expeditions.[14]

It is hardly a coincidence that the term Manifest Destiny received its rhetorical framing during his tenure and was coined shortly after it, in a magazine he endorsed.[15] All of these initiatives collided with the rem-nants of the Bank War and an economic panic. As Poinsett carried out a crusade for American opportunity, the economy became both a means and an end to war.

When he joined the cabinet, federal officials were still trying to figure out how best to "remove" Native peoples from their homes. Expulsion began as an ad hoc series of "voluntary" emigrations during the 1820s to make coveted land available for cotton plantations and gold mining, espe-cially after the discovery of gold on Cherokee lands in northern Georgia in the late 1820s.[16] Expulsion efforts combined with ongoing "civilization" policies targeted at education, religion, and husbandry.[17] On March 28, 1830, Jackson signed into law "An Act to Provide for an Exchange of Lands with the Indians Residing in Any of the States or Territories, and for Their Removal West of the River Mississippi," formally shifting US policy from one of "civilization" and assimilation to extermination.[18] This shift happened slowly on the ground, as representatives from Native na-tions and the United States signed treaties for the cession of tribal lands to the United States and the resettlement of members of those nations farther west. The treaties made it possible for individual investors and joint-stock companies to profit off dispossession, as speculators engaged in fraud and coercion to acquire land and agents ignored appeals to re-main on the land.[19]

The process of "removal" was at a critical juncture when Poinsett ar-rived in Washington and received the letter from Gaines requesting more troops.[20] The army stretched thin along the frontier because of military needs in Florida; a Cherokee delegation planned to visit Washington to negotiate terms of their treaty; and the Second Seminole War, which had begun several years before, seemed to some participants and onlookers to be over.[21] US Army officers pursued different strategies and different lev-els of force. Gaines advocated for an overall buildup; Alexander Macomb was interested in frontier roads; General John E. Wool tried to avoid bloodshed as he oversaw removals in Georgia and Tennessee; Winfield Scott and Thomas Jessup believed in uncompromising force in all frontier engagements.[22] "Removal" was neither inevitable nor inherently violent, but in a nation where land was tied to economic opportunity and federal officials were more than willing to use force, it resulted in what the Cherokee people would name "the Trail of Tears."[23] Here's how this happened.

Gaines's letter was one among many. Part of Poinsett's job was deciding whose interests to privilege, and it was not just army officers to whom he had to respond. The department was bombarded with letters from individuals all over the place who needed favors, offered policy advice, and complained about perceived injustices or insults. These ran the gamut from men trying to get their teenage family members into West Point to friends from home requesting plant and mineral samplings, squabbling between West Point faculty members, Indian agents soliciting more business, and the Mexican president requesting a stabilization of the Texas situation.[24] Poinsett spent a lot of time managing not only major military matters but egos and individual interests.

He took office as the economic recession known as the Panic of 1837 was setting in, and many of his correspondents wanted economic rescue.[25] This downturn had multiple causes, including the decision of banks in London and New York to raise interest rates and Jackson's Specie Circular, which required hard money for land purchases and drained the reserves of major banks. Jackson had won the Bank War officially when the bank's federal charter expired in January 1836.[26] Its economic consequences were long lasting and affected people of all classes all over the country, manifesting in flour riots in New York and abandoned plantations in Mississippi. Historians have not usually linked American Indian removal and the downturn, and yet, as bank president Nicholas Biddle realized, the expansion of the cotton kingdom into Native lands was key to recovery.[27] If we look at several of the routine requests for political favors Poinsett received in the first months of his tenure, we can see the economic context in which he made decisions about war and his understanding of his new obligations as secretary of war.[28]

On March 9, several days after Poinsett took office, Charleston Democratic newspaper editor J. N. Cardozo sent Poinsett a long letter that explained how his newspaper was struggling. The mail service took too long between Fayetteville and Charleston, and his delayed access to intelligence was causing his publication to "lose its interest and value." He wanted Poinsett's assistance in bringing this problem to the attention of

the postmaster general, in addition to more military advertising business and help settling his government debts. Cardozo also acknowledged
broader issues of political economy by noting that although people in
South Carolina were skeptical of Van Buren's politics, he was convinced
that Poinsett would help him change course from Jackson's monetary policy, which had been detrimental to commercial interests in Charleston.[29]

On April 3, West Point Foundry founder and soon-to-be congressman from New York Gouverneur Kemble sent a private letter to Poinsett. As the "symptoms of depression" set in, he was being accused by
other foundry owners of monopolizing government business. According to Kemble, his "brother founders" were upset that he kept his prices
low, while they wanted to charge the government more for their labor
and capital than it was worth. Kemble refused to acquiesce, believing it
would destroy competition. He wanted Poinsett to fight the battle between competition and monopoly, which was inherent in an economy
predicated on militarism and emerging capitalist values. Because their
accusations were holding up assignments for government work, Kemble
needed Poinsett to convince the colonel of ordnance—confidentially, so
as to avoid "unpleasant collisions" with the other founders—to continue
purchasing artillery from the West Point Foundry.[30]

Less than two weeks later, former Delaware customs collector Allen
M'Lane similarly tried to avoid the cruelties of an unfettered market. He
wrote to Poinsett after losing his business. He believed, wrongly, that the
war in Florida was over but thought "that some situation connected with
the emigration of the Indians might offer which would merit [him]."[31]
M'Lane wanted to profit from forced migration.

Poinsett's correspondence shows us how closely linked were American Indian removal and the economic downturn. His response to both
was to strengthen central control. This meant privileging national security over individual requests and prioritizing military power over all else.
This was why Kemble got more business providing munitions for the military and M'Lane did not get his appointment from Poinsett.[32] It was also
why Poinsett complied with Cardozo's requests, despite receiving advice
that he should not.[33] Cardozo printed military advertisements and financial news that aligned with Poinsett's military and economic initiatives.

These civilian requests intersected with military requests to combat
economic conditions.[34] General Winfield Scott, for example, wanted
Poinsett to reverse the cuts to the military's travel allowances. Pecuniary constraints, he said, should have little bearing on the fact that troops
needed to travel farther as a result of "the migrations of the Indians to the

west" and the "spread of our own people in that direction."[35] In the context of requests for personal financial betterment, military expansion, and desires to expel Native peoples from as much of the continent as possible, Poinsett adopted an aggressive stance that linked economic and military efficiency with American Indian extermination.

In early June, Poinsett received word that things in Florida were bad. James Gadsden, a former army officer and member of the Army Corps of Engineers and currently a member of the Florida territorial legislature, had left his plantation in middle Florida because he thought the war was over but had just received news suggesting otherwise. Negotiations had failed and hostilities had broken out.

Florida was supposed to be a land of opportunity for aspiring white planters. Gadsden was one among many men who had moved there hoping to take advantage of prime farming land and potential cotton profits.[36] The average yield of Sea Island cotton, whose market price was about twice that of short staple, was six hundred pounds per acre in Florida, versus South Carolina's three hundred.[37] Even more than in South Carolina was Floridian planters' well-being tied to cotton. Cotton functioned as cash, collateral, and credit, which meant that when cotton prices plummeted in 1837, planters needed to produce ever greater amounts to stay financially solvent. The renewal of "hostilities" with the Seminoles would make this impossible. Gadsden had no choice but to "to return and remain a sentinel and soldier at my own plantation."[38] He did not, however, want to be personally responsible for the fate of settler colonialism in Florida.

Later that month, Gadsden suggested the War Department begin preparations for "the hunt," a euphemism for the process of rooting out and killing Seminoles, who often hid from white perpetrators. Gadsden asked for an increase in troops "who cannot demand their discharge at 3 or 6 months" so that they could "speedily catch and transport every redman out of Florida."[39]

Poinsett turned to Jackson for advice. He apologized for bothering Jackson in his retirement, but he needed to know how best to "prosecute the war against them with rigor."[40] Just as Jackson had used Poinsett as his informant and clandestine military executor during the nullification crisis, Poinsett sent private letters to Jackson for help executing Jackson's own removal policy.[41] And Jackson delivered. He suggested Poinsett "urge congress to raise the rank and file to 1k bayonets" because "a well-chosen brigade with such officers as I could select, numbering 1000 bayonets and rifles, in addition to the regulars now in Florida would destroy the Seminole Indians in 30 days from the time of their reaching Tampa Bay."[42] It was very important, Jackson confided, that the governor of Florida have no role in organizing and assembling troops; that should be left to military men. Poinsett immediately launched a campaign to increase troop numbers.

He had to tread carefully. Removal was fairly popular among white Americans; brutal warfare was not. Many Americans hoped for a "philanthropic" resolution of the conflict.[43] Publicly, Poinsett authorized a peace delegation of Cherokee to negotiate an end to the war in Florida. He employed John H. Sherburne as a private agent to take advantage of the fact that a party of Cherokee led by John Ross was eager to renegotiate their treaty with the US government. Although a group of Cherokee had moved west in March 1837, a significant number remained and sought to annul the removal treaty.[44]

Poinsett gave Sherburne permission to offer the delegation treaty revisions and remuneration in exchange for their convincing the Seminoles to cease fighting and leave Florida. Because Poinsett did not trust individuals from the Cherokee Nation, he sent separate instructions to Major General Thomas Jesup, commanding general of US troops in Florida. The two agreed that Seminole submission took precedence over all else. Military men wanted an efficient end to the war, not a "philanthropic" one.[45] Poinsett himself never believed negotiations would work. When Poinsett presented his report on the war to Congress in September, he claimed that all humane measures had been exhausted. Vessels had been stationed off the coast of Florida, ready to transport willing Natives. These vessels were expensive, he said; it would be more "economical" to devote national resources to a "vigorous prosecution of the war."[46]

At the same time, Poinsett was engaged in a broader economic debate. The casualties of Jackson's Bank War were daily multiplying, and private citizens beseeched the administration to do something. The nation's economy was usually a partisan issue, but the cabinet split over the Specie Circular, which many Americans saw as the cause of their problems. Van Buren had asked Poinsett what he should do about Jackson's Specie Circular back in March. Poinsett suggested he repeal it. Van Buren ignored him.[47] Now, Poinsett weighed in again, advocating an independent treasury and stronger regulation of currency. This Van Buren accepted, partly to appease John C. Calhoun, who had become more amenable to the Democratic Party after the nullification issue.[48] However, Van Buren also understood the threats to government security. Things had gotten particularly bad over the summer, especially when New York banks refused to make specie payments. Van Buren, Poinsett, and other cabinet members and lawmakers were daily inundated with plans for repairing the economy. John H. Sargent of South Carolina, for example, sent a detailed plan for a bankruptcy law and a print mint.[49] Sargent believed both Jackson's policies and elite bankers had done him wrong. His appeals to injustice made little impact on Poinsett, and although his pamphlet got a showing in Congress on September 15, it went nowhere.

There were three major plans that seemed politically viable: revival of a national bank, continuance of the deposit system, and an independent treasury system.[50] Poinsett favored the latter. In July, he gave an interview explaining the need to separate the federal government from the state banks.[51] Poinsett knew better than anyone that the government needed to protect its reserves. An increase in military expenditures and Indian annuities were imminent. His solutions emphasized security, efficiency, and control and privileged federal stability and solvency over individual issues of equality.

Poinsett developed his ideas in conversation with others who were not necessarily associated with the military, such as New York merchant and congressman Churchill Cambreleng. Cambreleng had written to Poinsett over the summer, advocating that the government prioritize expenditures and American Indian treaties over the provisions of the 1836 Deposit Act, which required the federal government to deposit surplus revenue in state banks. The government had no surplus, given the economic crisis, but its revenue should be invested to promote national security and government credibility.[52] Cambreleng's recommendation, much more than Sargent's, accorded with Poinsett's worldview, in which sound political economy thrived on the solvency of a strong nation-state.[53]

Although Poinsett and Van Buren had diverged on the Specie Circular, Poinsett's advice on the federal regulation of the banking system appeared in Van Buren's special message to Congress in September.[54] The plan laid out in Van Buren's speech was supposed to transcend partisanship—indeed, the point of the Independent Treasury was to remove it from politics—but it ended up alienating many within their own party, particularly those who favored state banks. These included Poinsett's fellow South Carolina unionist Hugh Legare. During the week that the House took up the issue of the Treasury Bill, Legare determined to reach his own personal conclusion about the bill. On October 11, Legare asked to meet with Poinsett. He had a bad cold, he wrote in his note, but he planned to arrive at Congress at ten o'clock and wanted to see Poinsett in the hour before. Poinsett was apparently unable to sell the virtues of his plan. He scribbled a message to himself on the note Legare sent him: he

Figure 1 Henry R. Robinson, "Sub-Treasury System, or Office Holders Elysium"
(New York: H. R. Robinson, 1838).

had tried his best to convince Legare that the Treasury and currency were
not party issues but had lost Legare in the end.[55]

The Independent Treasury faced stiff opposition. One popular political cartoon criticized the plan, including Poinsett's role in it (see fig. 1).
In its depiction of a box labeled "Sub-Treasury" dropping bags of specie
on officeholders while common people are left with paper money, Van
Buren is handing money to Poinsett with a speech bubble saying, "With
the purse, and the sword of the nation firmly clutched in my hands we
can make the people submit!" Poinsett responds, "We must pass a bank-
rupt law against all State Banks, or else 'Cobblers and Tinkers' will get
credit, for we will have the Sub-Treasury in spite of the lamentations of
the people!"[56] Despite Poinsett's experience with public disparagement
of his actions in Mexico, he was sensitive to these attacks on his role in
Van Buren's administration. One criticism of the Treasury Bill was that
it would create unfair patronage, and Poinsett misinterpreted a letter he
received from E. B. Robinson, believing it implied that he was one of the
members of the administration who "try to control the government with

appointments." He confessed his "wounded feelings" to Gordon Moore, who solicited an apology from Robinson.[57]

While the public critiqued the Independent Treasury Bill and lawmakers battled over it in Congress, Poinsett continued the fight in Florida. He started by dooming to failure the Cherokee peace delegation in Florida. He and Van Buren met with John Ross in October to script a "talk" for Cherokee delegates to read to the Seminoles regarding peace negotiations. Poinsett gave military officers explicit instructions to "suppress Ross's talk" if it veered at all from the planned message.[58] Then, when Jesup's men captured a group of Seminoles under a flag of truce and refused to release them, Poinsett declined to issue a report on Jesup's behavior. Historians of the Seminole War do not fully know what happened regarding the deterioration of the peace negotiations, but it seems clear that Poinsett helped orchestrate their failure.[59]

For one, he employed former navy register John H. Sherburne, whose descriptions of cruelty manage to stand out among the dehumanizing letters regarding American Indian removal. Sherburne believed his job as Cherokee agent was to make removal "roll on unimpeded like an avalanche" over all remaining Natives.[60] This language may have been the norm for agents of removal, but that does not excuse how, during negotiations with the Seminole chiefs, Sherburne answered Osceola's question about what a match was by tapping it to the chief's leggings over and over—fifty times—because it garnered a few laughs from white Americans.[61] During negotiations in the fall of 1837, he misled the Cherokee delegates, lying about their compensation and the government's intentions.[62] Indian agents are often blamed for the corruption, mismanagement, and cruelty that characterized removal, but Poinsett was the one appointing people and calling the shots, and, as one army officer noted, "Poinsett goes for extermination."[63]

In the month leading up to the delegation, he sent out urgent calls for more troops. An upside of the economic recession was that it made recruiting easier.[64] Poinsett instructed governors that militia must arrive in Florida by November 15, shortly before the Cherokee delegation would begin talks with the Seminoles. Otherwise, they need not bother sending men.[65] The response was impressive; the army had so many troops it had to turn some away for fear of lack of supplies. The enlarged military presence emboldened Jesup to capture Seminole leaders Osceola and Micanopy, whom he claimed had violated their parole.[66] Reconciliation fell apart.

Poinsett used the failure of negotiations to justify increasing the army, especially as the concentration of troops in Florida left other frontiers unprotected. When Alabama slave owner William Smith requested that the War Department station permanent forces along the state's frontier, Poinsett had to tell him that was not possible at the present moment, even though he felt "particularly anxious for its safety."[67] Poinsett was, however, in the process of convincing Congress that they needed to expand the armed forces, especially in slaveholding states. He took seriously his duties to offer federal protection for the institution of slavery and the general prosperity of the enslaving class.

This request for troops appeared in his annual message to Congress. Like all such addresses, it included detailed reports from various bureau chiefs and army officers, but whereas his predecessor's first address stated that the army was adequate, Poinsett urged an increase in troop size.[68] Poinsett used the opportunity to make his case for military expansion and exploration for a national audience. He framed his argument around the need for both economic efficiency and force. He argued, for example, that it was more economical to increase regular troops than to rely on militia. There was an equilibrium between states and the federal government, he said, but the scales should tip toward the federal government. Poinsett addressed the need for ample arms supplies and proposed that in addition to production at the federal armories, the system of small flexible contracts with private arms makers, who have "no other market than that afforded by government demand," was best. He also opposed the trading companies in Indian Territory, whose interests he was "sorry to say" were "not identical with those of the government," and he wanted Indian trusts deposited in what he hoped would be the Independent Treasury.[69]

Of paramount importance was shoring up engineering capability. So much of the continent was unknown and unprotected. He advocated a major increase in the engineering corps, partly because he believed in science and discovery but also because he understood the challenges ignorance and underdevelopment posed to US power.[70] He took seriously the calls from government officials, military officers, and civilians to improve infrastructure, especially in vulnerable military areas.[71]

One year later, Poinsett would be able to announce that Congress had expanded the engineering corps and increased the size of the army.[72] In the meantime, it was up to him to make the most of military infrastructure, even as Congress insisted that peaceful measures be taken. When a group of Canadian militiamen and American rebels attacked an American steamship at a port on the Niagara River soon after his December address, Poinsett received further justification. Not a single coastal fortification was in defensible condition along the Canadian border.[73] Lives and livelihoods were at stake, and Poinsett had to commit fully to waging war against Indians, the economy, and nature—to maintaining "the authority of the government."[74]

Execution

After a very brief Christmas holiday, Poinsett was back at work. The attack on the *Caroline* appeared in print the day after New Year's. The whole northern frontier "was in commotion." The next day, Colonel William Jenkins Worth sent him a letter because, he wrote, "newspapers often fall short of fact." Worth wanted to give Poinsett the military perspective. Worth suggested that "a ranking officer will offer a soothing influence in that quarter in maintaining the authority of the government and the supremacy of the laws."[75]

Meanwhile, US diplomat Richard Rush had been keeping up on Poinsett's military reports while he was in London. Rush had recently secured the "Smithson bequest"—$500,000 left to the US government by British scientist James Smithson. Both Rush and Poinsett would later use this fund to help found the Smithsonian Institution (which would showcase the results of the exploring expeditions Poinsett endorsed), but for now, Rush was fixated on US security, even though he was worlds away from the realities of the frontier. He was shocked by some of the statistics Poinsett cited, especially the estimate that there were forty-five thousand Indian "warriors" ready to prevent US expansion. The other issue that worried him was the Canadian frontier. He had no official information, but he had heard "out of doors" that England was increasing her army to twenty thousand men. He hoped Congress had the good sense to heed Poinsett's call for fifteen thousand more troops. England, unlike the United States, had mastered the art of military investment.[76] Poinsett expressed Rush's intelligence in a letter to Van Buren on June 19.[77]

As the economic crisis became less acute, Poinsett could more easily legitimate an increase in military expenditure, but by no means was this easy. Another of his Philadelphia correspondents urged more moderation than Rush. Manufacturer and philanthropist James Ronaldson cautioned him against escalating the conflict on the Canadian border: "Never was thinking more necessary because our money resources are . . . now pretty much 'used up.'"[78] This was just the beginning of the resistance Poinsett would face. The first major hurdle to his proposed military increase was Congress. Both Ronaldson and Congress would come around on military

buildup, but at first, congressmen were none too pleased with the confus-
ing and contradictory financial statements they received from the War
Department. Why would they spend more money on an establishment
whose expenditures were in disarray? As letters poured into the office requesting appointments to various bureaus of the military, Poinsett could
only tell them that he was unable to offer an opinion on what Congress
would decide regarding the proposed increase.[79] He sent his own harried
letters to the chairman of the Committee on Military Affairs, blaming the
recent Canadian frontier disruption on the inefficiencies and size of the
army.[80] Poinsett's friend Churchill Cambreleng, as chairman of the Ways
and Means Committee, successfully pushed Poinsett's increase through
Congress. It became law in July.[81]

In the meantime, Poinsett decided to take full advantage of the newly
independent Topographical Corps of Engineers, whose work he hoped
would fulfill the economic promises of Indian extermination. Despite
long-standing resistance to military expenditures, there was a general
enthusiasm for, and romanticization of, exploratory expeditions, and
the corps became a focus for national patriotism.[82] And although topographical surveys and infrastructure served military purposes, they were
more expressly linked to civilian economic well-being than were military
campaigns. Poinsett himself had both a philosophical and pragmatic view
of exploration. He had long been an advocate of scientific discovery and
enjoyed learning about and disseminating geographical, botanical, and
mineralogical findings. However, he also got his start doing covert reconnaissance for the Department of State, whose aims certainly extended
beyond knowledge for its own sake, and his interest in Mexico's mineral
resources expressed itself in financial investment. Knowledge made possible US military security and economic conquest.

While Poinsett waited to hear the fate of military size, the reconnaissance of Cherokee Country was wrapping up.[83] Although Americans had
been mining gold there for about a decade, the US military intervened to
render the land more usable to its future inhabitants. One of the engineers
was John C. Fremont, a young explorer whom Poinsett had met when
Fremont was attending Charleston College and who had recently been
appointed as second lieutenant in the Topographical Corps. As Poinsett
issued military orders to remove Cherokee from the freshly surveyed
land—escalating his predecessor's policy of expulsion—he selected Fremont for a new mission to explore the territory between the Missouri
and Mississippi Rivers.[84] This was part of a broader initiative to update
maps of the Louisiana Purchase and assemble the information needed

to establish a chain of military forts across the continent. He sent Colonel Stephen Kearny on an expedition to locate a site for a new fort on the Missouri River.[85] Poinsett envisioned a "wooden curtain" of military forts that would separate Native peoples and American citizens. All of these initiatives reflected Poinsett's agenda of military pragmatism and informed opportunism.

They also overwhelmed him. In late March, Poinsett went home for over a month, "indisposed." Perhaps the DC climate he had worried about made him ill; certainly, though, the stress of juggling all these issues and interests at once was not good for his health. Poinsett was used to making things happen behind the scenes, used to covert government initiatives and controversy, but this was his first time doing so for a national constituency, when public funds and individuals' lives were at stake. Cherokee removal was especially troublesome because members of the Cherokee Nation continued to protest the treaty, even after he informed them that "the unreasonable pretentions put forth in your communications . . . have destroyed these hopes, and all that now remains for me to say in reply to your letter is that it is expected the Cherokee Indians will remove from the States at the period fixed by the Treaty of December, 1835."[86] He had to make it appear that he was upholding the treaty stipulations, even as he prepared to militarize the process.[87] (Army officers knew as soon as Poinsett took office that "Poinsett goes for extermination."[88]) Accomplishing his goals while protecting appearances meant simultaneously denouncing Georgia citizens and militia who disturbed "peaceful" removal and assembling the federal military capacity to compel Cherokee to leave their homes.[89] Like Georgia officials, Poinsett wanted removal to be unconditional, yet he wanted these unconditional terms based on federal, rather than state, mandates.

Being at home gave Poinsett a respite from the pressures of balancing federal and state sovereignty with his own aims on a public stage. Yet even as his chief clerk Samuel Cooper took care of day-to-day business and issued orders on his behalf, Poinsett continued to execute his agenda related to settler security and opportunity along the frontier.[90] The few official letters Poinsett sent while "indisposed" reflected the tensions and overlap between federal and state, covert and official action. When John Ross and other Cherokee delegates sought more amenable treaty terms, Poinsett handled the issue himself to ensure that the official response contained equal parts humanity and coercion. He made it clear that the Cherokee had no choice but to comply with removal, but his lengthy letter upheld government pretensions to protecting Cherokee rights. It feigned concern for Cherokee desires to remain in their homes and shifted the blame to the inexpediency of modifying the treaty terms without the consent of the states that would be affected.[91]

Several days later, he wrote to Winfield Scott to carry out removal in accordance to their "comfort" but also to "protect the interests of the United States, and prevent unnecessary delay."[92] Scott arrived on May 8 with the authority to expedite and brutalize removal, and several weeks later, Georgia troops organized under Scott to begin the process.[93] Poinsett offloaded much of the responsibility and decision-making to his officers. He gave Scott, for example, the power, once he was "possessed of the views of the government," to make "whatever arrangements you may deem it expedient to make with them."[94] He did, however, continue to manage things. In the summer of 1839, a fourteen-year-old boy forwarded Poinsett a letter that had been addressed to his father (the boy's father was away), confirming the murders of two prominent members of the Cherokee Treaty Party, who were viewed as allies of the US government. The boy wanted to make sure that justice was done. Poinsett immediately instructed his officers in Cherokee Country to find and arrest the alleged murderers.[95]

Once Cherokee removal was officially underway, Poinsett could devote time to his other wars. He was away from Washington off and on until the fall, including a trip to Sulphur Springs in Virginia, but he was around to see the passage of his bill in early July.[96] "An Act to Increase the Present Military Establishment of the United States and for Other Purposes" was his first major victory. The act expanded most branches of the service, including Poinsett's celebrated engineers, and increased term lengths. The act also added a professor of mineralogy and geology to West Point, a recognition of the importance of training officers in the science of making US territory more productive and secure. It gave legal legitimacy to Poinsett's agenda.

The immediate impact of the act was an escalation of war in Florida. With legislation in place to expand the nation's armed forces, Poinsett could more effectively respond to the concerns of white Americans in Florida, who urged more government intervention in the territory. Following the passage of the act, he received a private letter from a planter in Florida that pressed the urgency of Poinsett's agenda of submission and opportunity. Fear and uncertainty were destroying Florida's economic potential. Summer was deadly in Florida, and the summer of 1838 left many settlers dead and their homes abandoned. The worst part was the loss of fertile, productive land. The writer claimed that if the Indians "were totally pacified, it would induce a number of wealthy settlers now waiting to enter the country."[97] This was the point of settler colonialism, and Poinsett began to more seriously strategize over how and where to use the nation's financial and military resources to bolster settler security throughout the continent. This strategy was both racialized and economically rationalized. The protection of potential settler profits against Seminoles required a tremendous amount of resources, and Poinsett had to look for efficiencies to make this massive expenditure possible. Doing so meant first deciding not to send troops to Texas and Mexico. It also meant avoiding war with Great Britain on the northern frontier.

This reordering of priorities and legislative authority to expand the military coincided with a shift in his outlook on power. That summer Poinsett had a conversation with Francis Lieber, the well-known German American political philosopher who taught at Charleston College and would later compose the humanitarian code that President Lincoln issued during the Civil War. They talked both philosophically and practically about the treatment of expatriates during wartime. Poinsett was emphatically in favor of hanging any American who served in foreign navies. Lieber disagreed on humanitarian grounds. He asked Poinsett if his views might not be hypocritical, citing earlier American grievances against Great Britain for similar treatment. Poinsett argued that these earlier grievances had emerged from a position of weakness that no longer applied. When Lieber and Poinsett discussed the potential for war between the United States and Mexico in 1838, Poinsett emphasized that any American expatriates aiding Mexico should be executed; it was commensurate, he argued, with American strength and the importance of military order. Poinsett's comments reveal the predominance of military authority and violence in his vision for American development.[98]

This outlook existed alongside persistent insecurity, regarding not only the Seminoles but also Great Britain. However much Poinsett might have boasted about American strength, his officers still referred to Britain as the superior military force, especially when allied with Native groups. The solution to this insecurity, and a way to conserve financial resources, was to deploy enough military force to maintain order, while avoiding war. After a year spent monitoring "rebel" activity along the border with Upper Canada and seizing their arms, Colonel William Jenkins Worth reported that there was quiet along the Canadian frontier.[99] When hostilities broke out again in December, Poinsett publicly denounced the "reprehensible" actions of American participants and regretted that the army had to "coerce" American sympathizers of the Canadian patriots into submission.[100] Both Poinsett and the military officers despised the patriots. Also, neither he nor his officers had a desire for war against England, whose trade was important for the national economy.[101] The conflict mostly fizzled out in December, but not without provoking controversy over the reaches of federal authority.[102]

This border crisis bled into the next, renewing insecurities about Great Britain as well as tensions between state and federal authority. In 1838, the State of Maine wanted Congress to fund a survey of land it disputed with Great Britain. When the federal government declined to comply, the Maine legislature deployed local militia to secure the territory. Although there was enough national insecurity about Great Britain that Congress authorized the president to deploy force should tensions escalate, Poinsett did not necessarily want to use it. He criticized Maine's governor for calling out the militia and hosted a meeting of some of his officers several days later to decide what to do.[103] Although Poinsett stayed largely behind the scenes in these border crises, he made key decisions about whose advice to take. General Nathaniel Towson, for example, drew up a lengthy plan that advocated that the United States prepare for full-on war with Great Britain. Poinsett chose a different route. He dispatched General Scott to Maine in March 1839. He and Scott had no tolerance for American citizens who jeopardized the United States' trade or international reputation. They conflated Maine aggressors with the Canadian sympathizers of the previous border conflict, whose "lust of conquest and aggrandizement" would result in the "loss of the good will" of European nations.[104]

Once again, Poinsett privileged order and federal authority over states' rights or party politics. He also privileged secrecy. He authorized Scott to infiltrate the Maine legislature to convince lawmakers to recall the militia and submit to federal directives. Legislators split along party lines, with Whigs refusing to heed the Van Buren administration's wishes. Scott himself was a Whig but struggled with credibility because of his association with the administration.[105] During the debates, Scott sent Poinsett private letters around the clock—several times begging the postmaster to hold the mail for him—as he convinced state politicians to submit to federal authority.[106] Scott also sent Poinsett updates on his secret negotiations with Sir John Harvey, the British governor of Brunswick. Scott assured Harvey that the War Department was unlikely to follow through on Congress's act to raise a regiment of fifty thousand volunteers for Maine. Peace was more important, especially for "the interests of the mighty Saxon race."[107] Poinsett's agenda fared well in Scott's hands. After Scott succeeded in working with the Maine legislature and the British colonial government, Poinsett directed that the money Congress appropriated for the conflict be spent on "procuring information confidentially." Poinsett chose order over war. He authorized Scott to distribute funds to his subordinate commandants, who would hire covert agents as they saw fit and instruct them to inform local British commanders of any rebellious behavior.[108] Congress had been in the dark for over a year when they asked if and how the War Department had taken any measures in response to the March 1839 act.[109] Poinsett responded that no force had been necessary and dallied in releasing copies of Scott's secret negotiations with Harvey and the governor of Maine.[110]

The Maine crisis would ultimately be solved by diplomatic means several years later, but these two border experiences, in conjunction with the war in Florida, highlighted for Poinsett the importance of a more efficient system for waging war and securing the frontier. He had stayed behind the scenes in these conflicts but would become a much more visible military man during his last year in office.

Assessment

After the Maine crisis, Poinsett determined to remain in control. He joined a temperance society (despite his appreciation for fine wine) and issued an order that prohibited drinking in the army. The regulation extended to visitors of West Point, so that lodgers at the academy's hotel would no longer be treated to "dissipation."[111] Perhaps he thought the enforcement of asceticism would give more credibility to his claims that the militia—an unruly mass compared to the regular army—needed reform.

Congress asked Poinsett to present a plan for the reorganization of the militia on March 9, 1840. Civilians, soldiers, and lawmakers had long debated the proper relationship between the citizen soldier and national security. The militia was a source of both patriotic pride and military embarrassment. Poinsett believed that the regular army was more efficient than the militia, but with the increased security demand precipitated by the border crises, many officers began advocating for a larger, more competent militia on the borders. They also suggested that some of the regular troops in Florida be made available in case war with Britain broke out.[112] The logic was that Indian wars could be fought by the militia, while regular troops were needed against Britain. Poinsett disagreed.[113] He was paying close attention to Algiers, which France had been attempting to conquer with its professional army. (Poinsett would remain haunted by

Figure 2 Napoleon Sarony, "The New Era, or The Effects of a Standing Army"
(Washington, DC: H. R. Robinson, 1840).

France's inability to conquer the North African nation, and it would influence his opposition to the Mexican-American War). He sent several
Americans to France and Algiers to study the French military tactics used
against guerrilla warfare. Phillip Kearney produced a report that would
be distributed to the War Department in 1841.[114]

In the meantime, Poinsett generated his own solution for the nation's
militia woes. The plan called for a militia of two hundred thousand men—
half reserve, half a standing army—who were white, able bodied, and
between the ages of twenty and forty-five; they would receive military
training and serve for four years. His plan touched off a political mael-
strom (see fig. 2). Lawmakers and party leaders cried unconstitutional-
ity.[115] Newspaper editors lashed out at competitors for refusing to print it
or for printing only snippets.[116] Van Buren's opponents charged him with

complicity in the plan. Poinsett's plan went beyond what anyone in the administration was prepared to deal with.[117]

This public outrage was compounded by controversy over the "Bloodhound War." Around the time Poinsett was working out his plan for the militia, the public had become aware of the use of bloodhounds in Florida to locate Seminoles for execution. This was a strategy endorsed by Poinsett as an efficient way to end the war. By December 1838, Florida was effectively a military occupation zone, but even with increased personnel, the US military still could not defeat the Seminoles. Congress wanted a peaceful termination of the war. So did some of his officers. Poinsett, however, believed peace was futile.[118] He first advocated occupation by armed settlers but became increasingly convinced of the benefits of bloodhounds.[119] Poinsett received a letter from General Taylor advocating the use of bloodhounds in the summer of 1838, while he was away at Sulphur Springs in Virginia. Newspaper writers poked fun at Poinsett for being on vacation with Van Buren, but Poinsett's acquiescence to Taylor's request would have more significant consequences for his reputation.[120] Poinsett later claimed that the department knew little about bloodhound purchases in Florida, but it's important to note that Poinsett had told Taylor that it made sense to purchase them.[121] He in fact chose bloodhounds over the relatively new ballooning technology, which was expensive but would allow for "intelligence" gathering and scouting in Florida with less bloodshed.[122] Poinsett also helped appoint Robert R. Reid, a supporter of bloodhound warfare, as territorial governor of Florida.[123] Reid's successor, Richard K. Call, had contracted with an agent to transport several dozen dogs from Cuba for about $150 each.[124] During Reid's tenure, the US military attempted to train these dogs to locate Seminoles by scent. Bloodhounds had previously been trained to chase freedom-seeking slaves in Cuba and other parts of the Spanish Empire, which reflected the assumption that smells were somehow determined by "race."[125] Abolitionists would later accuse Jesup of intending to use bloodhounds to track down "all the negroes who belong to the white people."[126] Bloodhounds were increasingly used throughout the South in the 1840s and 1850s.[127]

As rumors about these bloodhounds trickled out of Florida, the public forced Poinsett to account for his role. Some charged that the thirty imported dogs were not enough to do anything, but arguments that the use of these dogs was inhumane were more common, especially among humanitarian activists who opposed slavery.[128] Opponents of the system demanded that Congress get answers from Poinsett. The petitioners wanted to know for what exactly the dogs were being used and at what cost. Poinsett deliberated over one memorial from Philadelphia, "remonstrating against the employment of Blood Hounds in the Florida war," which the Senate passed on to him in February 1840. The authors wanted to be "able authoritatively to contradict the idea that the administration are in any way connected with this matter."[129] A year earlier, Poinsett had told Taylor, "I have always been of opinion that dogs ought to be employed in this warfare, to protect the army from surprises and ambuscades," informing him that he was "therefore authorized to procure such number of dogs as he may judge necessary."[130] Poinsett wrote to the memorialists, however, that the dogs were "imported into Florida by the civil authorities of that territory, without any concert with the administration and without the knowledge of the Department of War." As Poinsett drafted his official response, he made notes that reflected his determination to remain an invisible agent. He changed I to Department.[131]

Poinsett's obsession with his appearance and reputation had intensified, especially after he was satirized in political cartoons.[132] Henry R. Robinson, the same cartoonist who had lampooned the Independent Treasury plan, printed "The Secretary of War Presenting a Stand of Colours to the 1st Regiment of Republican Bloodhounds," a moral condemnation of the administration's use of bloodhounds (see fig. 3). In the lithograph, Poinsett bears responsibility for the decision to employ Cuban dogs in the war, holding an American flag that depicts a Native head in the mouth of a dog as he looms over the bloodhound soldiers and Jacksonian editor Francis Blair.[133]

The cartoon was printed in an election year that proved to be a referendum on Van Buren's most unpopular policies. Poinsett had to explain both his management of the "Bloodhound War" and his militia plan. In the case of the bloodhounds, he argued that "inhuman murders lately perpetrated upon helpless women and children . . . render it expedient" and that employing bloodhounds earlier in the war could have prevented massacres.[134] The financial accounting relating to the dogs was hazy, and the military aimed to keep it opaque, but Poinsett claimed this was an economical use of military funds.[135] Likewise, his defense of the militia plan emphasized security and efficiency. He said he did not want to witness what could happen when untrained militia were brought into combat with regular troops. Men fought better when they had common training, and the federal government was best equipped to provide this. The current state system cost the American people upwards of $2 million, with little to show for it, while his national training plan, according to him, would cost no more than $1,362,093 and probably less than

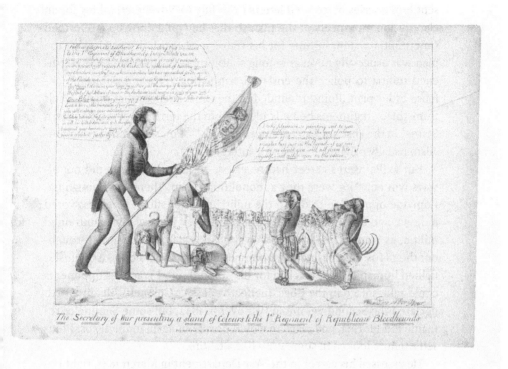

Figure 3 Henry R. Robinson, "The Secretary of War Presenting a
Stand of Colours to the 1st Regiment of Republican Bloodhounds"
(Washington, DC: H. R. Robinson, 1840).

$500,000.[136] Additionally, the sparse troop coverage along the frontier
jeopardized opportunities for expansion. An expanded active and reserve
force organized by large districts rather than states would solve this problem. Poinsett acknowledged that many Americans preferred to leave the
militia solely in the hands of the states and assured them of his respect for
constitutionality but emphasized that the current system was too decen-
tralized and unprofessional to provide effective security for impending
military needs.

Despite the congressional uproar and media ridicule Poinsett's plan
sparked, it was not without supporters. Defenders appealed to historical
precedent, referencing George Washington and citing prior plans to reform the militia.[137] Political supporters from all over the country wrote to
him asking for copies of the plan. He received enthusiastic endorsement
from several state governments. The Illinois quartermaster, for example,

sent him a series of frenzied letters from July to November, asking for an elaboration on aspects of the plan so that he could draw up a reformed state militia system in time for his state's next legislative session.[138] The plan was especially popular among southerners, who wanted a strengthened militia to police the enslaved population.[139] In the published defense of his plan, Poinsett alluded to the consequences that might result from "black regiments being landed within the territory of the Southern States" in the absence of a revamped militia.[140] Poinsett's military nationalism usually privileged enslavers' interests.

But as Poinsett's career had revealed, enslavers' interests did not always win out. Nor were they a monolithic group. There was enough nationwide opposition to doom the militia plan to failure. Congress voted it down, and the United States would carry on with a relatively untrained militia, as many states loosened or abolished state militia laws throughout the 1840s. Likewise, the bloodhound strategy was a bust. As Poinsett fielded humanitarian criticism for his "Bloodhound War," his opponents could take solace in the dogs' ineffectiveness.[141] Colonel William Worth declared the Second Seminole War over in 1842, but some Seminoles remained in Florida, and warfare would break out again in the 1850s. Poinsett's tenure looked in some ways like a failure.

He assessed his career in the War Department in March 1841, right before Van Buren left office. Overall, Poinsett was satisfied with his time in office. The first achievement he cited was a delusional one: "More than 40,000 Indians have been removed peacefully, and . . . are generally contented and are gradually advancing in the peaceful arts of life." He also noted that expenditures, notwithstanding Florida, had been reduced, while the military had been increased. Artillery was on good footing, the economy was improving, and things generally were looking up.[142] White plantation settlement in Florida seemed more secure, and Poinsett's contributions to artillery would later be credited for US victory in Mexico.[143] The Independent Treasury Bill eventually passed in 1840, was repealed, and then became a reality from 1846 to 1913.

Of particular note for Poinsett was the fact that "the Corps of Topographical Engineers is organized and employed so as to produce the most useful and beneficial results to the country."[144] This lined up with his next pursuit, to which he had already turned. Several months before Poinsett resigned as secretary of war, US diplomat Virgil Maxcy forwarded him a geological map of England and Wales, reflecting the latest in trigonometry and geology and completed under the order of the British government.[145] Maxcy wanted the map presented to the new National Institute for the Promotion of Science, of which Poinsett had recently been elected director. The larger goal was to turn the institute into something bigger: a great centralized repository for all the specimens, surveys, maps, and discoveries of the United States.[146] Right as Poinsett sent his resignation letter to Van Buren as secretary of war, he issued his last military order, a regulation for the Corps of Engineers to deposit all of their maps with the department.[147] The new institute, the Smithsonian, would house the tangible results of the engineers' efforts, as well as those of the exploring expeditions that Poinsett had recently seen off.

This new project would involve a battle with Congress, but Poinsett had grown accustomed to fighting. There were military supplies and objects from army reconnaissance in boxes in a Philadelphia museum storeroom waiting to be displayed. He would make sure national power received its showcase.

7

Final Battles, 1841–1851

On a winter evening in 1841, Henry Trescot read Poinsett's recent address on the National Institute for the Promotion of Science to his family by the fireside. Trescot was happy that it entertained and instructed his children. He was happier still that the "late political revolution" would likely return Poinsett to the "sunny fields of Carolina."[1]

The election of 1840 was a referendum on Van Buren's administration, and the results were resounding: William Henry Harrison won 234 of the electoral votes. During the inauguration, Poinsett took refuge with Van Buren and John Forsyth at Barnum's Hotel in Baltimore.[2] Despite Van Buren's decisive defeat, political supporters stopped by the hotel to see the former administration and to praise Van Buren as an "incorruptible patriot." This was comforting to Van Buren, who probably harbored desires to run again. It mattered less to Poinsett, whose public ambitions had mostly been sated after he served as a cabinet secretary and oversaw US military affairs. Poinsett claimed he wanted to avoid politics after the grueling election; he would, however, spend his last decade doing as he had always done, fighting political battles behind the scenes.

Poinsett's first battle was one that he started fighting while he was secretary of war. Just as he was leaving office, boxes were arriving from Rio by way of Philadelphia, with objects from the Exploring Expedition, a survey of the Pacific begun almost three years earlier. At the beginning of January, Poinsett had given an evening address at the Baptist Church on Tenth Street in Washington, advocating for the display of these objects and, more broadly, for the display of American greatness.[3] Trescot read a published version of this speech to his family. Americans, Poinsett argued, needed an institution to display and gather more knowledge.

He was serving as the first president of the National Institution for the Promotion of Science, which had been founded the previous year to stimulate the diffusion of knowledge by fostering ties between the federal government and the scientific community. It was a showcase of extractive imperialism, housing the spoils of Indian removal, such as tools and headdresses, as well as the mineral specimens of government geologist David Dale Owens's tour of Illinois and Wisconsin.[4] Poinsett had bigger ambitions for the institution and its showcase.

The US government had in its possession a pot of money that Poinsett wanted to use for a national museum and research establishment that would rival European institutions. Congress had recently received a $500,000 gift from British scientist James Smithson. Smithson's will stipulated that if his nephew died without heirs, his wealth should go to the United States to establish an institution for the "increase and diffusion of knowledge." When Smithson's nephew died in 1835, congressmen had to decide how exactly to spend the bequest. The debates would last a decade. Congressional indecision infuriated Poinsett and other proponents of a national scientific institution, especially when the money arrived in 1838—the same summer the Exploring Expedition went out—and the government had no plans for what to do with the anticipated spoils of the voyage.

Now, as he was leaving the War Department, he was concerned with the boxes that had been shipped to Philadelphia from Rio. How could the United States have a grand Exploring Expedition and nowhere to display the results? How could the government ignore the knowledge gained from the expedition and neglect to open new economic opportunities for its citizens? The project of establishing a national museum and research institute and using science for economic advancement would occupy much of Poinsett's retirement.[5]

As he retreated to his estates in the "sunny fields of Carolina," Poinsett's lifelong interests in natural philosophy intersected not only with his agenda of securing and consolidating American empire but also with his new goal of mastering his own plantation. He devoted more time to agricultural experimentation and investigation and became less militaristic, even as the nation geared up for war against Mexico. He was no less interventionist, however. As president of a prominent national institution, and as a perceived authority on Mexico, he still had a national platform, which he used to promote state-sponsored science, as well as restrained expansion and militarism in Mexican and Spanish territory. Poinsett's caution over Mexico reflected the experience and wariness of his age.

While Poinsett had gotten less militaristic, a large segment of the population had grown more so.

In many ways, the final decade of his life was a departure from the rest of his career, as he stayed local and stopped longing for war. However, he continued to manage events with both public messages and private correspondence. He also remained committed to federal strength, so much so that he challenged the dominant slaveholder position on secession.[6] His positions on secession, as well as slavery, expansion, and national science, often seemed contradictory but were in fact rational and related. As Poinsett's views ranged from conventional to unpopular, they were all linked by his self-interested belief in what was best for the country. By the 1840s, the inconsistent pairing of liberalism and exploitation defined US policy as much as it did Poinsett.

Poinsett took charge of the Exploring Expedition in early 1838, when he was secretary of war. As a maritime expedition, it technically fell under the purview of the Navy Department, but Van Buren requested that Poinsett, an able administrator, assist the less competent secretary of navy Mahlon Dickerson. This gave Poinsett the chance to consolidate his agenda for martial exploration. He envisioned the Pacific expedition as an integral component of his continental initiatives: Indian removal, mining ventures, ordnance tests, and Joseph Nicollett and John C. Fremont's western expeditions, as well as his lifelong collection of native plants and specimens. Nature, science, and the military built the nation's political economy. In one of his last acts before leaving office, Poinsett convinced Mahlon's successor James Kirke Paulding to have the collections of the Exploring Expedition sent to Washington.[7] There were currently some items stored in the basement of the Patent Office, where dampness and staff negligence threatened their survival.[8] All of what should have been signs of American greatness lacked a proper display.

These items would find a temporary home at the National Institution, which Poinsett helped found. Less than a year before leaving the War Department, Poinsett hosted a bipartisan gathering of seventeen men— including Whig congressman from Massachusetts John Quincy Adams and Democrat senator from Missouri Thomas Hart Benton, as well as John J. Abert from the Corps of Topographical Engineers and Dr. Henry King from the Ordnance Bureau—to discuss establishing a cabinet of natural history. At that time, natural history implied a broad study and collection of earthly occurrences and objects, including plants, minerals, and animals.[9] These men exceeded their goal by founding the National Institute for the Promotion of Science. The group appointed Poinsett as president and, in accordance with his wishes, created a board of "Counsellors" that included military men. Poinsett consulted army officers from all over the country for information collection.[10] He also made plans to secure a federal charter, which the institution received in 1842 (when it transitioned from institution to institute). Poinsett's ultimate goal was to inspire Congress to endow the institution with the Smithson bequest.[11] This linkage would help fulfill Poinsett's economic and military goals for the nation.

Poinsett's first annual address linked the institution's promotion of the arts and sciences to these goals. He connected several dozen practical and theoretical disciplines explicitly to the economy and said that the government must support them. The related fields of geology and mineralogy, for example, he said, "contribute many necessary and useful materials," yet too few Americans were trained as mineralogists, and therefore, "we pass unnoticed these [mineral] sources of individual and national wealth."[12] He wanted an "extensive cabinet, at the seat of Government . . . to present, at one view, all the mineral resources of each particular State . . . and a school of mining that cannot fail to be extensively useful, and lead to the early and full development of this great source of individual prosperity and wealth." Botany, too, was "desirable to every one."[13] Poinsett long had been fascinated by plants and had seen the popularity of the poinsettia grow; he also, for example, donated wood from Shakespeare's mulberry tree to the National Institute as an English souvenir for public display.[14]

Beyond these various specimens' status as objects of curiosity and decoration, however, were useful applications. Poinsett said that "a collection of models and paintings at Washington . . . would aid the cultivation of the art of design, which . . . multiplies the resources and enjoyments of the professional man, and is an essential accomplishment to the architect, the machinist, the artisan, and the mechanic." Here, he articulated the importance of science for capitalism, stating that "natural history is the basis of domestic and public economy" and that "it is to the study of natural history that civilized man is indebted for the use and enjoyment of the best races of domestic animals, food, and . . . the metals which multiply his force and contribute to his defence, and for most of the luxuries and enjoyments of his existence."[15] If European governments sponsored such establishments, he said, so too should the United States. National prosperity and international reputation depended on it.

When bad weather delayed Poinsett's departure from Washington that spring (after he had already sold the furniture from his H Street residence at public auction, including "handsome rosewood lounges" and two dozen parlor chairs with light haircloth seats), he used the opportunity to strategize with the old rival of his party John Quincy Adams about how to link the Smithson bequest to the institute.[16] Poinsett's party still controlled Congress, but the majority of Democrats opposed close ties between science and the federal government. Adams, a Whig, was serving as chair of the special House committee on Smithson's endowment and, like Poinsett, had long had overlapping interests in economic development and scientific progress.[17] They were both pragmatic nationalists.

Adams and Poinsett agreed about funding projects with the bequest's annual interest, without spending down the principal.[18] Adams wanted the first use of the interest payments to be for an astronomical observatory; he had begun promoting an observatory when he was president and spoke publicly about the virtues of astronomy. Poinsett also understood the applicability of astronomy to naval and commercial navigation and defense and had recently commissioned a report on observatories in Europe.[19] Both Adams and Poinsett were concerned that the United States had to rely on English almanacs for navigation and that it lagged embarrassingly behind Europe in such an important scientific field.[20] Adams was especially distraught about astronomy because the previous year, after both Poinsett and Adams had been approached by the American Philosophical Society to establish a system of observatories across the United States, Adams had presented the society's petition in Congress, where the Democratic majority voted resoundingly against it, 34–97.[21] Many congressmen wanted to use the Smithson funds instead to establish a public university, which, according to Poinsett and Adams, had dubious concrete benefits in comparison to naval and commercial navigation and defense. It is unclear whether Poinsett was much more in favor of an observatory than he was a public university; both were secondary to his main goal of making the National Institute the repository for the funds. He hoped, however, that ingratiating himself with Adams would further his own goals of gaining stewardship of the Smithson funds. Poinsett told Adams that he wanted to devote the next two years to organizing the institute and shoring up support for the Smithson bequest. Although Adams had been mildly suspicious of Poinsett's intentions and knew Poinsett would be spending most of his time in South Carolina, he was convinced that Poinsett was the best person to take charge of this objective.[22] Poinsett's combination of determined diplomacy and national and international connections to scientific networks was unparalleled.

When the weather improved, Poinsett left Washington to manage federal affairs from the comfort of his wife's plantation. This would be his first real experience with southern domestic life. Although he spent so much of his life outside the South, he was nonetheless influenced by the norms of southern manhood and mastery and was just as eager to assert control over his marital acquisitions as he was to further national science.[23] Poinsett returned to three homesteads from which he sought to reap both profit and pleasure; his domain of mastery now included familial relations, agricultural yield, and enslaved laborers. He and Mary owned a house in Charleston that they had purchased from her nephew and a plantation on the Pee Dee River near Georgetown, about sixty miles north of Charleston. The White House plantation had acres of rice fields, as well as fruit trees and grape vines. Poinsett followed the advice of landscape architect A. J. Downing of New York and planted a garden with magnolias, dogwoods, and Lamarque roses, which Downing gifted him.[24] The couple also had a vacation home in the mountains of Greenville, over two hundred miles away. Poinsett was upset that his wife's property had been badly managed in his absence.[25] He sold some of his Charleston properties to the bank to settle old debts and ensure that they had the means to enjoy retirement. Although he never treated Mary as anything close to his equal, he cared about her comfort and her health. When he and Mary married, Poinsett gained a stepson, John Julius Izard Pringle, who lived with his wife, New York native Jane Lynch, on the Greenfield plantation, only several miles away. The Pringles gave Poinsett four step-grandchildren (three boys and a girl), who were born throughout the 1840s.[26]

Poinsett's version of mastery was subtler than that of many southern men. He did not challenge other men to duels, nor did he maintain compulsive records of the individuals he kept in bondage. He owned slaves his whole life but devoted little of his written record to the people on whom his livelihood depended. As he became more accustomed to plantation life, his gendered and racialized obsession with appearance intensified. He said, for example, that he preferred that his plantation grew rice instead of cotton because, "where the latter is raised, the Negroes too often have a whitish hue, whereas here they look coal black with bright shining faces."[27] He told his granddaughter that he "liked best young ladies with their hair cut short and turned up in front with a comb to keep it out of their eyes, especially when the eyes are bright and cheeks tinged with health like those of my own dear grandchild."[28]

Ultimately, Poinsett sought to impose order on both people and land. He had always been interested in plants, and now he had a plantation to which he could apply his knowledge. In his retirement, he dedicated a lot of his time to the science and marketing of crops. He traded advice with Van Buren, Kemble, and others on new agricultural developments and the best varieties of seeds and invited them to see his plantation's improvements in irrigation and rice cultivation. Even in the last years of his life, Poinsett experimented with rice-cleaning fans from New York and sent back consumer reports to the manufacturers. Although he was more experimental than many planters, his approach to agricultural improvements was not unique. Agriculture is always about control and order, and in the second quarter of the nineteenth century, when agricultural productivity seemed to be on the decline as the nation industrialized, many planters looked to enhance the efficiency of their properties. Americans had been organizing agricultural societies since the 1780s, but these became more prevalent, and more dedicated to experiential reform, in the context of the antebellum era's social reform movements (the Agricultural Society of the United States, for example, was founded in 1841).[29] South Carolina had one of the oldest of these societies, founded in 1785, which Poinsett joined in his retirement. The Agricultural Society of South Carolina was well known, and its proceedings were consulted by such domestic and foreign groups as the American Philosophical Society and the Russian Economical Society.

Poinsett became increasingly active in the Agricultural Society in his retirement. In December 1841, he received a letter from the New York State Agricultural Society asking him for a report on agriculture in South Carolina. Poinsett politely expressed his annoyance at not having enough time to complete a comprehensive response, beginning his letter by writing that he received the request "too late to prepare such a paper as you desire for the period indicated in the printed communication." He went on to say, "I regret this the more as I was lately present at a meeting of our State Agricultural Society at Columbia, where information on the several subjects of your inquiries might have been obtained." He passionately rushed through a list of improvements but said he needed more time.[30]

Poinsett was appointed chairman of the Agricultural Society of South Carolina in 1844 and used the position to advocate agricultural innovations that would increase South Carolina's prosperity.[31] For example, he proposed that the South Carolina state legislature pass a measure related to the "scientific mode of culture with the application of manures, which in all civilized countries have become objects of national direction and will greatly advance our prosperity." He also praised the state-sponsored Agricultural and Geological Survey and successfully recommended that it issue a report on its finding that farmers would be obligated to consult.[32] Although his promotion of agricultural science for the sake of improvement was in line with that of other capitalist southern planters, he hoped to increase South Carolina's prosperity through the production of non-slave-grown agricultural commodities, and in this, he was not the norm. His friend naturalist John Bachman, for example, issued a report on the potential benefits of an agricultural survey and urged Carolinians to modernize their agricultural techniques—for example, implementing systems of underdraining and irrigation—to reap more slave-grown crops. He was in favor of the state legislature of South Carolina commissioning Virginia slaveholder and "father of soil science" Edward Ruffin to help conduct its agricultural survey, a job Ruffin accepted because of South Carolina's importance for the perpetuation of slavery.[33] Aware of the risks of monoculture, Poinsett was very concerned with crop diversity. He addressed the Greenville Agricultural Society with a very specific four-year program of crop rotation aimed at improving crop yield and diversity. He chastised Carolinians for blaming the state's hot weather for what was, he said, their own agricultural neglect, and he recommended a diet of turnips, potatoes, peas, and clover to make an "excellent race" of cattle.[34]

As Poinsett delved into the state's agriculture, he reveled in being away from Washington. He declined invitations to attend meetings and ceremonies all over the country, spending time with Mary at their summer home in Greenville and hosting family and friends at their various residences.[35] Members of the National Institute missed his presence at meetings, and members of various societies throughout the United States expressed their regret that he would not be gracing them with a speech.[36] Poinsett cited local business and scheduling conflicts, but he also wanted to minimize his interactions with the current "rulers of the land."[37] Although Poinsett had an easier time getting along with members of different political parties than did many politicians, he was not enthusiastic about the administration of President John Tyler, who was neither a Democrat nor a nationalist.

Poinsett made an exception to see the collections of the National Institution, which were now housed upstairs at the Patent Office, rather than in the basement.[38] Although he and Mary got a delayed start for Washington because Mary sprained her instep, the couple found the trip worthwhile. They were quite pleased with the collection, some of which they had contributed to. Among the collection were the skin of a tiger cat, boxes of shells, and the boot spur of a slain Mexican soldier from the battle of San Jacinto, as well as writings about Egyptian cotton and fossil reptiles. This was aspirational imperialism at its finest. Both Poinsetts had donated silver and gold coins to the institute. Poinsett had also given various medals and Indian pipes; Mary had gifted a marble bust of her husband.[39] This was all very gratifying for Poinsett and was made all the more so by his being in Washington in time to see Congress resoundingly pass a bill to incorporate the National Institute for the Promotion of Science, which confirmed its national legitimacy. Congress rarely did anything that Poinsett and his friends could celebrate, especially since their ongoing indecision over what to do with the Smithson funds. This made it seem as if Congress valued their society and might consent to their request for the Smithson funds.[40] That same year, a national observatory was built in Washington, albeit unconnected to the National Institute or future Smithsonian.[41]

After a brief stay at a boarding house across from the Treasury, the Poinsetts quickly left town. They wanted to relax at home in the garden chairs he had recently ordered from England.[42] Not that Poinsett spent much time relaxing, especially leading up to the presidential election of 1844. That year, he worked feverishly to get Van Buren appointed as the Democratic nominee in South Carolina. He traded news and strategies with friends in other states and assembled a South Carolina cohort to serve Van Buren if he were elected.[43] Poinsett's own name was proposed as a vice presidential candidate. At this point in his career, Poinsett was simultaneously content with retirement and still ambitious for office. He was oblique in his response, writing to a friend, "I am ready to accept office or decline it whenever the interests of the party or of its chief require it. . . . It is certainly a high and honorable station, but I do not much covet it."[44] He also wrote, "Whatever may be the decision, I shall be satisfied. All I require of my friends is not to expose me to Waterloo defeat in the convention."[45]

In the lead-up to the 1844 Democratic National Convention, Poinsett took a break from "arousing the young men of the state to activity" to travel to Washington.[46] On April 1, a bipartisan group of politicians and Washington notables, including Levi Woodbury and John Quincy Adams, assembled for the first annual scientific convention of the National Institute for the Promotion of Science. President Tyler introduced the weeklong meeting and celebration.[47] It was a well-attended event but did not have the impact its organizers had hoped for. Poinsett and others thought that this convention, combined with the upcoming election and a potential change in the political scene, would improve their chances of getting the Smithson bequest.

Unfortunately, Poinsett's beloved Exploring Expedition interfered. First, the expedition's commander, Charles Wilkes, had been court-martialed for losing a ship and for treating subordinates harshly, which did little to improve the reputation of a costly expedition that had been mismanaged in the years leading up to its departure in 1838. Poinsett counterattacked with an article in the *North American Review*. The nation's oldest literary magazine might have seemed an unlikely venue for such an attack, but he was paid twelve dollars for it and was assured an influential readership. Poinsett announced that "the results of this expedition will be the first contribution to science offered to the world by the government of the United States." The article praised the expedition's discoveries and data and cautioned against neglecting them on the basis of rumors of misconduct. He chided Congress and the public for focusing more on the negative news than on the positive. Poinsett spoke out against the expedition's detractors and about the disciplinary problems that would ensue if the government indulged suits brought against superior officers. He connected science to the military, writing, "In the peaceful pursuit of science, as in all the great attributes of a warlike nation, our navy has, to say the least, entered into honorable competition with the navies of the great maritime nations of Europe."[48]

Wilkes flouted Poinsett's support by insisting on only permitting a scientific corps to work with his collections. This was an odd move for a naval officer focused more on surveying than on science during the expedition.[49] When Congress appropriated money for the preservation of the expedition's collections, Poinsett volunteered the National Institute's cooperation in their "arrangement and preservation."[50] Wilkes, however, wanted to uncouple the expedition from government interference, which ran counter to Poinsett's preference for military control over national science and the expedition's activities.[51] Wilkes received reinforcement from influential Ohio congressman Benjamin Tappan.[52] Tappan, like Poinsett, was a Van Buren Democrat, and, like Poinsett, his vision for the national promotion of science did not track party lines. Unlike Poinsett, Tappan did not include the National Institute in his plan (although he supported the establishment of a Smithsonian Institution). Tappan was swayed by Wilkes into characterizing the National Institute as too self-promoting and bureaucratic to advance national science. Poinsett and John J. Abert, head of the Topographical Engineers and one of the Institute's co-organizers, also thought Tappan might be conspiring to set himself up as the head of an independent Smithsonian when his term in Congress ended the following March.[53] Either way, they were none too happy with this challenge. In the summer of 1844, Abert called on Poinsett to provide "courteous resistance" to Wilkes and Tappan.

Poinsett, though, was already back in South Carolina and would stay there, even as members of the institute wanted him to put more public pressure on Congress to pass legislation that would once and for all settle the debates over the Smithson funds. Members of the National Institute got a bill before Congress that proposed government control over the institute, in the hope that it would inspire lawmakers to grant them the Smithson bequest. The bill linked science and progress with military success in the institute's mission "of the rapid diffusion of scientific discovery and improvement in the arts; of giving character, consistency, and unity to national science; and of fostering that just pride which every American ought to feel in extending the fame of his country for her success in the promotion of the liberal arts, as well as in contributing to her martial renown, or her glory."[54]

Tappan proposed his own bill to establish a Smithsonian Institution with the bequest.[55] It, too, emphasized progress and strength but did so by adhering to Wilkes's desire to keep the institution entirely separate from the National Institute. Although the bill floundered in the House the following winter, Wilkes and Tappan ultimately won the battle. "An Act to Establish the 'Smithsonian Institution,' for the Increase and Diffusion of Knowledge among Men" on August 10, 1846, created a Smithsonian entirely independent of the National Institute.

In the meantime, Poinsett was preoccupied with election news. Van Buren had lost the Democratic nomination at the national convention in Baltimore at the end of May 1844, and Poinsett now claimed he could not support either Whigs or Democrats.[56] He and other Democrats like C. C. Cambreleng thought the dark-horse nominee James K. Polk was dangerous. Polk was too selfish, too indulgent of the conservative wing, not deferential to Van Buren.[57] Van Buren wrote to Poinsett soon after, thanking him for the indignation on his behalf, but claimed that the results did not interfere with his happiness. He had distracted himself by having a cottage built on his farm, which, he told Poinsett, Mary would like. Poinsett, though, was worried about the fate of the country. He feared that if Clay won, the South would threaten disunion again.[58] Poinsett thought this unlikely to succeed, but he was concerned nonetheless.[59]

When Polk won a narrow victory, Poinsett was glad at least that the South would not revolt. Polk's imperial posturing, however, made Poinsett uneasy. Polk had made the annexation of Texas a major part of his platform to appeal to southern slaveholders. Poinsett was not a typical

southern Democrat, if such a voter or politician existed. Although he supported territorial expansion in ways that often aligned with the interests
of southern enslavers and had just waged four years of war to secure settlement opportunities for white slaveholding Americans, he broke with his
party and with the dominant southern slaveholder opinion on the issue of
whether to annex Texas.

Aggressive expansionists all over the nation sought to acquire as much
territory as possible. Many southerners in particular wanted this empire
to include Texas, which was the fourth-largest slaveholding society in the
world.[60] They also wanted more Mexican territory on which to expand
American plantation society and create a bulwark against Mexican antislavery. Poinsett had once favored the annexation of Texas but no longer
saw it as politically, economically, or militarily expedient.

Poinsett was not an unbridled expansionist. His vision for US empire
had not included Texas in 1836, and it did not include Mexico now.[61] Poinsett did his usual cost accounting, influenced by the lessons of the Seminole War and his knowledge of Mexican military strength, and recognized
the expense and demoralization of war against another formidable foe. He
was also cognizant of French challenges in Algiers and urged others to
"recollect the fate of the . . . French armies in Algeria."[62] He warned that
the US military might find "in Mexico another Algiers."[63] To some extent,
he had soured on territorial expansion, commenting that "our hardy pio-
neers are not much more refined than the savages they dispossess."[64]

Additionally, he did not think slavery needed territory on which to
spread. When he was still dependent on his father's wealth, Poinsett had
viewed enslaved Africans as status objects; now, as a plantation owner, he
thought of them as capital—capital whose value was decreasing. He noted
that "slavery is too unprofitable in farming districts to be long maintained
there."[65] Poinsett was partly right. The average price of slaves hit a low in
the middle of the 1840s, when he made this statement, and for much of the
antebellum era, slave labor employed in rice production in South Carolina and Georgia was unprofitable. Poinsett, however, had an incomplete
view of the economic picture. Despite his perception that the South was
hindered by its dependence on a few agricultural staples, of which only
cotton had a comparative advantage, he never seemed to grasp the significance of slavery for the US economy as a whole.[66] Slave-grown cotton
was the nation's largest export, and the value of slaves would continue to
increase until the Civil War, as different regions of the country remained
linked by financial instruments whose value derived from enslaved bodies
and the crops they grew.[67]

In 1845, Poinsett gave the fullest presentation of his paradoxical position on matters of political economy in a speech to the Agricultural Society of South Carolina. His main message was that "the wealth and power
of a nation may be correctly estimated by its progress in husbandry."[68] As
the speech meandered among food production, irrigation, protectionism,
compulsory education, manure, domestic comforts, manufacturing, free
trade, hay, domestic table wine, and science, it was not always consistent
in its message. He criticized government regulation of economic matters
(despite his career-long promotion of unofficial intervention) while advocating government-mandated education for the purpose of creating
a population of farmers who understood advanced agricultural science.
He trumpeted the superiority of farming while claiming that good husbandry depended on robust industrial development. He argued against
protectionists who claimed that an import-heavy balance of trade harmed
society—citing an improvement in whites' quality of life over the preced-
ing decades—while also urging the domestic production of products that
grew better in other countries, such as olives, grapes, and *Sesamum ori-
entale*. Although he encouraged Americans to follow Britain's recent shift
toward free trade policies, he found much to criticize about its irrigation
practices, claiming that "if we sprang from any other nation than the English, our country would have been more generally cultivated by the use of
water."[69] He then went on to praise Peru, Chile, Persia, and China, places
he had previously disparaged (he had visited the first three), for their superior irrigation.

The speech revealed the intersection of Poinsett's patriotism and his
vision for political economy. He stressed that "as agriculturalists and patriots," southern planters must ensure that "every individual in the State
should have an abundance of wholesome food" because, according to
Comte de Buffon, "coarse, unwholesome and ill prepared food makes
the human race degenerate." Degeneration concerned Poinsett because
appearance and whiteness were so important to him. Just as Poinsett arranged for peach-tree-lined streets and whitewashed houses at his slave
labor camp, he remarked that Columbia was a sign of progress because it
possessed "handsome edifices, tasteful gardens, good hotels, and presenting in every particular, both the appearance and the reality of a thriving
place of business, scarcely surpassed in beauty of situation."[70] Poinsett did
not like the appearance of slavery, even as he and the state depended on
this "peculiar interest" and he supported investments in Texas and Cuba.[71]

Even though Poinsett had taken a close interest in his state, he was still
concerned with opportunities beyond its borders, particularly in Mexico

and Texas and eventually in Cuba. Although he never ended up profiting much from these investments, he remained motivated by the potential for financial opportunity, especially because he was regularly offered a stake in commercial ventures. Many of his associates' investment portfolios included schemes in Texas and Mexico, and the majority of them did not want annexation. The goal of most trading companies was to control trade; annexation or war would harm business. In Poinsett's last year in the War Department, two Carolinians, who both opposed annexation, approached him about a combination of related investment opportunities in Mexican trade and South Carolina state, bank, and manufacturing-company debt. Pierce M. Butler, former governor of South Carolina (and agent to the Cherokee at Fort Gibson), and Franklin H. Elmore, president of the Bank of South Carolina, were both major investors in various state bonds, including the state's 1838 fire-relief loan, and the Nesbit Manufacturing Company, a struggling iron foundry that depended heavily on loans from the Bank of South Carolina.[72] Both men were also keenly interested in the "overland" or "internal" trade with Mexico.[73] Trade was especially lucrative between Missouri and Santa Fe, New Mexico, and Butler planned to lead a company of men to take control of the route for the Republic of Texas.[74] To facilitate the mission, Elmore and Butler needed documents from Poinsett, including a department map of the southwest, letters from residents in Chihuahua, and invoices of goods sold in the region.[75] Butler offered Poinsett stock options in the Chihuahua Trading Company. He proposed that Poinsett purchase about $10,000, or 10 percent, of the shares. Butler was optimistic. He expected 100 percent profit and assumed it would be easy to raise the requisite 20 percent in advance funds from New York banks and from the Bank of South Carolina (where Elmore was president).[76] The expedition was thwarted by Mexican forces, and it is unclear that Poinsett ever saw any benefit from the trading company.[77] Regardless, the prospect of profit had influenced his stance on the issues of war and annexation.

Poinsett kept quiet about Mexico for a little while, as his health took a turn for the worse (so much so that he envied those in "convalescence"), and he dutifully congratulated Jackson on Polk's victory and the "triumph of the Democratic Party."[78] When Polk made good on his war promises, however, Poinsett took a more visible stance. Polk legitimated a war on Mexico by arguing that US troops needed reinforcement after Mexican troops unjustly attacked them on American soil. In reality, General Zachary Taylor helped instigate the conflict by invading Mexican territory.[79] The United States declared war on Mexico on May 13, 1846, after Congress voted decidedly in favor of it. It passed the Senate 42–2, and only fourteen members of the House of Representatives voted against it.

If Poinsett had been in Congress, maybe he would have voted for it, catering to voters. He no longer had constituents, or potential constituents, and he wrote to Lewis Cass in the Senate that he was so worried about war that he could not sleep. Poinsett had not become a pacifist in the face of a more jingoistic US population, but he feared that the United States would appear weak once faced with Mexican strength. He warned Cass that the United States should not invade with only fifty thousand volunteers. This would ruin America's military reputation.[80] He also wrote to expansionist Thomas Hart Benton that it was fruitless to throw men and money on a campaign in the interior. Instead of taking his advice, correspondents praised his role in strengthening the nation's artillery. Poinsett might have been anxious about American performance, but army officers assured him that they were indebted to him.[81]

Despite receiving military praise, Poinsett took to the press to warn Americans about the risks of incorrectly waging war against Mexico. He published a series of articles in *DeBow's Review*. "Our Army in Mexico" acknowledged the superiority of American arms and praised American gallantry and patriotism but warned against the "defective" composition of their forces.[82] He argued that the United States needed more and better-trained forces to win, and he cautioned that "we must not calculate upon compelling submission, by occupying their remote settlements, and harassing their commerce. Mexico would be less injured by such a proceeding than the commercial nations that traded with her, ourselves among the number."[83]

He sent a public letter to US senator from South Carolina Andrew P. Butler. Poinsett attacked Polk's strategy in Mexico, criticizing the president and secretary of war because they were not "military men." The article included Poinsett's usual cost accounting. On the basis of historical examples, such as the Peninsular War, he calculated a 20 percent loss of regular troops and 40 percent for volunteers. He referenced Russia, which had "conquered" the Caucasus in 1796, only to leave the region in a perpetual state of insecurity and overstretched military resources when Poinsett toured it a decade later. Poinsett advocated that the United States remove troops from the interior of Mexico and simply take whatever land it wanted. Mexico would eventually acquiesce, he conjectured, and American troops could be put to better use elsewhere along the frontier.[84]

Privately, Poinsett expressed his fear that the United States "would gain no honor in the contest with an inferior." Despite his opinion that there was much to "condemn" about the Mexican people, Poinsett doubted that the United States would be able to defeat them.[85] He was afraid of Mexican power in a way that he should have been of that of the Seminoles. He said Mexicans were proud and obstinate and would be backed by church money. He referenced the histories of Britain's disastrous invasion of Buenos Aires. He also suspected that the Mexican Army would procure arms secretly though Honduras.[86]

No one took his advice, and the United States won anyway. Military victory exacerbated sectional tensions in the United States. How much territory did Americans really need or want? What should be done with this territory? Most important, would it be slave or free? When Pennsylvania representative David Wilmot proposed a bill during the war that would prohibit slavery in any territory acquired from Mexico, it became a litmus test for loyalties to the institution of slavery. Although some slaveholders, like John C. Calhoun, opposed absorbing Mexico on the grounds that the United States was "the government of the white man," they wanted any territory that was appropriated to have slavery.[87] Poinsett was disgusted by these debates.[88] Treaty negotiators for the United States ultimately agreed to the Rio Grande as the boundary between the two nations, and Mexico forfeited large portions of the Pacific coast south of Oregon and a sizable chunk of the territory west of Texas.[89] The treaty the United States and Mexico signed on February 2, 1848, answered the question of how much territory but did nothing to resolve the issue of whether it would be slave or free.

While many southern slaveholders feared the fate of slavery in North America, they looked with hope at Cuba, which, if acquired from Spain, would allow the expansion of US slaveholding in the Caribbean. Cuban annexation was rational in a way that, to Poinsett, other popular southern positions, such as war against Mexico, were not.[90] He had earlier accepted Cuba as a Spanish colony because the status quo seemed safer and less costly than involvement in a Cuban revolution. The United States benefited from trade, and Spain helped maintain the institution of slavery and police British activities in the Caribbean. Now, however, Spanish power had weakened, ties had strengthened between Cuba sugar planters and US slave traders, and Americans feared what an independent Cuba meant for slavery or the health of the US economy.[91] British influence seemed especially detrimental as it sought to abolish slavery and to use the island to challenge US commerce.[92] Even if Poinsett was at times ambivalent about the profitability of slavery in his home state and the moral sustainability of the institution, he was never in favor of emancipation, and by the 1840s, the institution of slavery in Cuba seemed to be in jeopardy. Poinsett reasoned that "the possession of Cuba, and the ability to police the island's shores and waters" was also important to the "Gulf Coast frontier and consequently all western states."[93]

Here, Poinsett's interests lined up with the slaveholding status quo, in particular, former opponent James Hamilton Jr., South Carolina governor and nullifier.[94] Hamilton was one southern imperialist who coveted the Caribbean colony. He had recently been approached by one of the wealthiest men in the United States, and one of the largest investors in Cuba, in regard to a scheme to purchase the island secretly for the United States. Hamilton had been "solicited discreetly to sound our public men at Washington . . . to find an individual with the requisite tact, address, and ability to go as a secret agent to Madrid to conduct private negotiations there."[95] Hamilton did not hesitate in choosing whom to ask. Seventy-year-old Poinsett was the perfect candidate.

Poinsett had disagreed with Hamilton on nullification in 1832 (just as he did with Elmore and Butler) and on annexing Texas in the 1840s, but he was interested in this mission. He was no longer a government official; he did not even know with whom in the cabinet he should communicate. He was, however, used to negotiating and doing things behind the scenes. Hamilton promised him a $25,000 outfit and a handsome salary. Poinsett would also have access to a secret service fund and profits from Spanish public debt. These benefits would mean that Poinsett no longer had to depend on how well he marketed his crops in order to settle his debts.[96] He also seemed to believe the scheme was worthwhile. Once Cuba was independent, he thought, annexation would be a quick process.[97]

Hamilton and Poinsett had to decide how much the government should know. They wanted to work out a purchase agreement but were not exactly on friendly terms with Taylor's Whig administration. Hamilton had been "waiting anxiously" for cabinet changes, hoping the secretary of state would be replaced by Kentucky governor John J. Crittendon, who, although a Whig, was a southern enslaver and expansionist. Hamilton was pleased, however, that there seemed to be enough support in Washington for annexation, north and south, outside of the Free Soilers (the political party that opposed extending slavery to new territory) and abolitionists.[98] This support, though, was purely hypothetical. Hamilton had not disclosed their plan.

They decided to proceed with minimal involvement from the government. Poinsett was used to balancing official state power with covert operations. He wanted to be "above the board," but he also wanted to control the situation.[99] Hamilton assured Poinsett that he would work on getting the president and his cabinet to recommend to Congress that the government appropriate money to buy the island.[100] Although Poinsett claimed to live in "entire seclusion" from Washington, he forwarded a letter to their friend Senator Butler detailing the advantages of the Cuba purchase.[101]

Meanwhile, Poinsett would get ready to travel to Madrid to begin secret talks with the Spanish government. He requested to be furnished with information on Cuba's costs to Spain to more effectively bargain for its purchase.[102] The hope was that Spain would agree and the US government would shell out the money to close the deal. Cuba would then become US territory, adding lucrative slave-worked sugar plantations and naval bases, thus ensuring future profits for southerners and protection for US commerce.

Poinsett never made it to Spain because of a lung hemorrhage, among other ailments; instead, he spent the last year of his life in the United States, worrying about disunion, specifically South Carolinians' renewed threat to secede from the United States. In the late 1840s, a wave of secession movements swept the South, as Americans debated a host of issues, exacerbated by the Treaty of Guadalupe Hidalgo, which would determine the fate of slavery. These issues, which would result in the Compromise of 1850, included California's antislavery constitution, the Wilmot Proviso, the abolition of the slave trade in Washington, DC, and a new fugitive slave law. While Poinsett adhered to southern viewpoints in his enthusiasm for Cuba, he challenged them on this slate of issues.

In March 1850, Richard Yeadon approached him to represent South Carolina at the upcoming enslaver convention in Nashville, Tennessee, in early June. South Carolina planned to send delegates who represented the views of both the old nullifier and unionist parties. Poinsett knew the federal government was the surest way to preserve slavery. He believed that "nature and the Constitution assured that slavery would continue to exist and expand wherever it was profitable," regardless of any compromise. Yeadon was also a unionist, but he and others were also ready to stand firm should Congress not acquiesce to their demands. Poinsett quoted his old friend Jackson—"The union must be preserved"—and laid out the military numbers. When he had constructed his controversial militia plan as secretary of war, he had done a thorough examination of all the nation's military resources. He knew the South did not stand a chance. He half-heartedly offered to help the South organize defenses should they secede, but he said it would be hopeless. He initially planned to accept the nomination to the southern convention but realized he could not "yield to the torrent of public opinion" if public opinion approved secession.[103] He instructed Yeadon that should anyone else mention him as a delegate, the answer would have to be no. Yeadon, however, had already written a letter suggesting that Poinsett's refusal to lay secession on the table as an option would disqualify him for the position, anyway.[104]

Poinsett had diverged from many Carolinians in his unwillingness to secede from the Union in the name of slavery, as well as in his belief that Calhoun had inflicted evil on the state and the country by promoting disunion.[105] Even his old naturalist friend Dr. John Bachman, who had been a unionist in the 1830s, became a secessionist.[106] Poinsett's disagreement with many Carolinians was in line with his lifelong refusal to adhere to all dominant party and sectional lines, and it is worth examining. Although for most of his life Poinsett expressed reservations about the institution of slavery, and at times assumed it would die out, his disagreement with southern secessionists certainly did not stem from an antislavery position but rather from economic and military concerns.

By 1850, he, like other southern planters, admitted, "All I own in the world is vested in lands and negroes."[107] He also predicted that "slave labor will continue to go wherever it can be profitably employed" and its security would depend on the "large armies" of the United States.[108] In addition to considering the protection of other white men's enslaved property, Poinsett also most likely considered the economics of rice, which his plantation produced. "Clean rice" exports from Charleston found their biggest markets in the United States, unlike cotton and "rough rice," which sold more to Great Britain and Europe than domestically (many secessionists banked on securing cotton-based allies abroad).[109] Poinsett employed machinery specifically to produce clean rice and had no desire to split from his biggest consumer. Regardless of what crops a plantation produced, however, Poinsett championed the importance of the US government for economic prosperity, in general, and slaveholders' ambitions, in particular.

The Cuba scheme figured into Poinsett's reasoning. At the same time as Poinsett was discussing Cuban annexation with Hamilton, he argued against disunion to Yeadon on the grounds that it "would not extend the limits of the territory to which we might transport our peculiar property." Hamilton, a former nullifier and Calhoun supporter, agreed with Poinsett on this issue. Their plan for Cuba required federal resources, and they were part of a small cadre of southern militarists who advocated the bolstering of armed forces to protect and expand slavery.[110] Although Poinsett and Hamilton were right about needing the federal government for slavery, their Cuba strategy did not pan out, and the following year, Venezuelan Narcisco López was executed after leading a failed expedition of mostly US southerners to take the island from Spain.[111]

It bothered Poinsett to watch others take US empire into their own hands. His health was really starting to hinder him, and he "disliked his idle, aimless life."[112] Like many old men, Poinsett was growing increasingly cantankerous. When he and Mary hosted the Swedish feminist writer Fredrika Bremer, for example, he not only quibbled with all her positions on substantial issues like slavery but also took pleasure in criticizing the writings of Ralph Waldo Emerson right after she praised them. As if to illustrate that his preoccupation with appearance and proper roles for women had not changed in old age, he made sure to point out that Bremer was "not pretty."[113] Superficial pettiness aside, Poinsett was genuinely dismayed by the erosion of his plan for US imperialism. Although he believed Americans had a right to take Cuba, he thought López's filibustering crossed the line. Covert state action was one thing; extralegal organizing was another. Poinsett wished for, and correctly predicted, the expedition's failure and López's execution.[114] He also believed the United States had committed a "gross injustice" by taking California from Mexico; its punishment was the state's "sordid population."[115]

Most detrimental to Poinsett's vision for national empire was the continued threat of secession. The compromise legislation of September 1850 did not mollify southern extremists, who met again in Nashville in November. South Carolina secessionists held their own meeting in December. Before the meeting, Poinsett addressed the people of his state in a letter that ran in various newspapers. He argued that, yes, it seemed unjust to exclude slavery from California; however, he was confident that if the state's settlers voted, they would vote to exclude slavery because they were "unwilling to work side by side with the negro." Poinsett asked secessionists to put aside the resentment they felt toward fellow Americans for undermining slavery. He stressed military capability and prosperity, writing, "If there are any among us, so wild as to think of separate state action, to them I would say, that they mistake violence for strength. Let them examine the map and consult the census and they will see our relative weakness." He said that it was "to the Union, to which . . . we owe our unexampled prosperity as a nation."[116]

Secessionism, however, was persistent, and Poinsett continued to speak out. While on vacation in New York during the last summer of his life, he sent a letter to a July 4 celebration in Greenville: "I am aware that this is not popular language to hold to a people who are in the habit of hearing themselves lauded as being clothed with power to maintain this single State against the World in Arms, and possessing resources adequate to defray all the expenses of an independent government. This, fellow citizens, is a dream from which you must be roused by having the truth laid bare to you."[117] The truth, Poinsett wrote, was that the United States was a "great and prosperous nation" and that South Carolina would stand alone as an "insignificant state . . . unable to support or defend itself." Poinsett seemed to forget that the previous year he had blamed Calhoun for the "unmitigated evil" of disunion.[118] Referring to Calhoun and George McDuffie, he now argued that, "were these great statesmen now alive, they would be among the first to stem this torrent."[119] Despite the popularity of secession, it was defeated, temporarily, in the October 1851 election. Poinsett passed away that December, perhaps thinking the crisis had been averted. Ten years later, though, secessionists would make good on their threats. Poinsett's belief about the impracticability of an independent South Carolina and a confederacy of southern states was ultimately proved true.

His other predictions were mixed. Although there would never be an American Cuba, despite other attempts by schemers and government officials to purchase the island, the United States would finally establish a Smithsonian Institution that served as a showcase for American imperialism. For all the time Poinsett had spent lobbying for the Smithsonian, he said little about its foundation in the late 1840s, perhaps because the Smithson fund was not linked to the National Institute as he wanted. Yet the Smithsonian that opened in 1855 reflected his vision of an exhibition of all the specimens the various exploring expeditions had collected. In this respect, his plan beat out the others, including that of Joseph Henry, the institute's first president, who wanted the Smithsonian to serve solely as a research institution. The Smithsonian would be, as Poinsett intended, a display of imperialism. Although Poinsett had never wanted the Mexican-American War to happen, the relationship between its aftermath and the Smithsonian would have gratified him. The survey of the territories acquired from Mexico shaped the research and collection agenda of the new Smithsonian.[120] In 1858, the Smithsonian acquired the objects of the National Institute, whose collection Poinsett had helped create with his work on various surveys and exploring expeditions. Perhaps he would have viewed this as his greatest success, had he lived to see it. Perhaps he even viewed the Smithsonian that was under construction in 1851 this way.

Poinsett's letters give no hint of nostalgic career reflection in the last months of his life. Instead, he worried about his health and the consequences of political changes. In addition to fearing the declension of American empire, he expressed his doubts about the recent revolutions in Europe. In one of his last surviving letters, he wrote that only the English were capable of constitutional liberty and argued that Hungarian independence leader Lajos Kossuth, despite his popularity in the United States as a freedom fighter, was a "pestilent man."[121] Poinsett sent the letter from New York, where he spent the last summer before his death, hoping White Sulphur Springs would help his and Mary's health.[122] He had had bouts of serious illness since the previous Christmas, when he was too sick to entertain his step-grandchildren, nieces, and nephews as he and Mary had done the past few years.[123]

Before going home for the last time, the Poinsetts traveled to Niagara Falls, which, Poinsett noted in a letter to his cousin, impressed him. Despite the falls' splendor, Poinsett envied his cousin's recent tour of Normandy, France.[124] As much as the United States and South Carolina were his home, he was always lured by travel, always restless. As soon as he and Mary returned home, they set out again. This time it was for the pure air of Greenville because Poinsett's "pulmonary complaint" had intensified. They never made it.

Poinsett died on December 12, of a lung infection, probably tuberculosis or severe pneumonia. He died en route, between his city home and his mountain home, in Stateburg, South Carolina. He and Mary had stopped for rest along the way at the plantation of Dr. William Wallace Anderson, the husband of the niece of the recipient of Nathalie Sumter's letter about Poinsett's unrequited love all those years ago.

Poinsett was buried several days later in the Church of the Holy Cross Cemetery. The church was in Stateburg, not Charleston, or Greenville, or any other place Poinsett had called home, which was fitting for a man who was always on the go. News of his death caused a "deep sensation in the Senate Chamber" and prompted tributes in various forms.[125] On Christmas Day, 1851, the Christ Vestry Church in Greenville, where Poinsett "was for many years a zealous member," sent Mary a letter that read, "In his deceased our body has lost one of its brightest ornaments, the church one of its ablest defenders and society at large a generous sympathizer with the wants and ills of humanity."[126] That same day, the Southern Patriot published an obituary written by John Belton O'Neal, a South Carolina judge, plantation owner, and enslaver who wrote *Negro Law of the Carolinas*. The two had served briefly together in the South Carolina

House of Representatives. O'Neal wrote, "His long life has been devoted
to the honor of his native city and State."[127] Poinsett was similarly lauded
by the Charleston *Courier,* which announced "with deep and sincere regret the death of this eminent citizen and retired statesman" and praised
the "unabated vigor of his intellect and his patriotic interest in the welfare
of his country."[128] Despite Poinsett's commemoration in South Carolina,
in Mexico he was remembered as a man "of loathsome memory" whose
political meddling and "Machiavellian management" of diplomacy were
responsible for the "misery of Mexico."[129] He was not the same, anywhere.

Epilogue

....

Poinsett was an opportunist whose patriotism was a guise and a reality. To those who liked him or needed something from him, he was an "honest patriot" who exhibited "exalted patriotism."[1] To others, he was a proponent of despotism and "the cause of . . . miseries."[2] Alexander I considered the Poinsett who traveled to Russia in his early twenties worthy to dine at the imperial palace, while British officers in Chile accused him of "circulating poison . . . [and] contaminating the whole population."[3]

These different perceptions of Poinsett were matched by his changing takes on any number of issues. One such instance was when he helped US naval captain David Porter get a position in the Mexican Navy and then later said, "I should insist upon hanging every captain, officer or sailor of American birth [in the Mexican Navy]" should the United States and Mexico go to war.[4] Porter, having enlisted upon an "invitation" that Poinsett had solicited, might have found that assertion surprising.[5] We, however, should not. Poinsett also battled tariffs and then supported their collection, angered proslavery secessionists during the nullification crisis and later won their approval with his militia plan (which was, according to one enslaver, "vital to the independent existence of the south particularly at this time when in fact every free negro and even slave is openly enlisted on behalf of Tip and Ty").[6] Poinsett modified his positions on many issues, just as he made himself comfortable in many spaces—huts and palaces, bull fights, philosophical societies, and slave labor camps.

His changeability was part of his ambitious and pragmatic chauvinism as he sought to achieve his goals through the success of the republic. This meant, for example, competing with British imperial power in South America and Mexico to secure US national influence, while allying with individual British businessmen regarding personal land investments. For this reason, it's hard to know whether he would have remained committed to the Union. Nine years and eight days after his death, South Carolina seceded from the United States, an occurrence he had worked, until the end of his life, to prevent. His words were used to rally support for the Union. Newspapers reprinted the speech he had given during the nullification crisis in 1832, in which he argued that "we must maintain our place in the union," by saying that he had proudly waved the American flag during a political riot in Mexico City in 1828.[7] A New York article, for example, declared, "At this juncture in our national troubles, when the flag of the union is being treated with contumely and thrown aside to give place to those that were used in the days of our colonial vassalage, the following extract of the speech of Mr. Poinsett, delivered at Charleston, S.C., during the nullification excitement, will be perused with pleasure by all friends of the Union."[8] Union general John C. Fremont gave a speech in Boston recalling Poinsett's leadership of the Union Party in South Carolina.[9] In an article denouncing secession, Poinsett's name was included as a "first class name in the Southern States" who had "showed their accordance till a late date with Northern sentiment on the subject of slavery."[10] And yet, during the war, a twenty-year-old man named Poinsett, identified as a field hand, was sold in Charleston.[11] Regardless of Poinsett's feelings for the Union, he had been an enslaver, had contributed to the causes of the Civil War, and had started to join other enslavers in their desire for Cuba before he died. Another man who bore his name, Edward Poinsett Tayloe (the son of his private secretary in Mexico, Edward Thornton Tayloe), fought for the Confederacy.[12]

His complicated legacy extended past his death not only to the Civil War but beyond. He left traces in our modern world that most people no longer see, unless they happen to pick up *The Mountains Won't Remember Us: And Other Stories* and flip to the short story "Poinsett's Bridge" or happen to be in the section of unmarked forest in the upcountry of South Carolina where Poinsett's Bridge still stands today.[13] If you visit the Smithsonian, you might see his portrait as secretary of war but not a marker indicating that Poinsett was the first to argue that the institution should be a national museum.

You will, however, see his name every December, when the plant that the Nahua people used for medicine and red dye for hundreds of years before the Spanish began calling it the *Flor de Nochebuena* is marketed as a holiday flower. Of all the things Poinsett did, if he is remembered at all in the United States, it is for a plant he mailed to influential friends after searching for profit opportunities in southern Mexico. When we look at a poinsettia today, the vivid flower should call to mind more than December decorations: thanks to Poinsett, it should remind us of the blazingly selfish, confident statecraft that he helped pioneer. Poinsett's America was not our America, but his approach to politics is with us still. We should recognize it in all our elected and appointed officials who say one thing and do another. Poinsett's commitment to facades, militaristic and capitalist values, and his own self-interest were inseparable from his "exalted patriotism and devotion to [his] country."[14] This brand of patriotism persists, emblematic of the nature of the American experiment itself.

Acknowledgments

....

This feels like the hardest part of the writing process. I don't know how to express the proper gratitude required to the many individuals and institutions who have helped me write this book. All have made this work better.

This project began during a Program in Early American Economy and Society Post-Doctoral Fellowship at the Library Company in Philadelphia; I owe a tremendous gratitude to the intellectual and material resources provided by the Program, directed by Cathy Matson, and to the wonderful individuals I met during my time in Philadelphia. Emilie Connolly deserves a special thanks because she suggested I visit the Historical Society of Pennsylvania for the collections they had pertaining to individuals who worked in the War Department. I never expected to find boxes and boxes of materials for Joel Roberts Poinsett, an individual I kept encountering while I worked on my first book, but whose significance I did not yet understand. She also read chapters and offered insight in various conversations throughout the project. Her brilliant research has shaped how I understand Poinsett's life and the era in general.

Miami University allowed me to take that postdoctoral fellowship in my second semester of employment and provided support throughout the project, including the Robert H. and Nancy J. Blayney Assistant Professorship. I am fortunate to have wonderful colleagues at the university. I would like to give special thanks to Amanda McVety, Andrew Offenburger, Cam Shriver, Michele Navakas, Renee Baernstein, Steve Norris, and Steve Conn for reading chapter drafts, to Elena Jackson Albarrán for being an expert on Mexico, and to Wietse de Boer for being the best department chair. Katie Rogers and Grace Seifert provided skilled research assistance, and Karon Selm was always helpful. Thank you also to Tim

Melley and participants of the Humanities Center book proposal workshop, who helped shape the intellectual development of this project.

A number of other institutions made this book possible. A Kluge Fellowship at the John W. Kluge Center of the Library of Congress was instrumental in providing the resources and space to conduct research, consult with experts, discuss work in an enlightening intellectual environment, and meet wonderful friends. Special thanks to Sarah Mainwaring, Cydonie Banting, Jeanine Quené, Tom Bishop, Michael Stratmoen, John Haskell, and Travis Hensley. Daniel Tshiani and María Veronica Uribe provided helpful research assistance. A Beveridge Travel Grant from the American Historical Association and a Robert L. Middlekauff Fellowship at the Huntington Library also made research possible. The extraordinarily knowledgeable and helpful staffs at the South Carolina Historical Society; University of North Carolina at Chapel Hill; Washington, DC, branch of the National Archives; the American Antiquarian Society; the Historical Society of Pennsylvania; the Library Company of Philadelphia; the Library of Congress; and the Huntington Library answered questions and offered research leads and advice with patience and enthusiasm.

The opportunities to present portions of this book at the annual meetings of the Business History Conference, the American Historical Association Southeastern Conference for Latin American Studies, and the Society for Historians of the Early American Republic (SHEAR) improved the final outcome. My work benefited in particular from two workshops hosted by the latter. Many individuals spent precious time offering advice and reading portions (or all!) of this book. Andy Shankman helped shape the framing of this project at SHEAR's Second Book Workshop in Cleveland, and Caitlin Fitz provided incredibly generous and informative feedback, which helped me push the project over the finish line. I am appreciative of the helpful comments I received from Erika Pani Bano, David McKenzie, George Oberle, John Hall, Samuel Watson, Andrew Fagal, Cameron Shriver, and Tom Bishop. Jim Schakenbach has always stopped whatever he is doing to read my writing.

Mary McCudden and Mike Monteleone, Ania Borejsza-Wysocka and Chris Bender, Kiki Bolender and Chuck Capaldi, Michele and Gene Navakas, Allison Winacoo, Naomi Sussman, and John and Linda Schakenbach offered gracious hospitality and company during the research process. For writing and emotional support, thank you Youn Ki, Naaborle Sackeyfio, Kazue Harada, Kendra Leith, Carly Wilks, Meaghan Seelaus, Addie Capaldi, and Merritt Haswell. Also, wonderful neighbors make living away from family easier.

I am enormously indebted to my editor Tim Mennel, and I feel very fortunate for having the guidance of Stephen Mihm and the series editors of American Beginnings at the University of Chicago Press, as well as Susannah Engstrom, and the editorial staff.

And then, of course, there is my family. I could never repay my parents or my brother for their unwavering love and support and for the happiness they gave me growing up. And the Regeles have been wonderful family for the past two-plus decades.

Finally, Matt, Jack, and Emily: you make everything better. Jack and Emily: when I started this book, I didn't know if it would be possible to have you. You are my miracle babies. Matt: you are the only reason I ever get anything done. You are my best everything and for the past twenty-five years have believed in me more than anyone. Thank you for loving me and for caring about Poinsett.

Abbreviations

....

AJLC	Andrew Jackson Papers, MSS 27532 Library of Congress
BC-NARA	Bureau of the Census, RG 29, National Archives, Washington, DC
CLCP	Charles Lyon Chandler Papers, #3614, Southern Historical Collection, Wilson Library, University of North Carolina at Chapel Hill
HSP	Historical Society of Pennsylvania
JRP-LC	Papers of Joel R. Poinsett, Manuscript Division (MMC1421), Library of Congress
JRPP	Joel Roberts Poinsett Papers, Historical Society of Pennsylvania
NARA	National Archives and Records Administration
PPGC	Poinsett Papers, Henry D. Gilpin Collection, Gilpin Family Papers (0238), Historical Society of Pennsylvania
SCHS	South Carolina Historical Society
USDS-DC	United States Department of States, Despatches from US Consuls, RG59, National Archives, Washington, DC

Notes

....

Introduction

1. J. Franklin Jameson, ed., *Correspondence of John C. Calhoun* (Washington, DC, 1900), 1067, quoted in Charles Lyon Chandler and R. Smith, "The Life of Joel Roberts Poinsett," *Pennsylvania Magazine of History and Biography* 59, no. 1 (1935): 15.

2. Laura Trejo, Teresa Patricia Feria Arroyo, Kenneth M. Olsen, Luis E. Eguiarte, Baruch Arroyo, Jennifer A. Gruhn, and Mark E. Olson, "Poinsettia's Wild Ancestor in the Mexican Dry Tropics: Historical, Genetic, and Environmental Evidence," *American Journal of Botany* 99, no. 7 (July 2012): 1146–57.

3. I decided to use these terms rather than nationalism because of their historical usage, as well as the current relevance of American patriotism. Aviel Roshwald says it may be time to revisit "the role of patriotism in the context of the nation-state." Cemil Aydin, Grace Ballor, Sebastian Conrad, Frederick Cooper, Nicole Cunjieng Aboitiz, Richard Drayton, Michael Goebel, Pieter M. Judson, Sandrine Kott, Nicola Miller, Aviel Roshwald, Glenda Sluga, Lydia Walker, "Rethinking Nationalism," *American Historical Review* 127, no. 1 (March 2022): 311–71, esp. 321; Jill Lepore, *These Truths: A History of the United States* (New York: W. W. Norton, 2018); Lepore, *This America: The Case for the Nation* (New York: Liveright, 2019). There is, however, a tremendous amount of pertinent scholarship on nationalism. For several foundational works, see Carlton J. H. Hayes, *The Historical Evolution of Modern Nationalism* (New York: R. R. Smith, 1931); Benedict Anderson, *Imagined Communities: Reflections on the Origin and Spread of Nationalism* (London: Verso, 1983); Ernest Gellner, *Nations and Nationalism* (Ithaca, NY: Cornell University Press, 1983); Eric Hobsbawm, *Nations and Nationalism since 1780* (Cambridge: Cambridge University Press, 1990).

4. William Miller to JRP, April 27, 1819, folder 2, vol. 2, JRPP.

5. D. H. Mahan to JRP, December 27, 1837, folder 15, vol. 9, JRPP.

6. Stephen Elliott to JRP, November 16, 1824, folder 10, vol. 2, JRPP.

7. Chapman Levy, October 10, 1837, folder 8, vol. 9, JRPP.

8. T. Hartley Crawford to JRP, April 29, 1841, folder 11, vol. 16, JRPP.

9. JRP to Richard Yeadon, March 6, 1850, folder 19, vol. 16, JRPP.

10. While Poinsett's experiences reveal little about the common white man (to say nothing of women, Native peoples, or African Americans), they can tell us about the various expressions of masculine entitlement among both elites and the men he represented while serving in government.

11. John Belton O'Neal, "The Hon. Joel R. Poinsett," folder 51, folder 81, in CLCP. For an example of public criticism of Poinsett, see *Correo de la federacion mexicana* (Mexico City), August 17, 1827, 3–4, Readex: World Newspaper Archive.

12. Chapman Levy to JRP, October 10, 1837, folder 8, vol. 9, JRPP.

13. By "self-interested," I mean the motivations of certain businessmen to reap tangible benefits beyond what the larger community gained. However, I do not intend to imply that these businessmen were only driven by self-interest or that their interests did not also reflect a desire to benefit the nation. By the early 1800s, *interest* was no longer necessarily incompatible with the national good. Cathy Matson and Peter Onuf assert that after the Revolution, the "value of union . . . became identified . . . with the real needs of existing interest groups seeking to shape national policy." Cathy Matson and Peter Onuf, "Toward a Republican Empire: Interest and Ideology in Revolutionary America," *American Quarterly* 37, no. 4 (Autumn 1985): 530. For a discussion of the role of self-interest in the reconciliation of liberal capitalism with classical republicanism in the early republic, see Joyce Appleby, *Capitalism and a New Social Order: The Republican Vision of the 1790s* (New York: New York University Press, 1984); Steven Watts, *The Republic Reborn: War and the Making of Liberal America, 1790–1820* (Baltimore: Johns Hopkins University Press, 1987). For a discussion of the interconnectedness of merchants' individual interests and state apparatuses, see Hannah Farber, "State-Building after War's End: A Government Financier Adjusts His Portfolio for Peace," *Journal of the Early Republic* 38, no. 1 (Spring 2018): 67–76. See also John M. Belohlavek, "Economic Interest Groups and the Formation of Foreign Policy in the Early Republic," *Journal of the Early Republic* 14, no. 4 (Winter 1994): 476–84. I am using *self-interested* to complicate *patriotism*, which at its most basic means love and pride for one's nation, because Poinsett's service to his country was rooted in his political ambitions and concern with how others perceived him. Rick Kosterman and Seymour Freshbach, "Toward a Measure of Patriotic and Nationalistic Attitudes," *Political Psychology* 26, no. 2 (1989): 323–37. It has more positive connotations than, say *nationalism*, which suggests a corresponding "hatred for other countries." Lepore, *This America*, 23. Poinsett had an appreciation for other countries, even those about which he wrote condescendingly, like Mexico. For the United States' imperial nationhood, see Josep M. Fradera, *The Imperial Nation: Citizens and Subjects in the British, French, Spanish, and American Empires*, trans. Ruth MacKay (Princeton, NJ: Princeton University Press, 2018).

14. E. Anthony Rotundo, "Body and Soul: Changing Ideals of American Middle-Class Manhood, 1770–1920," *Journal of Social History* 16, no. 4 (Summer 1983): 25. See also E. Anthony Rotundo, *American Manhood: Transformations in Masculinity from the Revolution to the Modern Era* (New York: Basic Books, 1993). Dana Nelson argues that white manhood is a constitutive element of US citizenship and economic relations and enables men of different classes to bond over "fraternal sameness." Dana D. Nelson, *National Manhood: Capitalist Citizenship and the Imagined Fraternity of White Men* (Durham, NC: Duke University Press, 1998), 19. For masculinity, power relations, and national strength, see Joan W. Scott, "Gender: A Useful Cat-

egory of Historical Analysis," *American Historical Review* 91, no. 5 (1986): 1053–75. For a helpful overview of the past several decades of scholarship on masculinity, see Andrea Waling, "Rethinking Masculinity Studies: Feminism, Masculinity, and Poststructural Accounts of Agency and Emotional Reflexivity," *Journal of Men's Studies* 27, no. 1 (2019): 89–107. For an overview of characterizations of manhood in Poinsett's era, in particular, see Bryan C. Rindfleisch, "'What It Means to Be a Man': Contested Masculinity in the Early Republic and Antebellum America," *History Compass* 10/11 (2012): 852–65.

15. Watts, *Republic Reborn*; Joyce Appleby, *Inheriting the Revolution: The First Generation of Americans* (Cambridge, MA: Harvard University Press, 2000).

16. Raewyn Connell, *Masculinities* (Cambridge: Polity, 1995); R. W. Connell and James W. Messerschmidt, "Hegemonic Masculinity: Rethinking the Concept," *Gender and Society* 19, no. 6 (December 2005): 829–59; Christine Beasley, "Rethinking Hegemonic Masculinity in a Globalizing World," *Men and Masculinities* 11, no. 1 (October 2008): 86–103. Their demonstrations of respectability and refinement mirrored the activities of England's "gentlemanly capitalists," whose aristocratic disdain for work and market-based wealth belied their profit-generating activities. P. J. Cain and A. G. Hopkins, "Gentlemanly Capitalism and British Expansion Overseas I. The Old Colonial System, 1688–1850," *Economic History Review* 39, no. 4 (November 1986): 505.

17. For an analysis of theories and categories of masculinity, see Waling, "Rethinking Masculinity Studies," 89–107; Thomas A. Foster, ed., *New Men: Manliness in Early America* (New York: New York University Press, 2011). In writing about the gendered dimensions of US expansionism and imperialism, historian Amy Greenberg has identified two main types of masculinity in the nineteenth-century United States. "Martial" men embraced physical strength, domination, and aggression as markers of manhood, while "restrained" men valued self-discipline, morality, and the virtues of the private sphere (made possible by female domesticity). Amy Greenberg, *Manifest Manhood and the Antebellum American Empire* (New York: Cambridge University Press, 2005). For respectability in this era, see Brian P. Luskey, "Jumping Counters in White Collars: Manliness, Respectability, and Work in the Antebellum City," *Journal of the Early Republic* 26, no. 2 (May 2006): 173–219.

18. Francis Baring to JRP, August 27, 1833, vol. 2, JRPP.

19. Laurel Clark Shire describes how many white men of the Jacksonian era "were collectively convinced of their own racial superiority," which "enabled them to justify taking land from Indigenous peoples and stealing life and labor from Africans and African Americans." Laurel Clark Shire, "Sentimental Racism and Sympathetic Paternalism: Feeling like a Jacksonian," *Journal of the Early Republic* 39, no. 1 (February 2019): 115.

20. Emma Anna Bull to Charles Chandler, December 7, 1933, Emma Anna Bull research papers, 1933, Bull family of Ashley Hall collection, 1877–1977, (304.02) SCHS, *Charleston News and Courier*, January 15, 1899, p. 12, folder 82, CLCP.

21. Bertram Wyatt-Brown, *Southern Honor: Ethics and Behavior in the Old South* (New York, 1982), xv. For the role of mastery, honor, and violence among white male southerners, see Craig Thompson Friend and Lorri Glover, eds., *Southern Manhood: Perspectives on Masculinity in the Old South* (Athens: University of Georgia Press, 2004). For the importance of manhood over honor and of refined socializing, see

Lorri Glover, *Southern Sons: Becoming Men in the New Nation* (Baltimore: Johns Hopkins University Press, 2007).

22. Courtney Fullilove, *The Profit of the Earth: The Global Seeds of American Agriculture* (Chicago: University of Chicago Press, 2017), 5.

23. Andrea Wulf, *The Invention of Nature: Alexander von Humboldt's New World* (New York: Vintage, 2016).

24. Joel Roberts Poinsett, Thomas Pinckney, and State Agricultural Society of South Carolina, *Report of the Committee, Appointed by the South Carolina Agricultural Society, to Consider What Beneficial Effects Would Result to the Agricultural Interests of the State, by Importing Foreign Seeds, Plants and Implements of Husbandry: To Which Is Added, Gen. Thomas Pinckney's Letter on the Water Culture of Rice* (Charleston: A. E. Miller, 1823).

25. Emily Pawley, *The Nature of the Future: Agriculture, Science, and Capitalism in the Antebellum North* (Chicago: University of Chicago Press, 2020), 4.

26. John Annell to JRP, August 20, 1825, folder 10, vol. 17; James Ronaldson, November 6, 1828, folder 9, vol. 5, JRPP.

27. N. Herbemont to JRP, March 21, 1830, folder 6, vol. 6, JRPP.

28. James Ronaldson to JRP, November 6, 1828, folder 9, vol. 5, JRPP; St. Andrew's Society of Philadelphia, *An Historical Catalogue of the St. Andrew's Society of Philadelphia* (printed for the society, 1907), 1:305–6.

29. Ryan A. Quintana, "Planners, Planters, and Slaves: Producing the State in Early National South Carolina," *Journal of Southern History* 81, no. 1 (February 2015): 83.

30. Daniel Kilbride, *An American Aristocracy: Southern Planters in Antebellum Philadelphia* (Columbia: University of South Carolina Press, 2006).

31. Ernest M. Lander, "Manufacturing in South Carolina, 1815–60," *Business History Review* 28, no. 1 (March 1954): 62.

32. This challenges John Ashworth's argument that there was continuity in antebellum partisan ideologies and that ideologies protected class interests. John Ashworth, *Slavery, Capitalism, and Politics in the Antebellum Republic* (New York: Cambridge University Press, 1995). For another example of ideological inconsistency, see James M. Lundberg, *Horace Greeley: Print, Politics, and the Failure of American Nationhood* (Baltimore: Johns Hopkins University Press, 2019).

33. For Adams's contradictory positions on slavery and foreign relations, see Alastair Su, "'The Cause of Human Freedom': John Quincy Adams and the Problem of Opium in the Age of Emancipation," *Journal of the Early Republic* 40, no. 30 (Fall 2020): 465–96; Stephen Chambers, *No God but Gain: The Untold Story of Cuban Slavery, the Monroe Doctrine, and the Making of the United States* (New York: Verso, 2015).

34. Joel Roberts Poinsett, speech on the tariff bill (House of Representatives, Washington, DC, April 8, 1824).

35. Memorandum regarding the property of Joel Roberts Poinsett, folder 83, in CLCP. His will was recorded in Charleston but is not very detailed. Emma Bull to Charles Lyon Chandler, December 7, 1933, Bull family of Ashley Hall collection, 1877–1977, (304.02) SCHS.

36. Joel and Mary Poinsett to James R. Pringle, June 11, 1834, document 11/322/27, James Reid Pringle papers, 1745–1840, (1083.01.01) SCHS. As Michael Blaakman has contended, "large-scale investment in distant lands gave American

elites a self-interested, material reason to keep the states united." Michael A. Blaakman, "The Marketplace of American Federalism: Land Speculation across State
Lines in the Early Republic," *Journal of American History* 107, no. 3 (December
2020): 608.

37. Emma Bull to Charles Lyon Chandler, November 29, 1933, Bull family of
Ashley Hall collection, 1877–1977, (304.02) SCHS.

38. Francis Baring to JRP, August 27, 1833, vol. 2, JRPP.

39. JRP to James B. Campbell, [n.d., postmarked June 6, 1837], in Samuel Gail-
lard Stoney, "The Poinsett-Campbell Correspondence," *South Carolina Historical and
Genealogical Magazine* 42, no. 4 (October 1841): 163.

40. JRP to James B. Campbell, June 16, 1836, in Stoney, "Poinsett-Campbell Correspondence" (July 1841): 133.

41. Lester D. Stephens, "The Literary and Philosophical Society of South Carolina: A Forum for Intellectual Progress in Antebellum Charleston," *South Carolina
Historical Magazine* 104, no. 3 (July 2003): 156.

42. JRP to Isaac Johnson, July 9, 1821, March 31, 1825, May 27, 1826, Joel Roberts
Poinsett, Letters to Isaac A. Johnson, 1821–1826, (43/131) SCHS.

43. JRP to Isaac Johnson, July 9, 1821, Joel Roberts Poinsett, Letters to Isaac A.
Johnson, 1821–1826, (43/131) SCHS.

44. Certificate of Membership in the Freemason Lodge No. 1 in South Carolina, June 13, 1818, folder 3, JRPP, 1787–1851, SCHS. Freemasonry had a powerful
influence on early American society. Many statesmen were Masons, including over
a third of the signers of the Declaration of Independence. Freemasonry developed
in seventeenth-century England, and by the early 1800s, there were superintend-
ing grand lodges in every state and Freemasonry meetings in most cities and towns.
Lodges were and are the most basic local chapters of Freemasons, dealing with the
first three Masonic orders: Apprentice, Fellow, and Master Mason. Steven C. Bullock, "A Pure and Sublime System: The Appeal of Post-revolutionary Freemasonry,"
Journal of the Early Republic 9, no. 3 (Autumn 1989): 366.

45. For Freemasons' creation of bonds between white men, see Ami Pflugrad-
Jackisch, *Brothers of a Vow: Secret Fraternal Orders and the Transformation of White
Male Culture in Antebellum Virginia* (Athens: University of Georgia Press, 2010).
David G. Hackett argues that ritualism, tenets, ceremonies, and lodge activities in
America were especially appealing to members of Protestant denominations. David
G. Hackett, *That Religion to Which All Men Agree: Freemasonry in American Culture*
(Berkeley: University of California Press, 2014).

46. Bullock, "Pure and Sublime System," 368.

47. The British, too, used Freemasonry to serve imperial ends. Jessica Harland-
Jacobs, "'Hands across the Sea': The Masonic Network, British Imperialism, and the
North Atlantic World," *Geographical Review* 89, no. 2 (April 1999): 237–53.

48. For intimate friendships between men in the first half of the nineteenth century, see Thomas J. Balcerski, *Bosom Friends: The Intimate World of James Buchanan
and William Rufus King* (New York: Oxford University Press, 2019). For southern
male friendship and masculinity, see Anya Jabour, "Male Friendship and Masculinity in the Early National South: William Wirt and His Friends," *Journal of the Early
Republic* 20, no. 1 (Spring 2000): 83–111; Janet M. Lindman, "Histories of Friendship
in Early America: An Introduction," *Journal of Social History* 50, no. 4 (2017): 603–8.

49. See, for example, JRP to Joseph Johnson, February 4, March 3, March 27, 1825, and August 15, 1827, Poinsett Papers, Henry D. Gilpin Collection, Gilpin Family Papers (0238), HSP (PPGC).

50. Joseph Johnson to JRP, July 17, 1830, folder 9, vol. 6, JRPP.

51. JRP to James B. Campbell, April 16, 1836, in Stoney, "Poinsett-Campbell Correspondence" (July 1841): 131.

52. JRP to James B. Campbell, February 2, 1835, in Stoney, "Poinsett-Campbell Correspondence" (April 1941): 51.

53. JRP to James B. Campbell, May 30, 1835, in Stoney, "Poinsett-Campbell Correspondence" (July 1941): 126; Jacob Snider Jr. to JRP, March 4, 1832, folder 4, vol. 7, JRPP.

54. Fredrika Bremer, *The Homes of the New World*, p. 287, folder 81, CLCP.

55. Mary and Joel Poinsett to James R. Pringle, May 15, 1835, folder 11/322/27, James Reid Pringle papers, 1745–1840 (bulk 1800–1850), (1083.01.01) SCHS. According to Lorri Glover's characterization of southern manhood, Poinsett did not achieve full manhood until he was fifty-four. Glover, *Southern Sons*.

56. For a history of bachelorhood in early America and the privilege bestowed on elite, white bachelors by the Revolution, see John Gilbert McCurdy, *Citizen Bachelors: Manhood and the Creation of the United States* (Ithaca, NY: Cornell University Press, 2009).

57. JRP to James B. Campbell, October 5, 1833, in Stoney, "Poinsett-Campbell Correspondence" (April 1941): 35, 32.

58. JRP to James B. Campbell, June 16, 1836, in Stoney, "Poinsett-Campbell Correspondence" (July 1941): 132–35.

59. Michael Grossberg, *Governing the Hearth: Law and the Family in Nineteenth-Century America* (Chapel Hill: University of North Carolina Press, 1988), 282.

60. For marriage as the commonsensical foundation of the new nation and for the relationship between marriage and national identity, see Nancy F. Cott, *Public Vows: A History of Marriage and the Nation* (Cambridge, MA: Harvard University Press, 2000). For the companionate ideal of marriage and the separation of men's and women's spheres, see Anya Jabour, *Marriage in the Early Republic: Elizabeth and William Wirt and the Companionate Ideal* (Baltimore: Johns Hopkins University Press, 1998).

61. Ruth H. Bloch, "Untangling the Roots of Modern Sex Roles: A Survey of Four Centuries of Change," *Signs* 4, no. 2 (Winter 1978): 247.

62. Suzanne D. Lebsock, "Radical Reconstruction and the Property Rights of Southern Women," *Journal of Southern History* 43, no. 2 (May 1977): 208.

63. Grossberg, *Governing the Hearth*, 282.

64. Mary and Joel Poinsett to James R. Pringle, May 15, 1835, folder 11/322/27, James Reid Pringle papers, 1745–1840 (bulk 1800–1850), (1083.01.01) SCHS.

65. Joel and Mary Poinsett to James R. Pringle, June 11, 1834, document 11/322/27, and May 15, 1835, document 11/322/28, James Reid Pringle papers, 1745–1840, (1083.01.01) SCHS.

66. Stephanie E. Jones-Rogers, *They Were Her Property: White Women as Slave Owners in the American South* (New Haven, CT: Yale University Press, 2019).

67. Jan Lewis argues that during the nation's first few decades, women's status in society and in the family revolved around their identity as wives (she argues that

even Linda Kerber acknowledges that society depended on women's domestic, rather than maternal, activities, despite the emphasis on the "republican mother" in her scholarship). By the 1830s, women were celebrated for their role as mothers. Jan Lewis, "The Republican Wife: Virtue and Seduction in the Early Republic," *William and Mary Quarterly* 44, no. 4 (October 1987): 721.

68. JRP to Mary Izard Pringle, April 24, 1849, folder 13, Allston family papers, 1730–1901, (1164.00) SCHS.

69. Ray did this both in his official capacity as consul and as a private citizen, suggesting the blurred lines between state and nonstate actions. Caitlin A. Fitz, "'A Stalwart Motor of Revolutions': An American Merchant in Pernambuco, 1817–1825," *Americas* 65, no. 1 (July 2008): 35–62.

70. Decius Wadsworth to Roswell Lee, January 27, 1817, box 2, folder 4, Letters Received Miscellaneous, Records of the Springfield Armory, MA, RG 156, entry 1362, NM-59, 94-066, National Archives and Records Administration (NARA), Waltham, MA; "An Act for the Better Regulation of the Ordnance Department," February 8, 1815, 13th Cong., chap. 38, in Richard Peters, *United States Statutes at Large* (Washington, DC: US Government Printing Office, 1846), 3:203–4.

71. Wadsworth to Lee, July 25, 1818, November 10, 1818, Letters Received from Officials and Officers of the War and Treasury Departments, box 1, target #2, Records of the Springfield Armory, MA, RG 156, entry 1362, NM-59, 94-066, NARA, Waltham, MA; Wadsworth to Lee, August 30, 1817, box 3, folder 9, Letters Received Miscellaneous, Records of the Springfield Armory, MA, RG 156, entry 1362, NM-59, 94-066, NARA, Waltham, MA; Lindsay Schakenbach Regele, "Guns for the Government: Ordnance, the Military 'Peacetime Establishment,' and Executive Governance in the Early Republic," *Studies in American Political Development* 34, no. 1 (April 2020): 132–47.

72. Eda Kranakis, "Social Determinants of Engineering Practice: A Comparative View of France and America in the Nineteenth Century," *Social Studies of Science* 19, no. 1 (February 1989): 42; Hunter A. Dupree, *Science in the Federal Government: A History of Policies and Activities to 1940* (New York: Arno Press, 1980), 26, 64, 30; American Association for the Advancement of Science, "The United States Coast and Geodetic Survey and Its Early Superintendents," *Scientific Monthly* 3, no. 6 (December 1916): 616; Florian Cajori, *The Chequered Career of Ferdinand Rudolph Hassler, First Superintendent of the United States Coast Survey: A Chapter in the History of Science in America* (Boston: Christopher Publishing House, 1929).

73. Annals of Congress, "Coast Survey," H.R. Rep., December 15, 1806, 9th Cong., p. 151; Dupree, *Science in the Federal Government*, 30; American State Papers (ASP), "Survey of the Coast of the United States," S. Rep., April 4, 1816, 14th Cong., Commerce and Navigation, no. 198, p. 26; Annals of Congress, "Coast Survey," December 8, 1817, p. 2461; ASP, "Survey of the Coast," S. Rep., March 16, 1818, 15th Cong., Commerce and Navigation, no. 214, p. 106.

74. Dupree, *Science in the Federal Government*, 33.

75. Dupree, *Science in the Federal Government*, 54–55; T. C. Mendenhall, "The Geographical Work of the United States Coast and Geodetic Survey," *Geographical Journal* 11, no. 3 (March 1898): 290; Ferdinand R. Hassler, *Principal Documents Relating to the Survey of the Coast of the United States since 1816* (New York: printed by William Van Norden, 1834), 97–98.

76. Patent Act of 1790, Ch. 7, 1 Stat. 109 (April 10, 1790); Patent Act of 1793, Ch. 11, 1 Stat. 318–23 (February 21, 1793).

77. Robert C. Post, "'Liberalizers' versus 'Scientific Men' in the Antebellum Patent Office," *Technology and Culture* 17, no. 1 (January 1976): 27; Patent Act of 1836, Ch. 357, 5 Stat. 117 (July 4, 1836).

78. Vestry Christ Church to Mary Pringle, folder 1, JRPP, 1787–1851, (1164.03.03) SCHS.

79. Joel R. Poinsett, "Political Portraits with Pen and Pencil: (no. iii.)," *United States Magazine and Democratic Review (1837–1851)* 1, no. 3 (February 1, 1838); Ralph D. Gray, "Henry D. Gilpin A: Pennsylvania Jacksonian," *Pennsylvania History: A Journal of Mid-Atlantic Studies* 37, no. 4 (October 1970): 345.

80. Ralph D. Gray, "Henry D. Gilpin: A Pennsylvania Jacksonian," *Pennsylvania History: A Journal of Mid-Atlantic Studies* 37, no. 4 (October 1970): 345. Gilpin's material ended up at the Historical Society of Pennsylvania after he died.

81. John Belton O'Neal, "The Hon. Joel R. Poinsett," folder 51, folder 81, CLCP.

82. Emma Anna Bull research papers, Bull family of Ashley Hall collection, 1877–1977, (304.02) SCHS; Charles Lyon Chandler and R. Smith, "The Life of Joel Roberts Poinsett," *Pennsylvania Magazine of History and Biography* 59, no. 1 (1935): 1.

83. Dorothy Parton, *The Diplomatic Career of Joel Roberts Poinsett* (Austin: University of Texas Press, 1934), 150; James Fred Rippy, *Joel R. Poinsett: Versatile American* (Durham: University of North Carolina Press, 1935), vii; Herbert E. Putnam, *Joel Roberts Poinsett: A Political Biography* (Ann Arbor: University of Michigan Press, 1935), i.

Chapter 1

1. JRP to Joseph Johnson, March 7, 1807, notes from Gilpin Collection, folder 58, CLCP, #3614, Southern Historical Collection, Wilson Library, University of North Carolina at Chapel Hill.

2. Philip Yorke Royston and Henry Pepys, *The Remains of the Late Lord Viscount Royston: With a Memoir of His Life* (London: Murray, 1838), 109; Janet M. Hartley, *The Volga: A History* (New Haven, CT: Yale University Press, 2021).

3. Lauren Duval, "Mastering Charleston: Property and Patriarchy in British-Occupied Charleston, 1780–82," *William and Mary Quarterly* 75, no. 4 (October 2018): 594.

4. Richard Sorrenson, "Towards a History of the Royal Society in the Eighteenth Century," *Notes and Records of the Royal Society of London* 50, no. 1 (January 1996): 31, 41; R. Willach, "New Light on the Invention of the Achromatic Telescope Objective," *Notes and Records of the Royal Society of London* 50, no. 2 (July 1996): 195–210.

5. Charles Lyon Chandler and R. Smith, "The Life of Joel Roberts Poinsett," *Pennsylvania Magazine of History and Biography* 59, no. 1 (1935): 4n9.

6. Michael E. Stevens, "'To Be a Member of Congress Hereafter Will Be Like a Profession': New Letters from David Ramsay 1785, 1793," *South Carolina Historical Magazine* 116, no. 1 (January 2015): 55–79.

7. He owned seven slaves in 1790 and 1800. First Census of the United States, 1790; St. Phillips and St. Michaels, Charleston, SC, series M637, roll 11, p. 325; Re-

cords of the Bureau of the Census, RG 29, NARA, Washington, DC, Second Census of the United States, 1800, Charleston, SC, series M32, roll 48, p. 118; Records of the Bureau of the Census, RG 29.

8. Property was linked to "political loyalty and masculine authority," which was why Elisha Poinsett so readily switched wartime allegiances. Duval, "Mastering Charleston," 590.

9. Jane Turner Censer, "Planters and the Southern Community: A Review Essay," *Virginia Magazine of History and Biography* 94, no. 4 (October 1986): 391.

10. Arthur H. Shaffer, "David Ramsay and the Limits of Revolutionary Nationalism," in *Intellectual Life in Antebellum Charleston*, ed. Michael O'Brien and David Moltke-Hansen (Knoxville: University of Tennessee Press, 1986), 50.

11. Annabelle S. Wenzke, *Timothy Dwight, 1752–1817* (Lewiston, NY: E. Mellen, 1989); Marc L. Harris, "Revelation and the American Republic: Timothy Dwight's Civic Participation," *Journal of the History of Ideas* 54, no. 3 (July 1993): 449–68.

12. JRP to Eliza Poinsett, 1794, PPGC.

13. JRP to Eliza Poinsett, 1794, PPGC.

14. Poinsett Manuscript, chap. 1, folder 25, CLCP, #3614, Southern Historical Collection, Wilson Library, University of North Carolina at Chapel Hill.

15. JRP to Eliza Poinsett, 1796, PPGC.

16. Poinsett Manuscript, chap. 1, folder 25, CLCP.

17. Henry William DeSaussure to JRP, May 26, 1801, folder 1, vol. 1, JRPP.

18. Henry William DeSaussure to JRP, May 26, 1801, folder 1, vol. 1, JRPP.

19. To James Madison from Thomas Sumter Jr., August 6, 1801, abstract, in *The Papers of James Madison*, vol. 2, *1 August 1801–28 February 1802*, Secretary of State Series, ed. Mary A. Hackett, J. C. A. Stagg, Jeanne Kerr Cross, and Susan Holbrook Perdue (Charlottesville: University Press of Virginia, 1993), 20–21, quoted in *Founders Online*, National Archives, https://founders.archives.gov/documents/Madison/02-02-02-0024.

20. Joel R. Poinsett, "Political Portraits with Pen and Pencil: (no. iii)," *United States Magazine, and Democratic Review (1837–1851)* 1, no. 3 (February 1, 1838): 3–4.

21. Charles Lyon Chandler and R. Smith, "The Life of Joel Roberts Poinsett," *Pennsylvania Magazine of History and Biography* 59, no. 1 (1935): 10; Will of Dr. Elisha Poinsett, July 1803, folder 58, CLCP.

22. E. P. Richardson, "Allen Smith, Collector and Benefactor," *American Art Journal* 1, no. 2 (Autumn 1969): 5–19; R. A. McNeal, "Joseph Allen Smith, American Grand Tourist," *International Journal of the Classical Tradition* 4, no. 1 (Summer 1997): 64–91; Joseph Allen Smith to JRP, October 11, 1806, folder 1, vol. 1, JRPP.

23. Alfred W. Crosby, *America, Russia, Hemp, and Napoleon: American Trade with Russia and the Baltic, 1783–1812* (Columbus: Ohio State University Press, 1965). For early US-Russia relations, see Norman E. Saul, *Distant Friends: The Evolution of United States–Russian Relations, 1763–1867* (Lawrence: University Press of Kansas, 1991).

24. Franklin, Lee, Adams to President of Congress, July 20, 1778, *The Diplomatic Correspondence of the American Revolution*, ed. Jared Sparks, 12 vols. (Boston: N. Hale and Gray & Bowen, 1829–30), 5:410, quoted in Charles Stuart Kennedy, *The American Consul: A History of the United States Consular Service, 1776–1914* (New York: Greenwood, 1990), 7.

25. JRP to J. Johnson, February 10, 1807, folder 2, vol. 1, JRPP.

26. State of South Carolina to Joel Roberts Poinsett, December 10, 1806, folder 4, JRPP, 1787–1851, (1164.03.03) SCHS.

27. JRP to Joseph Johnson, March 7, 1807, notes from Gilpin Collection, folder 58, CLCP.

28. Royston and Pepys, *Remains of the Late Lord Viscount Royston*, 94, 96, 97, 107.

29. JRP to Joseph Johnson, August 12, 1807, folder 2, vol. 1, JRPP.

30. William Theobald Wolfe Tone to JRP, [June 16, 1819?], folder 2, vol. 8, JRPP; JRP to Joseph Johnson, August 12, 1807, folder 2, vol. 1, JRPP.

31. JRP to Joseph Johnson, August 12, 1807, folder 2, vol. 1, JRPP.

32. Royston and Pepys, *Remains of the Late Lord Viscount Royston*, 115.

33. JRP to Joseph Johnson, August 12, 1807, folder 2, vol. 1, JRPP.

34. Michael Khodarkovsky, *Russia's Steppe Frontier: The Making of a Colonial Empire, 1500–1800* (Bloomington: Indiana University Press, 2004); Charles King, *The Ghost of Freedom: A History of the Caucasus* (New York: Oxford University Press, 2009).

35. Royston and Pepys, *Remains of the Late Lord Viscount Royston*, 104, 166.

36. Alexander Martin, *Enlightened Metropolis: Constructing Imperial Moscow, 1762–1855* (New York: Oxford University Press, 2013).

37. JRP to John C. Calhoun, December 27, 1845, in John Franklin Jameson, *Correspondence of John C. Calhoun* (Washington, DC: Government Printing Office, 1899), 1067.

38. Chandler and Smith, "Life of Joel Roberts Poinsett," 17.

39. JRP to Joseph Johnson, March 20, 1809, folder 2, vol. 1, JRPP.

40. JRP to Joseph Johnson, March 1, 1812, notes from Gilpin Collection, folder 58, CLCP.

41. Will of Dr. Elisha Poinsett, July 1803, folder 58, CLCP.

42. Samuel was apparently under twenty-five; Poinsett's household lists two people, only one of whom was over twenty-five. Third Census of the United States, 1810, St. Phillips, Charleston, SC, series M252, roll 60, p. 393; Records of the Bureau of the Census, RG 29, NARA, Washington, DC.

43. JRP to Joseph Johnson, March 20, 1809, folder 2, vol. 1, JRPP.

44. Poinsett Manuscript, chap. 1, folder 25, CLCP.

45. Mrs. Thomas Sumter to Mrs. Thomas Hooper, January 6, 1811, folder 58, CLCP, #3614, Southern Historical Collection, Wilson Library, University of North Carolina at Chapel Hill.

46. SCHS, "Izard of South Carolina," *South Carolina Historical and Genealogical Magazine* 2, no. 3 (July 1901): 205–40; Robert F. Neville and Katherine H. Bielsky, "The Izard Library," *South Carolina Historical Magazine* 91, no. 3 (July 1990): 154.

47. Mrs. Thomas Sumter to Mrs. Thomas Hooper, January 6, 1811, folder 58, CLCP, #3614, Southern Historical Collection, Wilson Library, University of North Carolina at Chapel Hill.

48. JRP to Joseph Johnson, March 8, 1808, folder 2, vol. 1, JRPP.

49. James Fred Rippy, *Joel R. Poinsett: Versatile American* (Durham: University of North Carolina Press, 1935), 32.

50. To James Madison from Albert Gallatin, August 15, 1810, in Hackett, Cross, and Perdue, *Papers of James Madison*, 2:486–88, quoted in *Founders Online*, National Archives, https://founders.archives.gov/documents/Madison/03-02-02-0600.

51. For the beginnings of US commercial relations with Spanish America, see Roy F. Nichols, "Trade Relations and the Establishment of the United States Consulates in Spanish America, 1779–1809," *Hispanic American Historical Review* 13, no. 3 (August 1933): 289–313.

52. James R. Fichter, *So Great a Profit: How the East Indies Trade Transformed Anglo-American Capitalism* (Cambridge, MA: Harvard University Press, 2010), 113–14. Although Fichter emphasizes the importance of silver for the development of American capitalism, he downplays its Latin American origins while focusing instead on its role in East Indies exchange. Fichter, 4–5.

53. For US commerce after independence, see James F. Shepherd and Gary M. Walton, "Economic Change after the American Revolution: Pre- and Post-war Comparisons of Maritime Shipping and Trade," *Explorations in Economic History* 13, no. 4 (October 1976): 397–422; Claudia D. Goldin and Frank D. Lewis, "The Role of Exports in American Economic Growth during the Napoleonic Wars, 1793 to 1807," *Explorations in Economic History* 17, no. 1 (January 1980): 6–25; Donald R. Adams Jr., "American Neutrality and Prosperity, 1793–1808: A Reconsideration," *Journal of Economic History* 40, no. 4 (December 1980): 71; Brooke Hunter, "Wheat, War, and the American Economy during the Age of Revolution," *William and Mary Quarterly*, 3rd ser., 62, no. 3 (July 2005): 505–26. For the American Atlantic trade more broadly, see John H. Coatsworth, "American Trade with European Colonies in the Caribbean and South America, 1790–1812," *William and Mary Quarterly* 24, no. 2 (April 1967): 243–66; Javier Cuenca Esteban, "Trends and Cycles in U.S. Trade with Spain and the Spanish Empire, 1790–1819," *Journal of Economic History* 44, no. 2 (June 1984): 521–43; Javier Cuenca-Esteban, "British 'Ghost' Exports, American Middlemen, and the Trade to Spanish America, 1790–1819: A Speculative Reconstruction," *William and Mary Quarterly* 71, no. 1 (January 2014): 63–98; Michelle Craig MacDonald, "The Chance of the Moment: Coffee and the New West Indies Commodities Trade," *William and Mary Quarterly*, 3rd ser., 62, no. 3 (July 2005): 441–72; Linda Kerrigan Salvucci, "Development and Decline: The Port of Philadelphia and Spanish Imperial Markets, 1783–1823" (PhD diss., Princeton University, 1985); Jacques A. Barbier and Allan J. Kuethe, eds., *The North American Role in the Spanish Imperial Economy, 1760–1819* (Manchester: Manchester University Press, 1984); Edward P. Pompeian, "Spirited Enterprises: Venezuela, the United States, and the Independence of Spanish America, 1789–1823" (PhD diss., College of William and Mary, 2014); Pompeian, *Sustaining Empire: Venezuela's Trade with the United States during the Age of Revolutions, 1797–1828* (Baltimore: Johns Hopkins University Press, 2022); James Alexander Dun, "'What Avenues of Commerce, Will You, Americans, Not Explore!': Commercial Philadelphia's Vantage onto the Early Haitian Revolution," *William and Mary Quarterly*, 3rd ser., 62, no. 3 (July 2005): 473–504.

54. James E. Lewis Jr., *The American Union and the Problem of Neighborhood: The United States and the Collapse of the Spanish Empire* (Chapel Hill: University of North Carolina Press, 1998). In the context of British naval aggression in the Caribbean during the Napoleonic Wars, British influence in Spain's former colonies seemed especially detrimental to US interests. Daniel George Lang, *Foreign Policy in the Early*

Republic: The Law of Nations and the Balance of Power (Baton Rouge: Louisiana State University Press, 1985), 130.

55. To James Madison from Albert Gallatin, August 15, 1810, in Hackett, Cross, and Perdue, *Papers of James Madison*, 2:486–88, quoted in *Founders Online*, National Archives, https://founders.archives.gov/documents/Madison/03-02-02-0600.

56. Patent Act of 1793, chap. 11, 1 Stat. 318–323 (February 21, 1793); Robert C. Post, "'Liberalizers' versus 'Scientific Men' in the Antebellum Patent Office," *Technology and Culture* 17, no. 1 (January 1976): 24–54.

57. Robert Smith to JRP, August 27, 1810, folder 2, vol. 1, JRPP.

58. Kennedy, *American Consul*, 20, 24. US citizens were able legally to ship goods there as early as the 1790s. Bills of Lading, binder 5, Jay T. Last Collection of Maritime Prints and Ephemera, series 1, Huntington Library, San Marino, California.

59. Robert Smith to JRP, August 27, 1810, folder 2, vol. 1, JRPP. For issues over consular recognition, see Simeon Andonov Simeonov, "Consular Recognition, Partial Neutrality, and the Making of Atlantic Diplomacy, 1778–1825," *Diplomatic History* 46, no. 1 (January 2022): 144–72.

60. Robert Smith to JRP, August 27, 1810, folder 2, vol. 1, JRPP.

61. Mildred Amer, *Secret Sessions of Congress: A Brief Historical Overview* (Washington, DC: Congressional Research Service, 2004). John Adams relied on private correspondence to influence diplomacy during the Quasi War with France. Nathan Perl-Rosenthal, "Private Letters and Public Diplomacy: The Adams Network and the Quasi-War, 1797–1798," *Journal of the Early Republic* 31 (Summer 2011): 283–311; Katlyn Marie Carter, "Practicing Politics in the Revolutionary Atlantic World: Secrecy, Publicity, and the Making of Modern Democracy" (PhD diss., Princeton University, 2017); Katlyn Marie Carter, "Denouncing Secrecy and Defining Democracy in the Early American Republic," *Journal of the Early Republic* 40, no. 3 (Fall 2020): 409–33.

62. Ralph E. Weber, *United States: Diplomatic Codes and Ciphers, 1775–1938* (Chicago: Precedent, 1979).

63. Carter, "Denouncing Secrecy and Defining Democracy," 410.

64. Robert Smith to JRP, November 6, 1810, folder 2, vol. 1, JRPP.

65. Samuel C. Hyde, "Introduction: Setting a Precedent for Regional Revolution; The West Florida Revolt Considered," *Florida Historical Quarterly* 90, no. 2 (Fall 2011): 126; J. C. A. Stagg, "James Madison and George Mathews: The East Florida Revolution of 1812 Reconsidered," *Diplomatic History* 30, no. 1 (January 2006): 23–55.

66. Gilbert L. Lycan, "Alexander Hamilton's Florida Policy," *Florida Historical Quarterly* 50, no. 2 (October 1971): 148.

67. Robert W. Tucker and David C. Hendrickson, *Empire of Liberty: The Statecraft of Thomas Jefferson* (New York: Oxford University Press, 1990), 54.

68. Lindsay Schakenbach, "Schemers, Dreamers, and a Revolutionary Foreign Policy: New York City in the Era of Second Independence, 1805–1815," *New York History* 94, nos. 3–4 (Summer/Fall 2013): 267–82; Lewis, *American Union*, 6–24; Lawrence S. Kaplan, *Entangling Alliances with None: American Foreign Policy in the Age of Jefferson* (Kent, OH: Kent State University Press, 1987), 166.

69. Robert Smith to JRP, November 6, 1810, folder 2, vol. 1, JRPP.

70. For the limits to understanding diplomatic relations by considering official stances of "neutrality," see Simeonov, "Consular Recognition," 144–72.

71. Robert Smith to JRP, November 6, 1810, folder 2, vol. 1, JRPP.

72. For the United States' international colonization aims, see Brandon Mills, *The World Colonization Made: The Racial Geography of Early American Empire* (Philadelphia: University of Pennsylvania Press, 2020).

Chapter 2

1. Journal to Rio de Janeiro, Buenos Aires and Chile [rough draft] 1810–1811, Papers of Joel R. Poinsett, Manuscript Division (MMC1421), Library of Congress (JRP-LC).

2. Journal to Rio de Janeiro, Buenos Aires and Chile [rough draft] 1810–1811, JRP-LC.

3. JRP to Robert Smith, January 11, 1811, folder 1, vol. 1, JRPP.

4. Mathew Arnold Hoevel to President James Madison, September 29, 1810, folder 7, box 1, JRPP. For more on Hoevel and early US-Chilean relations, see Roland D. Hussey, "Some Articles in Spanish American Historical Reviews, 1938–1940," *Pacific Historical Review* 10, no. 3 (September 1941): 332. See also Estuardo Nunez, "Viajeros Norteamericanos En El Pacifico Antes De 1825," *Journal of Inter-American Studies* 4, no. 3 (July 1962): 344; William L. Neumann, "United States Aid to the Chilean Wars of Independence," *Hispanic American Historical Review* 27, no. 2 (May 1947): 205–6; Ferry DeGoey, *Consuls and the Institution of Global Capitalism, 1783–1914* (London: Pickering & Chatto, 2014), 96.

5. Robert Smith to JRP, August 27, 1810, November 6, 1810, folder 2, vol. 1, JRPP.

6. Andrea Wulf, *The Invention of Nature: Alexander von Humboldt's New World* (New York: Vintage, 2016).

7. When Poinsett returned home, for example, he received a letter from Secretary of States James Monroe, noting how important events in South America were for the United States and requesting to be kept apprised as Poinsett received information. James Monroe to JRP, October 10, 1815, vol. 1, folder 18, JRPP.

8. Alfred D. Chandler, *The Visible Hand: The Managerial Revolution in American Business* (Cambridge, MA: Belknap Press of Harvard University Press, 1977), 71–74.

9. Ferry DeGoey argues that consuls spread global capitalism. Ferry DeGoey, *Consuls and the Institution of Global Capitalism, 1783–1914* (London: Pickering & Chatto, 2014), 96. As Simeon Simeonov argues, "it is precisely because of their liminal diplomatic character, their ambiguous positionality between the public and the private, and their ambivalent relationship to the nation-state that consuls offer a unique transnational lens through which to examine the entangled history of the Spanish Empire and the young republic at the turn of the nineteenth century." Simeon Andonov Simeonov, "'With What Right Are They Sending a Consul': Unauthorized Consulship, U.S. Expansion, and the Transformation of the Spanish American Empire, 1795–1808," *Journal of the Early Republic* 40, no. 2 (Spring 2020): 20.

10. Brett Goodin, *From Captives to Consuls: Three Sailors in Barbary and Their Self-Making across the Early American Republic, 1770–1840* (Baltimore: Johns Hopkins University Press, 2020).

11. For the role of unauthorized consular agents in negotiating and challenging state sovereignties and institutions, see Simeonov, "'With What Right,'" 19–44. For Wilkinson specifically, see Simeonov, p. 33.

12. See, for example, Caitlin A. Fitz, "'A Stalwart Motor of Revolutions': An

American Merchant in Pernambuco, 1817–1825," *Americas* 65, no. 1 (July 2008): 35–62; Lindsay Schakenbach Regele, *Manufacturing Advantage: War, the State, and the Origins of American Industry, 1776–1848* (Baltimore: Johns Hopkins University Press, 2019), chap. 5.

13. As Caitlin Fitz has shown, profits generally trumped republican idealism, but when the two coincided, supporters of independence felt noble. Caitlin A. Fitz, *Our Sister Republics: The United States in an Age of American Revolution* (New York: W. W. Norton, 2016).

14. For a non-US-centric perspective on Poinsett's mission, see Guillermo Gallardo, *Joel Roberts Poinsett, agente norteamericano, 1810–1814* (Buenos Aires: Emecé Editores, 1984).

15. See, for example, Charles Stewart, Bill of Lading, April 1, 1811, United States Department of States, Despatches from US Consuls, RG59, National Archives, Washington, DC (USDS-DC), Rio de Janeiro, RG59 T172, roll 1.

16. Charles Stuart Kennedy, *The American Consul: A History of the United States Consular Service, 1776–1914* (New York: Greenwood, 1990), 20. US citizens legally were able to ship goods there as early as the 1790s. Bills of Lading, binder 5, Jay T. Last Collection of Maritime Prints and Ephemera 1, Huntington Library, San Marino, CA.

17. Mrs. Thomas Sumter to Mrs. Thomas Hooper, January 6, 1811, folder 58, CLCP.

18. Journal to Rio de Janeiro, Buenos Aires and Chile [rough draft] 1810–1811, JRP-LC.

19. For the prevalence of anti-Catholicism and the domination of Protestantism in the early United States, see Christopher Grasso, "The Religious and the Secular in the Early American Republic," *Journal of the Early Republic* 36, no. 2 (Summer 2016): 359–88. For pushback against this sort of argument, see Jeffrey R. Applehans, "The Creation of American Catholicism: From the Revolution to the Early Republic" (book manuscript, https://jeffappelhans.com/#work, January 15, 2022).

20. Journal to Rio de Janeiro, Buenos Aires and Chile [rough draft] 1810–1811, JRP-LC.

21. Brian R. Hamnett, *The End of Iberian Rule on the American Continent, 1770–1830* (New York: Cambridge University Press, 2017).

22. Charles E. Ronan, "Some Aspects of the Mission of Joel Roberts Poinsett to Buenos Aires and Chile 1810–1814" (master's thesis, Loyola University of Chicago, 1954), 33–34.

23. Journal to Rio de Janeiro, Buenos Aires and Chile [rough draft] 1810–1811, JRP-LC.

24. Journal to Rio de Janeiro, Buenos Aires and Chile [rough draft] 1810–1811, JRP-LC.

25. JRP to State Department, February 13, 1811, folder 4, vol. 1, JRPP.

26. Robert Smith to JRP, August 27, 1810, November 6, 1810, folder 2, vol. 1, JRPP.

27. Albert Gallatin's note on Poinsett's correspondence from March 8, 1811, vol. 1, JRPP. He was finally paid through Thomas Sumter in Rio. Thomas Sumter to Robert Smith, April 26, 1811, vol. 1, JRPP.

28. JRP to Thomas Sumter, [n.d.] 1811, folder 8, vol. 1, JRPP; JRP to James Monroe, November 2, 1811, folder 4, vol. 1, JRPP.

29. JRP to James Monroe, November 2, 1811, folder 4, vol. 1, JRPP.

30. Journal to Rio de Janeiro, Buenos Aires and Chile [rough draft] 1810-1811, JRP-LC.

31. JRP, March 5, 1811, folder 4, vol. 1, JRPP.

32. JRP to State Department, April 20, 1811, folder 4, vol. 1, JRPP.

33. JRP to State Department, June 29, 1811, folder 9, vol. 1, JRPP.

34. See Schakenbach Regele, *Manufacturing Advantage*, chap. 5.

35. JRP to Department of State, April 23, 1811, vol. 1, JRPP.

36. JRP to State Department, April 11, 1811, folder 6, vol. 1, JRPP.

37. JRP to State Department, February 13, 1811, folder 4, vol. 1, JRPP.

38. JRP to Thomas Sumter, October 25, 1811, folder 12, vol. 1, JRPP.

39. Early letters from the US consul in Havana complained of the "jealousies that appear by the officers of government against our trade" and the expectations that US trade with the island would "dwindle away to nothing." Bullock to Robert Livingston, December 14, 1783, USDS-DC Havana, microfilm T20, roll 1. The Crown believed in a "free," Crown-protected trade between European and American Spaniards, which operated to the detriment of American traders seeking outlets for European and Asian goods, as well as for American produce like tobacco. Bibiano Torres Ramirez and Javier Ortiz de la Tabla, eds., *Reglamento para el comercio libre, 1778* (Seville, 1979), quoted in John Fisher, "Imperial 'Free Trade' and the Hispanic Economy, 1778-1796," *Journal of Latin American Studies* 13, no. 1 (May 1981): 21-56, 21. The only sector in which Spain had encouraged truly "free" trade was slave trading, which Americans certainly took advantage of, both legally and illegally, but they soon needed to find other commodities to trade in South America, as many of Spain's former colonies enacted legislation that restricted slavery and the slave trade. James Ferguson King, "The Evolution of the Free Trade Principle in Spanish Colonial Administration," *Hispanic American Historical Review* 22, no. 1 (February 1942): 34-56, 55-56. For a discussion of changing attitudes toward the slave trade, as well as a discussion of the importance of Cuba as a market for American slave traders, see also Leonardo Marques, "Slave Trading in a New World: The Strategies of North American Slave Traders in the Age of Abolition," *Journal of the Early Republic* 32, no. 2 (2012): 233-60.

40. Neumann, "United States Aid," 205.

41. JRP to James Monroe, November 2, 1811, folder 12, vol. 1, JRPP.

42. See, for example, JRP to James Monroe, November 2, 1811; JRP to State Department, November 25, 1811, folder 12, vol. 1, JRPP.

43. Secretary of States James Monroe had changed his appointment to consul in April 1811. James Monroe to JRP, April 30, 1811, in *Diplomatic Correspondence of the United States Concerning the Independence of Latin American Nations*, ed. William R. Manning (New York, 1925), 1:11; JRP to State Department, March 1, 1812, folder 13, vol. 1, JRPP; Peter D. Eicher, "Inventing Interventionism: Joel Poinsett in Argentina, Chile, and Mexico," in *Raising the Flag: America's First Envoys in Faraway Lands* (Lincoln: University of Nebraska Press, 2018), 113.

44. JRP to State Department, March 8, 1812, folder 13, vol. 1, JRPP.

45. Patricia Vilches, "Not a Fox but a Lion: A Machiavellian Reading of Chile's First President, José Miguel Carrera," *Journal of the Midwest Modern Language Association* 44, no. 1 (Spring 2011): 123-44; Pedro Lira Urquieta, *Jose Miguel Carrera*

(Santiago de Chile: Editorial Andres Bello, 1960); Mary Lowenthal Felstiner, "Kinship Politics in the Chilean Independence Movement," *Hispanic American Historical Review* 56, no. 1 (February 1976): 58–80.

46. Neumann, "United States Aid," 206; James Monroe to JRP, May 1, 1811, folder 7, vol. 1, JRPP; Roland D. Hussey, "Some Articles in Spanish American Historical Reviews, 1938–1940," *Pacific Historical Review* 10, no. 3 (September 1941): 332; Estuardo Nunez, "Viajeros Norteamericanos En El Pacifico Antes De 1825," *Journal of Inter-American Studies* 4, no. 3 (July 1962): 344.

47. Paul Vanorden Shaw, *The Early Constitutions of Chile, 1810–1833* (PhD diss., Columbia University, 1938).

48. Eugenio Pereira Salas, *La influencia norteamericana en las primeras constituciones de Chile* (Santiago de Chile: Talleres Gnificos Valdes Hnos., 1945), 6–8.

49. Journal to Rio de Janeiro, Buenos Aires and Chile [rough draft] 1810–1811, JRP-LC.

50. Journal to Rio de Janeiro, Buenos Aires and Chile [rough draft] 1810–1811, JRP-LC.

51. Dorothy Parton, *The Diplomatic Career of Joel Roberts Poinsett* (Austin: University of Texas Press, 1934), 29; JRP to Joseph Johnson, August 18, 1812, folder 13, vol. 1, JRPP.

52. Eicher, "Inventing Interventionism," 115.

53. Anson Uriel Hancock, *A History of Chile* (Chicago: Charles H. Sergel, 1893), 149.

54. Neumann, "United States Aid," 207.

55. JRP, August 5, 1814, September 10, 1814, folder 15, vol. 1, JRPP.

56. Frank Lawrence Owsley Jr. and Gene A. Smith argue that early filibustering missions into the South and Southwest reveal an administration determined to expand by whatever means necessary and that the adventurers who embodied this expansionist policy usually carried out their operations to acquire land, as well as to spread democracy and liberty. Frank Lawrence Owsley Jr. and Gene A. Smith, *Filibusters and Expansionists: Jeffersonian Manifest Destiny, 1800–1821* (Tuscaloosa: University of Alabama Press, 1997), 3. For the *Leander* Expedition, see Lindsay Schakenbach, "Schemers, Dreamers, and a Revolutionary Foreign Policy: New York City in the Era of Second Independence, 1805–1815," *New York History* 94, nos. 3–4 (Summer/Fall 2013): 267–82. For US attitudes and policies toward Latin American independence, see Fitz, *Our Sister Republics*; James E. Lewis Jr., *The American Union and the Problem of Neighborhood: The United States and the Collapse of the Spanish Empire* (Chapel Hill: University of North Carolina Press, 1998); Harry Bernstein, *Origins of Inter-American Interest, 1700–1812* (Philadelphia: University of Pennsylvania Press, 1945); John J. Johnson, *A Hemisphere Apart: The Foundations of United States Policy toward Latin America* (Baltimore: Johns Hopkins University Press, 1990); James Johnston Auchmuty, *The United States Government and Latin American Independence, 1810–1830* (London: P. S. King & Son, 1937); Charles Carroll Griffin, *The United States and the Disruption of the Spanish Empire, 1810–1822* (New York: Columbia University Press, 1937); Arthur P. Whittaker, *The United States and the Independence of Latin America, 1800–1830* (Baltimore: Johns Hopkins University Press, 1941); Gordon S. Brown, *Latin American Rebels and the United States, 1806–1822* (Jefferson, NC: McFarland, 2015); Neumann, "United States Aid," 204–19. For the racial limits of US sympathy in comparison to the cause of Greek independence, see Piero Gleije-

ses, "The Limits of Sympathy: The United States and the Independence of Spanish America," *Journal of Latin American Studies* 24, no. 3 (October 1992): 481–505.

57. Rafe Blaufarb argues that an influx of arms from the United States and Europe after the Napoleonic Wars was responsible for the revival of patriot military successes in South America after 1816. Rafe Blaufarb, "Arms for Revolutions: Military Demobilization after the Napoleonic Wars and Latin American Independence," in *War, Demobilization and Memory: The Legacy of War in the Era of Atlantic Revolutions*, ed. Alan Forrest, Karen Hageman, and Michael Rowe (Basingstoke: Palgrave Macmillan, 2016), 100–116.

58. John J. Johnson, "Early Relations of the United States with Chile," *Pacific Historical Review* 13, no. 3 (September 1944): 267.

59. For a discussion of the interconnectedness of merchants' individual interests and state apparatuses, see Hannah Farber, "State-Building after War's End: A Government Financier Adjusts His Portfolio for Peace," *Journal of the Early Republic* 38, no. 1 (Spring 2018): 67–76.

60. Neumann, "United States Aid," 209.

61. Bernardo O'Higgins to JRP, October 28, 1813, folder 16, vol. 1, JRPP.

62. Juan Frances Sanchez, July 29, 1813, folder 16, vol. 1, JRPP.

63. JRP to [?], September 2, 1813, folder 14, vol. 1, JRPP.

64. JRP to [?], September 2, 1813, folder 14, vol. 1, JRPP.

65. JRP to State Department, August 5, 1814, September 10, 1814, folder 15, vol. 1, JRPP.

66. Samuel Curson to JRP, October 11, 1813, folder 15, vol. 1, JRPP.

67. Samuel Curson to JRP, October 11, 1813, folder 15, vol. 1, JRPP.

68. William Miller Collier and Guillermo Feliu Cruz, *La Primera Mision de los Estado Unidos de America en Chile* (Santiago de Chile, 1926), 159–60.

69. JRP to James Monroe, April 12, 1814, folder 15, vol. 1, JRPP.

70. Paul A. Gilje, "'Free Trade and Sailors' Rights': The Rhetoric of the War of 1812," *Journal of the Early Republic* 30, no. 1 (Spring 2010): 13.

71. David Porter, *Journal of a Cruise Made to the Pacific Ocean* (Philadelphia: Bradford and Inskeep, 1815), 159–60.

72. Peter D. Eicher, "The Commodore as Diplomat: David Porter at the Sublime Porte," in *Raising the Flag: America's First Envoys in Faraway Lands* (Lincoln: University of Nebraska Press, 2018), 182.

73. Ronan, "Some Aspects of the Mission," 107–8.

74. Parton, *Diplomatic Career*, 37.

75. David Porter to JRP, April 17, 1814, folder 15, vol. 1, JRPP.

76. JRP to James Monroe, April 21, June 21, 1814, folder 15, vol. 1, JRPP.

77. Ronan, "Some Aspects of the Mission," 112.

78. Journal to Rio de Janeiro, Buenos Aires and Chile [rough draft] 1810–1811, JRP-LC.

79. Charles H. Bowman, "Manuel Torres, a Spanish American Patriot in Philadelphia, 1796–1822," *Pennsylvania Magazine of History and Biography* 94, no. 1 (January 1970): 27.

80. JRP to State Department, March 9, 1811, folder 5, vol. 1, JRPP.

81. For American reexports of European arms to South America, see Caitlin A. Fitz, "Our Sister Republics: The United States in an Age of American Revolution"

(PhD diss., Yale University, 2010), appendix 3. For the links between US arms shipments and manufactured goods, see Schakenbach Regele, *Manufacturing Advantage*.

82. JRP to State Department, March 15, 1812, folder 13, vol. 1, JRPP.

83. Thomas Lloyd Halsey to US Department of State, February 11, 1815, USDS-DC Buenos Aires.

84. JRP to [?] March 6, 1815, folder 17, vol. 1, JRPP; Rippy, *Joel R. Poinsett*, 56.

85. James Leander Cathcart to JRP, February 5, 1815, folder 17, vol. 1, JRPP.

86. Peter D. Eicher, "To the Shores of Tripoli: James Cathcart, William Eaton, and the First Barbary War," in *Raising the Flag: America's First Envoys in Faraway Lands* (Lincoln: University of Nebraska Press, 2018), 34–71; Goodin, *From Captives to Consuls*; Hannah Farber, "Millions for Credit: Peace with Algiers and the Establishment of America's Commercial Reputation Overseas, 1795–96," *Journal of the Early Republic* 34, no. 2 (Summer 2014): 187–217; Michael Kitzen, "Money Bags or Cannon Balls: The Origins of the Tripolitan War, 1795–1801," *Journal of the Early Republic* 16, no. 4 (Winter 1996): 601–24.

87. For Americans' recent experimentation with the torpedo during the War of 1812, see Andrew J. B. Fagal, "Terror Weapons in the Naval War of 1812," *New York History* 94, nos. 3–4 (Summer/Fall 2013): 221–40.

88. James Leander Cathcart to JRP, February 5, 1815, folder 17, vol. 1, JRPP.

89. Cathcart would later work on linking trade between Mexico and the Barbary States. Roberto Narváez, "Dos Comunicaciones de James Leander Cathcart a Pablo Obregón. Sobre un Proyecto para Iniciar las Relaciones entre México y Berbería (1826)," *Historia Mexicana* 68, no. 4 (2019): 1793–830.

90. James Leander Cathcart to JRP, February 3, 1822, folder 6, vol. 2. Cathcart's request for over $1,600 for a payment for a brig captured in Spanish waters was granted. Annals of Congress, *Congressional Record Bound*, vol. 39, May 7, 1822, 17th Cong., 462.

91. JRP to State Department, May 30, 1815, JRPP.

92. James Monroe to JRP, July 16, 1815, JRPP.

93. JRP to José Miguel Carrera, September 16, 1814, folder 16, vol. 1, JRPP.

94. Rippy, *Joel R. Poinsett*, 62.

95. Felipe Santiago del Solar, "José Miguel Carrera. Redes masónicas y sociedades secretas durantelas guerras de independencia en América del Sur," XII Symposium Internacional de Historia de la Masonería Española (Almeria, October 8–10, 2009), 479.

96. "Certificate of Membership in the Freemason Lodge No. 1 in South Carolina," June 13, 1818, folder 3, Joel Roberts Poinsett Papers, SCHS.

97. José Miguel Carrera to JRP, July 30, 1816, folder 18, vol. 1, JRPP.

98. Charleston (SC) City Council, "Sketch of the Life of Joel R. Poinsett," in *Yearbook 1887: City of Charleston, South Carolina* (Charleston: Lucas, Richardson, Steam Book Printers, 1887), 409–14; Rippy, *Joel R. Poinsett*, 62–64.

99. Charleston (SC) City Council, "Sketch of the Life of Joel R. Poinsett," 409–14.

100. Rippy, *Joel R. Poinsett*, 70; Matthew Mason, "Slavery and Partisan Conflict during the Era of Good Feelings," in *Slavery and Politics in the Early American Republic* (Chapel Hill: University of North Carolina Press, 2006), 75–86; Andrew W. Robertson, "'Look on This Picture . . . and on This!': Nationalism, Localism, and Partisan Images of Otherness in the United States, 1787–1820," *American Historical*

Review 106, no. 4 (October 2001): 1263–80; Kim T. Phillips, "Democrats of the Old School in the Era of Good Feelings," *Pennsylvania Magazine of History and Biography* 95, no. 3 (July 1971): 363–82.

101. For internal improvements in the early republic, see John Lauritz Larson, *Internal Improvement: National Public Works and the Promise of Popular Government in the Early United States* (Chapel Hill: University of North Carolina Press, 2001); Roger Pickenpaugh, *The National Road, 1804–1852: America's First Interstate* (Kent, OH: Kent State University Press, 2020). For the relationship between internal improvements and the strengthening of government power in South Carolina, see Ryan A. Quintana, "Planners, Planters, and Slaves: Producing the State in Early National South Carolina," *Journal of Southern History* 81, no. 1 (February 2015): 79–116.

102. David J. McCord, ed., *The Statutes at Large of South Carolina* (Columbia, SC: A. S. Johnston, 1840), 6:277, 75; Joel Roberts Poinsett, Board of Public Works letters, folders 4–12, in Allston family papers, 1730–1901, (1164.00) SCHS, JRP-LC.

103. JRP to Joseph Johnson, [n.d.], folder 5, vol. 2, JRPP; McCord, *Statutes at Large*, 6:126.

104. E. W. Laight to JRP, March 30, 1821, Board of Public Works, JRP-LC.

105. Ulrich Bonnell Phillips, *A History of Transportation in the Eastern Cotton Belt to 1860* (New York: Columbia University Press, 1908), 86–88.

106. Roy Williams III and Alexander Lucas Lofton, *Rice to Ruin: The Jonathan Lucas Family in South Carolina, 1783–1929* (Columbia: University of South Carolina Press, 2018).

107. McCord, *Statutes at Large*, 8:277–78.

108. Thomas Pinckney Jr. to JRP, February 28, 1822, folder 7, vol. 2, JRPP.

109. Thomas Pinckney Jr. to JRP, February 28, 1822, folder 7, vol. 2, JRPP.

110. A. Blanding and D. J. McCord, *Carolina Law Journal* (Columbia: Times and Gazette Office, 1831), 218.

111. McCord, *Statutes at Large*, 8:277.

112. Harry Watson, "Slavery and Development in a Dual Economy: The South and the Market Revolution," in *The Market Revolution in America: Social, Political, and Religious Expressions, 1800–1880*, ed. Melvyn Stokes and Stephen Conway (Charlottesville: University of Virginia Press, 1996).

113. See, for example, "Conduct of Spain towards the United States," *Boston Patriot*, December 4, 1816, [2]; James Monroe to JRP, October 10, 1816, folder 18, vol. 1, JRPP.

114. D. Porter to JRP, March 19, 1816, folder 19, vol. 1, JRPP.

115. John J. Johnson, "Early Relations of the United States with Chile," *Pacific Historical Review* 13, no. 3 (September 1944): 267.

116. JRP to James Monroe, May 6, 1817, folder 1, vol. 2, JRPP.

117. Henry Bartholomew Cox, "Reasons for Joel R. Poinsett's Refusal of a Second Mission to South America," *Hispanic American Historical Review* 43, no. 3 (August 1963): 406.

118. Wayne D. Rasmussen, "Diplomats and Plant Collectors: The South American Commission, 1817–1818," *Agricultural History* 29, no. 1 (January 1955): 23. On returning to the United States, Henry Brackenridge published *Voyage to South America, Performed by Order of the American Government, in the Years 1817 and 1818, in the Frigate Congress* (Baltimore: printed by John D. Troy, 1819).

119. For a summary of the mission, see Watt Stewart, "The South American Commission, 1817–1818," *Hispanic American Historical Review* 9, no. 1 (1929): 31–59.

120. Rasmussen, "Diplomats and Plant Collectors," 31.

121. Merchants, for example, were very interested in the types of sheep in South America, especially as certain wool was better for certain American manufactures. David Curtis De Forest to George Dyson, March 7, 1814, De Forest family papers, Yale Collection of American Literature, Beinecke Rare Book and Manuscript Library, box 3, folder 15, letter book 5; Henry Hill to Captain Herman Perry, June 10, 1817, Henry Hill papers, Manuscripts and Archives, Yale University, box 1, folder 2. For discussions of the American extraction of raw materials outside the territory of the United States later in the nineteenth century, see Edward D. Melillo, "Debt Peonage and the Making of the Nitrogen Fertilizer Trade, 1840–1930," *American Historical Review* 117, no. 4 (October 2012): 1028–69; Christina Duffy Burnett, "The Edges of Empire and the Limits of Sovereignty: American Guano Islands," *American Quarterly* 57 (September 2005): 779–803.

122. William G. Miller to JRP, August 18, 1818, folder 3, JRPP.

123. This collection of and experimentation with natural flora marked a transition from the medieval and early modern elite European practice of assembling curiosity cabinets to modern bioprospecting. Lorraine Daston and Katherine Park, *Wonders and the Order of Nature* (New York: Zone Books, 1998); Stephen Greenblatt, *Marvelous Possession: The Wonder of the New World* (Chicago: University of Chicago Press, 1991); Christian F. Feest, "The Collecting of American Indian Artifacts in Europe, 1493–1750," in *America in European Consciousness 1493–1750*, ed. Karen Ordahl Kupperman (Chapel Hill: University of North Carolina Press, 1995). For the exploitation and extraction of natural resources and knowledge in the name of Western dominance, see Londa L. Schiebinger, *Plants and Empire: Colonial Bioprospecting in the Atlantic World* (Cambridge, MA: Harvard University Press, 2009).

124. *Message from the President of the United States at the Commencement of the Second Session of the Fifteenth Congress* (Washington, DC: E. De Kraft, 1818).

125. Rippy, *Joel R. Poinsett*, 67.

126. Henry Marie Brackenridge, *South America: A Letter of the Present State of That Country to James Monroe, President of the United States* (Washington, DC: Office of the National Register, 1817), 34, 37.

127. Rippy, *Joel R. Poinsett*, 67–68.

128. Lindsay Schakenbach, "From Discontented Bostonians to Patriotic Industrialists: The Boston Associates and the Transcontinental Treaty, 1790–1825," *New England Quarterly* 84 (September 2011): 377–401.

129. William Miller to JRP, April 27, 1819, folder 3, vol. 2, JRPP.

130. José Miguel Carrera to JRP, July 2, 1819, folder 4, vol. 2, JRPP.

131. Langdon Cheves to JRP, December 20, 1819, folder 4, vol. 2, JRPP.

132. John C. Calhoun to JRP, July 3, 1821, folder 5, vol. 2, JRPP.

Chapter 3

1. Edward Everett to JRP, August 3, 1820, folder 4, vol. 2, JRPP.

2. Edward Everett to JRP, June 2, 1821, folder 5, vol. 2, JRPP.

3. Stephen Elliott to JRP, January 9, 1822, folder 5, vol. 2, JRPP.

4. Peter Du Ponceau to JRP, October 9, 1820, folder 5, vol. 2, JRPP.

5. "State of South Carolina," December 12, 1820, folder 3, JRPP, SCHS.

6. "Communication," *City Gazette* (Charleston, SC), September 26, 1820, 2.

7. "Mechanics—Look at This!," *City Gazette* (Charleston, SC), October 9, 1820, 2.

8. James Burn to JRP, April 5, 1820, folder 6, Allston family papers, 1730–1901, (1164.00) SCHS. Burn also found Poinsett a map engraver and said that he could have maps made cheaper in the Philadelphia area than in South Carolina. James Burn to JRP, March 14, 1821, Board of Public Works of South Carolina, 1819–1821, JRP-LC.

9. Camillus, *Who Ought We to Send to Congress, John Geddes, or J.R. Poinsett? Dispassionately Discussed, and Respectfully Submitted to the Electors of Charleston District* (Charleston, SC, 1820), 15, 21.

10. Philip Lampi, comp., "South Carolina 1820 US House of Representatives, District 1," *A New Nation Votes*, American Antiquarian Society and Tufts University Digital Collections and Archives, accessed June, 2020, https://elections.lib.tufts.edu/catalog/q524jn87c.

11. Daniel Kilbride, "Philadelphia and the Southern Elite: Class, Kinship, and Culture in Antebellum America" (PhD diss., University of Florida, 1997), 354; Daniel Kilbride, *An American Aristocracy: Southern Planters in Antebellum Philadelphia* (Columbia: University of South Carolina Press, 2006).

12. Charles Ingersoll to JRP, October 26, 1820, folder 5, vol. 2, JRPP.

13. "Legislative Acts/Legal Proceedings," *City Gazette* (Charleston, SC), December 27, 1820, [2].

14. "Extract of a Letter from a Gentleman in Shelbyville, Dated 10th January, 1821, to His Friend in This City," *City Gazette* (Charleston, SC), February 12, 1821, 2.

15. Robert Mills to JRP, March 17, 1836, folder 17, vol. 7, JRPP. Mills would also request renewed employment when Poinsett was back in South Carolina.

16. John Johnson to JRP, October 24, 1820, folder 10, Allston family papers, 1730–1901, (1164.00) SCHS.

17. Robert Mills to JRP, June 5, 1821, Board of Public Works of South Carolina, 1819–1821, JRP-LC; David Kohn and Bess Glenn, *Internal Improvement in South Carolina, 1817–1828* (Washington, DC, 1938).

18. "[Col. Thomas Pinckney; Board; Public Works; President; Hon. Joel R. Poinsett]," *City Gazette* (Charleston, SC), July 10, 1821, [2]; Board of Public Works of South Carolina, 1819–1821, JRP-LC; A. Blanding to JRP, June 5, 1821, Board of Public Works of South Carolina, 1819–1821, JRP-LC; JRP to Joseph Johnson, June 19, July 10, 1821, PPGC, HSP.

19. JRP to Isaac Johnson, July 9, 1821, Poinsett, Joel Roberts, 1779–1851, Letters to Isaac A. Johnson, 1821–1826, (43/131) SCHS.

20. Churchill C. Cambreleng to JRP, March 3, 1825, folder 14, vol. 2, JRPP.

21. JRP to John Quincy Adams, June 8, 1827, folder 8, vol. 9, JRPP.

22. Robert Walsh to JRP, May 12, 1830, folder 8, vol. 6, JRPP.

23. JRP to Isaac Johnson, March 31, 1825, Poinsett, Joel Roberts, 1779–1851, Letters to Isaac A. Johnson, 1821–1826, (43/131) SCHS.

24. "Pennsylvania, Philadelphia City Death Certificates, 1803–1915," index, FamilySearch, Salt Lake City, UT, 2008, 2010, from originals housed at the Philadelphia City Archives, "Death Records."

25. JRP to Isaac Johnson, March 31, 1825, Poinsett, Joel Roberts, 1779–1851, Letters to Isaac A. Johnson, 1821–1826, (43/131) SCHS.

26. JRP to Joseph Johnson, July 10, 1821, PPGC.

27. JRP to Frances Tyrrell, July 15, 1847, PPGC.

28. JRP to Joseph Johnson, November 1821, PPGC.

29. John C. Calhoun to JRP, July 3, 1821, folder 5, vol. 2, JRPP.

30. ASP, "Reduction of the Army Considered," H.R., December 4, 1818, 15th Cong., Military Affairs, vol. 1, no. 168, 779; "An Act to Reduce and Fix the Military Peace Establishment of the United States," March 2, 1821, in Trueman T. Cross, *Military Laws of the United States* (Washington City [Washington, DC]: George Templeman, 1838), 213; John C. Calhoun to JRP, July 3, 1821, folder 5, vol. 2, JRPP. In July, the United States took control of Spanish Florida, fueling new concerns over national security. Andrew Jackson took over as governor with Henry M. Brackenridge as alcalde. Herbert J. Dougherty Jr., "Ante-bellum Pensacola: 1821–1860," *Florida Historical Quarterly* 37, nos. 3/4 (January–April 1959): 337–56.

31. William Johnson to JRP, January 3, 1822, folder 5, vol. 2, JRPP. For Johnson's career and views, see Irwin F. Greenberg, "Justice William Johnson: South Carolina Unionist, 1823–1830," *Pennsylvania History: A Journal of Mid-Atlantic Studies* 36, no. 3 (July 1969): 307–34.

32. W. B. Finch to Louis McLane, January 6, 1822, folder 5, vol. 2, JRPP.

33. Annals of Congress, *Congressional Record Bound*, vol. 39, April 15, 1822, 17th Cong., 1574.

34. Annals of Congress, *Congressional Record Bound*, vol. 39, April 19, 1822, 17th Cong., 1616.

35. Douglas R. Egerton, *He Shall Go Out Free: The Lives of Denmark Vesey* (Lanham, MD: Rowman & Littlefield, 1999); Edward A. Pearson, ed., *Designs against Charleston: The Trial Record of the Denmark Vesey Slave Conspiracy of 1822* (Chapel Hill: University of North Carolina Press, 1999); David Robertson, *Denmark Vesey* (New York: Alfred A. Knopf, 1999).

36. Scholars have debated the extent to which this was a conspiracy. James O'Neil Spady, "Power and Confession: On the Credibility of the Earliest Reports of the Denmark Vesey Slave Conspiracy," *William and Mary Quarterly* 68, no. 2 (April 2011): 287–304; Michael P. Johnson, "Denmark Vesey and His Co-conspirators," *William and Mary Quarterly* 58 (October 2001): 915–76; Robert L. Paquette and Douglas R. Egerton, "Of Facts and Fables: New Light on the Denmark Vesey Affair," *South Carolina Historical Magazine* 105, no. 1 (January 2004): 8–48.

37. James Hamilton Jr., *Negro Plot: An Account of the Late Intended Insurrection among a Portion of the Blacks of the City of Charleston, South Carolina* (Boston: Joseph W. Ingraham, 1822); Lionel H. Kennedy and Thomas Parker, eds., *An Official Report of the Trials of Sundry Negroes, Charged with an Attempt to Raise an Insurrection in the State of South-Carolina [. . .]* (Charleston, SC: James R. Schenck, 1822).

38. Hamilton, *Negro Plot*, 28.

39. Hamilton, *Negro Plot*, 28.

40. James O'Neil Spady, "Power and Confession: On the Credibility of the Earliest Reports of the Denmark Vesey Slave Conspiracy," *William and Mary Quarterly* 68, no. 2 (April 2011): 287–304.

41. Charles Jared Ingersoll, *African Slavery in America* (Philadelphia: T. K. and P. G. Collins, 1856), 4.

42. James Fred Rippy, *Joel R. Poinsett: Versatile American* (Durham: University of North Carolina Press, 1935), 88.

43. Irwin F. Greenberg, "Justice William Johnson: South Carolina Unionist, 1823–1830," *Pennsylvania History: A Journal of Mid-Atlantic Studies* 36, no. 3 (July 1969): 307–34.

44. Henry William DeSaussure to JRP, July 9, 1822, folder 7, vol. 2, JRPP.

45. This law mandated that free Black sailors would be jailed at their ship captain's expense or sold into slavery. The following year, William Johnson's court ruled the law unconstitutional, but Charleston continued to brutally police free Blacks. Elkison v. Deliesseline, 8 F. Cas. 493, 2 Wheeler, Cr. Cas. 56 (1823).

46. Timothy E. Anna, "The Rule of Agustin De Iturbide: A Reappraisal," *Journal of Latin American Studies* 17, no. 1 (May 1985): 82. For Mexican independence politics, see Timothy E. Anna, *Forging Mexico, 1821–1835* (Lincoln: University of Nebraska Press, 1998); Torcuato S. Di Tella, *National Popular Politics in Early Independent Mexico, 1820–1847* (Albuquerque: University of New Mexico Press, 1996).

47. Annals of Congress, "South American Governments," March 28, 1822, 17th Cong., 400.

48. Gregg Cantrell, "Mexico, 1821–1823," in *Stephen F. Austin: Empresario of Texas* (New Haven, CT: Yale University Press, 1999), 109.

49. For the beginnings of strain, see Josefina Zoraida Vázquez, "Los Comienzos," in *México y el Expansionismo Norteamericano* (Mexico City: El Colegio de Mexico, 2010), 37–48.

50. Stephen Elliott to JRP, July 24, 1822, folder 7, vol. 2, JRPP.

51. Dorothy Parton, *The Diplomatic Career of Joel Roberts Poinsett* (Austin: University of Texas Press, 1934), 49.

52. Joel Poinsett, *Notes on Mexico, Made in the Autumn of 1822* (Philadelphia: H. C. Carey and I. Lea, 1824), 9.

53. Poinsett, *Notes*, 9.

54. Poinsett, *Notes*, 6.

55. Parton, *Diplomatic Career*, 50.

56. Poinsett, *Notes*, 12.

57. Poinsett, *Notes*, 13.

58. Poinsett, *Notes*, 18.

59. Poinsett, *Notes*, 19.

60. Richard J. Salvucci, "The Origins and Progress of U.S.-Mexican Trade, 1825–1884: 'Hoc Opus, Hic Labor Est.,'" *Hispanic American Historical Review* 71, no. 4 (1991): 697–735, esp. 712.

61. Salvucci, "Origins and Progress," 699.

62. Poinsett, *Notes*, 20.

63. Poinsett, *Notes*, 21.

64. Poinsett, *Notes*, 23.

65. Poinsett, *Notes*, 30.

66. Poinsett, *Notes*, 36.

67. Poinsett, *Notes*, 37.

68. Poinsett, *Notes*, 38.

69. Poinsett, *Notes*, 42.

70. Poinsett, *Notes*, 43.

71. Poinsett, *Notes*, 65–67.

72. Poinsett, *Notes*, 83.

73. Poinsett, *Notes*, 81.

74. Poinsett, *Notes*, 91.

75. Poinsett, *Notes*, 23.

76. Di Tella, *National Popular Politics*, 105.

77. Poinsett, *Notes*, 164–65.

78. Poinsett, *Notes*, 92.

79. Poinsett, *Notes*, 93.

80. Poinsett, *Notes*, 93.

81. Margaret E. Rankine, "The Mexican Mining Industry in the Nineteenth Century with Special Reference to Guanajuato," *Bulletin of Latin American Research* 11, no. 1 (January 1992): 29–30.

82. Poinsett, *Notes*, 93–94.

83. Rankine, "Mexican Mining Industry," 29–30.

84. Poinsett, *Notes*, 104.

85. Poinsett, *Notes*, 128.

86. Poinsett, *Notes*, 183.

87. Poinsett, *Notes*, 243.

88. Poinsett, *Notes*, 246. This was Poinsett speaking from a radical liberal perspective, but Iturbide did start to lose support from progressive liberals. Di Tella, *National Popular Politics*, 119.

89. Poinsett, *Notes*, 254.

90. Poinsett, *Notes*, 257.

91. Poinsett, *Notes*, 266.

92. Poinsett, *Notes*, 265–66.

93. Poinsett, *Notes*, 274.

94. Poinsett, *Notes*, 276.

95. Benjamin Milam and Lorenzo Christie to JRP, December 3, 1822, folder 7, vol. 2, JRP.

96. Poinsett, *Notes*, 189.

97. Poinsett, *Notes*, 189.

98. Poinsett, *Notes*, 186.

99. Poinsett, *Notes*, 96.

100. Poinsett, *Notes*, 225–33.

101. Poinsett, *Notes*, 222.

102. Poinsett, *Notes*, 280.

103. Poinsett, *Notes*, 282.

104. Poinsett, *Notes*, 284–94.

105. Poinsett, *Notes*, 294. For the significance of the Cuban slave trade for US economic development and foreign policy, see Stephen Chambers, *No God but Gain: The Untold Story of Cuban Slavery, the Monroe Doctrine, and the Making of the United States* (New York: Verso, 2015).

106. Poinsett, *Notes*, 297–98.

107. JRP to Andrew Jackson, January 31, 1823, vol. 63, Andrew Jackson Papers, MSS 27532, Library of Congress (AJLC).

108. George B. Dyer and Charlotte L. Dyer, "A Century of Strategic Intelligence Reporting: Mexico, 1822–1919," *Geographical Review* 44, no. 1 (January 1954): 50.

109. Poinsett quotes, for example, Humboldt's description of the view from the convent of San Francisco and writes about Humboldt's experiment on the lake of Tezcuco, which contained "more of the muriate of soda than the Baltic sea." Poinsett, *Notes*, 35, 81.

110. Edith F. Helman, "Early Interest in Spanish in New England (1815–1835)," *Hispania* 29, no. 3 (August 1946): 339–51, 347.

111. Helmbrecht Breinig, "Invasive Methods: The Opening of Latin America in Nineteenth-Century U.S. Literature," *Amerikastudien/American Studies* 53, no. 1 (2008): 13–36.

112. José Antonio Aguilar Rivera, "Tocqueville in Mexico," *Journal of Iberian and Latin American Studies* 26, no. 2 (2020): 175–88.

113. T. Ford to JRP, May 26, 1823, folder 8, vol. 2, JRPP.

114. Chambers, *No God but Gain.*

115. In general, his speeches were shorter than others' because "his breast is not strong enough to deliver long speeches." "[Mr. Poinsett; Mexico]," *National Gazette* (Philadelphia), June 8, 1824, 2, Readex: America's Historical Newspapers.

116. "To the Planters," *City Gazette* (Charleston, SC), October 11, 1824, 2, Readex: America's Historical Newspapers.

117. Richard P. McCormick, *The Second Party System: Party Formation in the Jacksonian Era* (Chapel Hill: University of North Carolina Press, 1966); Richard Hofstadter, *The Idea of a Party System: The Rise of Legitimate Opposition in the United States, 1780–1840* (Berkeley: University of California Press, 1969).

118. Gary J. Kornblith, "Rethinking the Coming of the Civil War: A Counterfactual Exercise," *Journal of American History* 90, no. 1 (June 2003): 89; Adam Jortner, "Cholera, Christ, and Jackson: The Epidemic of 1832 and the Origins of Christian Politics in Antebellum America," *Journal of the Early Republic* 27, no. 2 (Summer 2007): 225.

119. Douglas Bowers argues that for the great majority of bills, parties offered little or no guidance. Douglas E. Bowers, "From Logrolling to Corruption: The Development of Lobbying in Pennsylvania, 1815–1861," *Journal of the Early Republic* 3 (Winter 1983): 439–74, quote 451. For other studies that make similar points, see John H. Aldrich, *Why Parties? The Origin and Transformation of Political Parties in America* (Chicago: University of Chicago Press, 1995), 97–125; Mark Voss-Hubbard, *Beyond Party: Cultures of Antipartisanship in Northern Politics before the Civil War* (Baltimore: Johns Hopkins University Press, 2002).

120. Annals of Congress, February 17, 1823, 17th Cong., 1040.

121. Annals of Congress, *Congressional Record Bound*, "Memorial of Masters of American Vessels," February 19, 1823, 1305–6.

122. Annals of Congress, *Congressional Record Bound*, "An Act to Establish a Competent Force to Act as a Municipal Guard, for the Protection of Charleston and Its Vicinity," March 3, 1823, 17th Cong., 1308–10.

123. President of the Franklin Society to JRP, May 20, 1823, folder 8, vol. 2, JRPP; Spain Frances Lander, "Libraries of South Carolina: Their Origins and Early History, 1700–1830," *Library Quarterly: Information, Community, Policy* 17, no. 1 (January 1947): 28–42.

124. For the importance of cultural aesthetics in early national politics, see

Catherine E. Kelly, *Republic of Taste: Art, Politics, and Everyday Life in Early America* (Philadelphia: University of Pennsylvania Press, 2016).

125. Stephen Elliott to JRP, January 16, 1824, folder 8, vol. 2, JRPP.

126. John Rodgers, "Examination and Survey of the Harbor of Charleston, South Carolina, and the Coast of Florida, with a View to the Establishment of Navy Yards," May 8, 1824, 18th Cong., ASP023 Nav.aff.246; Annals of Congress, "Standing Committees," December 3, 1823, 18th Cong., 797.

127. James Monroe, US Senate Journal, "Annual Message to Congress," December 2, 1823, 18th Cong., 11. For scholarly interpretations, see Dexter Perkins, *A History of the Monroe Doctrine* (Boston: Little, Brown, 1941); William Weeks, *John Quincy Adams and American Global Empire* (Lexington: University Press of Kentucky, 1992); Jay Sexton, *The Monroe Doctrine: Empire and Nation in Nineteenth-Century America* (New York: Hill and Wang, 2011). While Monroe's message lacked military teeth, it did informally bind the United States to take action should this declaration have been violated—an obligation to which Latin American officials held the US government accountable and to which it often complied. For examples of ministers asking the US State Department for clarification on its promise to resist foreign interference by the Holy Alliance and later requesting US military intervention against Britain and diplomatic intervention in negotiation with Spain, see José María Salazar to John Quincy Adams, July 2, 1824, USDS, Notes from the Colombian Legation, 1810–1906, RG59 National Archives, Washington, DC, 1943, microfilm M51, roll 2. Domingo Acosta to Louis McLane, April 17, 1834; Domingo Acosta to John Forsyth, February 25, 1837. See Pablo Obregon to Henry Clay (acknowledging the receipt of his note saying a US minister had been sent to Russia to request its influence with Spain in concluding peace with Mexico), January 4, 1824, USDS, Notes from the Mexican Legation, 1821–1906, RG59 National Archives, Washington, DC, 1960, microfilm M54, roll 1.

128. Worthington Chauncey Ford, "John Quincy Adams and the Monroe Doctrine," *American Historical Review* 8, no. 1 (1902): 685.

129. Poinsett, *Notes*, 93.

130. Stephen Chambers, "The American State of Cuba: The Business of Cuba and U.S. Foreign Policy, 1797–1825" (PhD diss., Brown University, 2008), 223; ASP, "Suppression of Piracy in the West Indies," May 19, 1824, 344.

131. Edward Mead Earle, "American Interest in the Greek Cause, 1821–1827," *American Historical Review* 33, no. 1 (October 1927): 44–63; Maureen Connors Santelli, *The Greek Fire: American-Ottoman Relations and Democratic Fervor in the Age of Revolutions* (Ithaca, NY: Cornell University Press, 2020).

132. Joel Roberts Poinsett, speech on the resolutions of Mr. Webster, of Massachusetts, recommending an appropriation to defray the expense of a mission to Greece (Charleston, A. E. Miller, 1824); Annals of Congress, *Congressional Record Bound*, "The Greek Cause," January 20, 1824, 18th Cong., 1104–11.

133. Jacques M. Downes, "American Merchants and the China Opium Trade, 1800–1840," *Business History Review* 42, no. 4 (Winter 1968): 418–42.

134. Jared Jacavone, "The Paid Vote: America's Neutrality during the Greek War for Independence" (master's thesis, University of Rhode Island, 2017). For Perkins and the opium trade, see Downes, "American Merchants," 418–42, esp. 431.

135. Annals of Congress, *Congressional Record Bound*, March 24, 1824, 18th Cong., 1894.

136. Frances Baring to JRP, August 27, 1823, folder 8, vol. 2, JRPP.

137. Annals of Congress, *Congressional Record Bound,* "The Tariff Bill," April 8, 1824, 18th Cong., 2252.

138. Daniel Peart, "Looking beyond Parties and Elections: The Making of United States Tariff Policy during the Early 1820s," *Journal of the Early Republic* 33, no. 1 (Spring 2013): 87–108.

139. Benjamin Pickman to JRP, February 10, 1824, folder 8, vol. 2, JRPP.

140. Annals of Congress, *Congressional Record Bound,* "The Tariff Bill," April 8, 1824, 18th Cong., 2240.

141. William Sampson to JRP, February 12, 1824; E.W. Laight to JRP, April 26, 1824, folder 9, vol. 2, JRPP.

142. Annals of Congress, *Congressional Record Bound,* "The Tariff Bill," May 17, 1824, 18th Cong., 2623.

143. Annals of Congress, *Congressional Record Bound,* "The Tariff Bill," May 17, 1824, 18th Cong., 2623; Douglas A. Irwin and Peter Temin, "The Antebellum Tariff on Cotton Textiles Revisited," *Journal of Economic History* 61, no. 3 (September 2001): 777–98.

144. Col. Blanding to JRP, February 12, 1824, folder 1, vol. 9, JRPP.

145. Act to Procure the Necessary Surveys, Plans, and Estimated, upon the Subject of Roads and Canals, 4 Stat. 22 (April 30, 1824).

146. John C. Calhoun to JRP, July 8, 1824, folder 10, vol. 2, JRPP.

147. Rippy, *Joel Roberts Poinsett,* 105.

148. Samuel L. Southard to JRP, July 17, 1824, folder 9, vol. 2, JRPP.

149. John C. Calhoun to JRP, July 8, 1824, folder 10, vol. 2, JRPP.

150. "To the Virtuous and Independent of All Parties," *City Gazette* (Charleston, SC), October 11, 1824, 2, Readex: America's Historical Newspapers; "To the Planters," *City Gazette* (Charleston, SC), October 11, 1824, 2, Readex: America's Historical Newspapers.

151. "[Determine; Gen. Jackson]," *Charleston (SC) Courier,* October 6, 1824, 2, Readex: America's Historical Newspapers; "[Amicus; Mr. Poinsett; Adams; Crawford]," *Charleston (SC) Courier,* October 7, 1824, 2, Readex: America's Historical Newspapers.

152. "[Amicus; Mr. Poinsett; Adams; Crawford]," *Charleston (SC) Courier,* October 7, 1824, 2, Readex: America's Historical Newspapers.

153. "To the Planters," *City Gazette* (Charleston, SC), October 11, 1824, 2, Readex: America's Historical Newspapers.

154. "[City; Gazette; Aristocrat; Hon. Joel R. Poinsett; Vice-President; Representative; Congress]," *City Gazette* (Charleston, SC), October 5, 1824, 2, Readex: America's Historical Newspapers.

155. "Report of the Committee Appointed to Prepare Rules to Be Observed by the House of Representatives in Choosing a President, &c.," 122 H.R. Rep. 41, January 26, 1825, 18th Cong.

156. Levatt Jarvis to JRP, December 13, 1824, folder 11, Vol 2, JRPP.

157. "Report of the Committee Appointed," 122 H.R. 41.

158. *Register of Debates,* February 9, 1825, 18th Cong., 525–27; Donald Ratcliffe, "Popular Preferences in the Presidential Election of 1824," *Journal of the Early Republic* 34, no. 1 (Spring 2014): 45–77.

159. Edward Everett to JRP, March 5, 1825, folder 11, vol. 2, JRPP.

160. Lawrence S. Kaplan, "The Monroe Doctrine and the Truman Doctrine: The Case of Greece," *Journal of the Early Republic* 13, no. 1 (Spring 1993): 18.

161. Edward Everett to JRP, March 5, 1825, folder 11, vol. 2, JRPP.

Chapter 4

1. James Madison to JRP, December 10, 1824, in *The Papers of James Madison Digital Edition*, ed. J. C. A. Stagg (Charlottesville: University of Virginia Press, Rotunda, 2010).

2. JRP to Daniel Webster, July 14, 1824, in *The Papers of Daniel Webster Digital Edition*, ed. Charles M. Wiltse (Charlottesville: University of Virginia Press, Rotunda, 2018).

3. William R. Manning, "Poinsett's Mission to Mexico: A Discussion of His Interference in Internal Affairs," *American Journal of International Law* 7, no. 4 (October 1913): 786; Curt Lamar, "Genesis of Mexican–United States Diplomacy: A Critical Analysis of the Alaman-Poinsett Confrontation, 1825," *Americas* 38, no. 1 (July 1981): 94.

4. J. Allen Smith to JRP, March 16, 1825, folder 12, vol. 2, JRPP.

5. Hezekiah Niles, William Ogden Niles, Jeremiah Hughes, and George Beatty, eds., *Niles' National Register* (Baltimore: Franklin, 1827), 32:234.

6. Poinsett would later oppose the annexation of Texas.

7. For Manifest Destiny as an American ideology from settlement to the twentieth century, see Anders Stephanson, *Manifest Destiny: American Expansionism and the Empire of Right* (New York: Hill and Wang, 1995). For expansion as a racial mission, see Reginald Horsman, *Race and Manifest Destiny: The Origins of American Racial Anglo-Saxonism* (Cambridge, MA: Harvard University Press, 1981).

8. Over a decade before the phrase *Manifest Destiny* was coined, British emancipation in 1833 prompted American slaveholders to protect jealously the institution in the hemisphere. Matthew Karp, *This Vast Southern Empire: Slaveholders at the Helm of American Foreign Policy* (Cambridge, MA: Harvard University Press, 2016).

9. Both contemporaries and historians used to argue that Britain had minimal imperial ambitions. Kinley Brauer, "The United States and British Imperial Expansion, 1815–60," *Diplomatic History* 12, no. 1 (Winter 1988): 20.

10. Alan C. Hutchinson, "General José Antonio Mexía and His Texas Interests," *Southwestern Historical Quarterly* 82, no. 2 (October 1978): 117–42, 123; Aaron Sachs, *The Humboldt Current: Nineteenth-Century Exploration and the Roots of American Environmentalism* (New York: Viking Books, 2006); Andrea Wulf, *The Invention of Nature: Alexander von Humboldt's New World* (New York: Vintage, 2016).

11. Poinsett notes specifically that Alexander von Humboldt had praised some of them. Joel Poinsett, *Notes on Mexico, Made in the Autumn of 1822* (Philadelphia: H. C. Carey and I. Lea, 1824), 71.

12. JRP to John Vaughan, March 5, 1829, Joel Roberts Poinsett, 1779–1851, American Philosophical Society.

13. For a definition of *corruption* that traces to the early modern era: in general usage, "moral deterioration or decay; depravity"; in government usage, "perversion or destruction of integrity in the discharge of public duties by bribery or favour; the

use or existence of corrupt practices, esp. in a state, public corporation, etc." *Oxford English Dictionary*, s.v. "corruption," http://www.oed.com, cited in Paula Baker, Mary Berry, Daniel Czitrom, Barbara Hahn, James Kloppenberg, Naomi Lamoreaux, and David Witwer, "Interchange: Corruption Has a History," *Journal of American History* 105, no. 4 (March 2019): 920. For another "corrupt bargain" of 1824, see Craig B. Hollander, "Corrupt Bargaining: Partisan Politics, the Election of 1824, and the Suppression of the African Slave Trade," *Journal of the Early Republic* 42, no. 3 (Fall 2022): 359–87.

14. The large body of scholarship dealing with the evolution and meaning of *interest* throughout the early national period does not quite capture Poinsett's experience in Mexico. For a discussion of this scholarship, see the introduction.

15. For example, five men sent introductory letters to Poinsett on behalf of the "most reputable" Captain Joseph Vidal from New Orleans, who had headed to Mexico to pursue the claims of his deceased friend. They stressed that Vidal was "disinterested." R. R. Call to JRP, April 16, 1825, folder 14, vol. 2, JRPP; David Holmes to JRP, May 7, 1825, folder 14, vol. 2, JRPP; Christopher Rankin, May 8, 1825, folder 14, vol. 2, JRPP.

16. Here, I am borrowing other historians' definitions of *corruption*. David Witmer defines *corruption* as "when someone violates the trust, duty, or obligation inherent in their position." Barbara Hahn defines it as "a way of using an institution to effect goals opposite to its purposes." Baker et al., "Interchange," 914–15.

17. Richard White, "Developing the West: Information, Markets, and Corruption; Transcontinental Railroads in the Gilded Age," *Journal of American History* 90, no. 1 (June 2003): 19–43.

18. Manning, "Poinsett's Mission to Mexico," 792.

19. For an overview of the origins of tension between Poinsett and some factions in Mexico and for a balanced treatment of Poinsett's interests in Mexico, see Lamar, "Genesis of Mexican–United States Diplomacy," 87–110.

20. E.W. Laight to JRP, March 29, 1825, folder 9, vol. 2, JRPP.

21. Joseph Johnson, March 17, 1825, folder 9, vol. 2, JRPP.

22. JRP to Joseph Johnson, April 4, 1825, PPGC, p. 13.

23. Lafayette to JRP, April 24, 1825, vol. 2, JRPP.

24. William Taylor to John Quincy Adams, December 19, 1824, USDS-DC Vera Cruz.

25. James Wilkson to James B. Wilkinson, September 1, 1824, HM27510, Correspondence of James Wilkinson, Huntington Library, San Marino, CA.

26. "[Mexico; United States; Successful]," *Georgian* (Savannah, GA), April 20, 1825, [2].

27. Manning, "Poinsett's Mission to Mexico," 788.

28. JRP to Miguel Barragán and Major Woolsey, May 5 and 22, 1825; José Coppinger to JRP, May 8, 1825, folder 15, vol. 2, JRPP.

29. JRP to James Wilcocks, May 14, 1825, folder 15, vol. 2, JRPP.

30. James Wilcocks to John Quincy Adams, August 2, 1822, USDS-DC Mexico.

31. To James Madison from Dennis A. Smith, February 21, 1825, in *The Papers of James Madison*, vol. 3, *1 March 1823–24 February 1826*, Retirement Series, ed. David B. Mattern, J. C. A. Stagg, Mary Parke Johnson, and Katherine E. Harbury (Charlottesville: University of Virginia Press, 2016), 476–78, quoted in *Founders Online*,

National Archives, https://founders.archives.gov/documents/Madison/04-03-02 -0477; Sharon Ann Murphy, "The Financialization of Slavery by the First and Second Banks of the United States," *Journal of Southern History* 87 (August 2021): 387.

32. Harris Gaylord Warren, "The Origin of General Mina's Invasion of Mexico," *Southwestern Historical Quarterly* 42, no. 1 (July 1938): 10–11.

33. James Wilcocks to John Quincy Adams, January 8, 1823, USDS-DC Mexico.

34. Marjorie Millace Whiteman, *Damages in International Law* (Washington, DC: US Government Printing Office, 1937), 3:1978. New Orleans was a hub for revolutionary activity throughout the nineteenth century. Kyle Jackson, "Port of Call to Arms: New Orleans and the Greater Caribbean in the Long Nineteenth Century" (PhD diss. in progress, UC Berkeley).

35. William Brent to JRP, March 29, 1825; R. R. Call to JRP, April 16, 1825, folder 14, vol. 2, JRPP; David Holmes to JRP, May 7, 1825, folder 14, vol. 2, JRPP; Christopher Rankin, May 8, 1825, folder 14, vol. 2, JRPP.

36. Joseph Johnson, April 13, 1825, folder 14, vol. 2, JRPP.

37. James Hawkins to JRP, March 25, 1825, folder 12, vol. 2 JRPP.

38. For information on the claims commission that commenced in 1839 to settle American claims against the Mexican government, see the digital work of David Mackenzie, George Mason University, http://davidmckenzie.info/claims/index.php.

39. JRP to James Wilcocks, May 18, 1825, folder 15, vol. 2, JRPP.

40. C. J. Ingersoll, July 9, 1830, Tlacotal mining company, folder 11, vol. 17, JRPP.

41. James Smith Wilcocks to John Quincy Adams, July 30, 1822, August 22, 1822, USDS-DC Mexico.

42. United States' Mexican Company, *Statement in Relation to the United States' Mexican Company* (Albany, NY: Websters and Skinners, 1826), 2.

43. This form of corruption is related to Barbara Hahn's definition as being the use of an institution for purposes other than its intentions, as well as Paula Baker's definition of violating the trust established with one's position. Baker et al., "Interchange," 914–15.

44. Manning, "Poinsett's Mission to Mexico," 792.

45. D. A. Smith to JRP, June 23, 29, July 3, 1825, folder 16, vol. 2, JRPP.

46. Mexican Company, *Statement*, 2–3.

47. D. A. Smith to JRP, June 29, July 3, 1825, folder 16, vol. 2, JRPP.

48. Michael P. Costeloe, "William Bullock and the Mexican Connection," *Mexican Studies/Estudios Mexicanos* 22, no. 2 (Summer 2006): 309.

49. Mexican Company, *Statement*, 5.

50. Robert Oliver to JRP, October 19, 1825, folder 3, vol. 3, JRPP; Camilla Townsend, *Tales of Two Cities: Race and Economic Culture in Early Republican North and South America* (Austin: University of Texas Press, 2012), 104; Stuart Weems Bruchey, *Robert Oliver, Merchant of Baltimore* (Baltimore: Johns Hopkins University Press, 1957).

51. Robert Oliver to JRP, October 19, 1825, folder 3, vol. 3; D. A. Smith to John Mason, January 30, 1826, folder 8, vol. 3, JRPP.

52. Documents related to mines, folder 12, vol. 17, JRPP.

53. Jay Sexton, *The Monroe Doctrine: Empire and Nation in Nineteenth-Century America* (New York: Hill and Wang, 2011).

54. JRP to Lucas Alamán, August 1825, folder 10, vol. 3, JRPP.

55. Ralph E. Weber, "Joel R. Poinsett's Secret Mexican Dispatch Twenty," *South Carolina Historical Magazine* 75, no. 2 (April 1974): 73–75.

56. "The Papers of Sir Charles Vaughan," *American Historical Review* 7, no. 2 (January 1902): 308.

57. María Eugenia Vázquez Semadeni, "Del mar a la política: Masonería en Nueva España, México, 1816–1823," *Revista de Estudios Históricos de la Masonería Latinoamericana y Caribeña*, December 2015, 122.

58. Vázquez Semadeni, "Del mar a la política," 129.

59. Lillian Estelle Fisher, "Early Masonry in Mexico (1806–1828)," *Southwestern Historical Quarterly* 42, no. 3 (January 1939): 203–4.

60. Manning, "Poinsett's Mission to Mexico," 800.

61. Certificate of membership in the Freemason Lodge No. 1, June 13, 1818, folder 3, JRPP, 1787–1851, (1164.03.03) SCHS; Steven C. Bullock, "A Pure and Sublime System: The Appeal of Post-revolutionary Freemasonry," *Journal of the Early Republic* 9, no. 3 (Autumn 1989): 359–73; Bullock, *Revolutionary Brotherhood: Freemasonry and the Transformation of the American Social Order, 1730–1840* (Chapel Hill: University of North Carolina Press, 1998).

62. Albert Mackey, *History of Freemasonry in South Carolina* (Columbia: South Carolina Steam Power, 1861), 207–9.

63. Grand Lodge of Philadelphia to JRP, June 5, 1826, folder 10, vol. 3, JRPP.

64. Manning, "Poinsett's Mission to Mexico," 796.

65. Manning, "Poinsett's Mission to Mexico," 793.

66. JRP to Isaac Johnson, May 27, 1826, Joel Roberts Poinsett, Letters to Isaac A. Johnson, 1821–1826, (43/131) SCHS. For the missionary impulse of Freemasonry, see Bullock, "Pure and Sublime System," 370.

67. Eric Van Young, *A Life Together: Lucas Alaman and Mexico, 1792–1853* (New Haven, CT: Yale University Press, 2021), 233. See, for example, *Correo de la federacion mexicana* (Mexico City), August 17, 1827, 3–4, Readex: World Newspaper Archive.

68. Thomas Kittera, "Joel Roberts Poinsett Masonic Authorization," June 5, 1826, JRPP; folder 4, JRPP, 1787–1851, (1164.03.03) SCHS.

69. R. W. H Hardy, *Travels in the Interior of Mexico in 1825, 1826, 1827 & 1828* (London: Henry Colburn and Richard Bentley, 1829), 13; Sanford A. Mosk, "Capitalistic Development in the Lower California Pearl Fisheries," *Pacific Historical Review* 10, no. 4 (1941): 461–68.

70. Hannah Farber, "Millions for Credit: Peace with Algiers and the Establishment of America's Commercial Reputation Overseas, 1795–96," *Journal of the Early Republic* 34, no. 2 (Summer 2014): 207; R. W. Hidy, "The House of Baring and the Second Bank of the United States, 1826–1836," *Pennsylvania Magazine of History and Biography* 68, no. 3 (July 1944): 269–85.

71. Poinsett, *Notes*, 64.

72. *The Jurist* (London: S. Sweet, 1839), 2:1033.

73. Peter E. Austin, *Baring Brothers and the Birth of Modern Finance* (London: Routledge, 2015), 21–26.

74. Credits Received from Mr. Baring, December 1, 1825, folder 14, vol. 17, JRPP.

75. Barings took Poinsett's advice on Mexican finance and investment prospects very seriously, especially in the wake of a rash of British overinvestments and failures

in Latin America. B. O. Wills to JRP, December 28, 1825, folder 6, vol. 3, JRPP; Austin, *Baring Brothers*, 21.

76. In the fall of 1825, Porter wrote to Poinsett and to Mexico's minister to the US, Pablo Obregon, offering to resign his commission in the US Navy if Mexico would make him a high-ranking officer. Elmer W. Flaccus, "Commodore David Porter and the Mexican Navy," *Hispanic American Historical Review* 34, no. 3 (August 1954): 366.

77. Stanley C. Green, *The Mexican Republic: The First Decade, 1823–1832* (Pittsburgh: University of Pittsburgh Press, 1987), 67.

78. Lois Garver, "Benjamin Rush Milam," *Southwestern Historical Quarterly* 38, no. 2 (October 1934): 79–121, 81; George R. Nielsen, "Ben Milam and United States and Mexican Relations," *Southwestern Historical Quarterly* 73, no. 3 (1970): 393–95.

79. Margaret Swett Henson, "Understanding Lorenzo de Zavala, Signer of the Texas Declaration of Independence," *Southwestern Historical Quarterly* 102, no. 1 (July 1998): 4; Karl E. Ashburn, "Slavery and Cotton Production in Texas," *Southwestern Social Science Quarterly* 14, no. 3 (December 1933): 257–71.

80. Ashburn, "Slavery and Cotton Production," 257–58.

81. Nielsen, "Ben Milam," 393; Garver, "Benjamin Rush Milam," 97.

82. JRP to Francis Baring, January 20, 1827, folder 2, vol. 4, JRPP.

83. Costeloe, "William Bullock," 309.

84. JRP to LeRoy Bayard and Co., December 6, 1825, Joel Roberts Poinsett, 1779–1851, Letter: Mexico, (43/834) SCHS.

85. Robert Oliver to JRP, March 6, 1826, folder 8, vol. 3, JRPP; Wyndham D. Miles, "A Versatile Explorer: A Sketch of William H. Keating," *Minnesota History* 36, no. 8 (December 1959): 294–99.

86. "Temascaltepec, Baltimore, March 10," *Enquirer* (Richmond, VA), March 17, 1826, 1.

87. For corporate insider privileges and the ability to shield business activities from public oversight, see Andrew Schocket, *Founding Corporate Power in Early National Philadelphia* (DeKalb: Northern Illinois University Press, 2007).

88. C. J. Ingersoll, July 9, 1830, folder 11, vol. 17, JRPP.

89. Henry George Ward, *Mexico: With an Account of the Mining Companies and of the Political Events in That Republic to the Present Day* (London: H. Colburn, 1829), 103.

90. John Mason to JRP, June 10, 1830, folder 8, vol. 6, JRPP.

91. JRP to John Quincy Adams, April 26, 1827, folder 4, vol. 4, JRPP.

92. Manning, "Poinsett's Mission to Mexico," 802–4.

93. JRP to John Quincy Adams, June 8, 1827, folder 8, vol. 4, JRPP.

94. JRP to Henry Clay, February 7, 1828, MS. Dept. of St., Mex., Desp., III, in William R. Manning, "Texas and the Boundary Issue, 1822–1829," *Southwestern Historical Quarterly* 17, no. 3 (January 1914): 243.

95. Ohland Morton, "Life of General Don Manuel De Mier Y Terán: As It Affected Texas-Mexican Relations (Continued)," *Southwestern Historical Quarterly* 47, no. 1 (January 1943): 35.

96. Morton, "Life of General Don Manuel De Mier Y Terán," 37.

97. Henry Clay to Pablo Obregón, April 30, 1828, box 4; August 2, 1828, box 5, Henry Clay papers, 1825–1829, mssHC 1-423, Huntington Library, San Marino, CA.

98. Eric Van Young, *A Life Together: Lucas Alaman and Mexico, 1792–1853* (New Haven, CT: Yale University Press, 2021), 237; W. S. Cleaves, "Lorenzo de Zavala in Texas," *Southwestern Historical Quarterly* 36, no. 1 (July 1932): 29–40, esp. 31.

99. Shara Ali, "Yucatecan-Mexican Relations and Yucatecan Politicking from 1829–1832: Centralism, Secession, and Federalism," *Mexican Studies/Estudios Mexicanos* 30, no. 2 (Summer 2014): 313–41, esp. 318, 323.

100. Ana Romero-Valderrama, "La coalición pedracista: elecciones y rebeliones para una re-definición de la participación política en México (1826–1828)" (PhD diss., Consejo Nacional de Ciencia y Tecnología, Mexico, 2011).

101. Torcuato S. Di Tella, *National Popular Politics in Early Independent Mexico, 1820–1847* (Albuquerque: University of New Mexico Press, 1996), 209.

102. Silvia M. Arrom, "Popular Politics in Mexico City: The Parián Riot, 1828," *Hispanic American Historical Review* 68, no. 2 (1988): 245–68.

103. JRP to [the recipient's name is missing, but based on subject matter, geographic reference, and date, it is likely that it was social reformer Robert Owen], April 25, 1829, folder 15, vol. 5, JRPP.

104. A. L. Fernet, "Statement" (Mexico City, 1828), box 27, cases not heard, claim 67, D. G. Jacques Company, 1839 Claims Commission, RG 76.7, Records of the United States and Mexican Claims Commissions, US National Archives, in David McKenzie, "Racing Ahead of Manifest Destiny: U.S. Migration, Citizenship, and Commercial Expansion in Mexico's Interior, 1821–53" (PhD diss., George Mason University, 2021).

105. Fernet, "Statement"; Laguerenne and Bourdel, "Memorial" (Mexico City, October 8, 1837), RG 76, 1839 US-Mexico Claims Commission, box 25, folder 34; Laguerenne and Bourdel to JRP, January 18, 1828, folder 2, vol. 5, JRPP.

106. Di Tella, *National Popular Politics*, 209.

107. Theodore G. Vincent, *The Legacy of Vicente Guerrero, Mexico's First Black Indian President* (Gainesville: University of Florida Press, 2001). He did, however, exempt Texas. Gerardo Gurza-Lavalle, "Against Slave Power? Slavery and Runaway Slaves in Mexico–United States Relations, 1821–1857," *Mexican Studies* 35, no. 2 (January 2019): 143–70, esp. 153.

108. JRP to John Quincy Adams, April 26, 1827, folder 5, vol. 4, JRPP.

109. Andreas Reichstein, "The Austin-Leaming Correspondence, 1828–1836," *Southwestern Historical Quarterly* 88, no. 3 (1985): 261.

110. "From Mexico," *Connecticut Journal* (New Haven), February 3, 1826, ; *Spectator* (New York), "Mexico and Mr. Poinsett," January 22, 1830, 4; Green, *Mexican Republic*, 167.

111. John Exter to JRP, September 17, 1829, folder 17, vol. 5, JRPP.

112. José María Herrera, "Vision of a Utopian Texas: Robert Owen's Colonization Scheme," *Southwestern Historical Quarterly* 116, no. 4 (April 2013): 346–50.

113. JRP to Robert Owen, April 25, 1829, folder 15, vol. 5, JRPP.

114. JRP to Robert Owen, April 25, 1829, folder 15, vol. 5, JRPP.

115. Lorenzo De Zavala, *Viage a los Estados Unidos del Norte de America* (Paris: Imprenta de Decourchant, 1834), 81.

116. JRP to Robert Owen, April 25, 1829, folder 15, vol. 5, JRPP.

117. Paul R. Bernard, "Irreconcilable Opinions: The Social and Educational Theories of Robert Owen and William Maclure," *Journal of the Early Republic* 8, no. 1

(Spring 1988): 21–44. Poinsett was in regular contact with Maclure. For example, Mary Carroll wrote to William Maclure care of Poinsett in Mexico. And Poinsett wrote to Maclure for a book. William Maclure to JRP, [n.d.] 1829, folder 21, series 1: New Harmony Correspondence, 1812–1871, Working Men's Institute of New Harmony, Indiana, New Harmony Manuscripts, 1812–1871.

118. William Maclure to JRP, April 25, May 8, December 31, 1828, folder 4, vol. 5, JRPP.

119. Herrera, "Vision of a Utopian Texas," 354–56.

120. Garver, "Benjamin Rush Milam," 109–11.

121. El Toro (Segunda Época, Diálogos 1–14), July 4, 1829, 65.

122. "Comunicado," *El Gladiador*, June 20, 1830, 3. *El Gladiador* was a progovernment newspaper. Henry Lepidus, "The History of Mexican Journalism," *University of Missouri Bulletin*, 29, no. 4 (January 1928): 3–87.

123. "Noticias Estrangeras," *El Gladiador*, May 8, 1830, 1.

124. Draft letter to US secretary of state explaining the request of Poinsett's removal. Legación Mexicana en Washington, 1829, Correspondencia con la Secretaría de Relaciones Exteriores, Archivo Histórico Genaro Estrada, Acervo Histórico Diplomático, Secretaría de Relaciones Exteriores, México.

125. Manning, "Poinsett's Mission to Mexico," 1814.

126. John Exter to JRP, September 17, 1829, folder 17, vol. 5, JRPP.

127. John Exter to JRP, August 20, 1829, folder 17, vol. 5, JRPP.

128. David Burnet to Stephen Austin, July 18, 1829, Austin Papers, 1676, 1765–1889, Center for American History, University of Texas at Austin, in Mary Virginia Henderson, "Minor Empresario Contracts for the Colonization of Texas, 1825–1834," *Southwestern Historical Quarterly* 31 (April 1928): 305.

129. Manning, "Poinsett's Mission to Mexico," 822.

130. James Treat to José M. Tornel, February 10, 1831, Correspondencia del James Treat Vice Consul Mexicano en New York, Archivo Histórico Genaro Estrada, Acervo Histórico Diplomático, Secretaría de Relaciones Exteriores, México.

131. "Por el presente document de covenio hecho en la ciudad de Mexico, el dia 10 de marzo de 1830 entre D. Lorenzo de Zavala, D. Joel R. Poinsett y el Col. D. Antonio Butler," March 10, 1830, folder 5, vol. 6, JRPP.

132. Hutchinson, "General José Antonio Mexía," 127.

133. Hutchinson, "General José Antonio Mexía," 127.

134. Quinton Curtis Lamar, "A Diplomatic Disaster: The Mexican Mission of Anthony Butler, 1829–1834," *Americas* 45, no. 1 (July 1988): 1–17; J. S. Wilcocks to JRP, February 12, 1833, folder 9, vol. 7, JRPP.

135. "Galveston Bay and Texas Land Company," *Boston Traveler*, January 7, 1831, 7.

136. George Fisher to JRP, October 14, 1829, folder 2, vol. 6, JRPP; Galveston Bay and Texas Land Company and Joel Poinsett, "J.R Poinsett—Galveston Bay and Texas Land Company Certificate," October 16, 1830, Kentucky Historical Society Special Collections and Archives, Frankfort, KY.

137. Henderson, "Minor Empresario Contracts," 307; Henson, "Understanding Zavala," 8.

138. Henderson, "Minor Empresario Contracts," 312.

139. James Treat to José M. Tornel, November 8, 1830, Correspondencia del

James Treat Vice Consul Mexicano en New York, Archivo Histórico Genaro Estrada, Acervo Histórico Diplomático, Secretaría de Relaciones Exteriores, México; Henderson, "Minor Empresario Contracts," 312.

140. Edward L. Miller, *New Orleans and the Texas Revolution* (College Station: Texas A&M University Press, 2004), 45.

141. Hutchinson, "General José Antonio Mexía," 128.

142. Hutchinson, "General José Antonio Mexía," 127–34.

143. Henderson, "Minor Empresario Contracts."

144. Hutchinson, "General José Antonio Mexía," 123.

145. John Exter to JRP, August 20, 1829, September 17, 1829, folder 17, vol. 5; William Exter to JRP, November 24, 1830, folder 13, vol. 6, JRPP.

146. David J. Weber, *The Taos Trappers: The Fur Trade in the Far Southwest, 1540–1846* (Norman: University of Oklahoma Press, 1971), 178.

147. John Martin Davis Jr., *Texas Land Grants, 1750–1900: A Documentary History* (Jefferson, NC: McFarland, 2016), 14.

148. Lucy Lee Dickson, "Speculation of John Charles Beales in Texas Lands" (master's thesis, University of Texas, 1941); Henderson, "Minor Empresario Contracts."

149. William Exter to JRP, November 24, 1830, folder 13, vol. 6, JRPP.

150. Miller, *New Orleans and the Texas Revolution*, 45.

151. C. C. Rister, "The Rio Grande Colony," *Southwest Review* 25, no. 4 (July 1940): 440.

152. Gerald D. Saxon, "Anthony Butler: A Flawed Diplomat," *East Texas Historical Journal* 24, no. 1 (March 1986): 12.

153. H.R. doc. 351, July 4, 1838, 25th Cong., US Congressional Serial Set, vol. 332 (Washington, DC: Government Printing Office, 1838).

154. "Manifesto of the Congress of Vera Cruz to the Mexican Nation," June 19, 1827, enclosed with Poinsett to Clay, July 8, 1827, MS. Dept. of State, Mex., Desp., III, in Manning, "Poinsett's Mission to Mexico," 802.

155. Flaccus, "Commodore Porter," 372.

156. "Affairs of Mexico," *Spectator* (New York), February 26, 1830, 3.

157. *Charleston (SC) Courier*, "Major Hamilton; Major Eaton; Mr. Poinsett," October 16, 1829, 6.

158. James Brown, March 12, 1830, folder 6, vol. 6, JRPP.

Chapter 5

1. Robert Gibbes to JRP, March 16, 1830, folder 6, vol. 6, JRPP.

2. Samuel Clarke, Paul Dean, Edward Livingston, Joel Roberts Poinsett, and Freemasons, Grand Chapter of Massachusetts, *Addresses Delivered at the Stated Communication of the Grand Chapter of Mass., June 8, 1830* (Boston: Marsh, Capen & Lyon, 1830), 21–22.

3. The *National Gazette*, founded in 1820, was a daily paper that published news related to arts, literature, science, and politics. Guy R. Woodall, "More on the Contributors to the 'American Quarterly Review' (1827–1837)," *Studies in Bibliography* 23 (1970): 199–207.

4. Robert Walsh to JRP, March 11, 1830, folder 6, vol. 6, JRPP.

5. Robert Gibbes to JRP, May 29, 1830, folder 8, vol. 6, JRPP.

6. Robert Gibbes to JRP, March 16, 1830, folder 6, vol. 6, JRPP.

7. Eric Hilt, "Rogue Finance: The Life and Fire Insurance Company and the Panic of 1826," *Business History Review* 83, no. 1 (Spring 2009): 100.

8. Joseph Anderson to JRP, March 13, 1830, folder 6, vol. 6, JRPP.

9. Richard B. Latner, "The Nullification Crisis and Republican Subversion," *Journal of Southern History* 43, no. 1 (February 1977): 21.

10. Richard R. Stenberg, "The Jefferson Birthday Dinner, 1830," *Journal of Southern History* 4, no. 3 (August 1938): 334–45.

11. Joshua Matthew Cain, "Jacksonian Nationalist: Joel R. Poinsett's Role in the Nullification Crisis" (PhD diss., Georgia Southern University, 2008), 46.

12. James M. Banner Jr. argues that South Carolina was the most "radical" and insular of the southern states. James M. Banner Jr., "The Problem of South Carolina," in *The Hofstadter Aegis: A Memorial*, ed. Stanley Elkins and Eric McKitrick (New York: Alfred A. Knopf, 1974), 60; James Haw, "'The Problem of South Carolina' Reexamined: A Review Essay," *South Carolina Historical Magazine* 107, no. 1 (January 2006): 9–25. For an excellent historiographic overview of slaveholders' political economy and the argument that "protecting slavery demanded sectional unity," see Harry L. Watson and John D. Majewski, "On the Banks of the James or the Congaree: Antebellum Political Economy," in *Reinterpreting Southern Histories: Essays in Historiography*, ed. Craig Thompson Friend and Lorri Glover (Baton Rouge: Louisiana State University Press, 2020), 166–96, esp. 188.

13. Bertram Wyatt-Brown's classic study of antebellum southern society defined honor as "the cluster of ethical rules . . . by which judgments of behavior are ratified by community consensus." Bertram Wyatt-Brown, *Southern Honor: Ethics and Behavior in the Old South* (New York, 1982), xv; Edward L. Ayers, "Honor," in *The New Encyclopedia of Southern Culture*, ed. Nancy Bercaw and Ted Ownby (Chapel Hill: University of North Carolina Press, 2009), 13:134–36; John Mayfield, "The Marketplace of Values: Honor and Enterprise in the Old South," in *The Field of Honor: Essays on Southern Character and American Identity*, ed. John Mayfield, Todd Hagstette, and Edward L. Ayers (Columbia: University of South Carolina Press, 2017), 5–20; Stephanie McCurry, "The Two Faces of Republicanism: Gender and Proslavery Politics in Antebellum South Carolina," *Journal of American History* 78, no. 4 (March 1992): 1245–64.

14. Joseph Johnson to JRP, February 20, 1830, folder 4, vol. 6, JRPP.

15. Haw, "'Problem of South Carolina,'" 9–10. Rice in particular suffered in the first part of the nineteenth century because of internal supply constraints and the incorporation of Southeast Asian rice in European markets. Peter A. Coclanis, "Distant Thunder: The Creation of a World Market in Rice and the Transformations It Wrought," *American Historical Review* 98, no. 4 (October 1993): 1056.

16. James Hamilton to JRP, September 14, 1828, folder 8, vol. 5, JRPP.

17. Haw, "'Problem of South Carolina,'" 13–14.

18. Joel Roberts Poinsett, speech on the tariff bill (House of Representatives, Washington, DC, April 8, 1824).

19. Historians have depicted Calhoun's articulate defense of a state's right to veto national legislation as principled, reactionary, conservative, liberal, and republican. For some he was a consistent defender of the Union, for others, a divisive states'

rights radical. Lacy K. Ford, for example, argues that Calhoun embodied "ancient republican ideals and the realities of modern capitalism." Lacy K. Ford, "Republican Ideology in a Slave Society: The Political Economy of John C. Calhoun," *Journal of Southern History* 54, no. 3 (August 1988): 405–22, esp. 422. See also Ford, "Recovering the Republic: Calhoun, South Carolina, and the Concurrent Majority," *South Carolina Historical Magazine* 89, no. 3 (July 1988): 146–59. W. Kirk Wood argues that Calhoun embraced the republican ideology of the framers of the Constitution. W. Kirk Wood, "History and the Recovery of the Past: John C. Calhoun and the Origins of Nullification in South Carolina, 1819–1828," *Southern Studies: An Interdisciplinary Journal of the South* 16, no. 1 (2009): 46–68. John Niven portrays Calhoun as a consistent protector of security. John Niven, *John C. Calhoun and the Price of Union* (Baton Rouge: Louisiana State University Press, 1991). For Calhoun's expression of "violent South Carolina radicalism," see William Freehling, "Spoilsmen and Interests in the Thought and Career of John C. Calhoun," *Journal of American History* 52, no. 1 (June 1965): 25–42, esp. 39. See also John Agresto, "John C. Calhoun and the Reexamination of American Democracy," in *History of American Political Thought*, ed. Bryan-Paul Frost and Jeffrey Sikkenga (Lanham, MD: Lexington Books, 2003), 316–23. Freehling also portrays Calhoun as equally committed to state and nation. William W. Freehling, *Prelude to Civil War: The Nullification Controversy in South Carolina, 1816–1836* (New York: Harper & Row, 1965).

20. In 1825, Poinsett owned more than $12,000 in stock. Joseph Johnson to JRP, March 17, 1825, folder 14, vol. 2, JRPP; Lawrence S. Rowland, "'Alone on the River': The Rise and Fall of the Savannah River Rice Plantations of St. Peter's Parish, South Carolina," *South Carolina Historical Magazine* 88, no. 3 (July 1987): 140.

21. Historians have long written about the connections among Webster, northern industrialists, and slave owners but have mostly focused on cotton as the commonality. Hamilton and Poinsett prove that this association extended to rice planters. Thomas H. O'Connor, *Lords of the Loom: The Cotton Whigs and the Coming of the Civil War* (New York: Charles Scribner's Sons, 1968).

22. Henry William DeSaussure to JRP, July 9, 1822, folder 7, vol. 2, JRPP; Robert L. Paquette, "Jacobins of the Lowcountry: The Vesey Plot on Trial," *William and Mary Quarterly* 59, no. 1 (January 2002): 185–92.

23. Marilyn McAdams Sibley, "James Hamilton, Jr., vs. Sam Houston: Repercussions of the Nullification Controversy," *Southwestern Historical Quarterly* 89, no. 2 (October 1985): 165–80, esp. 177–78.

24. Sibley, "James Hamilton, Jr., vs. Sam Houston," 167.

25. Virginia Glenn Crane, "Two Women, White and Brown, in the South Carolina Court of Equity, 1842–1845," *South Carolina Historical Magazine* 96, no. 3 (July 1995): 198–220.

26. William Keating to JRP, June 15, 1830, folder 9, vol. 6, JRPP.

27. Robert Gibbes to JRP, May 29, 1830, folder 8, vol. 6, JRPP.

28. Hannah Farber, "State-Building after War's End: A Government Financier Adjusts His Portfolio for Peace," *Journal of the Early Republic* 38, no. 1 (Spring 2018): 74.

29. William Keating to JRP, April 9, 1830, folder 7, vol. 6, JRPP.

30. Robert Walsh to JRP, May 12, 1830, folder 6, vol. 6, JRPP.

31. Robert Walsh to JRP, May 12, 1830, folder 6, vol. 6, JRPP.

32. "Commercial Record," *Patriot* (Baltimore), May 10, 1830, 2.

33. Robert Walsh to JRP, May 12, 1830, folder 8, vol. 6, JRPP.

34. *Baltimore Gazette and Daily Advertiser*, May 14, 1830, 3; *Baltimore Patriot*, May 24, 1830, 3; *Baltimore Gazette and Daily Advertiser*, June 7, 1830, 3; J. Meredith to JRP, May 29, 1830, folder 8, vol. 6, JRPP.

35. Stuart Bruchey, "Success and Failure Factors: American Merchants in Foreign Trade in the Eighteenth and Early Nineteenth Centuries," *Business History Review* 32, no. 3 (Autumn 1958): 272–92.

36. "Index to Claims on Naples," in ASP, *Documents, Legislative and Executive of the Congress of the United States*, no. 451 (Washington, DC: Gales and Seaton, 1859), 482; Robert Gibbes to JRP, October 4, 1830, folder 11, vol. 6, JRPP; William R. Nester, *The Age of Jackson and the Art of American Power, 1815–1848* (Lincoln: Potomac Books, University of Nebraska Press, 2003), 160–61; John Belohlavek, "Let the Eagle Soar! Democratic Constraints on the Foreign Policy of Andrew Jackson," *Presidential Studies Quarterly* 10, no. 1 (Winter 1980): 42.

37. Michael F. Conlin, *The Constitutional Origins of the American Civil War* (New York: Cambridge University Press, 2019), 75.

38. Oliver prided himself on being above politics. Stuart Weems Bruchey, *Robert Oliver, Merchant of Baltimore* (Baltimore: Johns Hopkins University Press, 1957).

39. Samuel Curson to JRP, April 8, 1830, folder 7, vol. 6, JRPP.

40. *Stimpson's Boston Directory* (Boston: Stimpson and Clapp, 1832), 24.

41. Much scholarship—extending from David F. Houston's 1896 *A Critical Study of Nullification in South Carolina* and Frederic Bancroft's 1928 *Calhoun and the South Carolina Nullification Movement* to William Freehling's *Prelude to Civil War* and to Manisha Sinha's more recent *The Counterrevolution of Slavery*—has identified fears about interference with slavery as the catalyst for the Nullifier Party, citing various economic and cultural factors behind these fears. David F. Houston, *A Critical Study of Nullification in South Carolina* (New York, 1896); Frederic Bancroft, *Calhoun and the South Carolina Nullification Movement* (Baltimore, 1928). The classic text is Freehling, *Prelude to Civil War*, which argues that Southern fears about interference with slavery drove nullification. For a refutation of Freehling's arguments, see Paul H. Bergeron, "The Nullification Controversy Revisited," *Tennessee Historical Quarterly* 35, no. 3 (Fall 1976): 263–75; J. P. Ochenkowski, "The Origins of Nullification in South Carolina," *South Carolina Historical Magazine* 83, no. 2 (April 1982): 121–53. Lacy K. Ford argues that nullification was a defensive reaction to economic crisis, racial fears, and market dependency, rooted in republicanism. Lacy K. Ford Jr., *Origins of Southern Radicalism: The South Carolina Upcountry, 1800–1860* (New York: Oxford University Press, 1988). For different perspectives on the meaning of the crisis, see Richard E. Ellis, *The Union at Risk: Jacksonian Democracy, States' Rights and the Nullification Crisis* (New York: Oxford University Press, 1987); Donald Ratcliffe, "The Nullification Crisis, Southern Discontents, and the American Political Process," *American Nineteenth Century History* 1 (May 2000): 1–30; Benjamin E. Park, "The Angel of Nullification: Imagining Disunion in an Era Before Secession," *Journal of the Early Republic*, 37, no. 3, (September 2017): 507–36; Kevin M. Gannon, "The Nullification Crisis," in *A Companion to the Era of Andrew Jackson*, ed. Sean Patrick Adams (Hoboken, NJ: Wiley-Blackwell, 2013), 376–90; William H. Denney, "South Carolina's Conception of the Union in 1832," *South Carolina Historical Magazine* 78, no. 3 (July 1977): 171–83; Latner, "Nullification Crisis," 19–38; George C. Rogers,

"South Carolina Federalists and the Origins of the Nullification Movement," *South Carolina Historical Magazine* 101, no. 1 (June 2000): 53–67. For southern decisions based on property in slaves, see James L. Huston, "Property Rights in Slavery and the Coming of the Civil War," *Journal of Southern History* 65, no. 2 (May 1999): 249–86. Manisha Sinha argues that secession was an elite slaveholder position; Poinsett defies this. Manisha Sinha, *The Counterrevolution of Slavery: Politics and Ideology in Antebellum South Carolina* (Chapel Hill: University of North Carolina Press, 2000).

42. Rowland, "'Alone on the River,'" 121–50, esp. 138–39.

43. For competing understandings of "states' rights," see Michael E. Woods, "'Tell Us Something about State Rights': Northern Republicans, States' Rights, and the Coming of the Civil War," *Journal of the Civil War Era* 7, no. 2 (2017): 242–68.

44. Jane H. Pease and William H. Pease, "The Economics and Politics of Charleston's Nullification Crisis," *Journal of Southern History* 47, no. 3 (August 1981): 349.

45. Pease and Pease, "Economics and Politics," 337–39.

46. Robert Gibbes to JRP, October 28, 1830, folder 12, vol. 6, JRPP.

47. "Copy of a letter from a Gentleman" to JRP, October 15, 1830, folder 12, vol. 6.

48. "Copy of a letter from a Gentleman" to JRP, October 15, 1830, folder 12, vol. 6, JRPP.

49. "Copy of a letter from a Gentleman" to JRP, October 15, 1830, folder 12, vol. 6.

50. Robert Gibbes to JRP, October 28, 1830, folder 12, vol. 6, JRPP.

51. Andrew Jackson to Robert Oliver, October 26, 1830, folder 12, vol. 6, JRPP.

52. Chauncey Samuel Boucher, *The Nullification Controversy in South Carolina* (Chicago: University of Chicago Press, 1916), 104–5.

53. "Editorial Correspondence Columbia," *City Gazette* (Charleston, SC), November 30, 1830, 2.

54. "Editorial Correspondence Columbia," *City Gazette* (Charleston, SC), November 30, 1830, 2; "New Magistrates Bill," *City Gazette* (Charleston, SC), February 3, 1831, 2.

55. Tinkler, *James Hamilton*, 121.

56. William Smith to JRP, February 16, March 1, 1831, folder 16, vol. 6. William Drayton, *The South Vindicated from the Treason and Fanaticism of the Northern Abolitionists* (Philadelphia, 1836).

57. Pease and Pease, "Economics and Politics," 351.

58. Bertram Wyatt-Brown ascribes a "brutal, even gothic" medieval code of honor to southern gentlemen, while Joanne Freeman finds a culture of honor in early national politics, arguing that a code of honor governed the actions of early republic political elites. Wyatt-Brown, *Southern Honor*, xv; Wyatt-Brown, "Andrew Jackson's Honor," *Journal of the Early Republic* 17 (Spring 1997): 2; Samuel J. Watson, "Flexible Gender Roles during the Market Revolution: Family, Friendship, Marriage, and Masculinity among U.S. Army Officers, 1815–1846," *Journal of Social History* 29 (Fall 1995): 84; Joanne B. Freeman, *Affairs of Honor: National Politics in the New Republic* (New Haven, CT; Yale University Press, 2002); Kenneth S. Greenberg, *Honor and Slavery: Lies, Duels, Noses, Masks, Dressing as a Woman, Gifts, Strangers, Humanitarianism, Death, Slave Rebellions, the Proslavery Argument, Baseball, Hunting, and Gambling in the Old South* (Princeton, NJ: Princeton University Press, 1996). For a different iteration of claims to early republican manhood, see Catherine O'Donnell Kaplan's study of the networks of male intellectuals who opted out of the more masculine realms of politics and commerce. Catherine O'Donnell Kaplan, *Men of Letters*

in the Early Republic: Cultivating Forums of Citizenship (Chapel Hill: University of North Carolina Press, 2008); Irving L. Janis, *Groupthink: Psychological Studies of Policy Decisions and Fiascoes* (Boston: Cengage, 1982), 174–75.

59. Alexander Spero to JRP, March 14, 1831, folder 17, vol. 6, JRPP.

60. Anthony Butler to JRP, November 30, 1830, folder 13, vol. 6, JRPP.

61. Theodore G. Vincent, *The Legacy of Vicente Guerrero, Mexico's First Black Indian President* (Gainesville: University of Florida Press, 2001).

62. *Baltimore Patriot*, March 10, 1831, 2.

63. Richard Willing to JRP, December 27, 1831, folder 3, vol. 7, JRPP; Peter E. Austin, *Baring Brothers and the Birth of Modern Finance* (Abingdon, UK: Routledge, 2015), 117; Ellis, *Union at Risk*, 85.

64. Anthony Butler to JRP, February 21, 1830, folder 16, vol. 6, JRPP.

65. Richard Willing to JRP, October 30, 1832, folder 6, vol. 7, JRPP.

66. John W. Jordan, ed., *Colonial and Revolutionary Families of Pennsylvania* (New York: Clearfield, 1911), 128.

67. Willing was the executor of Francis and Willing and petitioned the United States for not paying enough of its claims as a result of its treaty with Spain. *Documents Relating to the Foreign Relations of the United States*, vol. 6, *Memorial of the Philadelphia Claimants under the Florida Treaty*, February 7, 1826, doc. 84 (Washington, Gales & Seaton, 1826). Willing also had claims on France and was ultimately rewarded in 1832. US Senate, "List of Awards Made by the Commissioners Appointed under the Treaty with France, July 4, 1831" (Washington: Government Printing Office, 1886), 155.

68. "From the Charleston Mercury," *National Gazette* (Philadelphia), June 7, 1831, 3.

69. Frederic Cople Jaher, *The Urban Establishment: Upper Strata in Boston, New York, Charleston, Chicago, and Los Angeles* (Chicago: University of Illinois Press, 1982), 350–51; Tinkler, *James Hamilton*, 100. Although much has been written about southerners' opposition to internal improvements as an attempt to stymie federal power to abolish slavery, not all southern slaveholders shared this view. Daniel M. Mulcare, "Restricted Authority: Slavery Politics, Internal Improvements, and the Limitation of National Administrative Capacity," *Political Research Quarterly* 61, no. 4 (December 2008): 671–85.

70. Robert Gilmore to JRP, February 1, 1832, folder 3, vol. 7, JRPP.

71. For the history of southern barbecue and politics, see Daniel Dupree, "Barbecues and Pledges: Electioneering and the Rise of Democratic Politics in Antebellum Alabama," *Journal of Southern History* 60 (August 1994): 479–512; Robert F. Moss, *Barbecue: The History of an American Institution* (Tuscaloosa: University of Alabama Press, 2014).

72. Boucher, *Nullification Controversy*, 111; Tinkler, *James Hamilton*, 121.

73. Tinkler, *James Hamilton*, 124.

74. Pease and Pease, "Economics and Politics," 357.

75. Boucher, *Nullification Controversy*, 156.

76. John Aubry to JRP, June 27, 1831, folder 2, vol. 7, JRPP.

77. Cain, "Jacksonian Nationalist," 48.

78. Boucher, *Nullification Controversy*, 157.

79. Boucher, *Nullification Controversy*, 160–63.

80. Alexis de Tocqueville, "Conversations with Mr. Poinsett, January 12–17

(1832)," *American Notes*, in Encyclopedia Britannica, *The Annals of America*, vol. 5, *Steps toward Equalitarianism* (1821–1832) (Chicago: Encyclopedia Britannica, 1968), 500; James L. Crouthamel, "Tocqueville's South," *Journal of the Early Republic* 2, no. 4 (Winter 1982): 381–401; H. G. Nicholas, "Tocqueville and the Dissolution of the Union," *Revue Internationale De Philosophie* 13, no. 49 (3) (1959): 320–29.

81. ASP, "Memorial of the Minority of the Legislature of South Carolina, Praying That the Duties on Importations May Be Reduced," January 24, 1832, 22nd Cong., no. 34.

82. Free Trade Convention Philadelphia, "Memorial of the Committee Appointed by the 'Free trade Convention,' Held at Philadelphia, in September and October, 1831" (New York: W. A. Mercein, printer, 1832).

83. Thomas R. Mitchell to JRP, January 10, 1832, folder 3, vol. 7, JRPP.

84. C. [Robert Cunningham?] to JRP, January 23, 1832, folder 3, vol. 7, JRPP; Charles Grier Sellers, "Andrew Jackson versus the Historians," *Mississippi Valley Historical Review* 44, no. 4 (March 1958): 615–34.

85. During the Buckshot War in 1838, Poinsett told army captain George D. Ramsey, "Under the law of 1808, the States are not entitled to receive any munitions of war, other than arms and equipment; and no issue even of these ought to be made by an officer in charge of military stores, but on the order of the Department." Robert W. Coakley, *The Role of Federal Military Forces in Domestic Disorders, 1789–1878* (Washington, DC: Center of Military History, 1988), 109.

86. Poinsett's correspondents wrote to him with the subjects of the bank and the tariff intertwined. See, for example, William Drayton to JRP, April 5, 1832, folder 4, vol. 7, JRPP.

87. Norman Gasque Raiford, "South Carolina and the Second Bank of the United States: Conflict in Political Principle or Economic Interest?," *South Carolina Historical Magazine* 72, no. 1 (January 1971): 35.

88. In 1825, Poinsett had owned more than $12,000 in stock. Joseph Johnson to JRP, March 17, 1825, folder 14, vol. 2, JRPP.

89. Raiford, "South Carolina and the Second Bank," 40.

90. Robert Gilmore to JRP, February 1, 1832, folder 3, vol. 7, JRPP.

91. Boucher, *Nullification Controversy*, 166; William Drayton to JRP, April 5, 1832, folder 4, vol. 7, JRPP.

92. Robert Gibbes to JRP, May 2, 1832, folder 4, vol. 7, JRPP.

93. Boucher, *Nullification Controversy*, 169, 179.

94. N. G. Rolando to JRP, August 26, 1832; P. Chartrand to JRP and Thomas Bennett, September 22, 1832, folder 5, vol. 7, JRPP.

95. P. Chartrand to JRP and Thomas Bennett, September 22, 1832, folder 5, vol. 7, JRPP.

96. "Legislative Acts/Legal Proceedings," *Enquirer* (Richmond, VA), September 21, 1832, 2.

97. "South Carolina; Columbia; Hon. D. E. Huger; Joel R. Poinsett; Virginia; North Carolina; Hon. Henry Middleton; Mitchell King," *Spectator* (New York), October 8, 1832, 4.

98. Boucher, *Nullification Controversy*, 179.

99. Washington Society, "Address of the Washington Society to the People of South Carolina" (Charleston, SC: J. S. Burges, 1832), 5.

100. "South Carolina," *Salem (MA) Gazette*, November 2, 1832, 2.

101. Matthew Karp, "Slavery and American Sea Power: The Navalist Impulse in the Antebellum South," *Journal of Southern History* 77, no. 2 (May 2011): 283–324.

102. Claudio Saunt, *Unworthy Republic: The Dispossession of Native Americans and the Road to Indian Territory* (New York: Norton, 2020).

103. Sharon Ann Murphy, "The Financialization of Slavery by the First and Second Banks of the United States," *Journal of Southern History* 87 (August 2021): 385–426; Kathryn Boodry, "August Belmont and the World the Slaves Made," in Sven Beckert and Seth Rockman, eds. *Slavery's Capitalism: A New History of American Economic Development* (Philadelphia: University of Pennsylvania Press, 2016), 163–78.

104. For debates among leading textile manufacturers about tariffs and the expansion of slavery, see Robert F. Dalzell, *Enterprising Elite: The Boston Associates and the World They Made* (New York: W. W. Norton, 1987), 194–204. For classic studies of New England textile manufacturers and merchants who compromised morality for the sake of economic interests and unionism in their political support of the institution of slavery, see Kinley J. Brauer, *Cotton versus Conscience: Massachusetts Whig Politics and Southwestern Expansion, 1843–1848* (Lexington: University of Kentucky Press, 1967); O'Connor, *Lords of the Loom*. For the connection between industrialization and plantation slavery, see Beckert and Rockman, *Slavery's Capitalism*; Sven Beckert, *Empire of Cotton: A Global History* (New York: Vintage, 2015); Walter Johnson, *River of Dark Dreams: Slavery and Empire in the Cotton Kingdom* (Cambridge, MA: Harvard University Press, 2013); Philip S. Foner, *Business & Slavery: The New York Merchants & the Irrepressible Conflict* (Chapel Hill: University of North Carolina Press, 1941).

105. JRP to Richard Yeadon, March 6, 1850, folder 19, vol. 16, JRPP.

106. George Ticknor to JRP, December 28, 1832, folder 6, vol. 7, JRPP.

107. Richard Willing to JRP, October 30, 1832, folder 6, vol. 7, JRPP.

108. JRP to Jackson, November 25, 1832, series 6, vol. 162, AJLC.

109. Boucher, *Nullification Controversy*, 214–19; JRP to Jackson, November 25, 1832, November 29, 1832, series 6, vol. 162, AJLC.

110. Jackson to JRP, December 2, 1832, folder 6, vol. 7, JRPP; Lewis Cass to Winfield Scott, December 3, 1832, Records of the Office of the Secretary of War, Confidential and Unofficial Letters Sent, RG107, entry 11, vol. 309, NARA.

111. Matthew S. Brogdon, "Defending the Union: Andrew Jackson's Nullification Proclamation and American Federalism," *Review of Politics* 73, no. 2 (Spring 2011): 245–73.

112. JRP to Jackson, January 20, 1833, November 16, 1832, series 6, vol. 162, AJLC.

113. JRP to Jackson, January 20, 1833, series 6, vol. 162, AJLC.

114. JRP to Jackson, November 29, 1832, series 6, vol. 162, AJLC.

115. JRP to Jackson, January 27, 1833, series 6, vol. 162, AJLC.

116. Jackson to JRP, January 16, 1833, folder 7, vol. 7, JRPP.

117. JRP to Jackson, November 16, 1832, series 6, vol. 162, AJLC. The War Department supplied both new patent rifles and older Harpers Ferry models, which less experienced men would have to use. James Bankhead to JRP, January 30, 1833; Henry Saunders to JRP, January 30, 1833, folder 7, vol. 7, JRPP.

118. JRP to Jackson, February 22, 1833, series 6, vol. 162, AJLC.

119. David Hoffman, February 14, 1833, folder 9, vol. 7, JRPP.

120. Poinsett had gotten Captains Lawrence Kearny and William B. Shubrick to agree that Charleston would be a good base for the West India squadron. "Navy Yard Charleston, S.C.," in *The Army and Navy Chronicle*, vol. 6 (Washington City [Washington, DC]: B. Homans, 1838); JRP to Jackson, November 25, 1832, series 6, vol. 162, AJLC.

121. JRP to Andrew Jackson, January 7, 1833, AJLC; Brian Schoen, *The Fragile Fabric of Union: Cotton, Federal Politics, and the Global Origins of the Civil War* (Baltimore: Johns Hopkins University Press, 2009), 141.

122. Schoen, *Fragile Fabric of Union*, 143.

123. Andrew Jackson to JRP, March 6, 1833, folder 10, vol. 7, JRPP.

124. Joseph Grisham to JRP, March 12, 1833, folder 11, vol. 7, JRPP.

125. JRP to Andrew Jackson, March 23, 1833, PPGC.

126. Pease and Pease, "Economics and Politics," 362; Gannon, "Nullification Crisis," 388.

127. Stephanie McCurry, *Masters of Small Worlds: Yeoman Households, Gender Relations, and the Political Culture of the Antebellum South Carolina Low Country* (New York: Oxford University Press, 1995), 156.

128. W. J. Bennett, G. W. Reynolds, and R. E. Sutton to JRP, March 28, 1833, folder 11, vol. 7, JRPP; Robert Walsh to JRP, June 10, 1833, folder 12, vol. 7, JRPP.

129. James Wilcocks to JRP, February 12, 1833, folder 9, vol. 7, JRPP.

130. US Congressional Serial Set, vol. 332, 25th Congress, no. 351, p. 109.

131. JRP to J. B. Campbell, November 20, 1833, in Stoney, "Poinsett-Campbell Correspondence" (April 1841), 35.

132. Matrimony notice, *Charleston (SC) Courier*, November 1, 1833, 2.

133. JRP to J. B. Campbell, November 20, 1833, in Stoney, "Poinsett-Campbell Correspondence" (April 1841), 35.

134. JRP to Frances Tyrrell, March 25, 1833, PPGC, HSP.

135. JRP to Frances Tyrrell, August 8, 1833, PPGC; Fletcher M. Green, "On Tour with President Andrew Jackson," *New England Quarterly* 36, no. 2 (June 1963): 212–13.

136. "The Gazette. New-London, Wednesday, June 19, 1833. Reception of the President at New-London," *Connecticut Gazette* (New London, CT), June 19, 1833, 3.

137. "Progress of the President," *Boston Traveler*, June 25, 1833, 2.

138. Green, "On Tour with President Andrew Jackson," 226.

139. Poinsett had given a speech in 1830 urging voters not to retaliate against Masons. Clarke et al., *Addresses*.

140. "Letter to the High [Illegible]," *Painesville (OH) Telegraph*, August 9, 1833, 1. For anti-Masonic sentiment, see Steven C. Bullock, *Revolutionary Brotherhood: Freemasonry and the Transformation of the American Social Order, 1730–1840* (Chapel Hill: University of North Carolina Press, 1996), 277–307.

141. Bullock, *Revolutionary Brotherhood*, 282; Robert Gibbes to JRP, May 29, 1830, folder 8, vol. 6, JRPP.

142. John Forsyth to JRP, August 4, 1833, folder 12, vol. 7, JRPP.

143. Mary and Joel Poinsett to James R. Pringle, May 15, 1835, folder 11/322/27, James Reid Pringle papers, 1745–1840 (bulk 1800–1850), (1083.01.01) SCHS.

144. "Marriage Settlement," Joel R. Poinsett and Mary Pringle to J. R. Pringle and Benjamin Huger, October 24, 1833, folder 72, CLCP.

145. JRP to James B. Campbell, April 7, 1834, in Stoney, "Poinsett-Campbell Correspondence" (April 1841), 43–44.

146. "An Act to Provide for an Exchange of Lands with the Indians Residing in Any of the States or Territories, and for Their Removal West of the River Mississippi," March 28, 1830, 21st Cong., chap. 148, p. 411.

147. Maartje Janse, "'Anti Societies Are Now All the Rage': Jokes, Criticism, and Violence in Response to the Transformation of American Reform, 1825–1835," *Journal of the Early Republic* 36, no. 2 (Summer 2016): 247–82; Mary Hershberger, "Mobilizing Women, Anticipating Abolition: The Struggle against Indian Removal in the 1830s," *Journal of American History* 86 (June 1999): 15–40; Tiya Miles, "'Circular Reasoning': Recentering Cherokee Women in the Antiremoval Campaigns," *American Quarterly* 61 (June 2009): 221–43.

148. Joel R. Poinsett, *An Inquiry into the Received Opinions of Philosophers and Historians on the Natural Progress of the Human Race from Barbarism to Civilization: Read on the Anniversary of the Literary and Philosophical Society, May 14, 1834* (Charleston: The Society, 1834), 9.

149. JRP to James B. Campbell, December 25, 1834, in Stoney, "Poinsett-Campbell Correspondence" (April 1841), 46.

150. Poinsett, *Inquiry into the Received Opinions*, 17, 14, 39–40.

151. JRP to James B. Campbell, March 11, 1835, in Stoney, "Poinsett-Campbell Correspondence" (July 1841), 123.

152. JRP to James B. Campbell, April 16, 1836, in Stoney, "Poinsett-Campbell Correspondence" (July 1841), 131.

153. JRP to James B. Campbell, June 16, 1836, in Stoney, "Poinsett-Campbell Correspondence" Stoney(July 1841), 133–34.

154. JRP to James B. Campbell, April 16, April 21, May 13, 1836, in Stoney, "Poinsett-Campbell Correspondence" (July 1941): 131–33.

155. JRP to James B. Campbell, June 3, 1835, in Stoney, "Poinsett-Campbell Correspondence" (July 1941): 127.

156. JRP to James B. Campbell, May 30, 1835, in Stoney, "Poinsett-Campbell Correspondence" (July 1941): 126; JRP to James B. Campbell, August 25, 1836, in Stoney, "Poinsett-Campbell Correspondence" (July 1941): 135.

157. James Treat to José M. Tornel, March 3, 1831, Correspondencia del James Treat Vice Consul Mexicano en New York, Archivo Histórico Genaro Estrada, Acervo Histórico Diplomático, Secretaría de Relaciones Exteriores, México.

158. JRP to James B. Campbell, July 10, 1834, in Stoney, "Poinsett-Campbell Correspondence" (April 1841), 45.

159. JRP to James B. Campbell, June 3, 1835, in Stoney, "Poinsett-Campbell Correspondence" (July 1841), 127.

160. As one of Poinsett's friends noted, there would be difficulties with or without annexation. John Mason to JRP, May 28, 1836, folder 17, vol. 7, JRPP.

161. Barnard Bee to JRP, June 8, 1836, folder 18, vol. 7, JRPP.

162. JRP to Henry Clay, February 7, 1828, MS. Dept. of State, Mex., Desp., III, in William R. Manning, "Texas and the Boundary Issue, 1822–1829," *Southwestern Historical Quarterly* 17, no. 3 (January 1914): 217–61, esp. 243.

163. JRP to James B. Campbell, August 11, 1837, in Stoney, "Poinsett-Campbell Correspondence" (October 1841), 149–68, esp. 165.

164. JRP to James B. Campbell, May 30, 1835, in Stoney, "Poinsett-Campbell Correspondence" (July 1841), 126.

165. Tinkler, *James Hamilton*, 182–83.

166. JRP to John Graham, August 13, 1836, folder 1, vol. 8, JRPP.

167. Nina V. Potokova, "The British Policy toward Independent Texas as Seen by a Soviet Historian," *East Texas Historical Journal* 29, no. 1 (1991): 55–62.

168. JRP to J. B. Campbell, July 10, 1834, in Stoney, "Poinsett-Campbell Correspondence" (April 1841), 45. Poinsett also settled Burn's estate. Richard Willing to JRP, August 10, 1836, folder 2, vol. 8, JRPP.

169. Joseph Johnson to JRP, March 9, 1837, folder 4, vol. 8, JRPP.

170. JRP to James B. Campbell, [n.d., postmarked June 6, 1837], Stoney, "Poinsett-Campbell Correspondence" (October 1841), 163.

Chapter 6

1. "Affairs at Washington," *Vermont Patriot and State Gazette* (Montpelier, VT), March 27, 1837.

2. Cabinet officers in this era were much more independent of presidential control than they are today. William D. Adler, *Engineering Expansion* (Philadelphia: University of Pennsylvania Press, 2021), 75.

3. JRP to Joseph Johnson, February 4, 1837, folder 4, vol. 8, JRPP.

4. Andrew Jackson's first secretary of war, John Eaton, married a woman with whom he had allegedly had an affair, which sparked a campaign of misogynist slander in Washington.

5. See, for example, "From Washington," *Vermont Watchman and State Journal* (Montpelier, VT), February 28, 1837; "Correspondence of the Herald," *Herald* (New York), March 15, 1837; "Hon. Joel R. Poinsett," *Globe* (Washington, DC), April 1, 1837; "Correspondence of the Baltimore Patriot," *Daily Herald and Gazette* (Cleveland, OH), April 27, 1837; "The Correspondent of the N. Orleans True American, Dated Washington, May 25, 1837," *Daily Herald and Gazette* (Cleveland, OH), June 15, 1837. Not long after Poinsett started his post, however, some newspapers began printing negative coverage: "An inspection of the list of individuals appointed by the Secretary of War to visit the Military Academy at West Point, convinces us that the Secretary, Mr. Poinsett, is not the highminded man that his friends represent him." Excerpt from *Louisville Journal*, *Virginia Free Press* (Charlestown, WV), June 15, 1837; "Federal Tact," *Globe* (Washington, DC), June 16, 1837.

6. H. M. Rutledge to JRP, April 8, 1837; Charles H. Pond to JRP, May 1, 1837; John H. Jacocks to JRP, May 3, 1837, PPGC.

7. "Multiple News Items," *Daily National Intelligencer* (Washington, DC), January 23, 1837.

8. Poinsett's idea of masculinity was somewhere between Amy Greenberg's "restrained" and "martial" man but leaned toward "martial." Amy Greenberg, *Manifest Manhood and the Antebellum American Empire* (Cambridge: Cambridge University Press, 2005). For recent work on the role of masculine aggression in the politics of this era, see Joanne Freeman, *The Field of Blood: Violence in Congress and the Road to Civil War* (New York: Farrar, Straus & Giroux, 2018). For expansion as a racial mission, see Reginald Horsman, *Race and Manifest Destiny: The Origins of Ameri-*

can Racial Anglo-Saxonism (Cambridge, MA: Harvard University Press, 1981). For Manifest Destiny as an American ideology from settlement to the twentieth century, see Anders Stephanson, *Manifest Destiny: American Expansionism and the Empire of Right* (New York: Hill and Wang, 1995). According to Paul Frymer, one of the chief consequences of these pro-settler land policies was that they promoted the whitening of the American frontier. Paul Frymer, "Homesteading and Manufacturing Whiteness," in *Building an American Empire: The Era of Territorial and Political Expansion* (Princeton, NJ: Princeton University Press, 2017), 128–71, esp. 132.

9. "Regulation," April 3, 1837, March 1, 1841, Decisions, Orders and Regulations by the Secretary of War, vol. 1, Records of the Office of the Secretary of War, RG 107 E-41, NARA DC.

10. Report of the Secretary of War, December 2, 1837, 25th Cong., p. 185.

11. Martin van Buren, inaugural address, March 4, 1837, NARA.

12. Edmund P. Gaines to JRP, March 18, 1837, reel 16, Martin Van Buren Papers, Manuscript Division, Library of Congress, Washington, DC.

13. The process was also hastened by local white violence, as Adam Pratt has shown. Adam Pratt, *Toward Cherokee Removal: Land, Violence, and the White Man's Chance* (Athens: University of Georgia Press, 2020).

14. Samuel J. Watson, *Peacekeepers and Conquerors: The Army Officer Corps on the American Frontier, 1821-1846* (Lawrence: University Press of Kansas, 2013), 138–40. See also John P. Bowes, "American Indian Removal beyond the Removal Act," *Native American and Indigenous Studies* 1, no. 1 (Spring 2014): 65–87; Alfred A. Cave, "Abuse of Power: Andrew Jackson and the Indian Removal Act of 1830," *Historian* 65, no. 6 (Winter 2003): 1330–53. For the original "frontier thesis," which argued that the existence of a frontier provided opportunities for white Americans that were unavailable in Europe, see Frederick Jackson Turner, "The Significance of the Frontier in American History," *Annual Report of the American Historical Association* (1893): 197–227. Although Turner associated this frontier with violence, Patricia Nelson Limerick, Richard White, and others have done more to reveal the violence and economic exploitation involved in territorial expansion. James R. Grossman, *The Frontier in American Culture: Essays by Richard White and Patricia Nelson Limerick* (Berkeley: University of California Press, 1994). Historians disagree over the usage of *frontier* versus *borderlands*. The term *frontier* has more commonly been associated with Anglo-American dominance and colonial binaries, while *borderlands* often signifies more fluid zones of interaction. Andrew R. L. Cayton and Fredrika J. Teute, eds., *Contact Points: American Frontiers from the Mohawk Valley to the Mississippi, 1750-1830* (Chapel Hill: University of North Carolina Press, 1998); Pekka Hämäläinen and Samuel Truett, "On Borderlands," *Journal of American History* 98, no. 2 (2011): 343–44; Jeremy Adelman and Stephen Aron, "From Borderlands to Borders: Empires, Nation States, and the Peoples in between in North American History," *American Historical Review* 104, no. 3 (1999): 815–16. David Silverman has compellingly defined *frontier* as a "zone of contact in which indigenous people exercised significant and sometimes even disproportionate power and the outcome was uncertain and contested." David Silverman, *Thundersticks: Firearms and the Violent Transformation of Native America* (Cambridge, MA: Belknap, 2016), 19.

15. Jane Cazneau, using the pen name Cora Montgomery, coined the term *Manifest Destiny* in 1845 and laid the historical and political justification for it in 1839, in the

United States Magazine and Democratic Review. Laurel Clark Shire, *The Threshold of Manifest Destiny: Gender and National Expansion in Florida* (Philadelphia: University of Pennsylvania Press, 2016), 13. *Manifest Destiny* has also been attributed to John L. O'Sullivan, but it is likely that Cazneau wrote the anonymous editorial associated with O'Sullivan.

16. Michael Morris, "Georgia and the Conversation over Indian Removal," *Georgia Historical Quarterly* 91, no. 4 (Winter 2007): 410.

17. Christine Snyder, *Great Crossings: Indians, Settlers, and Slaves in the Age of Jackson* (New York: Oxford University Press, 2017).

18. "An Act to Provide for an Exchange of Lands with the Indians Residing in Any of the States or Territories, and for Their Removal West of the River Mississippi," March 28, 1830, 21st Cong., chap. 148, p. 411.

19. Claudio Saunt, "Financing Dispossession: Stocks, Bonds, and the Deportation of Native Peoples in the Antebellum United States," *Journal of American History* 106, no. 2 (September 2019): 315–37, esp. 320–22.

20. Poinsett subscribed to Jackson's position that Native peoples could and should forcibly be removed from their homes. Some Jacksonian apologists read benevolence into Jackson's plans, associating relocation with desires to protect and preserve Native life and culture. They blame its consequences on poor midlevel management and individual corruption. The responsibility, however, lay with top-ranking executives. Jackson revealed his intention for genocide in unofficial marginal scribblings to Poinsett in 1829, which touted the advantages of acquiring Texas for land that could be used for "concentrating the Indians." Cave, "Abuse of Power," 1338; Robert Remini, *The Legacy of Andrew Jackson: Essays on Democracy, Indian Removal, and Slavery* (Baton Rouge: Louisiana State University Press, 1988); Francis Paul Prucha, "Andrew Jackson's Indian Policy: A Reassessment," *Journal of American History* 56, no. 3 (December 1969): 527–29. For the efficacy of the Creek state in retaining sovereignty and checking white expansion until the 1810s, see Kevin Kokomoor, *Of One Mind and of One Government: The Rise and Fall of the Creek Nation in the Early Republic* (Lincoln: University of Nebraska Press, 2019). For sketchy government financing relating to Native dispossession, see Emilie Connolly, "Panic, State Power, and Chickasaw Dispossession," *Journal of the Early Republic* 40, no. 4 (Winter 2020): 683–90.

21. Laurence M. Hauptman, "General John E. Wool in Cherokee Country, 1836–1837: A Reinterpretation," *Georgia Historical Quarterly* 85, no. 1 (Spring 2001): 20.

22. Robert Wooster, *The American Military Frontiers: The United States Army in the West, 1783–1900* (Albuquerque: University of New Mexico Press, 2012), 71, 76.

23. Patrick Minges, "Beneath the Underdog: Race, Religion, and the Trail of Tears," *American Indian Quarterly* 25, no. 3 (Summer 2001): 453–79; Ethan Davis, "An Administrative Trail of Tears: Indian Removal," *American Journal of Legal History* 50, no. 1 (January 2008): 49–100. There was also a check on US military power. Catherine Denial, "Pelagie Faribault's Island: Property, Kinship, and the Meaning of Marriage in Dakota Country," *Minnesota History* 62, no. 2 (Summer 2010): 48–59. Although the act led to approximately fifty thousand people being forced from their homes and over four thousand deaths, some Natives successfully resisted removal. Jane Dinwoodie, "Evading Indian Removal in the American South," *Journal of American History* 108, no. 1 (June 2021): 17–41. For the story of one family's experience,

see Tiya Miles, *Ties That Bind: The Story of an Afro-Cherokee Family in Slavery and Freedom* (Berkeley: University of California Press, 2005).

24. Robert M. Walsh to JRP, October 22, 1838, box 5, Kane-American Collection, msHM32944, Huntington Library, San Marino, CA; N. Herbemont, August 12, 1837, PPGC, HSP; Anastasio Bustamante y Oseguera to JRP, May 22, 1837, folder 10, vol. 8, JRPP.

25. Jessica Lepler, *The Many Panics of 1837: People, Politics, and the Creation of a Transatlantic Financial Crisis* (New York: Cambridge University Press, 2014).

26. Stephen W. Campbell, *The Bank War and the Partisan Press: Newspapers, Financial Institutions, and the Post Office in Jacksonian America* (Lawrence: University Press of Kansas, 2019).

27. Stephen W. Campbell, "'A Very Large Extent of Virgin Land': Nicholas Biddle, Cotton, and the Expansion of Slavery, 1823–1841," *Pennsylvania Magazine of History and Biography* 145, no. 1 (January 2021): 33–65, esp. 60.

28. Article II, Section II of the Constitution gave the executive the power to appoint officers of the government. Executive departments fielded an endless stream of solicitations from individuals seeking positions for themselves or their friends, even though, as Ellen Hartigan-O'Connor has shown, Americans increasingly began to view patronage as anathema to democracy and manly independence. Lawmakers regularly railed against the "rapid growth of patronage, with all its attending evils." Ellen Hartigan-O'Connor, "'Auctioneer of Offices': Patronage, Value, and Trust in the Early Republic Marketplace," *Journal of the Early Republic* 33, no. 3 (Fall 2013): 464–65, esp. 487. Although merit-based appointments did not supplant political ones until the 1883 Pendleton Civil Service Act, throughout the first half of the nineteenth century there existed an uneasy tension between patronage and democracy.

29. J. N. Cardozo to JRP, March 9, 1837, folder 4, vol. 8, JRPP. For the links among the press, the post office, and Bank War tactics, see Stephen W. Campbell, *The Bank War and the Partisan Press: Newspapers, Financial Institutions, and the Post Office in Jacksonian America* (Lawrence: University Press of Kansas, 2019).

30. Gouverneur (G.) Kemble to JRP, April 3, 1837, folder 5, vol. 8, JRPP.

31. Allen M'Lane to JRP, April 12, 1837, folder 6, vol. 8, JRPP.

32. ASP, "Steam Frigate Fulton," June 11, 1838, 25th Cong., 84.

33. T. Maxey to JRP, April 7, 1837, vol. 40, Galloway-Maxcy-Markoe Families Papers, Manuscript Division, Library of Congress, Washington, DC.

34. See, for example, John H. Jacocks to JRP, May 3, 1837; Thomas Hunt (New Orleans) to JRP, July 23, 1837, PPGC. Both men wanted Poinsett to encourage government regulation of banking and the repealing of the Specie Circular. C. G. Memminger to JRP, May 20, 1837, folder 9, vol. 8, JRPP.

35. Winfield Scott to JRP, April 8, 1837, folder 6, vol. 8, JRPP.

36. C. S. Monaco, *The Second Seminole War and the Limits of American Aggression* (Baltimore: Johns Hopkins University Press, 2018), 15.

37. Julia F. Smith, "Cotton and the Factorage System in Antebellum Florida," *Florida Historical Quarterly* 49, no. 1 (July 1970): 36.

38. James Gadsden to JRP, June 5, 1837, folder 12, vol. 8, JRPP.

39. James Gadsden to JRP, June 22, 1837, folder 14, vol. 8, JRPP.

40. JRP to Andrew Jackson, August 19, 1837, folder 2, vol. 9, JRPP.

41. JRP to Andrew Jackson, August 19, 1837, folder 2, vol. 9, JRPP.

42. Andrew Jackson to JRP, August 27, 1837, folder 3, box 9, JRPP; Andrew Jackson to JRP, October 1, 1837, folder 7, vol. 9, JRPP.

43. See, for example, "Cherokee Deputation to Florida," *Connecticut Herald* (New Haven, CT), November 14, 1837, 2; "Domestic from the Augusta Constitutionalist," *Enquirer* (Richmond, VA), December 8, 1837, 4.

44. Watson, *Peacekeepers and Conquerors*, 156.

45. Gary E. Moulton, "Cherokees and the Second Seminole Wars," *Florida Historical Quarterly* 53, no. 3 (January 1975): 297–98.

46. ASP, "Appropriations—Seminole War," September 15, 1837, 25th Cong.

47. Congress revoked Jackson's executive order the following spring by a joint resolution.

48. William G. Shade, "'The Most Delicate and Exciting Topics': Martin Van Buren, Slavery, and the Election of 1836," *Journal of the Early Republic* 18, no. 3 (Autumn 1998): 481; John C. Calhoun, *Speech of Mr. Calhoun, of South Carolina, on the Subtreasury Bill: Delivered in the Senate, February 15, 1838* (Washington, DC: Hamilton & Denham, printers, 1838).

49. John H. Sargent to JRP, September 4, 14, 1837, folder 5, vol. 9, JRPP; *Journal of the House of Representatives*, September 15, 1837, 25th Cong. (Washington, DC: Thomas Allen, 1837), 59.

50. David Kinley, *The Independent Treasury of the United States and Its Relations to the Banks of the Country* (Washington, DC: Government Printing Office, 1910), 35–36.

51. J. W. Cardozo to JRP, July 26, 1837, folder 17, vol. 8, JRPP.

52. C. C. Cambreleng to JRP, August 4, 1837, folder 8, vol. 8, JRPP. See also Thomas and Randell Hunt [New Orleans] to JRP, July 23, 1837, PPGC.

53. JRP to Martin Van Buren, September 4, 1837, reel 18, Martin Van Buren Papers, Manuscript Division, Library of Congress, Washington, DC.

54. Martin Van Buren, "Special Session Message," September 4, 1837, https://millercenter.org/the-presidency/presidential-speeches/september-4-1837-special-session-message.

55. Hugh S. Legare to JRP, October 11, 1837, folder 8, vol. 9, JRPP.

56. Henry R. Robinson, *Sub-Treasury System, or Office Holders Elysium* (New York: H. R. Robinson, 1838).

57. E. B. Robinson to JRP, January 5, 1838, folder 17, vol. 9, JRPP.

58. JRP to Thomas Jesup, November 10, 1837, vol. 18, Letters Sent by the Secretary of War Relating to Military Affairs, RG107, M6, NARA, Washington, DC.

59. Monaco, *Second Seminole War*, 99. John W. Hall argues that Sherburne was the chief architect of the Cherokee mission. John W. Hall, *Dishonorable Duty: The U.S. Army and the Removal of the Southeastern Indians* (Cambridge, MA: Harvard University Press, forthcoming). Poinsett, however, bears much of the blame for the mission's failure.

60. John H. Sherburne to JRP, October 4, 1837, folder 7, vol. 8, JRPP.

61. John H. Sherburne to JRP, November 13, 1837, folder 12, vol. 8, JRPP.

62. ASP, "Memorial of the Cherokee Mediators," March 26, 1838, 25th Cong., no. 285.

63. Truman Cross to Thomas Jesup, July 27, 1837, box 5, Ethan Allen Hitchcock

Collection on Indian Removal, Western Americana Collection, Beinecke Rare Book and Manuscript Library, Yale University.

64. Monaco, *Second Seminole War*, 101.

65. JRP to Wallace Warrenton, November 4, 1837; JRP to William Marcy, November 11, 1837, vol. 18, Letters Sent by the Secretary of War Relating to Military Affairs, RG107, M6, NARA, Washington, DC.

66. Thomas Sidney Jesup to JRP, June 6, 1838, box 25, Thomas Sidney Jesup papers, 1780–1907, MMC 0318C, Library of Congress.

67. JRP to William Smith, December 11, 1837, vol. 18, Letters Sent by the Secretary of War Relating to Military Affairs, RG107, M6, NARA, Washington, DC.

68. ASP, "Report of the Secretary of War," November 21, 1831, 22nd Cong., p. 708. Poinsett's push for more troops in some ways countered the general federal policy, which tended to prefer the payment of annuities to Native peoples as a means to disincentivize armed resistance. Emilie Connolly, "Fiduciary Colonialism: Annuities and Native Dispossession in the Early United States," *American Historical Review* 127, no. 1 (March 2022): 233.

69. ASP, "Report of the Secretary of War," December 2, 1837, 25th Cong., p. 181. See Emilie Connolly, "Indian Trust Funds and the Routes of American Capitalism, 1795–1865" (PhD diss., New York University, 2019); Connolly, "Fiduciary Colonialism," 223–53.

70. ASP, "Report of the Secretary of War," December 2, 1837, 25th Cong., p. 576.

71. JRP to Levi Woodbury, April 6, 1837, vol. 18, Letters Sent by the Secretary of War Relating to Military Affairs, RG107, M6, National Archives, Washington, DC.

72. ASP, "Report of the Secretary of War," November 28, 1838.

73. Watson, *Peacekeepers and Conquerors*, 261.

74. William J. Worth to JRP, January 3, 1838, folder 6, vol. 9, JRPP.

75. "Highly Important from the Frontier," *Albany (NY) Argus*, January 2, 1838, 3. William Jenkins Worth to JRP, November 24, 1838, vol. 1, William Jenkins Worth papers, MMC-2944, Manuscript Division, Library of Congress, Washington, DC.

76. Richard Rush to JRP, January 13, 20, 1838, folder 17, vol. 9, JRPP.

77. JRP to Martin Van Buren, June 19, 1838, vol. 3, Letters Sent to the President, 1800–1865, M127, NARA, Washington, DC.

78. Richard Rush to JRP, January 13, 20, 1838, folder 17, vol. 9, JRPP.

79. JRP to John Boyle, February 22, 1838, vol. 18, Letters Sent by the Secretary of War Relating to Military Affairs, RG107, M6, NARA, Washington, DC.

80. JRP to J. J. McKay, February 28, 1838, vol. 18, Letters Sent by the Secretary of War Relating to Military Affairs, RG107, M6, NARA, Washington, DC.

81. C. C. Cambreleng to JRP, February 17, 1838, folder 5, vol. 10, JRPP.

82. William Goetzmann, *Army Exploration in the American West, 1803–1863* (Austin: Texas State Historical Association, 1991), 17. Cameron Strang argues that at no time were Native peoples' efforts to use exploration to defy imperialism clearer than during the era of Indian removal. Cameron B. Strang, "Pursuing Knowledge, Surviving Empire: Indigenous Explorers in the Removal Era," *William and Mary Quarterly* 78, no. 2 (April 2021): 285.

83. Tom Chaffin, *Pathfinder: John Charles Fremont and the Course of American Empire* (Tulsa: University of Oklahoma Press, 2014), 32–33; Samuel Cooper to Edward Bishop Dudley, April 6, 1838, vol. 19, Letters Sent by the Secretary of War Relating to Military Affairs, RG107, M6, NARA, Washington, DC.

84. Hauptman, "General John E. Wool," 1.

85. Stephen W. Kearny to JRP, March 18, 1838, folder 8, vol. 10, JRPP; JRP to Francis Malloy, March 26, 1838, vol. 19; Milton E. Holtz, "Old Fort Kearny, 1846–1848: Symbol of a Changing Frontier," *Montana: The Magazine of Western History* 22, no. 4 (Autumn 1972): 49.

86. JRP to John Ross, Edward Gunter, R. Taylor, James Brown, Samuel Gunter, Situwake, Elijah Hicks, and White Patch, December 27, 1837, in US Congress, *House Memorial of a Delegation of the Cherokee Nation Remonstrating against the Instrument of Writing (Treaty) of December, 1835* (Washington, DC: Thomas Allen, printer, 1838), 49.

87. US Congress, *House Memorial of a Delegation*.

88. Truman Cross to Thomas Jesup, July 27, 1837, box 5, Ethan Allen Hitchcock Collection on Indian Removal, Western Americana Collection, Beinecke Rare Book and Manuscript Library, Yale University.

89. Hauptman, "General John E. Wool," 1; Letters Sent by the Secretary of War Relating to Military Affairs, RG107, M6, NARA, Washington, DC.

90. For example, when Felix Huston of Natchez confessed his fear that southern security might be jeopardized by a union of Mexicans and Indians, Poinsett launched an investigation and consulted with Van Buren on relations with Mexico and Texas. JRP to Martin Van Buren, May 2, 1838, folder 11, vol. 10, JRPP.

91. JRP to John Ross, Edward Gunter, R. Taylor, James Brown, Samuel Gunter, Situwake, Elijah Hicks, and White Patch, May 18, 1838, vol. 19, Letters Sent by the Secretary of War Relating to Military Affairs, RG107, M6, NARA, Washington, DC.

92. JRP to Winfield Scott, May 23, 1838, vol. 19, Letters Sent by the Secretary of War Relating to Military Affairs, RG107, M6, NARA, Washington, DC.

93. Carl J. Vipperman, "The Bungled Treaty of New Echota: The Failure of Cherokee Removal, 1836–1838," *Georgia Historical Quarterly* 73, no. 3 (Fall 1989): 558.

94. JRP to Winfield Scott, June 27, 1838, vol. 19, Letters Sent by the Secretary of War Relating to Military Affairs, RG107, M6, NARA, Washington, DC.

95. Wilson Lumpkin to JRP, July 31, 1839, Confidential and Unofficial Letters Received, RG107, entry 21, NARA, Washington, DC.

96. Samuel Cooper to JRP, August 11, 1838, vol. 19, Letters Sent by the Secretary of War Relating to Military Affairs, RG107, M6, NARA, Washington, DC.

97. L. Kingsley to JRP, August 24, 1838, folder 17, Volume 10, JRPP.

98. Francis Lieber, "Right of Search Political Ethics," January 1842, Francis Lieber papers, mssLI 1-5222, Huntington Library, San Marino, CA.

99. William Jenkins Worth to JRP, November 24, 1838, vol. 1, William Jenkins Worth papers, MMC-2944, Manuscript Division, Library of Congress, Washington, DC.

100. William Jenkins Worth to JRP, November 24, 1838, vol. 1, William Jenkins Worth papers, MMC-2944, Manuscript Division, Library of Congress, Washington, DC.

101. Watson, *Peacekeepers and Conquerors*, 266–67.

102. ASP, "Petition and Remonstrance of E. P. Walton and 215 Other Legal Voters of Washington County, in the State of Vermont, against the Passage of Any Law Prohibiting the Selling, Transporting, or Giving to the Canadians, Arms, Ammunition, or Provisions, or Giving Any Authority to Seize or Detain the Same, beyond What Is Given by Existing Laws," February 21, 1838, 25th Cong.

103. ASP, Statute 3, March 3, 1839, 25th Cong., pp. 355–56.

104. Winfield Scott to JRP, March 20, 1839, Confidential and Unofficial Letters Received, RG107, entry 21, NARA, Washington, DC.

105. Howard Jones, "Anglophobia and the Aroostook War," *New England Quarterly* 48, no. 4 (1975), 524.

106. Winfield Scott to JRP, March 20, 21, 22, 1839, Confidential and Unofficial Letters Received, RG107, entry 21, NARA, Washington, DC.

107. Winfield Scott to J. H. Harvey, March 25, 1839, Confidential and Unofficial Letters Received, RG107, entry 21, NARA, Washington, DC.

108. Winfield Scott, Confidential Circular, April 15, 1839, Confidential and Unofficial Letters Received, RG107, entry 21, NARA, Washington, DC.

109. JRP to Martin Van Buren, January 22, 1840, Letters Sent by the Secretary of War to the President, RG107, M127, roll 2, NARA, Washington, DC.

110. JRP to Martin Van Buren, January 22, March 27, March 23, 1840, Letters Sent by the Secretary of War to the President, RG107, M127, roll 2, NARA, Washington, DC.

111. Zanesville Aurora, "Commendable," *Newark (OH) Advocate*, May 25, 1839; NY Journal of Commerce, "Domestic," *Vermont Chronicle* (Bellows Falls, VT), July 3, 1839, 107.

112. George Croghan to JRP, March 8, 1839, Col. General George Gibbon to JRP, March 9, 1839; Nathaniel Towson to JRP, March 11, 1839; J. R. Fenwick to JRP, March 15, 1839, Confidential and Unofficial Letters Received, RG107, entry 21, NARA, Washington, DC.

113. He and Scott, for example, disagreed about the need to move troops from the northern border to Florida. Winfield Scott to JRP, October 18, 1839, Confidential and Unofficial Letters Received, RG107, entry 21, NARA, Washington, DC.

114. Timothy Mason Roberts, "The Role of French Algeria in American Expansion during the Early Republic," *Journal of Western Society for French History* 43 (2015): 153–64.

115. Robert P. Wettemann Jr., *Privilege vs. Equality: Civil-Military Relations in the Jacksonian Era* (Santa Barbara, CA: Praeger, 2009).

116. "The Tippecanoe Club, No. 1, of Richmond, at a late meeting, passed a resolution for the appointment of a committee, to wait on the Editor of the Enquirer and request him to publish Mr. POINSETT'S scheme for organizing the militia, and, in the event of his refusal, to endeavor to get it inserted in his paper as an advertisement." *Virginia Free Press* (Charlestown, WV), May 28, 1840.

117. Mahlon Dickerson to JRP, June 21, 1842, folder 13, vol. 16, JRPP.

118. John T. Sprague, *The Origin, Progress, and Conclusions of the Florida War* (New York: D. Appleton, 1848), 236–37, 199–202.

119. ASP, "Report of the Secretary of War," November 28, 1838, p. 101.

120. "General Intelligence," *Virginia Free Press* (Charlestown, WV), August 30, 1838.

121. JRP, War Department, February 10, 1840, Confidential and Unofficial Letters Received, RG107, entry 21, National Archives, Washington, DC; ASP, "Letter from the Secretary of War, to the Chairman of the Committee on Military Affairs, in Relation to the Employment of Bloodhounds against the Hostile Indians in Florida," February 17, 1840, 26th Cong., p. 4.

122. Charles B. Van Pelt, "The Army's Introduction to the Air Arm," *Air Power Historian* 9, no. 4 (October 1962): 241–47. Sherburne advocated ballooning as a way to locate and capture large encampments of Seminoles. Michael G. Schene, "Ballooning in the Second Seminole War," *Florida Historical Quarterly* 55, no. 4 (1977): 480–82.

123. James W. Covington, "Cuban Bloodhounds and the Seminoles," *Florida Historical Quarterly* 33, no. 2 (October 1954): 115.

124. Sprague, *Origin, Progress, and Conclusions*, 240.

125. John Campbell, "The Seminoles, the 'Bloodhound War,' and Abolitionism, 1796–1865," *Journal of Southern History* 72, no. 2 (2006): 259–302, esp. 267.

126. Joshua R. Giddings, *The Exiles of Florida: Or the Crimes Committed by Our Government against the Maroons, Who Fled from South Carolina and Other Slave States, Seeking Protection under Spanish Laws* (Columbus, OH: Follett, Foster, and Company, 1858), 154.

127. Campbell, "Seminoles, the 'Bloodhound War,'" esp. 268; Tyler D. Parry and Charlton W. Yingling, "Slave Hounds and Abolition in the Americas," *Past & Present* 246, no. 1 (February 2020): 69–108.

128. "The Bloodhound War," *Emancipator* (New York), November 21, 1839, 118; "The Bloodhound Expedition," *Tennessee Whig* (Jonesborough, TN), February 27, 1840.

129. Senate Chamber to JRP, February 7, 1840, Confidential and Unofficial Letters Received, RG107, entry 21, NARA, Washington, DC.

130. Sprague, *Origin, Progress, and Conclusions*, 241.

131. JRP, War Department, February 10, 1840, Confidential and Unofficial Letters Received, RG107, entry 21, NARA, Washington, DC.

132. Pictorial reporting had become popular during Jackson's presidency. Peter C. Welsh, "Henry R. Robinson: Printmaker to the Whig Party," *New York History* 53, no. 1 (January 1972): 25–53, esp. 28.

133. *The Secretary of War Presenting a Stand of Colours to the 1st Regiment of Republican Bloodhounds* (Washington, DC: H. R. Robinson, 1840).

134. ASP, "Letter from the Secretary of War, to the Chairman of the Committee on Military Affairs, in Relation to the Employment of Bloodhounds against the Hostile Indians in Florida," February 17, 1840, 26th Cong.

135. "Memo in Relation to the Expenses of Purchasing or Keeping Bloodhounds in Florida," box 25, Thomas Sidney Jesup papers, 1780–1907, MMC 0318C, Library of Congress.

136. US Senate, *Public Documents*, 26th Cong. (Washington, DC: printed by Blair and Rives, 1840).

137. Valley Star, "Poinsett's Report," *Ohio Statesman* (Columbus, OH), April 22, 1840.

138. J. C. Bennett to JRP, July 27, August 25, November 20, 1840, Confidential and Unofficial Letters Received, RG107, entry 21, National Archives, Washington, DC.

139. John L. Eaton to JRP, October 18, 1840, folder 12, box 15, JRPP. Poinsett was in line with Karp's argument about southern statesmen who were not secessionists but nationalists and worked to modernize the US military while using the federal government to protect slavery. Matthew Karp, *This Vast Southern Empire: Slavehold-*

ers at the Helm of American Foreign Policy (Cambridge, MA: Harvard University Press, 2016). The militia was limited to whites, but Blacks did serve in some states, a reality that made many slaveholders nervous. Roland C. McConnell, *Negro Troops of Antebellum Louisiana: A History of the Battalion of Free Men of Color* (Baton Rouge: Louisiana State University Press, 1968).

140. Thomas Ritchie and Joel Roberts Poinsett, "Interesting correspondence" (Richmond, 1840), 2.

141. "Scraps Preserved by N.M. for H.W.M.," April 3, 1840, HM4020, Merrill Collection, Huntington Library, San Marino, CA.

142. JRP to Martin Van Buren, March 2, 1841, Letters Sent by the Secretary of War to the President, RG107, M127, roll 2, NARA, Washington, DC.

143. Stanley L. Falk, "Artillery for the Land Service: The Development of a System," *Military Affairs* 28, no. 3 (1964): 103; Benk Huger to JRP, December 9, 1846, folder 17, box 16, JRPP.

144. JRP to Martin Van Buren, March 2, 1841, Letters Sent by the Secretary of War to the President, RG107, M127, roll 2, NARA, Washington, DC.

145. V. Maxcy, "National Institution," *Daily National Intelligencer* (Washington, DC), February 1, 1841.

146. Correspondence of the Register, "Congress." *Raleigh Register and North-Carolina Gazette* (Raleigh, NC), January 5, 1841.

147. "Regulation," April 3, 1837, March 1, 1841, Decisions, Orders and Regulations by the Secretary of War, vol. 1, Records of the Office of the Secretary of War, RG 107 E-41, NARA DC.

Chapter 7

1. Henry Trescot to JRP, February 6, 1841, folder 8, vol. 16; Mahlon Dickerson to JRP, June 21, 1842, folder 13, vol. 16, JRPP.

2. "Advertisement," *Daily National Intelligencer* (Washington, DC), March 12, 1841, 2; *Ohio Statesman* (Columbus, OH), March 23, 1841.

3. "Multiple Classified Advertisements," *Daily National Intelligencer* (Washington, DC), January 1, 1841.

4. Correspondence of the Inquirer and Courier, "From Washington," *Pennsylvania Inquirer and Daily Courier* (Philadelphia), December 17, 1841.

5. For an understanding of early national "science," I rely on the definition posed by Conevery Bolton Valencius, David I. Spanagel, Emily Pawley, and Sara Stidstone Gronim: "systematic work of observation, data collection, theorizing about natural causes, or experimental production of knowledge. These activities were typically categorized as either natural philosophy or natural history, but were mainly pursued in the context of seeking 'useful' knowledge." Conevery Bolton Valencius, David I. Spanagel, Emily Pawley, and Sara Stidstone Gronim, "Science in Early America: Print Culture and the Sciences of Territoriality," *Journal of the Early Republic* 36, no. 1 (February 2016): 82. The American Journal of Science was founded in 1818. Valencius, Spanagel, Pawley, and Gronim, "Science in Early America," 87.

6. Interestingly, Lawrence T. McDonnell argues that some of the major movers in the secession movement were not slaveholders but "young, single, unpropertied men." Lawrence T. McDonnell, *Performing Disunion: The Coming of the Civil War in Charleston, South Carolina* (New York: Cambridge University Press, 2018), 15.

7. William Stanton, *The Great United States Exploring Expedition of 1838–1842* (Berkeley: University of California Press, 1975), 292.

8. John J. Abert to JRP, July 12, 1841, PPGC, 148.

9. Valencius, Spanagel, Pawley, and Gronim, "Science in Early America," 85.

10. Meeting, August 10, 1840, *Bulletin of the Proceedings of the National Institute for the Promotion of Science* (Washington, DC, 1840), 6.

11. Stanton, *Great Exploring Expedition*, 292–93.

12. Joel Roberts Poinsett, *Discourse on the Objects and Importance of the National Institution for the Promotion of Science, Established at Washington, 1840, Delivered at the First Anniversary* (Washington, DC: P. Force, Printer, 1841), 31.

13. Poinsett, *Discourse*, 32.

14. Meeting, April 12, 1841, *Bulletin of the Proceedings of the National Institute for the Promotion of Science* (Washington, DC, 1841), 75.

15. Poinsett, *Discourse*, 47, 22.

16. "Advertisement," *Daily National Intelligencer* (Washington, DC), March 12, 1841, 2; *Ohio Statesman* (Columbus, OH), March 23, 1841.

17. Marlana Portolano, "John Quincy Adams's Rhetorical Crusade for Astronomy," *Isis* 91, no. 3 (September 2000): 492.

18. John Quincy Adams and Charles Francis Adams, *Memoirs of John Quincy Adams: Comprising Portions of His Diary from 1795 to 1848* (Philadelphia: J. B. Lippincott, 1874–1877), 10:462–64; "Extract from the Memoirs of John Quincy Adams," folder 78, CLCP.

19. Portolano, "John Quincy Adams's Crusade," 480–503; Elias Loomis, *The Recent Progress of Astronomy: Especially in the United States* (New York: Harper & Brothers, 1850), 171–72.

20. Portolano, "John Quincy Adams's Crusade," 489.

21. American Philosophical Society Memorial to JRP, December 20, 1839, in Nathan Reingold et al., ed., *The Papers of Joseph Henry*, vol. 4, *The Princeton Years: January 1838–December 1840* (Washington, DC: Smithsonian Institution, 1981), 315–20; Christopher Carter, "Magnetic Fever: Global Imperialism and Empiricism in the Nineteenth Century," *Transactions of the American Philosophical Society*, n.s., 99, no. 4 (2009): 129.

22. Harley Harris Bartlett, "The Report of the Wilkes Expedition, and the Work of the Specialists in Science," *Proceedings of the American Philosophical Society* 82, no. 5 (June 1940): 620; W. Jones Rhees, *The Smithsonian Institution: Documents relative to Its Origin and History* (Washington, DC: Smithsonian Institution, 1879), 780.

23. For just a sampling of the field of scholarship that deals with southern masculine mastery over agriculture, enslaved Africans, racial and gender politics, and social and economic activities, see Eugene Genovese, *Roll, Jordan, Roll: The World the Slaves Made* (New York: Vintage Books, 1974); Lorri Glover, *Southern Sons: Becoming Men in the New Nation* (Baltimore: Johns Hopkins University Press, 2010); Craig Thompson Friend and Lorri Glover, *Southern Manhood: Perspectives on Masculinity in the Old South* (Athens: University of Georgia Press, 2004). For the classic work on southern honor, see Bertram Wyatt-Brown, *Southern Honor: Ethics and Behavior in the Old South* (New York, 1982); Drew Gilpin Faust, "The Rhetoric and Ritual of Agriculture in Antebellum South Carolina," *Journal of Southern History* 45, no. 4 (November 1979): 541–68; Caitlin Rosenthal, "From Memory to Mastery: Accounting for Control in America, 1750–1880," *Enterprise & Society* 14, no. 4 (December 2013):

732–48; Rosenthal, *Accounting for Slavery: Masters and Management* (Cambridge, MA: Harvard University Press, 2018). For capitalism and agricultural more generally, see Courtney Fullilove, *The Profit of the Earth: The Global Seeds of American Agriculture* (Chicago: University of Chicago Press, 2017).

24. William Thomas Okie, "Beauty and Habitation: Fredrika Bremer and the Aesthetic Imperative of Environmental History," *Environmental History* 24, no. 2 (April 2019): 258–81.

25. JRP to G. Kemble, June 4, 5, 1841, PPGC, 146.

26. Mary Pringle Fenhagen, "Descendants of Judge Robert Pringle," *South Carolina Historical Magazine* 101, no. 4 (October 2000): 305–6.

27. JRP to G. Kemble, November 12, 1843, folder 79, CLCP.

28. JRP to Mary Izard Pringle, April 24, 1849, folder 13, Allston family papers, 1730–1901, (1164.00) SCHS.

29. As Drew Gilpin Faust argues, "Because agriculture appeared to be a foundation of both social and moral order, perception of decline in its objective social and economic importance created considerable uneasiness among Americans already apprehensive about the widespread changes affecting their early-nineteenth-century world." Drew Gilpin Faust, "The Rhetoric and Ritual of Agriculture in Antebellum South Carolina," *Journal of Southern History* 45, no. 4 (November 1979): 542; Dana G. Dalrymple, "The Smithsonian Bequest, Congress, and Nineteenth-Century Efforts to Increase and Diffuse Agricultural Knowledge in the United States," *Agricultural History Review* 57, no. 2 (2009): 218; Timothy K. Minella, "A Pattern for Improvement: Pattern Farms and Scientific Authority in Early Nineteenth-Century America," *Agricultural History* 90, no. 4 (Fall 2016): 434–58.

30. Joel R. Poinsett, "Agriculture of South Carolina," December 10, 1841, in *Transaction of the New York State Agricultural Society* (Albany, NY: T. Weed, printer to the state, 1842), 164–65.

31. State Agricultural Society of South Carolina, *Proceedings of the Agricultural Convention and of the State Agricultural Society* (Columbia, SC: Summer and Carroll, 1846); "South Carolina State Agricultural Society," *Southern Cultivator*, vol. 2, (October 1844), 156–57.

32. "South Carolina State Agricultural Society," *Southern Cultivator*, vol. 2, (October 1844), 156–57; Edmund Ruffin, *Report of the Commencement and Progress of the Agricultural Survey of South Carolina, for 1843* (Columbia: A. H. Pemberton, 1843); M. Tuomey, *Report on the Geological and Agricultural Survey of the State of South Carolina, 1844* (Columbia, SC: printed by A. S. Johnston, 1844).

33. John Bachman, *An Inquiry into the Nature and Benefits of an Agricultural Survey of the State of South Carolina* (Charleston: Miller & Browne, 1843), 10; Peter McCandless, "The Political Evolution of John Bachman: From New York Yankee to South Carolina Secessionist," *South Carolina Historical Magazine* 108, no. 1 (January 2007): 25.

34. *Southern Cultivator*, 390.

35. Mary, for example, was friends with Gouverneur Kemble's wife. G. Kemble to JRP, April 2, 1842, PPGC, 159.

36. John J. Abert to JRP, August 23, 1842, PPGC, 165.

37. JRP to G. Kemble, May 24, 1842, PPGC, HSP, 162; "An Act to Incorporate a Society in the District of Columbia by the Name of the National Institute for the

Promotion of Science," July 27, 1842, 27th Cong., chap. 105, pp. 845–46; Sally Kohl-stedt, "A Step toward Scientific Self-Identity in the United States: The Failure of the National Institute, 1844," *Isis* 62, no. 3 (Autumn 1971), 345.

38. Daniel Webster to Peter Force, John Abert, W. Ellsworth, August 9, 1841, box I:7, Peter Force papers and collection (MSS20990), Library of Congress.

39. National Institute for the Promotion of Science, *Bulletin of the Proceedings of the National Institute* (Washington, DC, 1841), 83, 236.

40. JRP to G. Kemble, May 24, 1842, PPGC, HSP, 162; "An Act to Incorporate a Society in the District of Columbia by the Name of the National Institute for the Promotion of Science," July 27, 1842, 27th Cong., chap. 105, pp. 845–46; Kohlstedt, "Step toward Scientific Self-Identity in the United States," 345.

41. Loomis, *Recent Progress of Astronomy*, 171–72; Portolano, "John Quincy Adams's Crusade," 501.

42. Richard Harrison to JRP, April 18, 1842, PPGC, 160.

43. JRP to Henry D. Gilpin, July 8, 1844, PPGC, 184.

44. G. Kemble to JRP, [n.d.] 1843; JRP to Kemble, September 13, 1843, folder 79, CLCP.

45. JRP to G. Kemble, November 12, 1843, folder 79, CLCP, #3614, Southern Historical Collection, Wilson Library, University of North Carolina at Chapel Hill.

46. JRP to G. Kemble, March 8, 1844, PPGC, 181.

47. John Carroll Brent, *Letters on the National Institute, Smithsonian Legacy, the Fine Arts, and Other Matters Connected with the Interests of the District of Columbia* (Washington, DC: J and G. S. Gideon, 1844), 87–90.

48. Joel Roberts Poinsett, "The Exploring Expedition," *North American Review* 56, no. 2 (April 1843): 257–58, 270.

49. Kohlstedt, "A Step toward Scientific Self-Identity in the United States," 347.

50. National Institute for the Promotion of Science, *Bulletin of the Proceedings of the National Institute* (Washington, DC, 1841), 259.

51. John J. Abert to JRP, November 9, 1842, folder 14, vol. 16, JRPP. In general, Poinsett wanted to protect decisions about national scientific initiatives from public interference.

52. John J. Abert to JRP, July 3, 1844, folder 16, vol. 16, JRPP; Kohlstedt, "Step toward Scientific Self-Identity in the United States," 347.

53. John J. Abert to JRP, December 28, 1844, PPGC, 191.

54. ASP, "National Institute for the Promotion of Science," February 15, 1845, 28th Cong., no. 130.

55. "Benjamin Tappan's Bill for Smithson Bequest," June 6, 1844, in William Jones Rhees, *The Smithsonian Institution: Documents relative to Its Origin and History: 1835–1899*, vol. 1, *1835–1887* (Washington, DC: Government Printing Office, 1901), 266–68.

56. Although many historians have linked Van Buren's loss to Southern Demo-crats' Texas extremism, Michael Morrison identifies a host of nonsectional reasons. Michael A. Morrison, "Martin Van Buren, the Democracy, and the Partisan Politics of Texas Annexation," *Journal of Southern History* 61, no. 4 (November 1995): 695–724; JRP to G. Kemble, June 18, 1844, PPGC, 182.

57. C. C. Cambreleng to JRP, November 25, 1845, folder 16, vol. 16, JRPP.

58. JRP to G. Kemble, July 1, 1844, PPGC, 183, 184.

59. JRP to [?], October 14, 1844, folder 79, CLCP.

60. Poinsett, however, reveals that not all white southerners felt this way. In this, he was not alone. For example, among New Orleans merchants, opinions varied widely on whether uninterrupted silver imports from Mexico or the potential for access to land for a railroad were more important and thus whether conflict with Mexico was advantageous. Kyle Jackson, "'Those from Louisiana, Who Are to Be Considered as Brothers': Southern Expansion, Mexican Federalism, and the 1835 Secret Pact of New Orleans" (paper presented at the Society for Historians of the Early American Republic, New Orleans, July 22, 2022).

61. Although Poinsett had offered Mexico $1 million in the 1820s for territory for the United States, his opinions changed. Curt Lamar, "Genesis of Mexican–United States Diplomacy: A Critical Analysis of the Alaman-Poinsett Confrontation, 1825," *Americas* 38, no. 1 (July 1981): 97.

62. JRP to Thomas Hart Benton, May 13, 1846, folder 17, vol. 16, JRPP.

63. JRP to Frances Tyrrell, January 18, 1847, PPGC, 210.

64. JRP to Frances Tyrrell, February 24, 1845, PPGC, 192.

65. JRP to [?], October 14, 1844, folder 79, CLCP.

66. Peter A. Coclanis and Stanley L. Engerman, "Would Slavery Have Survived without the Civil War? Economic Factors in the American South during the Antebellum and Postbellum Eras," *Southern Cultures* 19, no. 2 (Summer 2013): 70, 76.

67. Samuel H. Williamson and Louis Cain, "Measuring Slavery in 2016 dollars," Measuring Worth, 2020, accessed October 1, 2020, https://www.measuringworth.com/slavery.php; Robert Evans Jr., "The Economics of American Negro Slavery, 1830–1860," in *Aspects of Labor Economics*, ed. National Bureau Committee for Economic Research (Princeton, NJ: Princeton University Press, 1962), 199.

68. State Agricultural Society of South Carolina, *Proceedings of the Agricultural Convention and of the State Agricultural Society* (Columbia: Summer and Carroll, 1846), 242.

69. State Agricultural Society of South Carolina, *Proceedings of the Agricultural Convention*, 243.

70. Fredrika Bremer, *The Homes of the New World*, p. 287, folder 81, CLCP; State Agricultural Society of South Carolina, *Proceedings of the Agricultural Convention*, 255.

71. State Agricultural Society of South Carolina, *Proceedings of the Agricultural Convention*, 254–55.

72. Ernest M. Lander, "The Iron Industry in Ante-bellum South Carolina," *Journal of Southern History* 20, no. 3 (August 1954): 337–55; Miles S. Richards, "Pierce Mason Butler: The South Carolina Years, 1830–1841," *South Carolina Historical Magazine* 87, no. 1 (January 1986): 26; Lander, "Manufacturing in South Carolina, 1815–60," *Business History Review* 28, no. 1 (March 1954): 60.

73. For the importance of the overland trade between the United States and Mexico, see Richard J. Salvucci, "The Origins and Progress of U.S.-Mexican Trade, 1825–1884: 'Hoc Opus, Hic Labor Est.,'" *Hispanic American Historical Review* 71, no. 4 (1991): 697–735.

74. George Wilkins Kendall, *Narrative of the Texan Santa Fé Expedition: Comprising a Tour through Texas* (London: Sherwood, Gilbert, and Piper, 1846), 5.

75. Pierce M. Butler to JRP, September 4, 5, 1840, folder 6, vol. 15, JRPP; F. H. Elmore to JRP, September 18, 1840, folder 8, vol. 15, JRPP.

76. Pierce M. Butler to JRP, February 3, 1841, "Notes from the Gilpin Papers," folder 78, CLCP.

77. William Campbell Binkley, "New Mexico and the Texan Santa Fé Expedition," *Southwestern Historical Quarterly* 27, no. 2 (October 1923): 85–107.

78. JRP to Frances Tyrrell, February 24, 1845, PPGC, 192; JRP to Jackson, November 12, 1844, folder 78, CLCP.

79. Amy Greenberg, *A Wicked War: Polk, Clay, Lincoln and the 1846 US Invasion of Mexico* (New York: Penguin Random House, 2013), 103–8. For Mexican domestic politics during the war, see Pedro Santoni, *Mexicans at Arms: Puro Federalists and the Politics of War, 1845–1848* (Fort Worth: Texas Christian University Press, 1996). For a longer military history of Mexico, see William A. DePalo Jr., *The Mexican National Army, 1822–1852* (College Station: Texas A&M Press, 1997).

80. JRP to Lewis Cass, May 16, 1846, folder 17, box 16, JRPP.

81. See, for example, J. G. Totten to JRP, November 27, 1846; Benjamin Huger to JRP, folder 17, vol. 16, JRPP.

82. Joel Roberts Poinsett, "Our Army in Mexico," *DeBow's Review* 2, no. 6 (December 1846): 426–30.

83. Joel Roberts Poinsett, "Mexico and the Mexicans," *DeBow's Review* 2, no. 2 (September 1846): 177.

84. JRP to A. P. Butler, December 12, 1847, newspaper clipping, folder 18, vol. 16, JRPP.

85. JRP to Frances Tyrrell, January 18, 1847, folder 80, CLCP.

86. JRP to G. Kemble, February 8, 1847, folder 80, CLCP.

87. John C. Calhoun, speech to Congress on Mexico, January 4, 1848, in Ernesto Chávez, ed., *The U.S. War with Mexico: A Brief History with Documents* (Boston: Bedford/St. Martin's, 2008), 118–20.

88. JRP to G. Kemble, October 29, 1847, PPGC, 217.

89. For treaty negotiations, see Greenberg, *A Wicked War*, 256–60; Joel H. Silbey, *Storm over Texas: The Annexation Controversy and the Road to Civil War* (New York: Oxford University Press, 2007), 96.

90. Melvin Johnson White, *The Secession Movement in the United States, 1847–1852* (New Orleans: Tulane University Press, 1916), 107.

91. Raúl Rodríguez, and Harry Targ, "US Foreign Policy towards Cuba: Historical Roots, Traditional Explanations and Alternative Perspectives," *International Journal of Cuban Studies* 7, no. 1 (Spring 2015): 18–20; Amy S. Greenberg, "Cuba and the Failure of Manifest Destiny," *Journal of the Early Republic* 42, no. 1 (Spring 2022): 1–20.

92. Simeon Simeonov, "The Consular Caribbean: Consuls as Agents of Colonialism and Decolonisation in the Revolutionary Caribbean (1795–1848)," in *Memory, Migration and (De)Colonisation in the Caribbean and Beyond*, ed. Webb Jack, Westmaas Rod, Del Pilar Kaladeen Maria, and Tantam William (London: University of London Press, 2020), 129.

93. JRP to J. Hamilton, May 11, 1850, folder 18, vol. 16, JRPP.

94. Miles S. Richards, "Pierce Mason Butler: The South Carolina Years, 1830–1841," *South Carolina Historical Magazine* 87, no. 1 (January 1986): 20.

95. James Hamilton to JRP, January 16, 1850, folder 18, vol. 16, JRPP.

96. JRP to G. Kemble, October 2, 1841, PPGC, 150.

97. JRP to James Hamilton, May 11, 1850, folder 18, vol. 16, JRPP.

98. James Hamilton to JRP, March 1, 1850, folder 19, vol. 16, JRPP.

99. JRP to James Hamilton, May 11, 1850, folder 18, vol. 16, JRPP.

100. James Hamilton to JRP, March 1, 1850, folder 19, vol. 16, JRPP.

101. JRP to James Hamilton, May 11, 1850, folder 18, vol. 16, JRPP.

102. JRP to James Hamilton, April 1, 1850, folder 19, vol. 16, JRPP.

103. JRP to Richard Yeadon, March 18, 1850, folder 19, vol. 16, JRPP.

104. Richard Yeadon to JRP, March 1, March 9, 1850, folder 19, vol. 16, JRPP.

105. JRP to G. Kemble, April 26, 1850, PPGC, 231.

106. Bachman, *Inquiry*.

107. *Charleston (SC) Courier*, December 5, 1850, folder 81, CLCP.

108. JRP to Richard Yeadon, March 6, 1850, folder 81, CLCP.

109. See, for example, "Exports-Charleston," *DeBow's Review* 2 (1846): 415–16.

110. Matthew Karp argues that there was a "vigorous military wing of southern foreign policy," who advocated for the use of federal power to bolster slaveholding imperialism. Matthew Karp, *This Vast Southern Empire: Slaveholders at the Helm of American Foreign Policy* (Cambridge, MA: Harvard University Press, 2016), 33.

111. JRP to G. Kemble, February 10, 1851, PPGC, 233.

112. JRP to G. Kemble, July 11, 1851, PPGC, 231.

113. JRP to G. Kemble, April 26, 1850, PPGC, 231.

114. JRP to G. Kemble, September 6, September 9, 1851, PPGC, 238.

115. JRP to Frances Tyrrell, April 20, 1849, PPGC, 224.

116. JRP to Fellow Citizens, *Charleston (SC) Courier*, December 5, 1850, folder 52, CLCP.

117. JRP to Greenville, June 13, 1851, folder 54, CLCP.

118. JRP to G. Kemble, April 26, 1850, PPGC, 231.

119. JRP to Greenville, June 13, 1851, folder 54, CLCP.

120. Cameron B. Strang, "Perpetual War and Natural Knowledge in the United States, 1775–1860," *Journal of the Early Republic* 38, no. 3 (Fall 2018): 408.

121. JRP to Frances Tyrrell, November 5, 1851, PPGC, 239–40.

122. For white Anglo-American appropriation of these springs, see Will B. Mackintosh, "Red Jacket Bathed Here: Creating Race and Nation at Early National Mineral Springs," *Journal of the Early Republic* 42, no. 3 (Fall 2022): 421–50.

123. JRP to Frances Tyrrell, January 1851, PPGC, 233.

124. JRP to Frances Tyrrell, November 5, 1851, PPGC, 239.

125. "Thirty-Second Congress—First Session," *Philadelphia Inquirer*, December 20, 1851, 2.

126. Vestry Christ Church to Mary Pringle, folder 1, Joel Roberts Poinsett Papers, 1787–1851, (1164.03.03) SCHS.

127. John Belton O'Neal, "The Hon. Joel R. Poinsett," folder 54, CLCP.

128. Mortuary notice, *Alexandria (VA) Gazette*, December 20, 1851, 2.

129. Mortuary notice, *Alexandria (VA) Gazette*, December 20, 1851, 2; *El Universal: periódico independiente*, August 6, 1851; *El Universal: periódico independiente*, January 28, 1853.

Epilogue

1. Samuel Curson to JRP, April 8, 1830, folder 7, vol. 6, JRPP; Chapman Levy to JRP, October 10, 1837, folder 8, vol. 9, JRPP.

2. "Comunicados," *El Sol*, May 2, 1829, 3.

3. "Llegada del consul Joel Roberts Poinsett," *Aurora de Chile*, March 2, 1812; Edward Tagart, *A Memoir of the Late Captain Peter Heywood, R.N.* (London: E. Wilson, 1832), 256–57.

4. Francis Lieber, "Right of Search Political Ethics," January 1842, Francis Lieber papers, mssLI 1-5222, Huntington Library, San Marino, CA.

5. David Porter to JRP, August 21, 1825, PPGC.

6. John L. Eaton to JRP, October 21, 1840, folder 12, box 15, JRPP.

7. "South Carolina," *Salem (MA) Gazette*, November 2, 1832, 2; "The History of Nullification. Its Origin and Progress. An Inside View. Fourth Article," *Evening Post* (New York), December 21, 1860, 1.

8. "The American Flag," *Alexandria (VA) Gazette*, November 30, 1860, 2.

9. "Great Speech of Gen. John C. Fremont, at Boston," *Wooster (OH) Republican*, September 11, 1862, 1; "Gen. Fremont's Speech," *Milwaukee Sentinel*, September 19, 1862, 2.

10. "Is Secession a Constitutional Right, or Is It Revolution?," *Farmers' Cabinet* (Amherst, NH), July 19, 1861, 1.

11. "Advertisement," *Charleston (SC) Mercury*, September 11, 1862, 2.

12. C. Harvey Gardiner, ed., *Mexico, 1825–1828: The Journal and Correspondence of Edward Thornton Tayloe* (Chapel Hill: University of North Carolina Press, 1959).

13. Robert Morgan, *The Mountains Won't Remember Us: And Other Stories* (Atlanta: Peachtree, 1992).

14. Chapman Levy, October 10, 1837, folder 8, vol. 9, JRPP.

Index

....

masculinity, 186n14; and aggression, 5,
229n8; and authority, 193n8; and
commerce, 223n58; and comparison
to other males, 13; and entitlement,
186n10; and friendships between
men, 189n48; martial, 21, 187n17,
229n8; and national interest, 128–29;
and national strength, 186n14; and
politics, 223n58, 229n8; and power
relations, 186n14; and property,
193n8; refined aspect of, 4–5; and
respectability, 187n17; restrained,
187n17, 229n8; scholarship on,
187n14; southern, 5, 189n48, 239n23;
and southern male friendship,
189n48; and southern mastery, 157,
239n23; theories and categories of,
187n17; transnational business, 4–5;
white, 3. *See also* manhood
Mason, John, Jr., 82
Masons. *See* Freemasons
Matson, Cathy, 186n13
Matthews, William, 51
Maxcy, Virgil, 150–51
Mayan people, 93
McDonnell, Lawrence T., 238n6
McDuffie, George, 105, 111, 113, 115, 125,
172
McLane, Louis, 60, 114–15
Medical Society of South Carolina, 19
Mediterranean, 47
mercantilism, 29, 34, 38, 47, 81, 90, 107,
109; and capitalism, 26; and militarism, 26. *See also* commerce
Metternich, Klemens von, 26
Mexía, José Antonio, 99
Mexico, 6, 35, 61–71, 159, 163–66,
218n117, 235n90; affairs, Poinsett's
intervention in, 14; American claims
against, 214n38; British imperial
power in, 175–76; and capitalism,
70, 81, 97; capitalist writings on, 70;
church/mass in, 68; claims against
government for revolutionary aid,
83–84; and commerce, 1, 64, 69, 79,
92, 94, 166; constitutional monarchy of, 62; consul in, 101; covert

interference in, 82; and democracy,
70; domestic politics during war,
243n79; and Europe, 82; and foreign
relations, 86; and immigration, 96–
97; independence, 62, 67, 77, 83, 86,
97, 207n46; interests in, 1, 78–101,
164–65, 213n14, 213n19; investments
in, 28, 89, 97, 111, 176–77, 215n75;
liberty, 61, 97; manufacture interests
in, 74–75; minister to, 1, 10, 56, 58,
62–71, 76–101, 125, 174; Navy, 89,
100–101, 175, 216n76; and New Orleans, conflict with, 242n60; peace
with, 210n127; Poinsett as ambassador to, 1, 3, 28; politics of, 3–4, 58,
62–71, 89–90, 93–97, 125, 174, 176,
207n46, 243n79; and prosperity,
100; and racism, 70; racist writings
on, 70; and republican similarities,
85; and revolutionary similarities,
85; and slavery, 96; social equality in, 93–95; and southern honor,
102–5, 108–9, 111–12, 116, 120,
124; and Spain, 82–83, 86, 89, 97,
100–101; and trade, 70, 80, 82, 165,
242n73; transportation issues in, 69;
treaty with, 92–93, 96, 167; US as
model for development, 93; and US
territory, 242n61; and war, 62, 67,
128, 136, 140, 150, 153, 165–67, 172,
175, 243n79; York Rite (Freemason)
lodges in, 10
Michaux, François, 59
Mier y Terán, Manuel de, 96–97
Milam, Benjamin R., 90, 95–96
militarism, 1–5, 7–9, 18, 21–32, 42–44,
47–53, 56, 71–72, 78, 80, 102, 132–
33, 143–46, 150, 153–55, 163, 175,
236n116; and arms/munitions, 14,
35, 39, 43–48, 53, 63, 83, 93, 106, 114,
116–19, 132, 138, 143, 166–67, 172,
201n57, 202n81, 225n85; and asceticism, 145; and business interests, 71;
and capitalism, 26, 47, 128–29, 132,
177; and coercion, 143–44; and com-
merce/mercantilism, 26, 47, 51–52,
71; and early American politics and

258   INDEX

Pedro I (emperor of Brazil), 14
Peninsular War, 166
*Pennsylvania Magazine of History and
    Biography,* 17
Perkins, Thomas Handasyd, 73, 210n134
Perry, Matthew, 60
Persia, 25–26, 164
Peru, 30, 34, 40, 42, 44–45, 74–75, 164,
    176
Petigru, James, 106
Philadelphia, PA, 6–8, 14, 19–20, 35,
    48–50, 52, 55–58, 60, 77, 82–83, 88,
    106–7, 112–14, 117, 120, 139, 148, 151–
    53, 205n8; American abolitionism,
    as birthplace of, 8; commercial hor-
    ticulture, as center of, 6; Hispanic
    studies, as unofficial center of, 46; as
    marketplace for wealthy southern-
    ers, 8; Poinsett's mansion house
    in, 107; and publishing, 102–3; and
    revolutionaries, 48–49; scientific
    community of, 79
Pinckney, Charles, 24
Pinckney, Thomas, Jr., 51
piracy, 59, 63, 69–72; anti-, 70
Poinsett, Ann Roberts (mother), 3, 5,
    19, 21
Poinsett, Elisha (father), 5, 10, 12, 17, 19–
    24, 26–28, 51, 89, 163, 193n8
Poinsett, Joel Roberts, 1; and aggres-
    sion, 4; ambitions, 3, 7, 57, 120,
    152, 175–76, 186n13; and American
    experiment, 2; as archenemy of
    England, 45; biographers, 16–17;
    birth, 16, 18–19; changeability of,
    175–76; in Charleston, 22, 48–54, 81,
    102, 108; in Charleston, childhood
    and adolescence, 16, 18–19; concern
    with others' perception of him,
    14, 36, 102–3, 104, 106–7, 148, 164,
    186n13; as Congressman (US), 1, 55–
    62, 71–78; death, 2, 16, 172–74, 176;
    as Democrat, 7; democratic princi-
    ples, 17; as Democratic-Republican,
    8; desires, 26–27; diplomatic affairs,
    career, service, 17, 21–22, 28–30, 45,
    78, 90, 93, 174; education and learn-
    ing, 5, 8, 20–21, 106; as eminent

citizen and retired statesman, 174; as
    entitled, 25–26; facades, commit-
    ment to, 177; financial interests, 9,
    11–13, 18, 20, 22, 24, 26–28, 51, 72,
    103–4, 106–8, 163, 221n20; French
    Huguenots, descended from, 3, 5;
    genteel upbringing, 5; gentility of,
    4; as gentleman, 13, 24–25, 27, 39,
    104, 109; as "good Christian," 2; and
    governance, 7; health, 112, 141, 165,
    169, 171, 173; individualistic ideals,
    95; inheritance, 23–24, 26–28; and
    interventionism, 43–44, 153; as
    Jacksonian Democrat, 7–8; lan-
    guages, interest and fluency in, 20–
    21, 24, 28, 42; law studies, 22; legacy,
    complicated, 176; letters, 173; as
    loner, 21; manhood, full, 190n55;
    as market oriented and feudal, 51;
    marriage, 12–13, 16, 120–24, 128, 157;
    medical studies, 21; in Mexico, 1, 3,
    6, 10, 28, 56, 58, 61–71, 76–101, 125;
    as naturalist, 5–6, 34, 55, 154, 157–
    59; natural philosophy, interest in,
    153; order and regulation, reverence
    for, 5, 36, 128–29, 144; as pestilent
    man, 173; as plantation "master"
    and owner, 5, 11–13, 122–24, 127,
    153, 157–58, 170; political battles
    behind the scenes (1841–51), 152–74;
    political record, 9; and power of
    US, 18, 56; predictions of, 172; and
    privilege, 19, 21, 27, 36, 109, 131,
    144; as radical liberal, 208n88; as
    reputable figure nationwide, 55;
    science, interest in, 20, 55, 79, 91,
    128, 150–51, 154–56, 161, 241n51;
    as secretary of war, 1, 2, 4, 51, 123,
    126–52, 176; and self-presentation,
    14; self-righteousness of, 43–44; as
    self-serving, 3; and slavery, 3, 7, 12,
    16, 26–27, 51, 114, 116–17, 122–23, 157,
    163–64, 169–70; son of (James), 9,
    57–59, 75, 107; in South America,
    1, 6, 29, 33–55; as South Carolina
    state legislator, 1; as southerner, 2,
    7, 8; and southern honor, 102–26;
    Spain, as secret agent in, 168; and

railroads, 4, 8, 109, 112–13, 122, 242n60
Ramsay, David, 19–20
Ramsey, George D., 225n85
Ray, Joseph, 14–16, 191n69
Reding, Alois, 23
regionalism, 104
Registro Oficial, 112
Reid, Robert R., 147
republican idealism/ideals, 198n13,
    221n19
republicanism, 67; anti-, 102; and
    capitalism, 186n13, 221n19; classical,
    186n13; and governance, 14; mania
    for, 17; and militarism, 22–23; and
    nullification, 222n41; and revolu-
    tion, 85; and self-interest, 186n13;
    and sovereign executive power, 42;
    symbols of, 41
Republican Party, 71; and era of "good
    feelings," 49
respectability, 187nn16–17
Revolutionary War, 22, 36. *See also*
    American Revolution
rice, 13, 20, 59, 108–9, 157–58, 163,
    221n21; clean, 158, 170; and internal
    supply constraints, 220n15; planta-
    tions, 6, 11–12, 27–28, 106, 122;
    rough, 170; Southeast Asian in
    European markets, 220n15
Rich, Dr., 82
rifles, 43, 118–19, 133, 226n117. *See also*
    guns
Rio de Janeiro, Brazil, 33, 36–38, 41, 52,
    152, 198n27. *See also* Brazil
Rio Grande river, 86, 167
Rippy, James Fred, 17
Robert Gilmore & Son (merchants and
    collectors), 4
Robinson, E. B., 136–37
Robinson, Henry R., 136, 148–49
Rodney, Caesar Augustus, 52
Ronaldson, James, 6, 139–40
Roshwald, Aviel, 185n3
Ross, John, 134, 137, 141
Royal Botanical Garden (Spain), 6
royalists, 37, 40, 42–44
Royston, Lord. *See* Yorke, Philip
Ruffin, Edmund, 159

Rush, Richard, 59, 139
Russia, 1, 18, 24–30, 39, 103, 166, 175,
    193n23, 210n127
Russian Economical Society, 158

Sanchez, Juan Frances, 43
Santa Anna, Antonio López de, 64, 70,
    97, 124
Sargent, John H., 135
Sarony, Napoleon, 146
science, national, 154, 157, 161–62,
    241n51; defined, 238n5
Scott, Winfield, 131–32, 142, 144–45,
    236n113
secession, 2, 7, 120, 154, 169–72, 175–76,
    223n41, 237n139, 238n6
secrecy, 10, 30–31, 54, 56, 59, 61, 76–77,
    144
"Secretary of War Presenting a Stand of
    Colours to the 1st Regiment of Re-
    publican Bloodhounds, The" (H. R.
    Robinson), 148, *149*
self-interest, 4, 53, 101, 175–77; and
    capitalism, 186n13; and economic
    development, 14–15; and investment
    in distant lands, 188n36; and national
    policy, 186n13; and patriotism, 3, 44,
    154, 177, 186n13; and politics, 49–50;
    and profiteering, 84–85; and repub-
    licanism, 186n13; and state appara-
    tuses, of merchants, 186n13, 201n59
Seminole people, 4, 31, 133–34, 137, 143,
    147, 150, 167, 237n122
Seminole War, Second, 130, 137, 150, 163
separation of powers, 41
Sherburne, John H., 134, 137, 233n59,
    237n122
Shire, Laurel Clark, 4, 187n19
Shubrick, William B., 227n120
silver: and capitalism, 195n52; dona-
    tions, 160; and East Indies exchange,
    195n52; and gold, 83, 160; imports,
    242n60; mining, 29, 64, 66–67;
    trade, 29
Silverman, David, 230n14
Simeonov, Simeon, 196n59, 196n70,
    197n9, 197n11
slavery, 3–4, 7–8, 12, 16, 26–27, 51, 56,

60–61, 73–75, 114–17, 122–25, 157, 163–64, 169–71, 175–76, 187n19, 212n8, 221n21; and colonialism, 90; and commerce, 8, 71, 87, 159, 169; and economic development, 109, 167, 170, 208n105; expansion of, 79, 117, 167, 170, 226n104; as financial instruments, 163; and foreign policy, 208n105; and foreign relations, 188n33; and freedom, 123; illegal, 71, 73; and militarism, 170; "negro cloth" for cheap clothing, 75, 119; and nullification, 108–9, 119–20, 222n41; perpetuation of, 159; and political economy, 220n12; preservation and protection of, 109, 117, 138, 169–70, 220n12, 237n139; and race, 63, 147; restricted, 199n39; and tracking, 147; and unionism, 226n104; and wealth, 104. *See also* abolitionism; antislavery; nullification crisis (1832–33)
Smith, Dennis A., 82, 83–86, 90–91, 99–100, 106
Smith, Gene A., 200n56
Smith, Joseph Allen, 24, 30–32
Smith, Robert, 30, 198n27
Smith, William, 110–11, 138
Smithson, James, 139, 153, 155–56, 160, 162, 172
Smithsonian Institution, 1, 16, 139, 151, 153–56, 159–62, 172, 176
social equality, 93–95, 135
social reform, 94, 158, 217n103
South America, 1–2, 6, 70, 78; American property in, 61; American reexports of European arms to, 201n81; and British, challenged, 35, 37; British imperial power in, 175–76; commodities to trade in, 199n39; diplomatic and intelligence-gathering mission in, 28–30, 106; economic opportunism/opportunity in, 33–35; independence, 42, 52, 56, 76; infrastructure, 50; interests in, 30; international and domestic politics (1811–19), 33–56; military involvement in, 56; patriot military successes

in, 201n57; Poinsett's financial arrangements in, 38; Poinsett's travels in, 49–50, 54, 62, 70; political and military affairs in, 16; revolutionaries in, 2; sheep, merchants' interest in, 204n121; social control in, 73–74; and trade, 199n39; transportation issues in, 50, 69; US economic success in, 31; US relations with, 197n7. *See also* Argentina; Brazil; Chile; Latin America; Peru; Uruguay
Southard, Samuel, 76
South Carolina: and agricultural improvements, 158; commercial interests in, 132; government power, strengthening in, 203n101; independence, 172; insular politics of, 104, 220n12; internal improvements in, 48, 203n101; and national political decisions, 105; and Panic of 1819, 104–5; as radical state, 220n12, 221n19; secession debates, 2; secession from US, 176; and slavery, 159; and violent radicalism, 221n19. *See also* Charleston, SC
South Carolina General Assembly, 1
South Carolina Historical Society, 9
South Carolina Philosophical Society, 55
South Carolina Society, 19
southern honor, 5, 20, 102–26, 220n13, 223n58, 239n23
Southern Review, 111
southwest, North American, 42–43
sovereignty, 29, 31, 41–42, 69, 73, 92, 126, 141, 197n11, 231n20
Spain, 28–34, 37–38, 45–48, 53–54, 59, 62–63, 67–70, 78–79, 86–89, 96–97, 167–71; British influence in former colonies, 195n54; and commerce, 30, 86; diplomatic intervention in negotiation with, 210n127; and free trade, 45–46, 199n39; independence, 28, 38, 45–46; interests in, 86; and Mexico, 82–83, 86, 89, 97, 100–101; revolution, 29; Royal Botanical Garden, 6; and slavery, 167, 199n39; and trade, 32, 79; treaty with, 53, 92–93, 224n67; warfare in, 64